Museums of the Mind

Museums of the Mind

German Modernity and the Dynamics of Collecting

Peter M. McIsaac

THE PENNSYLVANIA STATE UNIVERSITY PRESS
UNIVERSITY PARK, PENNSYLVANIA

Library of Congress Cataloging-in-Publication Data

McIsaac, Peter.
Museums of the mind : German modernity and the dynamics of collecting /
Peter M. McIsaac.
p. cm.
Includes bibliographical references and index.
ISBN 978-0-271-05870-2 (pbk : alk. paper)
1. Museums—Social aspects—Germany.
2. Museums in literature.
I. Title.

AM7.M39 2007
069.0943—dc22
2007003712

Copyright © 2007 The Pennsylvania State University
All rights reserved
Printed in the United States of America
Published by The Pennsylvania State University Press,
University Park, PA 16802-1003

The Pennsylvania State University Press is a member of the Association of American University Presses.

It is the policy of The Pennsylvania State University Press to use acid-free paper. Publications on uncoated stock satisfy the minimum requirements of American National Standard for Information Sciences—Permanence of Paper for Printed Library Material, ANSI Z39.48–1992.

FOR KARYL, INÉS, AND LUCAS

Contents

Illustrations

Acknowledgements

It will likely not come as a large surprise that a great many people—more than I can properly recognize—have helped me conclude this project. Its beginnings reach back to my early graduate work. In those years, most prominent in their support, guidance, and inspirational critiques were Jann Matlock, Eric Downing, Dorit Cohn, Maria Tatar, and Beatrice Hanssen. Harvard University and the Whiting Foundation provided financial support for the project in these stages.

Many people have since contributed to the growth of my project. I am grateful to Ann Marie Rassmussen, Liliane Weissberg, and Michael Cornett for their critical feedback. Yvonne Ivory, James Rolleston, and Claudia Koonz deserve special recognition for their unflagging and selfless efforts to help me get this project into print. Since coming to Duke University, I have received research support from the Center for European Studies and the Arts and Sciences Committee on Faculty Research. The Deans of Arts and Sciences, the Center for European Studies, and the German Department generously subsidized the publication of this book.

I owe just as much to my friends and family—they have probably never thought the day would come that it would be over. Special thanks are due to Patricia Garcia Rios for her help in the dissertation phase, and to my mother, Karyl Hare, for stepping in with support of all kinds at critical moments. Most of all, I am indebted to my wife, Inés Ibáñez, and son Lucas Samuel McIsaac, who have sustained me in the later stages of this project.

Finally, some of the material in Chapters 3 and 4 has been previously published in journal form. This material is reproduced with the kind permission of the American Association of Teachers of German (*The German Quarterly* 70, 4 [1997]: 347–57) and Blackwell Publishing ("The Museal Path to *Bildung:* Collecting, Gender, and Exchange in Stifter's *Nachsommer,*" *German Life and Letters* 57 [2004]: 268–89)

I

Historical and Theoretical Coordinates of Museal and Literary Discourses

SIGHTS SEEN IN THE MIND'S EYE CAN NEVER BE DESTROYED.
STRABO (64 BCE–CE 21)

SOMEONE READS ALOUD, YOU CLOSE YOUR EYES, AND YOU "SEE" EXACTLY AS MUCH AS IF YOU WERE STROLLING THROUGH A MUSEUM.
DURS GRÜNBEIN IN CONVERSATION WITH HEINZ-NORBERT JOCKS

I

The Museum Function, Inventoried Consciousness, and German-Speaking Literature

Imagine Berlin's Pergamon museum, a neoclassical building housing a series of ancient architectural wonders. Approach and ascend, in your mind's eye, the Pergamon Altar, a full-size Hellenistic temple moved from Asia Minor and painstakingly reconstructed for display in Berlin (Fig. 1). Turn the corner into the space created by the Market Gate of Miletus (Fig. 2), pass through the Ishtar Gate (Fig. 3) and Procession Street of Babylon, and stand before the façade of the Umayyad palace from Mshatta, Jordan (Fig. 4). Built on such a scale that it dwarfs these and many other ancient monuments, the Pergamon museum is supposed to radiate greatness. This greatness is manifested in the brute fact of possession, to be sure, insofar as the museum was built at the height of Germany's imperialistic ambitions. But the Pergamon also manifests the commitment of German culture to the contemplative aesthetic cultivation of the self (*Bildung*). Indeed, there could be no higher testimony to the values of *Bildung* than a museum like the Pergamon, an institution meant to inspire individual nobility in proportion to the sense of its treasures' historical permanence and rarified aesthetic magnificence.

Peter Weiss's novel *Die Aesthetik des Widerstands* [The Aesthetics of Resistance] transforms this bastion of *Bildung* into a site of political contestation, using the mind's eye. In the opening scene, a small group of young, anti-fascist resistance fighters stands precisely before the Pergamon Altar. The young men seek a figure to whom they liken themselves in their struggle against overwhelming odds—Herakles, the only mortal to rise up against the triumph of godly force as depicted in the Pergamon's battle friezes.[1] Their visit makes the Pergamon into a space where the struggle to resist oppression pits not only mind against history and power, but also mind against matter. For in the museum display, all that remains of Herakles is his lion skin and the briefest of labels, a kind of

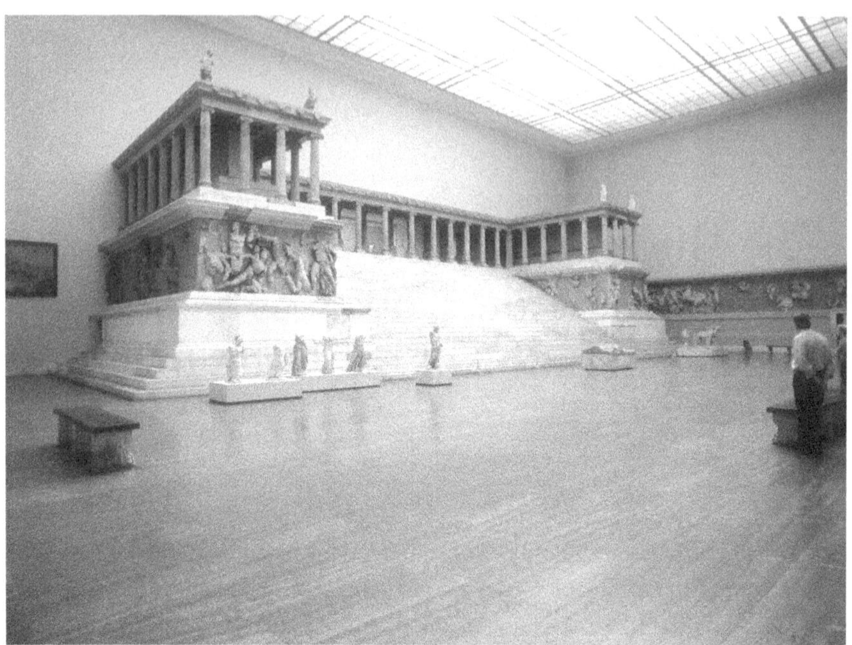

Figure 1 Pergamon Altar, ca. 180–160 B.C.E., as reconstructed in the Pergamon Museum, Berlin. Marble, 9.66 × 34.2 × 36.44 m. Antikensammlung, Staatliche Museen zu Berlin.

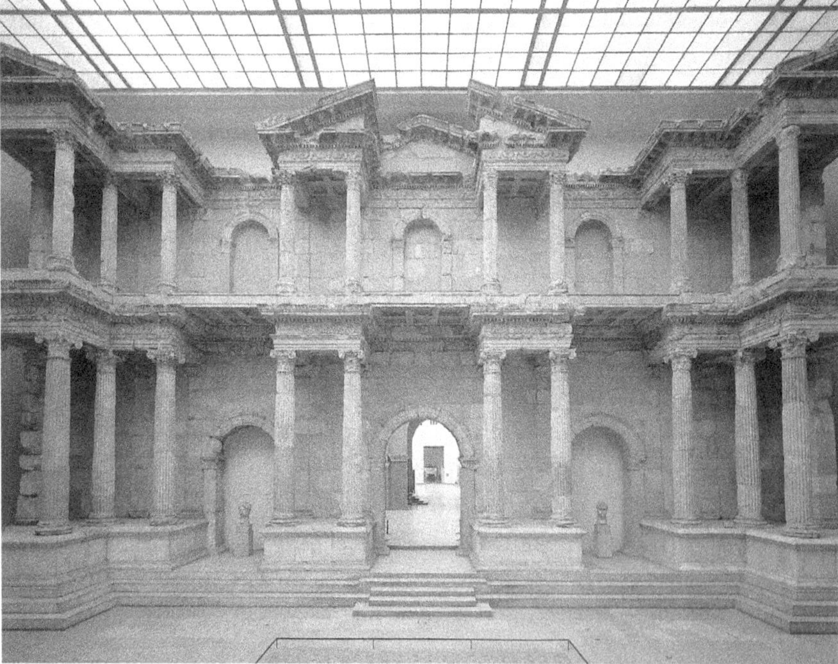

Figure 2 The Market Gate of Roman Miletus, ca. 120 C.E., as reconstructed in the Pergamon Museum, Berlin. Marble, 16.68 m. The visitor reaches this room after passing before the Pergamon Altar. Antikensammlung, Staatliche Museen zu Berlin.

material and curatorial erasure that can be confronted only in the beholder's mind.[2] Weiss's narrative makes the reader into just such a beholder, a person who can challenge the myths constructed by the museum display in order to find Herakles in the mind's eye. Writing such as Weiss's that intervenes in the museal construction of the world is the topic of this book, a study of museum culture and German literature.

The premises of this book, to which Weiss's text speaks, are twofold. This study ventures, first, that the forces that lead curators, artists, and politicians in a given culture to produce museums lead authors to produce certain kinds of literary writing. And second, the values and priorities that make a museum possible and desirable are also articulated in literary form. These are not simple premises, and they require some justification in relation to what, in the following pages, I call the "museum function."[3] But as becomes clear, good reasons exist for wanting to understand the relationship between collecting, exhibiting, and cognition. The relationship is of utmost importance in contemporary museum culture and German literary writing, where a mode of cognition I call inventoried consciousness has become predominant in shaping how people organize, classify, and interpret real and imagined environments. But it also true that this mode of cognition is not new or even, precisely speaking, a creation of modernity. Modern museal and literary institutions, rather, inflect this mode of cognition. Coming some 175 years after the invention of the first public museums, modern German literature, and the program of *Bildung,* the cultural and political coordinates of Weiss's text appear at a fairly late juncture in the evolving relationship of modern collecting and writing. Yet the *Ästhetik des Widerstands* addresses both *Bildung* and museal conventions with a logic that is vital for understanding the trajectories of German literature, the museum, and what it means to be acculturated.

It is not hard to see that Weiss's novel uses literary techniques to intervene in the museal presentation of the world. In the book's opening pages, the reader encounters a fascinating literary rendering of the museal display. The book begins:

> All around us the bodies rose from the stone, pressed together into groups, swallowed into each other or burst into fragments, with a torso, a propped-up arm, a cracked hip, an encrusted chunk indicating their form, always in the gesture of battle, evading, surging back, attacking, covering themselves, startled straight or bent, wiped out here and there, yet still with a free-standing foot jutting out, a back turned, the contour of a calf, yoked into a single common movement.[4]

This long and demanding sentence represents nothing less than the literary casting of a sculpture. Replicating the reconstructed frieze from the remaining bits and body parts, the grammatical fragments ("with a torso," "a propped-up arm") are fused together into a single sentence whose progressive adjectives ("evading," "surging back") impart ongoing motion, following both the action of the pitched battle and the movement of the eye across the statue. As it mimics the cognitive and sensual work of taking in the sculpted block, the sentence culminates in the phrase "yoked into a single movement" that joins the various present and absent parts ("wiped out here and there") into a unified sweep. In this way, content and grammar combine to form a meaningful unit with a sense of completion and aesthetic fulfillment.

In the next eight pages, Weiss presents a narrative consciousness ekphrastically infused with the protagonists' movements, perceptions, and cognitive acts:

> We were standing in front of the sculpted torsos of the weeping Ge's sons, giants who had sacrilegiously risen up against the gods, though it seemed other battles that once passed over Pergamon's Empire were hidden behind these representations. . . . Historical events appeared disguised as myth, events that were incredibly palpable, frightening, awesome but nonetheless not penetrable on a human scale, events we could only accept as the expression of a superhuman power wanting innumerable bondsmen and slaves and an elite few who could determine fates with a flick of the wrist. Passing by in holiday processions, the common people hardly dared to gaze up at their own history in effigy, the temple where the artists arriving for the occasion, the philosophers and the poets, together with the priests, had already been gathering in their expert knowledge, and what for the ignorant lay in a magical darkness was, for the knowledgeable, something to be soberly appreciated. The initiated, the specialists, spoke of art; they praised the harmony of movement, the interlocking gestures, while the others, who were unfamiliar with the concept of *Bildung,* stared furtively into the gashed throats, felt the blow of the animal's paw in their own flesh. (9)

Stepping into the ekphrastic flow, Weiss's figures envision the historical conditions of production and ownership that the artists, elites, and museum staff have, at various points, all left unrepresented (see, for instance, Fig. 5). Elided information fills the mind's eye, telling here of the forgotten souls who performed the artistic labor and those who, without the knowledge and experience of privilege, were and are excluded from this magnificent space and its traditions. The subtle but telling reference to *Bildung* signals that the frieze's epic mythmaking is to be understood not only in the past. Via the museum setting, the frieze also contributes to the modern myth of *Bildung*.

Moreover, the less educated or less traveled reader has, via the text, a chance to have his or her ignorance dispelled. The grammar and images of Weiss's opening lines manifest those same aesthetic qualities—harmony of movement and

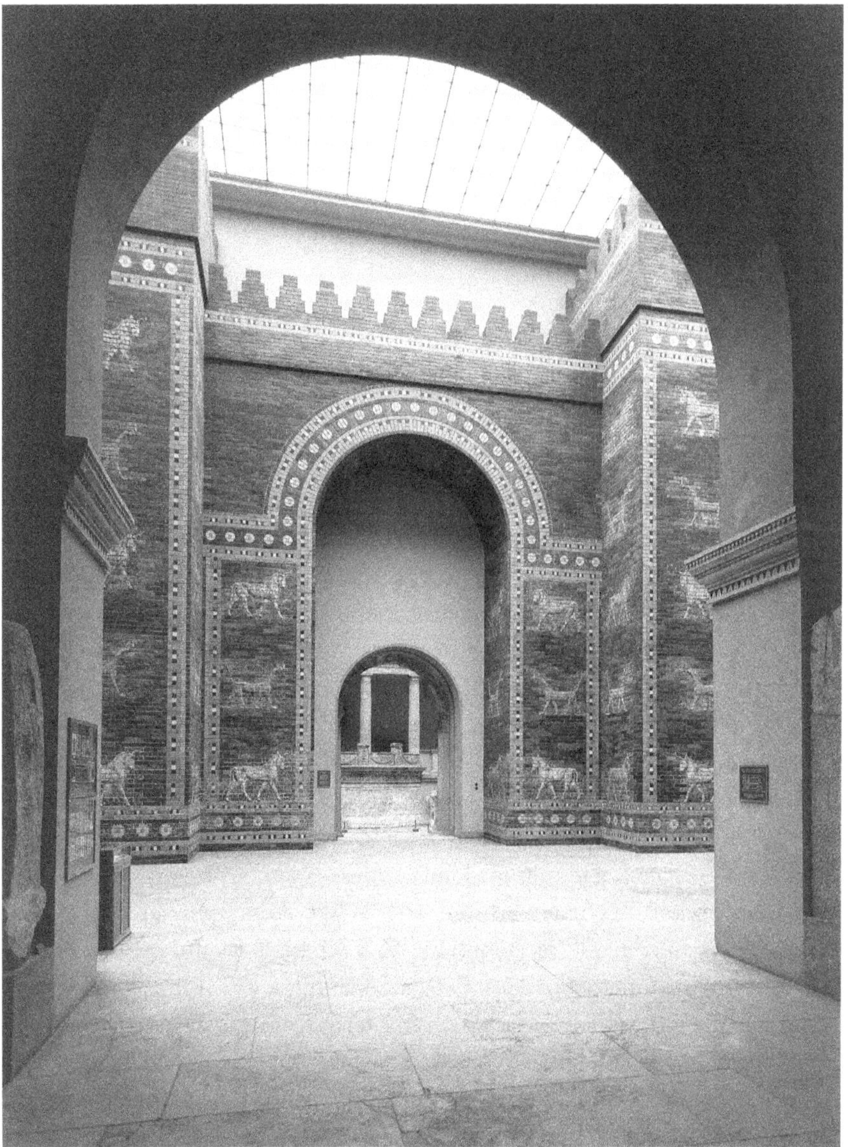

Figure 3 Ishtar Gate of Babylon, sixth century B.C.E., as reconstructed in the Pergamon Museum, Berlin. Mud brick, glazed brick relief mosaic decoration, 14.73 × 15.80 × 4.36 m. After passing through the Miletus Market Gate, the visitor emerges on this side of the Ishtar Gate. Vorderasiatisches Museum, Staatliche Museen zu Berlin.

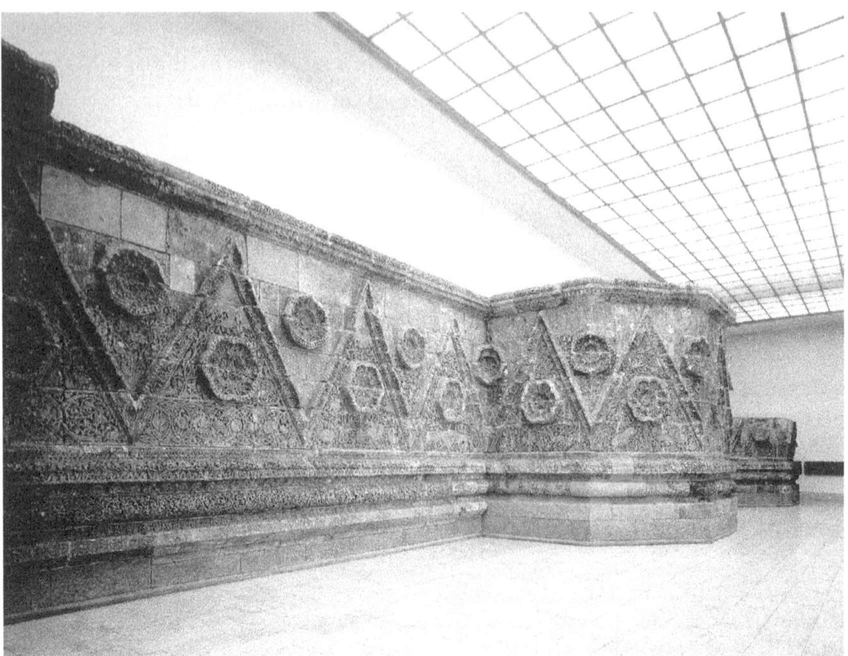

Figure 4 Facade from the Umayyad palace in Mshatta, Jordan, ca. 743–44 C.E., as reconstructed in the Pergamon Museum, Berlin. Limestone, 5.07 × 33 m. Inv. J. 6163. Museum für islamische Kunst, Staatliche Museen zu Berlin.

interlocking gestures—that constitute the specialists' art. By exposing the savagery and oppression that museal displays often render invisible, Weiss's opening disrupts the construction of mythic narratives. It ruptures what Walter Benjamin, in his critique of Wilhelmine state museums such as the Pergamon, called *Kulturgeschichte* (cultural history).[5] In this cultural mode, past culture is presented only as a string of glorious high points, shorn of the barbarity Benjamin thought had to accompany each human triumph.[6] Weiss's narrative dynamically recasts the place of the aesthetic and material reality in our consciousness and in the world. Indeed, through Weiss's literary imagination, the museum's complex mode of articulating beauty and knowledge is brushed against the grain, transformed, and re-staged, generating a kind of museal counterdiscourse.

Such a counterdiscourse works because it, like the museum, refers to and shapes a particular mode of cognition. This mode of cognition expresses a paradigmatic way of organizing, acting, and making sense of the world, which I call inventoried consciousness.[7] With this term I want to designate the mental activity involved not only in the making of lists, but also more differentiated orderings such as illustrated catalogs, three-dimensional displays, and topographies of memory. Such a term also resonates with notions such as Hans Haacke's,

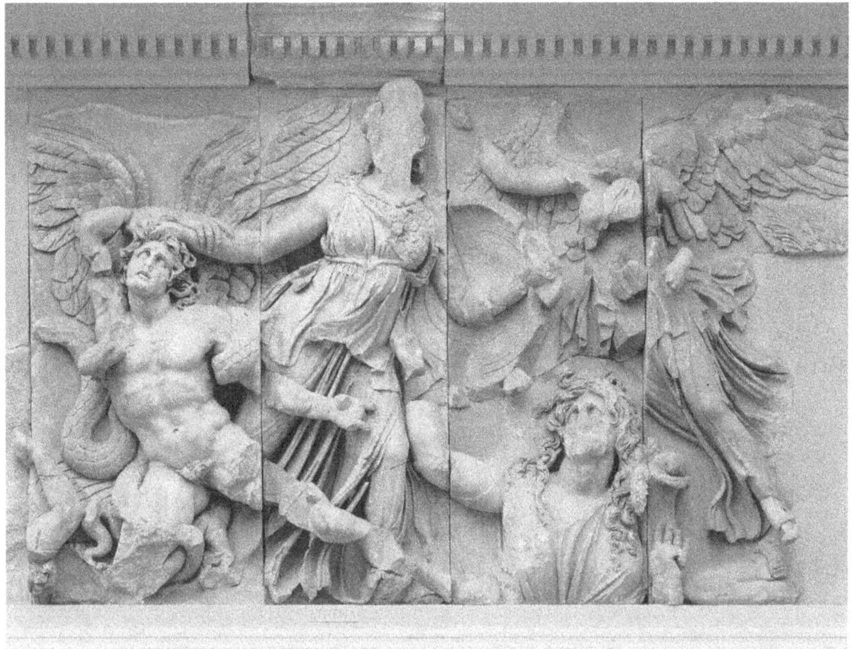

Figure 5 Relief from the Pergamon Altar, ca. 180 B.C.E. Curators and archaeologists have been able to reconstruct the relief only partially, leaving gaps. Antikensammlung, Staatliche Museen zu Berlin.

when he calls modern museums "managers of consciousness."[8] Yet in elaborating what inventoried consciousness is and how it is that literary writing and museum culture are related to it, it quickly becomes clear that no one novel, by Weiss or anyone else, can on its own adequately account for this phenomenon. This is partially a historical question, insofar as inventoried consciousness has clearly existed for far longer than modern novels and museums and in fact continues to evolve to this day. One might think of ancient stories like Noah's Ark, in which the ability to account for and assemble "the world" according to its core categories (individual animal species, male and female) is the key to envisioning its redemption, or narratives like *Beowulf,* in which the loss of a world is made complete by relating the mental catalog of exalted items that once were but no longer remain.[9] And people have seemed always to collect things and show them off in some fashion, sometimes, as with early modern *Wunderkammern* (Fig. 6), in ways radically other to our own organizational habits.

Gaining access to inventoried consciousness is complicated by the disciplinary and institutional configurations that shape our own thought and practice. Since the late eighteenth century inventoried consciousness has been transformed following what Michel Foucault described in *The Order of Things* as the shift to the modern episteme, a shift that would eventually give rise to the differentiated arts and sciences disciplines and their attendant institutions such as laboratories, libraries, archives, and museums.[10] Before 1800, the term "museum" tended to be understood as a "cognitive field of ideas, words, and artifacts"—potentially a place, but very often a text—whose "semiotic inventorying operations made the world readable."[11] In Renaissance collections, as Paula Findlen argues, the "museum" was in fact thought to reside most enduringly in

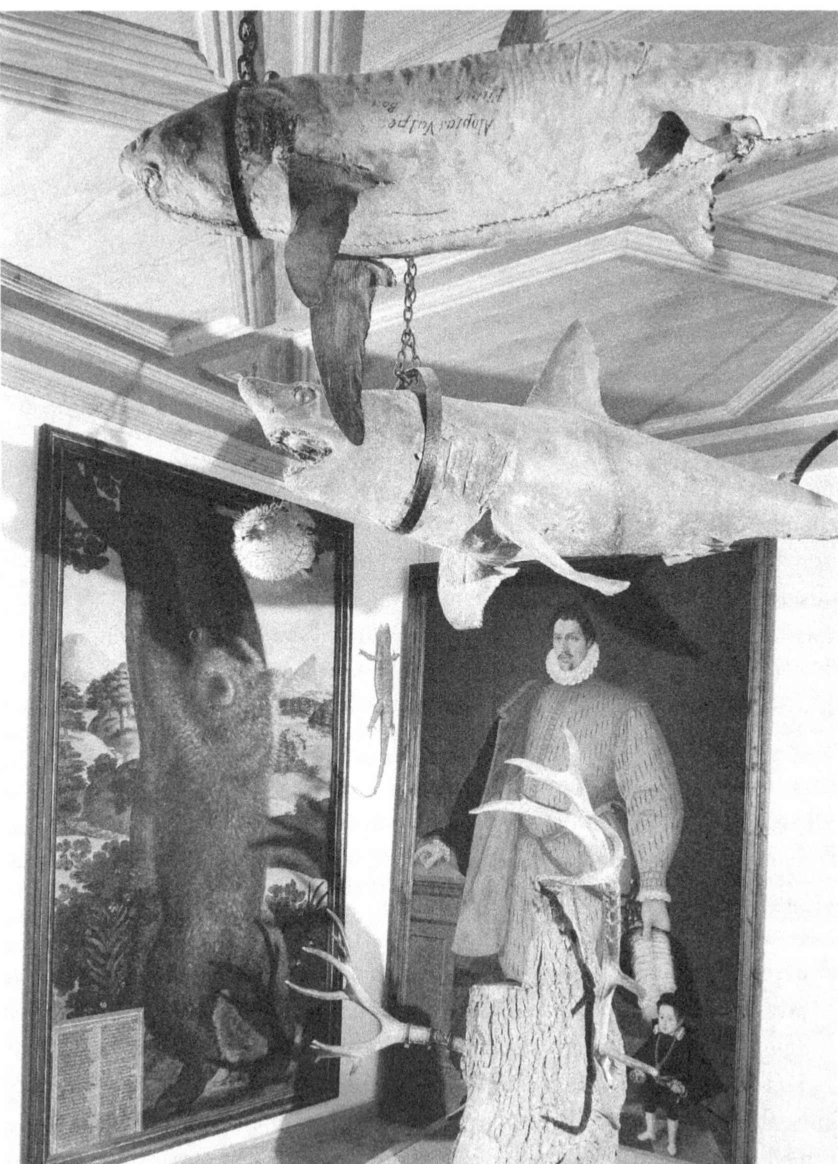

Figure 6 Objects from Archduke Ferdinand II's "Wunderkammer." In a combination of objects typical of such a collection, two sharks and one deep-sea fish hang from the ceiling. On the walls, a painting of a bear shot by the archduke is situated next to a small crocodile and a painting of a giant and a child. In the foreground are the antlers of a stag, around which a tree has grown. Schloss Ambras, Innsbruck, Austria.

the mind of the collector.[12] This idea figures in my study in relation to what I call the "notional museum," a term that recovers this Renaissance concept without losing sight of the epistemic shifts that have accompanied the rise of modern museum culture.

With regard to those epistemic shifts, it is worth pointing out that over the course of the nineteenth century, museums came to function as material repositories of disciplinary-specific objects, addressed by but no longer contiguous with discursive and textual registers.[13] As Wolfgang Ernst puts it, "[T]wo forms of processing the past took shape in the eighteenth century: the architectural and institutional container of the (art-) historical museum was created, serving as a grid for memory; and the implementation of historical imagination, based on the literary medium of narrative, led to an 'in/formation' of the imaginary."[14] As a result of the perceived antagonism between material objects and imaginary narratives, inventoried consciousness tends from this point forward to be inflected by the epistemological constraints of each disciplinary context, particularly in light of history, art history, and literature undergoing further discursive and disciplinary differentiation. Literary writing, in traditional conceptions the art form least bound to materiality, might be collected in books and libraries, perhaps also in manuscripts and archives, but almost never in museums.[15] Museums, in their classifying and ordering function now primarily linked to physical storage, retain a more narrowly circumscribed, but still deeply palpable relationship to forms of inventoried consciousness. At first glance, intense literary and museal exchanges might not be expected across these cultural and disciplinary divides. A genealogy of inventoried consciousness in the age of the public museum cannot, however, be constructed anywhere but in the exchanges between literature and museum culture.

The fact that literary and museal divides were always to some extent arbitrary, shifting, and permeable makes inventoried consciousness appropriate for study in the interstices of museum culture and the literary imagination. Yet what necessitates this study is that inventoried consciousness stands at the nexus of crucial, unresolved issues confronting contemporary scholarship, literature, and culture. The museum has become a dominant cultural paradigm shaping ever more areas of thought, particularly as they are affected by the exchanges between traditional and "new" media and culture. For a host of reasons, museums have in the past thirty years been dynamically expanding their purposes and audiences. This period has seen the rate and variety of new museums and museum types rapidly increase, some of which, as in Bilbao (Guggenheim), Milwaukee (Milwaukee Art Museum), New York (MoMA), Berlin (Jewish Museum), and Los Angeles (Getty), have been carried out in spectacular architectural idioms.[16] Offerings in traditional museum fields such as the fine arts have become both wider and more differentiated, while areas previously outside museums' purview, for instance, rock music or commodities from chocolate to Coca Cola, have entered the museum. No longer fittingly described as dusty vaults for elite edification (if they ever actually were), museums almost across the board have redefined their rationales for addressing the public, with some institutions becoming expansive cultural centers, others staging ever more extravagant blockbusters (in the minds of some a form of "dumbing down"), and still others opting for self-critical modes of interaction with visitors.[17] By all accounts, visitors are responding with unprecedented attendance and interest.

How easy is it, then, to envision today's world without museums? This thought experiment is a challenging one, particularly for anyone invested in prevailing notions of history, popular science, tourism, heritage, and/or art. In a variety of accounts, the appeal of museums and their ongoing cultural relevance have been explained in terms of their singular ability to supply organized material presence and uniqueness ("aura") in an age of simulation.[18] This is not to suggest that museums stand in some simple opposition to the onslaught of television and digital reproduction. But if a host of computerized presentation methods and cinematographic design techniques are finding their way into museum layouts at the same time as virtual museums are promoting the off-site exploration of holdings, it can be noted that museums' spatial and material constraints also shape and interrogate the meaning of virtuality.[19] This is no doubt one reason that computer companies such as Oracle, Microsoft, and Siemens-Nixdorf, among others, have turned to high-concept art and technology museums to aid in the discovery of software and hardware more capable of mediating through virtual means how people think and act in so-called material environments.[20] But even without knowing how these efforts impact it, today's world is clearly experiencing the expansion of "musealization" into aspects of everyday life previously not subject to relentless recording, categorizing, storing, and displaying. As old ways of organizing and interpreting knowledge and experience are disrupted, the spatial environments of museums represent important venues for exploring and negotiating new modes of inventoried consciousness.

In my approach, I describe inventoried consciousness in the museums and literary texts of a particular period in terms of what I call the "museum function." I define the museum function as the way objects are valorized, acquired and discarded, organized, displayed, and hidden in a particular society and historical period. If the museum function refers to processes, then inventoried consciousness is the related discursive register that organizes and shapes the perception and comprehension of people and the world. Because it refers to processes, the museum function extends beyond institutional walls in important and subtle ways. This means that the prevailing social impulses and exigencies that give rise to museums can also be detected in the behavior and activities of noninstitutional agents such as private collectors and in a variety of discourses circulating at the time.

The museum function does not explain literary texts as the mere product of their time of production, as if the text's ultimate "truth" could be elucidated through its straightforward alignment with a historical narrative. The museum function operates rather as a specific, consciously deployed hermeneutic, used to foreground the act of interpretation performed in the present while gaining access to prevailing cultural dynamics of a particular past. One of the things I show is the way that collections and exhibitions depend on narratives, such as those describing the formation of a collection, the stories people tell about it, and the values placed on the collection's objects. Studying literary texts alongside museum practices enables me, moreover, to expand understandings of how museums are situated dialectically within the processes of the creation and preservation, storage, reproduction, and circulation of objects. In turn, I demonstrate how literary narratives collect, arrange, and display objects, characters, and other stories as they establish "obvious truths" by telling object-oriented stories.

The museum function enables an approach with a dialectical notion of history, which helps in three ways. First, collecting and exhibiting still exert a tremendous cultural force in our day, inevitably shaping the questions asked of the past. Without an awareness of potential historical difference, the events of the past turn into a mere anticipation of the present state of things. Second, inventoried consciousness was in existence, and in different configurations with respect to processes of collecting and display, long before the age of the public museum. If a society without modern museums can still possess a museum function—and the museum function has been formulated so as to permit its application to pre-Enlightenment practices of collecting—then it is far easier to understand what happened to those practices and thought patterns when the public museum was invented.[21] And third, a nuanced historicizing of collecting and exhibiting draws attention to the larger cultural context in a particular time, requiring the examination of all the fields and discourses that contributed to the museum's development, successes, and failures. The same is true of literary texts. Rather than see the establishment of a particular museum and a particular literary text as isolated phenomena, the museum function prompts us to look for a confluence of cultural discourses capable of producing a particular museum and a particular literary text. I claim in particular that this function finds poignant and revealing expression in narrative projects. Delineating this function in narratives yields insights not only into how people collect and exhibit, but also into how the experiences of these processes profoundly affect perceptions, values, and behavior. Through collecting and museum going, visitors not only interact with objects; they also establish relationships with other people, certainly with collectors and exhibitors, but also with other visitors. The museum historically has been deemed capable of exerting a civilizing and enlightening effect on public behavior, or of helping to transform a citizenry into individuated members of a regional, superregional, or even national community, through what Carol Duncan has called "civilizing rituals."[22] In the German-speaking world, these civilizing and enlightening rituals have, in many ways, been related to the important and evolving concept of *Bildung*.

From the standpoint of collecting and literature, however, always speaking strictly in terms of *Bildung* does not provide the greatest insight into what these rituals of acculturation mean over time, and, as a corollary, how they relate people to one another by telling stories with objects. This is another way of saying that the quasi-private notion of *Bildung* needs to be superseded by a master category—the museum function—that accounts for both the public and the private.[23] The museum function is attuned to models of culture such as that of Walter Benjamin, in which "the present moment (which a priori cannot understand itself) relates to the entirety of the past (which has never ceased speaking) through mutual translation."[24] Such a "translational" view of culture, as James Rolleston has shown, regards the past in terms of a "simultaneous functioning of dissonant language systems" that produce a great variety of texts: "buildings, administrative organizations, utopian fantasies, advertisements, social chatter."[25] Sharing the same social processes, all language systems, from discarded objects and advertisements on the sidewalk to rarified poetry, can reveal aspects of social change, but only when the process of closure in the present can be forestalled and the assumptions of the present inquiry allegorized. In this model, quotation represents one strategy available for accomplishing this allegorizing task, though, as Benjamin writes in the *Passagenwerk* (Arcades Project), collecting represents another. While it does not privilege political discourse over any other, the museum function—because it is tied to the processes of collecting—remains capable of recovering repressed political moments, of reconstituting "events that can be read as the text of a single story."[26]

The necessity of language for understanding social processes, as, for instance, manifested in Benjamin's thinking, resonates with the notion that the study of literature is necessary for a full comprehension of the processes of collecting and exhibiting. This point is reflected, moreover, not merely in that artistic and literary practice of late has frequently entered into intermedial relationships, challenging a whole array of notions such as permanence, memory, and stable cultural tradition upheld by traditional conceptions of the monument and the museum. Nor is it, strictly speaking, because "[poetry] was at home in the virtual, long before the introduction of the computer and any neuro-Romanticism," as the poet and essayist Durs Grünbein insists.[27] Or perhaps Grünbein's point needs to be put differently. For it is not only that literary discourses have failed to become obsolete per se with the advent of computer technology, but also that *for the time period of this study,* literary discourses represent a crucial, if not the most crucial, site where the boundaries of imaginative constructions and metaphorical regimes are interrogated and revised.[28]

Insisting on the need to study literary discourses does not exclude consideration of nonlinguistic and/or multimedial discourses. Indispensable for thinking about the ways the museum operates on prevailing imaginative constructions is Mieke Bal's theorization of the museum in terms of what she calls a "multi-medialization" of discourse.[29] In this conception, various linguistic and nonlinguistic elements (images, architecture) are seen to contribute to the museum's ability to make its core gesture of exposure signify, though what is true of literary discourse is also true of multimedial discourse. As Bal argues, "[D]iscourse implies a set of semiotic and epistemological habits that prescribes ways of communicating and thinking that others who participate in the discourse can also use.... It also includes unexamined assumptions about meaning and about the world."[30] These qualities of discourse enable Bal to elucidate a "grammar of display" regulating the production of symbolic meaning in the museum.

Now, Bal can then show not only why the museum's core gesture of exposure inevitably leads to the production of narrative (a fascinating proposition in the context of literary museum narratives), but also that the multimedialized grammar of display acts on the imagination in much the same way as literary discourse. In both, according to Bal, narratives are structured by "myth models," Gananath Obeyesekere's term for "the powerful, paradigmatic myths that serve as models for the construction of similar myths.... The term also refers to underlying combinations of ideas deployed in a variety of narrative forms.... Discourses are repositories for myth models that become 'naturalized'—taken for granted as obvious truths. Narrativization is a highly efficient way of inserting myth models into the stories of everyday life."[31] When Bal then drives home the point that "the realist novel flourished in the same age as the development of the great museums" because both narrativize in a profoundly similar fashion, she gives her own project traction on terms that compel us to attend to the main mode of narrativization from the age of Goethe to the present: literary writing. Literature must be studied with multimedialized discourse in order to understand the role of inventoried consciousness in converting myth models into "obvious truths."

The concerns of a growing number of contemporary writers require probing the relationship of inventoried consciousness to literature. Since the 1970s, writers and literature scholars have become increasingly fascinated by the relationship of memory and culture to records, spaces, and artifacts. Titles such as *Heimatmuseum* (1977; literally Local History Museum, translated as The Heritage), *Die Archive des Schweigens* (1980–91; Archives of Silence), and *Das Echolot* (1990; The Echo Sounder) indicate an expanding paradigm that has tended to be analyzed under the scholarly rubrics of cultural memory and the archive. Though recent approaches to archival processes have foregrounded some of the concerns that interest us here, for the most part, these approaches cannot provide the theoretical precision necessary to account for the way inventoried consciousness has been shaped by the rise of the public museum.

Three points can be made here. For one thing, the notion of the archive is problematically overdetermined in contemporary scholarship, with the "archive" serving as a repository for any theory using the name.[32] For another, the "archive" too often subsumes any and all forms, real or imagined, of knowledge production based on accumulation and classification.[33] Too few "archival" approaches seem capable of, or interested in, making necessary distinctions between libraries, archives, and museums and their respective historical processes.[34] Museums are archival institutions, to be sure, and the impact that libraries and archives have on how people make sense of the world is worth understanding.[35] That impact cannot, however, become the main focus of this study. In insisting on the particularity of the museum, this study recognizes the specificity of museum culture in ways that require my full attention. Many critical issues—among them the layout and ordering of exhibition spaces, the identity and practices of collectors, the behavior of exhibition visitors, the circulation of collected objects, and the relationship of material objects to medial reproductions—pertain only to museum culture. Moreover, and just as important, these and several other issues are central to the concerns of contemporary writers, not to mention their historical predecessors, when their work is read with these questions in mind. To establish the link between contemporary writing and museum processes, this book's first chapter focuses on two prominent German writers, W. G. Sebald and Durs Grünbein, in whose work scholars have tended to label any process of accumulation and classification as "archival." Refining this view, this chapter establishes that these writers' approaches and thought manifest specifically museal processes that bear on the contours of their writing and reveal the contemporary shape of inventoried consciousness.[36]

Within my argument, the chapter on Sebald and Grünbein provides the present-day coordinates for the genealogy that follows in the remainder of this book.

I have chosen this structure to generate, using prominent contemporary texts, a number of questions that inform the investigations of earlier literary texts. Part of this project involves showing that the cultural processes that now demand attention have in some sense been "with us" in the German literary canon for at least the last two centuries, even if they have never before received careful and sustained scholarly attention. Scholars in English-language literature have recently undertaken comparable efforts in their fields. Since the year 2000, Eric Gidal's *Poetic Exhibitions,* Barbara Black's *On Exhibit: Victorians and Their Museums,* and Catherine Paul's *Poetry in the Museums of Modernism* have demonstrated that literary writing has much to tell us about the ways museal institutions shaped English-language thought and culture in the respective Romantic, Victorian, and modernist periods. Of these studies, Gidal's emphasis on literature as "documented accounts of the [museal] institution as imaginative acts and encounters" is perhaps closest to my own in how it motivates the conjoined study of literature and museum culture, though many of the underlying ideas running through Black's and Paul's studies resonate with the premises of my study.[37] What distinguishes my work from these allied approaches are three related points: the German-speaking traditions I work on, the time frame of my study (1800 to the present), and the theoretical framework (the museum function) I develop to gain access to inventoried consciousness in the age of the public museum.

With respect to the first point, I contend that the larger project of understanding the intersections of museum culture and the literary imagination remains deficient if it fails to account for the perspectives of German-language writers and thinkers. Many German-speaking writers and thinkers were avid collectors and/or drawn to museum-related work in one manner or another (so many as to provide one useful criterion for selecting texts). One of the most significant was Johann Wolfgang von Goethe, during whose lifetime the concept of the public museum suddenly began to exert its hold on European bodies and minds. The cultural shockwaves created by the looting carried out during the Napoleonic conquest of Europe—much of which ended up in the Louvre—were acutely felt by Goethe, a collector also attuned to the German neoclassical and Romantic thought that would allow the museum idea to take hold swiftly in the German-speaking universe. By portraying this rapidly changing world in penetrating fashion in the remarkable novel *Die Wahlverwandtschaften* (Elective Affinities) and in several essays including "Der Sammler und die Seinigen" (The Collector and His Circle), Goethe subtly revealed the relationship of collecting and exhibiting to emerging aspects of modernity such as *Bildung.* The perspicacity with which Goethe treated these issues and his status as a paragon of modern German culture caused his writing to be read and reread by many subsequent generations, permitting these ideas to radiate into German culture again and again under varying circumstances.

Perhaps the readers most sensitive to these issues in Goethe's writing were other writers likewise attached to collecting projects, such as Adalbert Stifter and Walter Benjamin.[38] While each took away very different lessons from Goethe, both developed Goethean ideas in highly significant ways with respect to collecting and exhibiting. Stifter's writing was appreciated by the likes of Rainer Maria Rilke, Thomas Mann, and Friedrich Nietzsche, though Nietzsche never made clear whether his professed admiration for *Der Nachsommer* (Indian Summer) enabled his important critique of the historicism and museum culture of late nineteenth-century Germany.[39] When it comes to collecting and exhibiting, however, even more significant than Stifter, Nietzsche, and even Goethe is Walter Benjamin. Few thinkers in any language can rival the nuance Benjamin brings to bear on these questions, though even scholars of museum studies familiar with his work have yet to take full stock of the cultural traditions that Benjamin consolidates, inflects, and transmits in his essays.

In focusing on Benjamin's writing, I am not arguing that a single line of influence can be traced between Goethe and Benjamin. I seek, rather, to underscore Benjamin's importance for transmitting collecting-related concerns to post–World War II German-speaking intellectuals. Hannah Arendt's observation—that "collecting was Benjamin's central passion," which, after his youth, "soon extended into something far more characteristic, not so much of the person as of his work"—serves as a reminder that Benjamin's writings are especially likely to sensitize his readers to the ways that processes of collecting shape inventoried consciousness.[40] The Benjaminian resonance in Peter Weiss's writing is one that I noted previously. Similarly, W. G. Sebald, Siegfried Lenz, Ingeborg Bachmann, and Durs Grünbein all explore Benjaminian conceptions of history, collecting, media and reproducibility, and/or "imaginary topographies" of memory.[41] And from a theoretical perspective, Benjaminian thought offers productive conceptions for understanding the writing considered in this study, even by earlier writers whom Benjamin either did not analyze, or at least did not from the angle of collecting and exhibiting.

Certain perspectives offered by Michel Foucault also lend themselves for thinking about collecting, exhibiting, and discourse. Though Foucault himself wrote relatively little about museums, his notions of order, power/knowledge, and discipline offer sophisticated means for generating critical accounts of how display environments produce knowledge and regulate the conditions for social relationships.[42] Foucault's notion of the episteme makes it possible to think of the discursive spaces of public museums and exhibitions in terms of a grid, anterior to words, perceptions, and gestures, which governs the basic conditions and categories according to which people can perceive and make sense of the world. The world becomes comprehensible according to a set of primary organizing principles that determine which artifacts can and cannot appear in relation to other artifacts. How objects are collected and arranged, then, grounds the knowledge and narratives that a discourse based on the display of objects can generate. By the same token, different arrangements of objects would permit different ways of knowing and relating a subject position to the world and other people.

A focus on the semiotic encodings of exhibitions can be justified on this basis, a focus that sheds light on the crucial interplay between the ordering of visible elements and gaps in generating meaning. Such a semiotic approach makes it clear that museal displays—for instance, the use of frames and spacing to set off objects as aesthetically autonomous wholes—determine certain disciplinary conventions in fields such as art history and anthropology, without those operations necessarily being acknowledged.[43] The power of exhibitions derives not only from the ability of exhibitions to make certain things and relationships visible and thus seemingly self-evident, but also in their ability to render alternative narratives and ways of knowing invisible, and thus more or less unthinkable. It also follows from this semiotic conception that certain levels of education and training are necessary to make sense of display environments, thereby suggesting ways competing social groups might use display techniques to differentiate and legitimate themselves.[44] In other words, discursive regimes of exhibitions are capable of defining the constituencies they address and possibly also exclude, both with respect to agents in control of the collections (curators, state institutions, scientific bodies, private collectors, and so on) and to the relationships among these constituencies. Something like this was depicted in *Die Ästhetik des Widerstands,* where Weiss's working-class protagonists resist their exclusion from the museum space by decoding and contesting the curatorial gaps particularly likely to frustrate the approach of those uninitiated in art history to the display.

More than symbolic inclusion and exclusion is at stake in public exhibition spaces. This can be seen in Tony Bennett's subtle grasp of Foucauldian discipline in what he calls the exhibitionary complex, a term that serves to capture the work done by the differentiated set of display-oriented institutions, from permanent museum displays to temporary exhibitions and fairs. Bennett's account is instructive because he recognizes that telling stories in museum spaces involves ideologies *and* the interaction of bodies with architecture and other bodies. Visitors would learn ways of thinking about the world by moving through exhibition spaces, to be sure, but they would also discern how to regulate their behavior by being subjected to a series of real and imagined looks. Thus on one level, the mechanisms of discipline offer a profitable way of understanding how display environments represent an uninterrupted exercise of power in the Foucauldian sense, potentially reforming or at least altering visitors' sense of embodiment and behavior. At the same time, display space is organized differently from that of institutions of confinement. In contrast to schools, hospitals, and prisons, the exhibitionary complex offered environments promoting the sense among visitors that they were not only to be seen, but they were also, at least in principle, to look from the vantage point of some real or imagined eye of power.[45] That is, "as micro-worlds rendered constantly visible to themselves, expositions realized some of the ideals of panopticism in transforming the crowd into a constantly surveyed, self-watching, self-regulating, and as the historical record suggests, consistently orderly public—a society watching over itself."[46] Though it is possible to think of ways in which this equalizing potential would fail to materialize fully—particularly for women, minorities, and the lower classes—the point remains that museal architectures organize the properties of discourse in unique ways, transforming them into embodied modes of belonging and behaving in modern, "cultured" society.

The implications these notions have for the important questions of personal and collective memory as well as identity formation emerge by turning to Benjamin's linkage of the private collector to the problems generated by modernity. The collector is a privileged figure in Benjamin's thought, for, in modernity, he is uniquely capable of communicating experience, in an age when true experience (*Erfahrung*) has generally become inaccessible. This is not the place to rehearse Benjamin's intricate unraveling of the paradox of experience in modernity; suffice it to say that the labyrinthine path by which experiences can pass into memory is negotiable for him in only a few forms of cultural practice that can produce open-ended or dialectical images, two of which are writing and collecting.[47] When inflected by the collector's instinct and knowledge, collections and narratives offer interlocking strategies by which, in the words of Ackbar Abbas, the "experience of possession can become the possession of experience."[48]

Collecting, as understood by Benjamin, offers the opportunity for individuals to enter into a peculiarly intimate relationship with objects, so that the collector seems to live in them. The nature of this investment goes far beyond some simple identification. If, as Benjamin notes, the collector imposes order as a means of holding a dangerous flood of personal memories at bay, the collection represents a highly complex and fascinating means of constructing consciousness, with inventories listing what is known not in some positivistic fashion, but in the form of a habituated, perhaps even ritual, forgetting. Moreover, the collector's personal investment in his objects obligates him to treat his objects in a way that ensures they are handled appropriately—not (just) utilized, bought, or sold—in the present as well as in future societies. The collector has this capability because of his knowledge of the object's total history, or "fate" (*Schicksal*), which Benjamin describes thus: "[E]verything remembered and thought, everything known, becomes the pedestal, the frame, the base, the lock of his property. The period, the region, the craftsmanship, former owners—for the true collector the whole background of an item adds up to a magic encyclopedia whose quintessence is the fate of the object."[49] Indeed, that history or "fate" of an object might include all kinds of information on the object, including reproductions, lengthy descriptions, interpretations, any thought connected to the object. This combination of confrontation with material reality and awareness of the past's fullness permits the collector to become, in the words of Michael P. Steinberg, "an allegory of the allegorist."[50] Moreover, through acquisition, the object and its interlocking narratives pass into the collector's life, renewing and enriching it. This strategy of renewal, embedded as it is in a process of narrative being added to narrative, works against cultural history's fetishization of art objects, presenting images whose ambiguity keeps them unfolding and open to interpretation.

Benjamin's valorization of the figure of Eduard Fuchs reveals important political and historical implications of this strategy of renewal. Fuchs was a turn-of-the-century private collector whose collecting and publishing techniques were directed at reading the museums and society of his day against the grain. For Fuchs as for Benjamin, as noted above, official state museums such as the Pergamon rankled for their propensity to show culture "in its festive Sunday dress, and only very rarely in its ragged work clothes."[51] Expanding how one might think about state collections and museums as politicized instruments of power, Fuchs advanced a mode of collecting and reading existing collections that represented one way of challenging the omissions and elisions made by state museums. This critique translated into tactics by which Fuchs rescued, and then put back into cultural circulation, officially neglected and endangered art objects such as Tang sculpture, erotic art, and political caricature. With respect to caricature, Fuchs took advantage of his thorough knowledge of the history of such images, creating book publications whose text and reproductions sought to keep these once mass-produced images in circulation.

The kind of encounter promoted by this strategy, of reproductions bringing the original into new contexts, is a form of renewal that likewise represents a crucial way of shattering tradition and renewing the object in the modern world as it is described in Benjamin's seminal essay "The Work of Art in Its Age of Mechanical Reproducibility." There, Benjamin argues that collecting has from the outset been embedded in a process of circulation that transfers objects from an original context into new orders dictated by the collector, following a system of values that has implications for how one might think about collecting, writing, and the body. This value-based conception is an integral part of Benjamin's theorization of auratic art, which is thoroughly couched in terms of collecting and exhibiting.[52] In explaining aura in terms of its value, Benjamin insists that the only true value a work of art can have, its use value (*Gebrauchswert*), arises from its use as a religious or cult object. When the dynamics of secularization and collecting bring artifacts into circulation, a new value Benjamin terms the exhibition value (*Ausstellungswert*) dialectically supplements, but does not replace, its original use value. "*With the emancipation of the various art practices from ritual,*" Benjamin writes, "*go opportunities for the exhibition of their products.*"[53] While Benjamin observes that the concept of authenticity displaces that of originality, he makes clear that originality always precedes authenticity and remains in some form, even when authenticity predominates.[54] It should not be surprising, then, to find a ritual function in secular environments such as museums, even in an age when aura was supposed to have been shattered. Indeed, as Hal Foster observes, the successful dissolution of aura through photography and digital media might well tend to increase demand for auratic objects, for, "as new aura is difficult to produce, established aura skyrockets in value."[55] This value can also be understood as respective increases in both the objects' exhibition value *and* their exchange value (price). Though both values are dialectically tied to use value in Marxian fashion, these terms must remain differentiated for Benjamin. Indeed, as he took pains to point out to Adorno, many modes of acquisition and possession are available to collectors (arguably also to institutions) that do not involve direct monetary exchange (for instance, donation) and/or that are driven by considerations other than financial benefit (for instance, prestige). It is precisely because the collector resists universal commodification by reworking what possession means that his practices are of interest to Benjamin.

"Possession and having are allied with the tactile [*taktisch*]," Benjamin writes with respect to the collector, meaning that they can be key terms by which the collector's body and identity figure in what it means to collect, preserve, and write in modernity.[56] The increase in exhibition value does not take place at the expense of cult value of the object. It instead alters the human beings' sensory perception (*Sinneswahrnehmung*) of them. As Benjamin puts it, "[T]he manner in which human sense perception is organized, the medium in which it is accomplished, is determined not only by nature but by historical circumstances as well."[57] Benjamin's conception opens up the possibility that human beings might learn to perceive and respond to their environment in a new way, should a quantitative increase in display and exhibition at some point become qualitative. This insistence on the body can be understood in part as a rejection of German idealist aesthetics, based on illusory notions of autonomous art coupled with a mode of disembodied, contemplative reception.[58] In contrast, the collector's relationship to his objects is at once tactical and tactile (*taktisch*), guided as it is by passion and an instinct that works like a "divining rod," turning "him into a finder of new sources" that need to be renewed, which he accomplishes by taking possession.

Of all the possibilities for taking possession available to the collector—finding or purchasing an object, receiving a gift or inheritance, "neglecting" to return a borrowed object—for Benjamin the most praiseworthy was to reproduce the object in one's own hand.[59] The greatest example of this Benjamin sees in Jean Paul's story of poor little Wutz, the impoverished schoolmaster who acquires a collection of great books by writing them himself on the basis of titles he sees in advertising catalogs. This example represents for Benjamin nothing less than the ability of collecting and writing, indeed, of writing *as* collecting, to work as media in touch with experience. When Benjamin explains on this basis that from the standpoint of the collector, "writers are actually people who write books not because of poverty but rather because they are dissatisfied with the books they could buy but do not like," he is stressing the value, seen by the collector, of allowing objects and narratives to enter into human lives, from which they can emerge enriched with additional traces of thought and action.[60] Over time, such a cultural practice accumulates traces the way rings grow on a tree, enabling the enriched object to "grow" with the people who possess it. Resonant with what Benjamin calls "memory" in the "Storyteller" essay, this practice enables the fragile possibility of cultural transmission, of passing "a happening from generation to generation."[61] This practice figures at the beginning of our opening example, the *Aesthetics of Resistance,* which leaves traces of the protagonists' thought embedded in an ekphrastic rendering of the Pergamon frieze.

The texts in this study similarly develop narrative modes—albeit to a variety of ends—that can be read from the perspective of Benjamin's collector. That is, all contain traces of how lives and thought changed when objects in certain arrangements or organized environments entered them. In Goethe's *Wahlverwandtschaften* (1809), a collector's images and ancient funerary objects "organize [the characters'] imagination toward that time," inspiring cultural practices and a built environment resulting in a modern type of grave mound (as Benjamin himself noted in his "Wahlverwandtschaften" essay). In Stifter's *Nachsommer* (1857), learning to collect scientific specimens puts that novel's hero on the royal road to the aesthetic and societal heights of *Bildung,* with the collections he creates reflecting his current state of mind. Or one might speak of Raabe's "Celtic Bones" (1861), in which the display of unearthed bones and artifacts sparks desires for the wealth, academic prestige, or both in those who would possess or control them. And whereas Rilke's *Neue Gedichte* (1907) represents an imaginary museum resulting from a complex mental process that situates objects, people, thoughts, and stories within a notional museal space, Lenz's *Heimatmuseum* (1977) presents a textual museum, layering story upon story of the lives touched by objects destroyed to prevent their abuse by unapologetic fascists. In a different and even more intricate way, the "imaginary topography" constructed in Bachmann's novel *Malina* (1971) depicts the creation of authorial consciousness as a function of the legacies of historical violence, in Viennese museums and their related organizing paradigms.[62] Sebald's method of composing text around images rescued from junk shops and old photo albums and Grünbein's approach to exhibition spaces as a means of exploring the contours of the poetic mind represent two contemporary efforts that reveal, through the confrontation with collecting, the valences and ambivalences of human thought and memory in the digital age.

Other criteria, in addition to being readable from the standpoint of Benjamin's collector, justify this selection of texts. Each of the literary projects examined here openly thematizes or comments on its relationship to museums and/or collecting and exhibiting. Though a text with an "unannounced" relationship to museums and/or collecting might still have something to tell us about inventoried consciousness in the age of the public museum, part of what I wish to establish is that these instances are not isolated cases. When text after text presents evidence that museum culture figures as part of its design, the inadequacy of prevailing approaches to these texts becomes apparent, particularly in light of the fact that more texts can be analyzed from the standpoint of the museum function than I can accomplish here (worth mentioning is Benjamin's point that from the collector's standpoint, the collection's incompleteness is what makes it a patchwork and thus a form of allegory).[63]

In any case, some sort of explanation is necessary to account for instances when, as in Goethe's *Wahlverwandtschaften,* characters comment soberly on the need to develop norms of behavior for the newly devised practice of encountering real art in museums and art collections, or when, as in Ingeborg Bachmann's *Malina,* the novel's murderous namesake is from the very first page described as having gone underground at a real existing institution whose catalog the novel quotes at length. The possibility that this kind of evidence can be accounted for *without* considering processes related to collecting and exhibiting is even less when these writers, and sometimes their informed readers, confirm that reading for the museum function is not only possible, but in fact necessary. It is, for instance, significant that a figure such as the architect in the *Wahlverwandtschaften* was read as a like-minded collector by the Boisserée brothers, Romantic collectors whose assembly of religious art helped inspire the completion of the Cologne cathedral and eventually formed the core of Munich's Alte Pinakothek—a fact from the historical record that justifies a focus on this particular novel. It is also significant that the writers in this study are themselves collectors (Goethe or Sebald), verifiably involved in museum- or object-based activities (Stifter, Raabe, Rilke, Grünbein), or, demonstrable interpreters of Benjamin's projects (Bachmann, Lenz, Grünbein, Sebald). Benjamin's own writing suggests why this third set of criteria should gain in importance. As he writes in "Ich packe meine Bibliothek aus," "Even though public collections may be less objectionable socially and more useful academically than private collections, the objects get their due only in the latter. I do know that time is running out for the type [the private collector] I am discussing here and have been representing before you a bit *ex officio*. But, as Hegel put it, only when it is dark does the owl of Minerva begin its flight. Only in extinction is the collector comprehended."[64] If Benjamin's insight proves right, fewer personal collectors as he understands them surfaced over the course of the twentieth century, at the same time as comprehension of the collector and his processes grows.

A separate point regarding the array of texts in this study is that certain features of the development of German-speaking museums must figure in deciding the sequence of texts within the trajectory of my argument. In selecting texts, I drew on some twenty years of museum-studies scholarship, which offers not only a critical vocabulary for studying museums in a variety of cultural contexts but also a number of issues that have particular importance in the German-speaking realm.[65] One of these factors, as I have already suggested, has to do with the ways that the meaning of being acculturated (often, but not completely the same as being *gebildet*) has been constructed and changed over time. Though it makes sense on one level to regard museums as champions of *Bildung,* this concept is valorized and naturalized as a function of many other discourses and practices, not the least of which are forms of identity as refracted by notions of history, nationhood, class, and gender. Not only can these issues be interrogated by appropriately selected texts, but the study of their museum functions can also disaggregate and sharpen the views of them and how they develop alongside one another. This is particularly the case with gender constructs, which most of the texts in this study show to be related to questions of inventoried consciousness in ways the study of nonliterary museum culture tends to be less able to do.[66] But it is the same with other cultural configurations, whose relationship to acculturation, on the one hand, and to processes of accumulation and classification, on the other, is worth thinking about in disaggregated ways. Even though *Bildung* has generally lost the cachet it once had, what it means to be acculturated and have access to related exhibitionary environments continues to have deep significance when it comes to practices such as tourism.

Even though each of the texts discussed here proves to be a rich vehicle in its own right for exploring its respective museum function, I make particular headway into the question of inventoried consciousness in the age of the public museum by organizing the chapters of the text into pairs around certain critical issues. In the first pairing of texts, in Chapter 2, I analyze the projects of Sebald and Grünbein as a means of probing two significant contemporary modes in which classified material culture interacts with modern media in shaping memory and consciousness. In Part 2, consisting of analyses of Goethe's *Wahlverwandtschaften* (Chapter 3) and Stifter's *Nachsommer* (Chapter 4), I study collecting and exhibiting as the first public museums were being founded in German-speaking Europe. Examining the competing forces and discourses that made German-speaking museums possible, in these two chapters, I account for the establishment and naturalization of German-speaking museum culture, precisely for the ways in which collecting served various registers of *Bildung*. In both chapters, references to the material and historical record are used to corroborate the view of inventoried consciousness generated by my readings of the respective museum functions. In Part 3, I examine the expansion of museum culture from the 1860s to the early twentieth century in Raabe's "Keltische Knochen" (Chapter 5) and Rilke's *Neue Gedichte* (Chapter 6). These two chapters trace the growing number and differentiation of museal offerings, on the one hand, and the emerging inflection of acculturation by cultural tourism, on the other, showing how the German-speaking literary imagination navigates national and foreign cultures through an orientation on exhibitionary institutions ranging from spectacles such as the Viennese Prater and the Parisian morgue to archaeology, history, and a host of fine-art museums. Even more than in the first two chapters, the respective material records from the Hallstatt archaeological digs and Rilke's residency in Rodin's studio-museums play a significant role in illuminating these museum functions.

Shifting to the post-1945 era, in the final part of this book I take up two institutions that played a peculiar and understudied role in the Nazi mobilization of the German home front during World War II: Heimat museums and army museums.[67] In Chapter 7, I again turn to the material record of a museum, this time the Heeresgeschichtliches Museum im Arsenal (the Austrian Military History Museum in the Arsenal), the first purpose-built museum in Austria with a long and peculiar past. Unpacking that past helps us understand Bachmann's *Malina* to be a subtle but unmistakable literary intervention into the oppressive discourses constructed by this museum, discourses that, as this text states on its first page, had since the Second World War largely operated out of sight but not out of mind. Examining a different kind of narrative intervention into museal discourses, in Chapter 8 I analyze Lenz's *Heimatmuseum,* a novel named for a local history museum that is burned down in order to prevent its postwar takeover by unrepentant fascists. A text that revealingly anticipates the practices of later German Holocaust antimonuments—built environments often designed to disappear and be actively recalled through the mediation of photographs and texts—this textual museum comes into being when its curator, Zygmunt Rogalla, unpacks objects in his memory for an interlocutor. Their dialogue produces a series of textual "guided tours," representing objects' multivalent meanings in a serially unfolding form, beckoning readers to detect museal processes at work and actively to interpret the text in ways valorized by Benjamin. In some sense, this project has then returned, richer than when it began, to its opening coordinates: intellectually, with a project of writing as collecting very much in the spirit of Walter Benjamin, and chronologically, to the problems of the contemporary era. One of the outcomes of the journey is the concept of the "notional museum," which, I show, pertains to thinking shaped by museums, certain literary texts, or both, in a fashion that once appealed to Renaissance thinkers on the museum.

Before turning to the next chapter, I should say a word about my use of sources and translations in this book. I have analyzed source texts in the original German, but because it is often necessary for me to quote large blocks of source material, offering original and translation in parallel would have led to an unwieldy presentation. I have chosen to work with published English translations unless otherwise indicated. I hope that German readers of this discipline-crossing study do not mind too much. Citations of German source materials are still provided, so that those wishing to look at the original language may readily locate quoted passages. In so doing, I present the page numbers of the German source first, followed by those of the English translation. Where key words or concepts are untranslatable or have no single English equivalent, I supply the original word in parentheses and sometimes elaborate further in a note. I follow the German titles of works, indicating in parentheses titles of standard translations. Where no translation has been published of either a title or passage, I offer my own rendering.

2

Inventoried Consciousness Today: Durs Grünbein and W. G. Sebald

At one point in an interview, the contemporary poet and essayist Durs Grünbein was prompted to explain why museum spaces seemed crucial to comprehending his views of art and literature. Confirming that museums have a privileged place in his reflections, Grünbein responded, "[T]here [in museums], you can see without interference how the battles of memory work [*Schlachten der Erinnerungsarbeit*] were fought. Where else could I, in the briefest amount of time, learn more about the way my brain works?"[1] For Grünbein, a writer and theorist with a keen knowledge of neurology and the natural sciences, museums are privileged realms for exploring the brain and its production of artistic and linguistic images. In this model of thought and artistic production, consciousness stands in an exact relationship to language, on the one hand, and the structuring of display environments, on the other. Grünbein's writing is promising territory for mapping the contemporary contours of consciousness, memory, and space in literary writing. And Grünbein is not alone. The prominent writer W. G. Sebald is equally clear that collecting and exhibiting are key terms in how he constructs literary texts and how the figures in these texts act and make sense of their world.

Recent scholarship has argued that these issues are part of a more general "archival" trend in literary writing of the 1990s, exemplified by the texts of Michael Krüger, Gerhard Roth, Walter Kempowski, and W. G. Sebald, among others.[2] Yet for Grünbein and Sebald, meaningful distinctions can and should be made between archives and museum culture, defined in terms of collecting and exhibiting at personal and institutional levels. Refining the current state of scholarship on these two representative writers, which until now has tended to regard museums and other exhibitionary institutions as just another variant of the trope of the "archive," represents a necessary step in establishing the contours of contemporary inventoried consciousness. Establishing the contours of inventoried consciousness as it is shaped by the museum function of the digital age, in turn, helps clarify the stakes in generating a genealogy of inventoried consciousness since the invention of the public museum. For structural reasons, then, this chapter appears at the outset of the study rather than at the end, though its concerns surface again and again throughout the text.

In this chapter I examine first Grünbein and then Sebald, eliciting the centrality of contemporary museum culture for their thought and literary production. In terms of authorial approach and reflective trope, collecting, museums, and materiality emerge as significant factors that can help unlock these texts. By isolating the museum function in these texts, it also becomes easier to comprehend that the impact of the museum on consciousness and writing has a cultural genealogy reaching back at least two centuries.

Exhibitionary Spaces in the Writing of Durs Grünbein

In contemporary German letters, Durs Grünbein is often thought of as a poet of postunification Germany, particularly of Berlin. The rapidly changing cultural landscape following the fall of the Berlin wall provided the backdrop for Grünbein's meteoric rise to literary prominence. Though relatively unknown before 1989, by 1995 Grünbein had received major awards such as the Peter Huchel and Georg Büchner prizes for his writing, which is often associated with the urban experience and the problems of the modern subject in the digital age. But while modern-day concerns drive his projects, most of his work stands out for the maintenance of intertextual dialogues with literary tradition, guided sometimes by a thematic affinity to a particular poet and sometimes by poetological concerns that can be explored in the corpus of earlier bodies of writing.[3] Grünbein's deep interest in ancient literatures became much more apparent with his publication of *Nach den Satiren* (After the Satires), a collection of poetry written in dialogue with the Roman poet Decimus Iunius Iuvenalis, better known as Juvenal, as a means of exploring modern concerns via the "bread and circuses" of ancient Romans.[4] In general, this kind of movement between ancient and modern city spaces represents a multitiered act of translation for Grünbein, an attempt to interrogate the ancients' use of language for insights into key components of modern thought. As Grünbein himself explains,

> [T]he artistic element in modern literature is composed of both components; it owes the Greeks as much as it does the Romans. Put differently, the literature of antiquity generally represents the nontrivial, that which is not banal, in linguistic reflection. Only in this way can one understand its enormous effects on all later intellectual trends. Ancient literature is the hinterland of all the unsolved problems, the source of all the aporias that hold us

> breathless today. Ancient literature is the nutrient medium of our languages, the original collection of categories, the founding act behind our cultural routines.[5]

But because ancient literature cannot be directly accessed today—partly because of the intervention of Christianity but also for reasons I delve into in a moment—it must be treated as a kind of act of recovery, of elements that are "with us" but whose presence is suppressed from consciousness. As Grünbein puts it, "[T]o speak of ancient poetry means, as Nietzsche showed, to speak of the repressed. . . . Reading the Greeks, the Romans, helps us to re-discover the physical human being, this mortal existence that accepted transience with the quiet soul of the stoic."[6] As becomes clear, the condition Grünbein diagnoses in the relationship of ancient and modern is profoundly bound up in dynamics shaped by today's museum culture.

Reading Grünbein's work for its museum function traces out dynamics faced by the museum in the digital age, illuminated by Grünbein's pronounced awareness of the dialectical interrelationship of media and materiality to language. Grünbein's approach to writing can be productively thought of as a post-post-structuralist "poetics of presence," to use the phrasing of Wolfgang Riedel.[7] Riedel describes Grünbein's project as an "invalidation of the poststructuralist abolition of the [Derridean] 'hors-texte,'" of any referentiality to human or ontological reality outside language.[8] For Grünbein, the *only* reality that exists for us is that generated by the human brain, situated in the body. From this perspective, what one perceives or designates to be "presences"—feelings, perceptions, dreams, memories, and any other cognitive operations—derive from our neurophysiology. The same is true for everything deemed to be "absence," whether in a physical or metaphysical sense.[9]

Language does not precede this neurophysiological reality. Before words can be used, Grünbein posits the occurrence of psychic acts ("imagination," either *Vorstellung* or *Imagination* in German) resulting from the interplay of the body and the human brain. As this notion is expressed in the central essay "Mein babylonisches Gehirn" [My Babylonian Brain], this is so "because the word, this most specious of all aesthetic media, is only a pretense: behind it there is a psychic act that demands transformation" into linguistic expression with full semantic perfidy.[10] As a consequence, lyric can be thought of as "a protocol of internal gazes. The body determines what the method is. Behind the semantic order stands the anatomical; under the layers rolled up by hermeneutics, living tissue appears, the stuff the lines [of poetry] have been made of since the beginning of lyrical fumbling. For the poem presents thought in a series of physiological short circuits."[11]

Language and poetry are thus understood to express and, in the recipient, to produce, neurological firings. These interactions and reactions between language and the body produce effects people variously (and to some extent erroneously, according to Grünbein) ascribe to spirituality and (self-)reflection.[12] Since aesthetics, history, memory, and, in some ways, politics remain crucial and carefully articulated concerns for him, Grünbein seeks not to reduce all meaning to some neurochemical level. But in a crucial way, a view that ignores the role of the brain in generating words and images is bound to misrecognize what he considers to be the fundamental bases of the human condition.[13]

The implications of this view are compelling. For Grünbein, the model for all poetry can be found in the Greek poet Simonides of Ceos. Since Cicero, Simonides has often been credited as the inventor of a mnemonic device based on pictorial-spatial representation. Faced with the need to identify friends killed and dismembered at a feast by the sudden collapse of the roof, Simonides, who had just gone outside to relieve himself, relied on a mental picture of where each friend had sat to supply order to the turmoil of memories and impressions. Grünbein writes, "The simile could hardly have been chosen in more fortunate a manner: as surviving witness, [Simonides] showed the way for the mourning of the survivors and found as an epigrammatist and poet of lamentations the key to memory, the prerequisite of every obituary."[14] As is also the case with Sebald's writing, architectural spaces offer a highly effective means of structuring consciousness as a set of relations within an imaginary realm. Such a model represents for Grünbein a lyric evocation of presence ("it could easily serve as the basis for all future poetry"), guided by an imaginary picture space that can trigger memories in an ordered manner.[15] Building on the notion that words flow from internally generated images, an organizational paradigm for structuring thought is an essential component of all art and literature.

Part of what Grünbein means can be expressed in terms of ekphrasis and *ut pictura poesis,* traditions that allow image and language to produce similar effects and draw on each other's techniques. As he states in an interview,

> In literature there is the genre of ekphrasis [*Bildbeschreibung*], the attempt to achieve painterly effects with words, in essence a transposition. The whole thing remains completely unclear, however, for in the end only mental images are produced instead of the visual stimuli triggered by paintings. . . . Even today I do not know how the presence of that which is absent functions in the mental image. Someone reads aloud, you close your eyes, and you "*see*" exactly as much as if you were walking through a museum.[16]

Coming close to John Hollander's concept of notional ekphrasis, a concept developed to account for poetic genres that describe imaginary art objects in the mind's eye as if they existed materially, Grünbein is fascinated by the ability of sheer language to generate the stimuli that might be felt during a gallery walk.[17]

This is a problem—one that I am subsuming under the category of the "notional museum" or the "museum of the mind"—that occupies almost every writer in this study in one way or another. Grünbein's thinking offers one way of understanding how "notional museums" work. Insofar as Simonides' spatial-mnemonic images represent the basis for all poetic endeavors, Grünbein's reference to the intersection of the museum and the linguistic imaginary is highly revealing, for it again points to his sensitivity to the impact of museal organization on thought. Indeed, museal spaces occupy a central place in Grünbein's reflections on art and physiology. For Grünbein, museums are not only a metaphor for delineating mental functions, but are also realms directly related to the way one thinks and acts in the world.

The implications of museums for the literary imagination are complex in Grünbein's oeuvre. On the one hand, the museum and the gallery are a key paradigm for Grünbein's conception of the poet. As he writes in his essay, "Das babylonische Gehirn,"

> [T]he Babylonian brain, the basic equipment of the poet today, moves through the scenes of cities *as through painting galleries.* It approaches the stars telescopically while nearing the corner of a building in ancient Rome. . . . Always in transit on its journey through the times (the journey of its own body as well as that of the species, history), it finds in the poem a place to pause, a sojourn among the unjustified speeches, among the wretched views. It finds a showplace of signs and images that amounts to life.[18]

In the space provided by the poem, the contemporary poet is able to cope with the chaotic bombardment of images and the flood of memories in present-day society by relating them to spatially configured environments like city spaces or painting galleries. For the poetic mind, the showcase of perceived signs and images seems to exist in a simultaneous temporal context that fundamentally resembles a museum space. One of the hallmarks of display environments lies in their ability to situate objects and artifacts from various times of production in a single time, the present (a fact that is often not perceived, when, for instance, objects are arranged so as to represent some notion of change over time).[19] As Helmut Böttiger observes with regard to Grünbein's classically informed poetry, the simultaneity of physical remnants of the past and present allows him to create a kind of spiraling montage in linguistic form. "The strict form, the verbose tone, the classical enclosures enable Grünbein to move from close ups to long shots, to switch from the language of present-day newspapers into the language of the authors of antiquity, to confront today's slang with the transmitted tone of yesterday."[20] Standing at a dialectical remove from the world's unceasing movement, both poem and picture gallery enable reflection and attribution of meaning by relating past and present remains.

On the other hand, Grünbein defines the Babylonian brain in terms of a failed archive. Grünbein is highly aware that the historical specificity of prevailing cultural conditions—as affected by the workings of traditional and technological media and the catastrophes of modern experience—profoundly constrains poetic consciousness. Moreover, because memories are at once personal and societal for Grünbein, the contemporary poet cannot escape the implications of the twentieth century's worst catastrophes.[21] Thus Grünbein writes, "[T]oday, at the end of the twentieth century, Baudelaire's formula of the Babylonian heart can be varied: the new setting, less passionate, and in a colder desire, is the Babylonian brain. As in *an archive that has collapsed under the weight of its murderous files, of the documents of notorious inhumanity,* the verses of antiquity lay scattered . . . elegy on top of psalm on top of satire, a pile of loose pages."[22] As if physically damaged by the experience and the evidence of civilization's transgressions, the Babylonian brain undergoes a breakdown in order, akin to an archival failure.[23] It is a failure caused *not* by information overload per se, but instead by the inescapable evidence of unspeakable inhumanity. Past traditions, conceptions, and works continue to exist, yet, as an unorganized pile of loose pages, their retrieval is not secure or predictable. This point cannot be brushed aside, insofar as the archive is typically described as a repository organized to facilitate the reliable storage and retrieval of documents and information.[24] Grünbein's writing thus raises a question that this study takes up in a variety of subsequent contexts: how should museums and archives be differentiated in their effects on consciousness?

Museums and archives, though related, are not interchangeable in Grünbein's thinking: museums and galleries continue to represent suggestive if complex ways of describing the operations of the Babylonian brain, while the archive's systematizing effects apply today only in negative form. A critic could be forgiven for missing these distinctions, for Grünbein's use of the word "archive" is subtle. Grünbein uses the term when, for instance, he discusses Stasi files and the arrangement of animals and specimens in zoos and scientific museums.[25] It is plausible to say that zoos perform an archival function in preserving animals and being capable of returning them to some original habitat (often more of a theoretical proposition as humankind intrudes upon ever-growing segments of the environment). Yet accounting for the zoo in Grünbein's writing, to take it as an example, requires additional thinking about a large number of issues that are only tangentially related to the zoo's arguable "archival" functions.[26] As can be seen in Grünbein's zoo poetry and especially in his essay on the Berlin zoo, topics such as the long history of zoo architecture, specific display techniques, historically differentiated collecting practices, and a typology of visitor behaviors (derived from the animal trader Carl Hagenbeck, who invented the cageless animal display) fascinate Grünbein. Since the storage and retrieval functions of the zoo do not sufficiently account for all the functions of interest to Grünbein, using the term "archive" to refer to institutions like zoos and museums offers inadequate theoretical precision and invites unnecessary confusion.

Similarly, while science museums also perform archival functions, Grünbein makes it clear that these functions are performed within a larger institutional framework. In an essay on the growth of nineteenth-century science collections, Grünbein writes that the assembly of "great osteological archives" then required people to "collect, prepare specimens, create inventories" so that "a provisional sense of order comes into being."[27] In light of the processes Grünbein associates with archive building, one would, at first glance, be justified in speaking of them either as archival or museal processes. But later in the same essay, Grünbein discusses the differences between scientific uses of specimen collections and displays created for the production of lay knowledge.[28] The knowledge that the different orderings produce varies as a function of collecting process and display environment, making it clear that display and archiving are not interchangeable for him. Though museums and related institutions such as zoos archive, for Grünbein, museums and zoos represent *more* than storage and retrieval systems.

Treating archives and museum collections as simple equivalents for each other also runs the risk of overlooking the nuance with which Grünbein grasps the effects of digital databases, electronic media, and the Internet on contemporary thought and culture. As I mentioned previously, all modes of artistic production rely on the creation of images. But as Grünbein explained to Heinz-Norbert Jocks, that production of images depends on the specific medium, meaning that each medium has distinct qualities and advantages:

> Now, writing has the same prerequisite [as art]; it is a genuine process of creating images, only with the difference that it spares you from taking the detour of canvases, computer monitors, or exhibition walls. That is of great advantage in purely ecological terms. For the production of an imagistic vision I need a single line. Poetic images are less impressive probably only because people want to see or touch objects in a three-dimensional space in order to comprehend them.[29]

The differentiation Grünbein makes between poetry, the visual arts, and computer screens is worth dwelling on. For one thing, writing, digital display, and material art objects each occupy distinct realms in his thinking. Moreover, in contrast to the economy of writing or the shimmer of computer monitors, exhibition spaces offer a distinct and attractive experience of materiality and three-dimensionality. According to Grünbein, objects with physical presence continue to fascinate. In understanding the appeal of material objects in space, Grünbein's argument comes very close to Andreas Huyssen's emphatic point that the advent of photographic and electronic reproduction has by no means spelled the end for the object-laden museum: if anything, in the age of the Internet and digital databases, it is possible to register an increased craving for material objects.[30] Moreover, for some time, electronic media and cinematically inspired exhibition layouts have themselves been moving into traditional museum spaces.[31]

Many of Grünbein's remarks and arguments resonate with these notions, suggesting that reproducible media, museums, zoos, and literature respectively perform indispensable functions. When Grünbein therefore observes, "[L]ong before the introduction of the computer and any neuro-Romanticism, [lyric] was at home in the virtual," he means to suggest that the poem is all the more valuable today for two reasons. It can operate in a manner that approximates the workings of the Internet and digital media while offering, as a mechanism for establishing spatial order and presence, respite from the ceaseless mental wanderings exacerbated by the chatter of images in contemporary society.[32] The same logic underlies Grünbein's views of museums and zoos. Moreover, Grünbein valorizes museums for their unequaled opportunity for reflection and insight into that central fascination of Grünbein's, the brain. These two features make display spaces crucially important for an increasingly digital age.

The particular ability of the museum diorama to structure personal memory, and thereby consciousness, is elaborated in the essay "Kindheit im Diorama" [Childhood in the Diorama]. Here, Grünbein writes of his childhood love for natural history museums and the ecstasies of gazing at animal dioramas:

> The changing showcases behind glass, concentrated tableaux of the typical habitat of the five continents: they corresponded precisely with the combinatorial consciousness of a child who was out to conquer the world. As soon as the curtain was pulled back I gazed spellbound at scenes that were as strange as they were familiar. . . . [The frozen display elements] sent me into small ecstasies and followed me into my dreams, long before I knew what an epiphany is.[33]

Looking back as an adult, Grünbein realizes how these experiences continue to structure his consciousness and his knowledge of his own and the historical past.

> Today it seems to me that in such moments, my entire childhood entered the diorama. Like the Chinese painter of whom legend has it that he was absorbed into his finished landscapes, the child's imago slipped into those fantastic middle realms of near and far, its ideal place to be. As if a magic word had been uttered, everything that was there, the exotic and strange and the familiar objects from home, was intermingled with the fragments of lived experience (*Erlebnisfragmente*) from my early years. . . . Here in the museum they were inventoried as archetypal dream images, and it had to be possible to call them back up when their time came. The diorama was the "open sesame" [realm] in which my memories lie stored as primal geographical motifs.[34]

Describing the effect of mental absorption with the same language as Benjamin's "Work of Art" essay (the Chinese painter who enters the landscape), the passage places the child's imago in the display with two important consequences. First, the display becomes doubly encoded in the sense that a personal level of meaning is inscribed on the display's general, or public, encoding. Such double encoding of exhibition space results from the ability of exhibitions to structure identity, though in many variants such as Stifter's *Nachsommer* [Indian Summer], it is easier to achieve when the collector assembles the collection himself.

Second, the three-dimensional diorama technique structures the dream images, allowing them to function in terms of a mental inventory. Crucially, however, this transformation is twice described as a magic one, suggesting that conscious criteria do not organize it. For Walter Benjamin, transferring lived experiences (*Erlebnisse*) into memory without conscious intervention represents a crucial precondition for lived experiences in modernity to be converted into "true" experience (*Erfahrung*). One way such successful conversion seems possible, as Benjamin writes in "On Some Motifs in Baudelaire," is through a ritual process resembling Proustian *mémoire involontaire*. "This concept," Benjamin explains, "bears the marks of the situation which gave rise to it; it is part of the inventory of the individual who is isolated in many ways. Where there is experience in the strict sense of the word, certain contexts of the individual past combine with material of the collective past."[35] With this mixing of personal and collective pasts being precisely what Grünbein's diorama achieves, the diorama bears thinking about as a productive ritual site in the sense Benjamin goes on to describe: "the rituals with their ceremonies, their festivals (quite probably nowhere recalled in Proust's work) kept producing the amalgamation of these two elements of memory over and over again. They triggered recollection at certain times and remained handles of memory for a lifetime. In this way, voluntary and involuntary recollection lose their mutual exclusiveness."[36]

But the diorama represents not only an apt site for placing recollected personal and collective dream images into a kind of mental inventory. Rather, this inventorying function arises from the diorama's particular display techniques, which impart order and create illusion through one and the same gesture. As Grünbein analyzes it, this gesture produces a phenomenological "feast for the eyes" (*eine Augenweide*) constructed through collecting and exhibiting techniques that produce effects akin to those of filmmaking. Specifically, the diorama represents

> a "feast for the eyes" in which both display and mirrored nature meld in a long shot. In its illusionary space the appearance of the natural is completed as a perfect memory of nature. By remaining invisible, montage, applied here in instrumentalized form, helps to speculate with the probable. . . . The impression of spatial depth is produced through a slight curving of the rear wall. Sculpted foreground and painted backdrop diverge here by miles; this and the painted trompe-l'oeil manipulation of space create the low-level hypnotic effect that awakened the sense of vertigo in the child. Is this perhaps one of the reasons for the long-lasting psychological effects of the diorama?[37]

Beyond performing an organizing function, dioramas also permit a Benjaminian ritualization of memory by means of hypnotic, three-dimensional display techniques that reveal the structure of inventoried consciousness in modernity.[38] The structuring of inventoried consciousness via exhibition can be recognized because humankind has reached a point in history when the display techniques born out of the technological, modernizing spirit of the nineteenth century have fallen out of favor and therefore seem obsolete.[39] Yet their apparent obsolescence is deceiving in two ways. First, in Benjamin's terms, contemporary culture has yet to awaken from the dream of the nineteenth century because the worn-out cultural forms of the nineteenth century remained those of the twentieth and the twenty-first. This is another way of saying that museum culture operates on consciousness today without people's general awareness.[40] And second, the modernizing processes that first led to natural history dioramas—the form of obsolescence called the destruction of the environment and extinction—have yet to take their full toll on the world and humankind. This is part of what Grünbein means when he writes, "[E]xtinction is the future of the diorama" (more on this is a moment).[41]

All of these complex issues are in play, and they are what Grünbein wants to explore, when he deploys the trope of the diorama as memory space. Such an instance occurs in the poem "Hälfte des Ohres" [Half of the Ear], where the sensory pathways by which aural signals reach the brain and trigger memory and the unconscious are described in terms of neurological processes and three-dimensional display. After the sound has passed through the cochlea and into memory, it passes

. . . further on to the unconscious, until every individual tone
    In the phonic gelatin congeals into cartilage,—
. . . .
Like the space that gets narrow behind you forming memory,
    Expands in front of you without knowing you,
        In each moment returning as a diorama.
Bio-savanna; and all the chaos gets integrated.
    But the languages do not really take hold.
        Farther, then, into the poem, deeper into the diagram,
Where numbers turn like Möbius strips,
    Incalculable because they are silent
        Like the ping-pong between the brain's right and left hemispheres
The ping-pong of lightning-fast sensory data and their decay.
    Thinking in real-time, and how things go on from here
        Is shown by Zeno's arrow, the frozen flight.
Cagey are the jokes, space is encoded through and through.[42]

In light of his depiction of the diorama, Grünbein's point about the value of the museum space for understanding the brain ("in museums you can see without interference how the battles of memory work were fought") can now begin to be unpacked. Returning again and again where the physiological signal processing, consciousness, memory, and poetic language converge, the natural history diorama this passage deploys functions as a rich trope for the interweaving of personal *and* collective memory as well as the chaos of the outside world as mediated by the senses. This explains why the poem, staged as a "soliloquy" (*Selbstgespräch*), produces a "protocol of internal gazes" that shifts between fragments from the history of brain exploration (with references to figures such as Pavlov, Skinner, and Rorschach) and potentially lived experiences such as a bungee jump. The natural history dimension is perhaps also why the poem employs a series of animal metaphors that cast both the urban realm described at various points and the internal anatomy of the ear in terms of an undersea space. It is because the diorama provides the possibility for Benjaminian memory and experience in a way that accords with Grünbein's neurological conception of image and language production that he turns to the museum as a means of exploring the way for contemporary consciousness out of mere "sound and urban trance."

This structuring of memory and consciousness occurs in a space Grünbein claims is "liberating" because it is dialectically enmeshed in, but at a remove from, the dynamics of present-day existence.[43] Similarly, Grünbein thinks that zoos, places where the tantalizing physical "presence of the animals is sensed from far away," employ processes of collecting and exhibiting that are multiply enmeshed in the dialectic of modernization and human conquest that threaten to annihilate the world. Paradoxically, to their human visitors zoos promise escape from modernity: "[F]or a few hours, mankind seeks a forgetting of history and the everyday in the museum of evolution."[44] Yet even this attempt at what might be called a "creative forgetting" partakes in, perhaps even underwrites, the progress of modernity.[45] Recalling Theodor W. Adorno's analysis of zoos and extinction in *Minima Moralia,* Grünbein writes, "[I]n a diabolical dialectic, the animal display spaces inside that are becoming more comfortable correspond to the disappearing habitats outside. . . . Today, zoos justify their existence with a responsibility for protecting the species, for so-called preservation breeding."[46] What can be seen most clearly in the zoo, but nevertheless also in the art museum, is the fact that institutions that collect, preserve, and display are anything but losing relevance in a world driven by processes of obsolescence and the new.[47]

Today, these processes are inflected by digital media and a glut of reproduced images, making museums ever more valuable as places to explore what modes of consciousness remain open in the present day. The contemporary poem similarly provides an irreplaceable means of constructing meaning in the world, precisely at a time when the textual cultural archive has collapsed under the weight of human-wrought catastrophe. Dialectically related to the processes of modernization and advancing dematerialization, neither museum nor poem offers mere compensation. In fact, the two institutions might be viewed not as limping along behind the relentless march of computer networks and television broadcasting, but rather as the harbingers of a new stage in cultural development. While it seems improbable that museums and poems will be able to take us (far) outside the culture industry or prepare the way for a utopian future in some straightforward fashion, it bears keeping in mind that many contemporary thinkers such as Grünbein are notoriously allergic to any and all notions of utopia and especially the offering of utopian pronouncements.[48] The dynamics are likely too complex and too contingent to be predicted with any certainty. At the very least, however, the study of a writer such as Grünbein offers an unparalleled opportunity to reverse what seems to be an unceasing tendency with respect to museums in our society, namely to fade into the background and seemingly become invisible. If Grünbein's writing is any indication, museum spaces and poetic writing represent a unique chance of "waking from the dreams" of the nineteenth century (Benjamin).

Collecting in the Writing of W. G. Sebald

W. G. Sebald is no less aware of the relationship of his writing to museum processes than is Durs Grünbein. Like Grünbein, Sebald is a writer whose literary texts are located squarely in the postunification cultural milieu, though, as a scholar of German literature, Sebald had been publishing for some three decades before the appearance of his first "fiction." But whereas Grünbein emerged from East Germany to become one of the main poets of united Berlin, Sebald had spent most of his adult life in a kind of self-imposed exile in East Anglia in Britain. Troubled acutely by the traumas inflicted by Germans in World War II but also highly sensitive to the human and environmental devastation seen by Europe in the age of capitalism, Sebald found Britain a place where he could explore language and the (German) past without being utterly overwhelmed by them. But neither the German language nor the German past were things Sebald could actually escape. In nearly every work, from his break-through collection *Die Ausgewanderten* [The Emigrants] to seminal texts such as *Schwindel. Gefühle* [Vertigo], *Die Ringe des Saturn* [The Rings of Saturn], and *Austerlitz*, Sebald feels compelled to revisit the topoi of the ruined German and European past, peregrinating through the physical vestiges and wrecked lives strewn throughout the continent (and sometimes farther). His writing represents a peculiar kind of search and recovery effort, one beset by melancholy but unable to turn away from the piling wreckage of the past.

In interviews, W. G. Sebald readily discusses the characteristic way his collecting relates the recovery of elements from the past and writing. When, in an interview for Dutch television, Sebald was asked, "You collect photographs?" he responded, "I do. I have for years. Anything that comes my way I put in a box but I also have a small cheap camera."[49] Elsewhere in the same interview he elaborates on his methods of composition, "About two months ago in a junk shop in Bungay, which is the nearest small town to where I live, I fished out of a box of cheap prints a little card, which had a lichen on it, a dried lichen, and underneath in very neat handwriting it said: *Gathered from the tomb of Marshall Ney, Paris, on 7 July 1833.* And something like this, totally valueless as such, somehow gets me going."[50] Sebald's rummaging through junk shops for seemingly discarded or valueless objects vividly recalls the collector's tactics depicted by Walter Benjamin. As Benjamin writes in "Unpacking my Library," "[C]ollectors are people with a tactical/tactile (*taktisch*) instinct; their experience teaches them that when they capture a strange city, the smallest antique shop can be a fortress, the most remote stationery store a key position. How many cities have revealed themselves to me in the marches I undertook in the pursuit of books!"[51] A collector in the Benjaminian mode, Sebald uses tactile and tactical instincts. Driven instinctually to find new sources, by a passion likened to a "divining rod," collectors such as Sebald acquire objects for reasons other than utility or monetary value. In the process, they defy wholly conscious planning or organization. Nonetheless, as Benjamin's metaphors of conquest suggest, the collector's approach to objects is also tactical, in the sense that taking possession of any object, no matter how obscure, can be indispensable for chasing down past social processes and their dissonant languages. Such an object might be the misprinted streetcar ticket, found discarded on the sidewalk by "the great collector Pachinger" after being "in circulation for only a few hours," making it an indispensable addition to his collection of proscribed, damaged, and erroneous cultural goods.[52] Or the object might be a small card with dried lichen, found with the traces of past human ownership.

Part of what collectors such as Sebald sense is that the objects lying ignored or discarded are at risk of disappearing or being destroyed. Should those objects be lost, they would take with them the evidence of human handling and investment of meaning that, for reasons unknown in the present, could well prove highly meaningful in the future. Indeed, Sebald selects photographs and other items because he feels he can rescue them from the ravages of history. As Sebald explains,

> I realize that, in prose, making a decent pattern out of what happens to come your way is a preoccupation, which, in a sense, has no higher ambition than to rescue something out of that stream of history that keeps rushing past, for a brief moment in time. . . . The photograph is meant to get lost somewhere in a box in an attic. It is a nomadic thing that has only a small chance to survive. I think we all know that feeling when we come accidentally across a photographic document being of one of our lost relatives, being of a totally unknown person. We get this sense of appeal; they are stepping out, having been found by somebody after decades or half centuries. All of a sudden they are stepping back over the threshold and are saying, "We were here too once and please take care of us for a while."[53]

Echoing Benjamin's point that "one of the finest memories of a collector is the moment when he rescued a book to which he might never have given a thought . . . because he found it abandoned on the marketplace and bought it to give it its freedom," Sebald plucks objects out of the stream of history.[54] His stories are in some sense stories of rescue, of objects and anecdotes given a chance to survive in his characters' hands and a chance to become meaningful in today's contexts and language. Part of this becoming meaningful has to do with a collector's memories of acquisition and possession, as Benjamin observes, meaning that the collector's life story becomes intertwined with the collection. When Sebald speaks of his stories emerging from the quest to find patterns in the details in the photographs, traces written on them, accompanying documents, and the like, it must be realized that his method is fundamentally embedded in a dynamics of collecting. At the same time, collecting in this fashion also tells the collector's story.

Arising from his use of collecting to generate texts, Sebald's writing possesses a dialectical interplay between media and display environments, between strategies of reproduction, collecting, and exhibiting. This interplay has been partially accounted for in recent scholarship from the standpoint of the "archive," an approach that has yielded some important insights but that, as a conceptual regime, lacks enough subtlety to account for how Sebald's texts work with libraries, archives, and museums, not to mention certain dimensions of personal identity.[55] A dialectical conception of collecting offers more precision for approaching Sebald's narratives.

Particularly revealing in this regard is Sebald's final book, *Austerlitz*. A novel whose features are in many ways representative of Sebald's writing, *Austerlitz* is, in the main, a recounting of the life of Jacques Austerlitz, a Czech Jew whose parents perished in the Holocaust after sending him from Prague to Wales as part of the *Kindertransport*. This fictional biography is constructed not by Austerlitz per se, but by a narrator recalling his twenty-plus years of conversations with Austerlitz, an architectural historian whom the narrator encountered several times while Austerlitz was researching, exploring, and photographing built environments from the bourgeois era. The story that emerges has been (re)collected in more than one sense: it is drawn out of the narrator's memory, at points triggered by photographs, documents, other memories, and a variety of other sources. Though some of these sources must be attributed to Austerlitz's collection and some are the narrator's, in some cases it is impossible to decide their provenance.

In my approach, taking photos of and telling stories about objects can be a form of collecting and exhibiting, precisely because I aim to respect distinctions between reproductions and material originals on the one hand and specific architectural and institutional environments on the other. Maintaining such distinctions would matter for textual reasons if all the narrator and the most important characters did was report on their visits to exhibitions and museums, libraries and archives, streets, store fronts, and all sorts of architectural structures. In this regard, it is significant that Austerlitz's cognitive experiences vary according to the kinds of archival institutions in which they occur. As Russell Kilbourn argues with reference to topological theories of the art of memory, for Austerlitz, the discovery of a "radically negative mnemonic content" occurs through "the transformation of concrete built space, through narrative description, into the exteriorized space in which memory operates."[56] Yet not all spaces are equally conducive for these operations in the text. When Austerlitz recounts his walk through the ghetto museum in Terezín (Theresienstadt), for instance, the individual objects on display are carefully distinguished in memory. Austerlitz recalls,

> I studied the maps of the Greater German Reich and its protectorates, which had never before been more than blank spaces in my otherwise well-developed sense of topography, I traced the course of the railway lines running through them, felt blinded by the documentation recording the population policies of the National Socialists, by evidence of their mania for order and purity, which was put into practice on a vast scale through measures partly improvised, partly devised with obsessive organizational zeal. . . . I saw pieces of luggage that were brought to Terezín by the internees from Prague and Pilsen, Würzburg and Vienna, Kufstein and Karlsbad, and countless other places, objects like handbags, belt buckles, clothes brushes, and combs, which they had made in the various workshops; I saw precisely elaborated production plans and plans for the agricultural exploitation of the open spaces in the ramparts and glacis, where neatly separated parcels of oats and hemp were to be farmed alongside hops and pumpkins and corn. I saw balance sheets, registers of the dead, lists of every imaginable kind, and endless rows of numbers and figures, which must have served to reassure the administrators that nothing ever escaped their notice. (282–83, 190–97)

Reminiscent of the literary technique used in the opening pages of Peter Weiss's *Ästhetik des Widerstands* (Chapter 1), the objects are presented with traces of Austerlitz's thought, creating a linguistic inventory of the museum space infused with an additional human layer.

In contrast to his museum visit, Austerlitz is thoroughly unable to use the holdings of the new French National Library to discover clues about his earlier life and family. Following a highly detailed description of the labyrinthine path a library user needs to use to request materials and enter the reading room (276–80), Austerlitz sits, reflecting on the sterility of his thinking in this archival institution:

> [S]everal times, said Austerlitz, birds which had lost their way in the library forest flew into the mirror images of trees mirrored in the reading room windows, struck the glass with a dull thud, and fell lifeless to the ground. Sitting at my place in the reading room, said Austerlitz, I thought at length about the way in which such unforeseen accidents, the fall of a single creature to its death when diverted from its natural path, or the recurrent symptoms of paralysis affecting the electronic data retrieval system, relate to the Cartesian overall plan of the Bibliothèque Nationale, and I came to the conclusion that in any project we design and develop, the size and degree of complexity of the information and control systems inscribed in it are the crucial factors, so that the all-embracing and absolute perfection of the concept can in practice coincide, indeed ultimately must coincide, with its chronic dysfunction and constitutional instability. At any rate, as far as myself was concerned, a man who, after all, had devoted almost the whole of his life to the study of books and who had been equally at home in the Bodleian, the British Museum, and the rue Richelieu, I for my part, said Austerlitz, found that this gigantic new library, which according to one of the loathsome phrases now current is supposed to serve as the treasure house of our entire literary heritage, proved useless in my search for any traces of my father, who had disappeared from Paris some fifty years ago. (394–95; 281–82)

As the descriptions of the library structure make clear, the architecture and surroundings of the new building disrupt his dialogue with the past. Such a dialogue might be possible in some libraries such as the Bodleian or the old French National Library, but that dialogue is not secured just because an institution or apparatus is archival, and certainly not because the apparatus implements high technology. Only by differentiating between archival institutions and apparatus on a textual level can *Austerlitz* diagnose the present as an age that often seems to accumulate the entirety of the past in so-called treasure houses, not to keep the past speaking to the present, but in fact to promote amnesia. Indeed, one can recognize so clearly that the "fullness of the past" must be constructed through an interaction of the human mind with the material world, and not through some massive storage of records per se, precisely because the narrative mode of this text is so sensitive to the ways various physical environments, repositories, and objects can shape consciousness. Specific attention to display environments (museums, zoos, shop windows), particularly their spatial arrays and dimensions, is warranted, moreover, because they represent one of the few modern sites where encounters with the past can still be brought into context with the present-day mind.

Even more significant than this discriminating textual mode is that Austerlitz is plagued with bouts of memory loss that force him to reconstruct his visits and walks from photographs, ticket stubs, stories of the people around him, and documents. For Austerlitz, who lacks a conscious memory of his childhood prior to arriving in Wales, this reconstructive project is further related to his trying to piece together the elements of his early, obscured life and identity. Trying to fill these memory voids produced in part through the collaboration of his own psyche, Austerlitz ends up having to pursue his subject (himself) indirectly and associatively (see his comments on 64–65; 44). The "blank spaces" in his mental topography must be filled in by a process of reading for and in the gaps of the public past.

This aspect lends Austerlitz the appearance of the flâneur, the ragpicker, and the detective, Benjaminian figures whose characteristics are also shared by the figure of the collector.[57] As an architectural historian and amateur photographer, Austerlitz turns to his detailed professional knowledge about when and to what specific ends institutions such as museums, libraries, and archives, not to mention train stations and fortresses, were created. His project takes form as an accumulation of any and all seemingly relevant details, some mental, others physical, contributing to the reconstruction of the social changes taking place since the rise of capitalism (174–210; 120–46). In the manner of a Benjaminian collector (though not necessarily with the same valences), he constructs the "story" of suppressed social processes that can become legible by "listening" to the "dissonant language systems" of the past as articulated by various anecdotes, objects, and buildings.[58]

Such a revelation of these suppressed processes occurs when Austerlitz visits the streets of Terezín (Theresienstadt). Looking at the objects in the window of an antique shop, he thinks, "[T]hey were all as timeless as that moment of rescue [depicted in a small statue in the window], perpetuated but forever just occurring, these ornaments, utensils, mementos stranded in the Terezín bazaar, objects that for reasons one could never know had outlived their former owners and survived the process of destruction, so that I could now make out my own faint shadow image among them" (281; 197). Seeing these objects in terms that recall the fragility of photographs in the stream of history, here Austerlitz portrays social and historical change as generally destructive. Only after he has visited the Theresienstadt museum and returned to Prague does his statement receive full valence. Back in his hotel room, memories from his visit to Terezín and its museum pass before Austerlitz's mind as he tries to fall asleep:

> But whether I kept my eyes wide open or closed, all through the night I saw pictures from Terezín and the Ghetto Museum, the bricks of the fortification walls, the display window of the Bazaar, the endless lists of names, a leather suitcase with the double sticker from the Hotel Bristol in Salzburg and Vienna, the locked gates that I had photographed, the grass that grew between the cobblestones, a pile of briquettes in front of a cellar entrance, the glass eye of the squirrel [in the shop window]. (287; 201–2)

By mixing objects from the shop window of the Terezín Bazaar with museum displays, Austerlitz's thoughts are inventoried in a way that reveals, as much to the attentive reader as to Austerlitz, a hidden dimension to his earlier comment on history's destructiveness. In the seemingly abandoned ghetto and concentration camp city, the process of annihilation that led to these objects being stranded in the shop display becomes hard to differentiate from the process of destruction that led to artifacts being available for the Holocaust museum. The stylistic similarity in the descriptions of the respective antique shop and museum objects reinforces this perception for the reader.

Regarding Austerlitz as a collector makes it possible, moreover, to understand that Austerlitz's own story can emerge in parallel with the story of the collective past, thanks to the peculiarly intimate relationship the collector can have with his acquired anecdotes, sources, and objects. When Benjamin writes that the collector fondly recollects those moments when he rescues objects, he is pointing out that the collector is in some sense contributing to his own life story by taking possession of objects and stories. Generating and organizing a certain form of personal memory by collecting, the collector inscribes a level of personal history into the full or total history (the "fate") of the objects, making them a kind of proxy of self. This is one way of understanding why, as Austerlitz considers the fates of the objects in the shop window, his image appears among them (280–81; 197). By "living in his objects," as Benjamin puts it in "Unpacking My Library," personal and historical pasts can be intermingled in the collector's mind.[59] The "twist" in Austerlitz's approach to recollecting his past—and Sebald's writing projects often share this tendency—consists in allowing the admixture of personal and collective memories generated by the process of collecting to stand in for a narrative of self that does not consciously exist prior to the moment of collecting in a conventional sense.[60]

Following Benjamin's "translational" view of the present's relationship to the past, moreover, the worn-out languages of the past speak to and through Austerlitz. Not only does Austerlitz function as a kind of translator into the future, but his sense of self will also be allegorized; that is, Austerlitz will never construct more than a patchwork narrative of self for very long. The collector's chaos of memories may be held in place and at bay by a sense of habitual order, as Benjamin writes in "Unpacking My Library." But this means two things. First, such a construction of a personal narrative allows certain memories and aspects of the past to recede from active awareness. Paradoxically, constructing consciousness via collecting can, at least provisionally, place memories out of consciousness, helping us to think about museum practices in the digital age in terms of Andreas Huyssen's notion of "creative forgetting."[61] And second, if the habitual order is disturbed, the ordered, suppressed memories readily dissolve into chaos.[62] The fragility of this model of memory and identity seems well suited for depicting Holocaust survivors and the heirs to the other catastrophes of European modernity who populate Sebald's novels.[63] The incessant flood of images in Austerlitz's mind following his visit to Terezín represents a moment (of crisis) before habitual order has been established.

Helping to generate something like a storyline out of Austerlitz's meanderings is a first-person narrator who shares much with the public figure of Sebald the author. Not only does Sebald share the same core personal information such as birth date, biography, and impulse to write with all of his narrators, but this (and every) Sebaldian narrator is also a writer-collector.[64] Rather than explaining Austerlitz's condition per se, Austerlitz's "story" is produced via his relationship to the narrator, making the story appear to proceed out of the interaction between the two figures. Moreover, the narrator inserts photographs and other visual elements into a textual fabric interspersed with quotes from Austerlitz (sometimes quoting others) and fragments from a host of learned and "trivial" sources. Corresponding on one level to Levi-Strauss's notion of bricolage, this assemblage of heterogeneous elements is also a Benjaminian personal collection.[65] Thus it provides a fullness that prevents it from being explained in the moment it is encountered. What Austerlitz says of his passage through the Theresienstadt museum represents in some sense a condition of the narrative as a whole: "[E]very detail that was revealed to me as I went through the museum from room to room and back again far exceeded my comprehension" (283; 199). Unpredictable, associative, and brimming with multiple meanings, the narrative exceeds Austerlitz's and the narrator's control.

For the narrator, his personal recollection of Austerlitz's recollections also structures his own consciousness and identity. For one thing, *Austerlitz* is written in some sense to resolve a kind of conjoined bodily and psychological crisis sparked by the narrator's sudden loss of vision in one eye (50–56; 35–40). Such a crisis sets nearly every Sebald narrative in motion, with the narrator performing a series of Proustian-style rituals that trigger his memory.[66] As with Austerlitz's recollection, the narrator inscribes an additional personal narrative onto the personal and collective levels of meaning already put in place by Austerlitz. I have argued elsewhere that Sebald's writings are characterized by a peculiar sense of Sebald's authorial presence, which seems palpable everywhere *and* necessary for a text's interpretation.[67] Understood in terms of collecting, this ubiquitous authorial presence can be understood to emanate from the manner in which the personal collector organizes discourse. Like Austerlitz, the narrator's assemblage of heterogeneous elements allegorizes the resulting story, leaving his sense of identity (and his story) forever incomplete, a patchwork, as it were. This relentless allegorizing of the present's construction of the past, together with the conscientious capturing of how objects are enriched by having passed into the lives of figures such as Austerlitz and/or the narrator, permits Sebald's writings to appear to be writing in touch with "true" experience in the Benjaminian sense. As objects and anecdotes are passed from one person to the next, personal traces are left behind the way rings grow on a tree.

Or so it seems at first glance. Sebald's methods possess a fundamental ambivalence that complicates the apparent satisfaction of Benjaminian categories, making its Benjaminian modes potential traps when they are not reflected upon. Austerlitz, though resembling the figure of the flâneur in some ways, tends to head not into the urban fray but out of town, moving as far as possible from the crowd.[68] Such a decoupling of the flâneur from the crowd suggests that certain modes of Benjamin's thinking might need to be historicized in Sebald's writing, making them revealing for their having passed into a kind of cultural obsolescence or anachronism. At the same time, Sebald's writing derives from processes of collecting that, at first glance, seem to provide access to "experience" in an intellectually and ethically responsible way. Many of Sebald's writings on the German past, particularly *The Emigrants* and *Austerlitz*, have been interpreted as taking this responsibility with supreme seriousness and sensitivity. Ernestine Schlant, for instance, makes the debatable claim that Sebald is the first German writer to successfully mourn the victims of the Holocaust.[69] But though it is true that the collector feels charged with the utmost responsibility to the objects and their stories, insofar as it is through him that they are passed down to posterity, Sebald's writing plays with the authenticity of this experience.

The point is not merely that authentic experience might amount to little more than a discursive effect, but that there might be no way to distinguish between factual and fictional "experience." Centered on found objects and physical remains, Sebald's language leaves the impression that it refers to an extratextual reality.[70] As Sebald puts it in an interview, his compositional method employs conventions of referentiality that recall, and complicate, techniques of literary realism:

> Most of [the photographs and documents] are true but there are several which I made up so the reader must be constantly asking, "Is this so or isn't it so?" Of course, this is one of the central problems of fiction. Nineteenth-century authors are always at pains to point out that they found this manuscript in a bedroom in Husum and that therefore it is true. They're not telling a story they've made up; they're recording real life. Of course, in a sense, we still have that problem as narrators. Many writers fudge it or obscure it, but I think it is still a crucial problem to deal with, this legitimization.[71]

Sebald's writings deal with the problem of legitimization by systematically suspending the reader's ability to discern fact from forgery, resulting in what Amir Eshel calls a "poetics of suspension."[72] Even though, as Carolin Dittlinger observes, the photographs in *Austerlitz* correspond more tightly to the text than the photographs in other Sebald narratives, it remains difficult to establish beyond a doubt whether a particular photograph or document relates most directly to Austerlitz's or to the narrator's reconstructive efforts.[73] It may well be that the "poetics of suspension" mean that the reader should remain wary of just what "story" a descendent of the "perpetrator" culture—even a well-intentioned one—makes out of the shattered life of a Holocaust victim.

Yet when it becomes impossible to decide fact versus fiction, as in this text, questions also arise about the general relationship of "memory" and "experience" to artifice. It is precisely because Sebald's texts succeed in making objects, spaces, and stories appear to have passed through others' lives that they raise the question of whether "experience" has been or can be more than artifice. To put it another way: the resonance of Sebald's writings says perhaps more about the desires of its (approving) readers to partake in the transmission of "experience" than it can about the actual wisdom or counsel available in Sebald's writings. The point is not that fictional personae cannot serve as vehicles by which to transmit experience. Rather, one might ask how to think about the notion that certain modes of collecting and writing might help us "wake from the dreams of the nineteenth century"—which Grünbein suggested they might—when they, too, represent nothing but artifice. One way to probe this issue is by constructing a genealogy of inventoried consciousness in literary writing as it has been shaped in the age of the public museum. I advance that genealogy in the next chapter by exploring Goethe's *Wahlverwandtschaften* [Elective Affinities], an artful text that openly comments on the growing cultural impact of newly developing public museums and encounters with actual art objects, encounters that seem to induce, rather than dispel, dream images.

2

The Rise of the Public Museum and *Bildung*

3

Ottilie Under Glass:

Collecting as Disciplinary Regime in Goethe's *Wahlverwandtschaften*

The social world of Goethe's age was only beginning to establish protocols and expectations for encounters with art objects.[1] In the course of the eighteenth century, rulers in a number of German principalities who sought to appear enlightened had begun to expand access to select scholars and artists to their royal holdings.[2] Moreover, from the 1790s until the 1830s, events ranging from the French Revolution and the Napoleonic wars to secularization led to profound changes in the ways objects were valorized, collected, displayed, and experienced. As old methods of organizing the world met their demise, huge numbers of aesthetic objects were moved from one place to another, within existing collections, and through transfers of ownership. Driven by political and ideological forces whose fault lines ran along the new principle of public access and by market pressures responding to fluctuating valuation and circulation of goods and information, the ensuing dynamics spawned new, experimental practices and remade traditions.

By the time of Goethe's death in 1832, rulers in the German states had begun to establish and even expand public art museums, believing that exposure to art collections would promote social cohesion, educate and refine the public, and define identity through common ownership of cultural property. In many cases, museums eventually invented ways to shape behavior through *Bildung*. For much of the period in which Goethe was a collector and observer of the emerging museum landscape, however, the direction these developments would take was unclear. In those years, political and financial constraints limited the scope and effectiveness of the projects that leaders could undertake, and private collectors had also become established cultural figures who could rescue art objects from the ravages of the art market (or junk shop) and exert strong influences on the cultural functions that art collections could have. While Goethe's voice was not

I owe the suggestion of treating the *Wahlverwandtschaften* in terms of collecting to Jann Matlock, who also gave me helpful critiques on an early draft of this chapter.

the only one to be heard, his concerns about the ways collecting and exhibiting were beginning to shape culture are insightful and intriguing in the analysis of the museum function of a culture learning to encounter art.

Despite growing access to collections in the eighteenth century, public viewing of collections in most places was a dispensed privilege that "could be revoked at any time, restricted for the use of artists at work, or made difficult by surly attendants."[3] A 1792 decree opened the imperial collections in Vienna on Mondays, Wednesdays, and Fridays. Yet even then, visitors had to come "with clean shoes," a condition that likely kept out those who had to muck through the streets on foot, even if they did not have to work on those days.[4] But despite the rising interest in collecting in German-speaking circles, the notion of all classes visiting collections remained largely a hypothetical one until the leaders of the French Revolution established the Musée Français in the Louvre and the Musée des Monuments Français in 1793.[5]

Though the invention of these museums as truly public institutions irrevocably shifted the terrain of aesthetic ideology, the implications of that shift for the German-speaking principalities were shaped by the philosophical, economic, and political conditions that prevailed there. German intellectuals, among them Wilhelm von Humboldt, Friedrich Schlegel, Adolph Müller, Karl Friedrich Schinkel, Gustav Waagen, Carl-Friedrich von Rumohr, and the Boisserée brothers, carefully and critically studied the quickly changing French developments. Germans responded to the French concepts of the museum—first developed during the Revolution and then instrumentalized by Napoleon—by appropriating those principles that were useful to them and critiquing and rejecting others. Indeed, the Germans were already developing certain highly specific ideas about collecting and exhibiting as a function of culture and aesthetics. Though their responses were not limited to the creation of public museums, significant German museal institutions eventually arose out of this constellation of ideas.[6]

One aspect of Revolutionary museums that fascinated Germans was the sheer quantity of cultural richness anyone could now symbolically claim as one's own. As a principle, the Louvre and the Musée des Monuments Français allowed all classes to inspect the previously inaccessible art and treasures of churches, aristocratic homes, and palaces.[7] Although its condition and organization were quite different when first made public than they are today, in 1793 the Louvre represented a breathtakingly vast accumulation of aesthetic and cultural treasures (Fig. 7). When it opened on August 10th of that year, only half the space of the palace was available, and still "a total of 537 paintings, plus 124 assorted marble and bronze sculptures, precious marbles, pieces of porcelain, clocks, and 'other objects'" were shown.[8] The Musée des Monuments, which was dissolved in 1815 when the church was permitted to reclaim its property, contained façades and other elements of important historical architectural structures. Illustrating vividly the principle that collecting involves a circulation of objects from an older context into a new one, this museum offered a walk through French architectural history in one centralized place. For Revolutionaries, contact with these collections represented one step toward educating and producing a citizenry of equals who were to make up the French nation and possess all the national treasures collectively.[9] Museum collections defined and directed identity formation and were an important tool for converting masses into individuated citizens.

The Louvre underwent significant changes after Napoleon assumed power. It continued to be a central national symbol and open to the public, but in the course of his military conquests, Napoleon carried out a policy of looting art from conquered countries. The confiscations from Italy and Germany generated particular attention, although the spoils came from many other lands and as far away as Egypt. Under Napoleon, the Louvre became the depository for this stolen art and a preferred site for representative state functions, thus underscoring the function of the museum as a symbol of French culture and state power.[10] Furthermore, objects in the Louvre were repeatedly reorganized so as to fulfill certain ideological goals. Napoleon showed the art of vanquished countries in parades and temporary exhibits to evoke the notion of French triumph over cultures now

Figure 7 Hubert Robert. Project for the Disposition of the Grand Galerie of the Louvre, 1796. Note the multiple activities envisioned in this space, from copying art to promenading. Louvre, Paris.

held to be lesser than the culture of France, with unconquered countries like England receiving no representation in the displays, thus rendering them in some sense invisible as cultural entities.[11] These displays were all the more effective in that they resonated with the public. As Andrew McClellan notes, the press excitedly followed the daily progress of art convoys toward Paris.[12] And as German visitors often complained, the galleries were so full of French visitors that it was practically impossible to see the art on the walls, let alone contemplate it (that this situation seemed not to bother the public at large further dismayed many German visitors). In a single decade, public museum going had developed from a highly unconventional practice to a chief means of recreation and entertainment, as well as a pivotal way for the state to win the hearts, minds, and bodies of its populace.[13]

To be sure, the majority of German-speakers could not themselves directly take part in the expanding museum culture in Paris. Leading German writers, artists, and architects, however, closely followed and debated the relative merits and drawbacks of the policies implemented by the French. Sulpiz Boisserée observed that German newspapers were full of stories about the remarkable riches of the French museums and the unprecedented opportunity they offered to see in one place the combined heritage of so many far-flung countries.[14] Even Goethe, who for some time was considered to have been uncritical, and even ignorant, of French art policy, has recently been shown to have worried about its implications.[15] The German concern with these policies arose in no small part because many of the best German-owned pieces had been carted off to Paris by Napoleon. But it also stemmed from an increasing public awareness of the unfavorable state of collections in the German-speaking territories, which the French helped to highlight.

In some crucial respects, the new French museums in Paris offered a marked contrast to the conditions of German museums. With the relative abundance of original artworks, the impressive grandeur, and the institutions' unmistakable national importance, an opportunity to visit them was hard to resist for German intellectuals.[16] This was particularly true since German collections were scattered around various politically fragmented courts and palaces, leading Germany's art to be more spread over its territory than in many other European countries. Even the most impressive eighteenth-century displays in the courts of Dresden, Vienna, and Munich did not represent the totality of their respective princely collections, since many important works were kept in inaccessible settings. Conditions for experiencing art were also not optimal in most places. In addition to most important works being off limits, displays had what was felt to be antiquated and bewildering modes of organization, as Goethe, for instance, noted in 1801 when he recalled an earlier visit to the Dresden gallery.[17]

When German observers visited the French public museums, they tempered their admiration of certain aspects with criticisms of the institutions, revealing acute museum-making sensibilities.[18] After having gone to Paris, Wilhelm von Humboldt complained in 1797 about improper care damaging works in the Louvre.[19] The clutter in the Louvre's main rooms four years later in 1801 caused Heinrich von Kleist to liken the museum to a *Polterkammer.* Continued overcrowding, insufficient lighting, and poor displays offended Friedrich Schlegel in 1803.[20] In 1806, however, Johann Georg von Dillis and Crown Prince Ludwig of Bavaria inspected the Louvre, with the future form of Munich's Glyptothek and Pinakothek eventually emerging from the favorable and critical observations they took from the Parisian galleries.[21] That the populace seemed to promenade past rather than contemplate the works of art dismayed the architect Karl Friedrich Schinkel. For Schinkel, access to the museum for all classes was lost on a populace of museum goers who tended to deny art an appropriate, contemplative reverence and the museum its rightful status of "sanctuary of art."[22] Inappropriate behavior in the presence of art was thus diagnosed in Parisians, at this time the society most experienced with public art collections in all of Europe. On top of poorly organized display environments, the Parisians lacked German *Bildung.*

Most Germans were also insufficiently *gebildet* at this time, however, though von Humboldt and Schinkel expended considerable effort to promote *Bildung* through school and university reform and through museums. Both men were central to the development of the first purpose-built museum in Prussia, today known as Berlin's Altes Museum. Humboldt's impact on the museum was felt most profoundly through his stewardship of an influential commission that reviewed planning for the museum's implementation in 1829.[23] With the paintings looted by Napoleon having now been returned en masse, and with the purchase of private collections to improve its coverage, the museum commission was able to produce a hang of paintings by historical period and school.[24] This strategy served the mutually conducive purposes of keeping the collections together in one place after their having been unified by the French and of presenting the general public an organized history of Western art.

In Schinkel's conception, in fact, the art museum was to be a rarified space that overlaid art historical knowledge production with functions intended to lead visitors through a set of rituals, to promote the formation of specific social bonds, and to transport the viewer away from the quotidian world.[25] As the museum's architect, Schinkel exerted influence on nearly all aspects of the design down to the deep red color of the walls and the size of the pedestals supporting each piece of sculpture. By presenting such an architectonic and unified arrangement of building façades, sculptures, and paintings, and by emphasizing individual

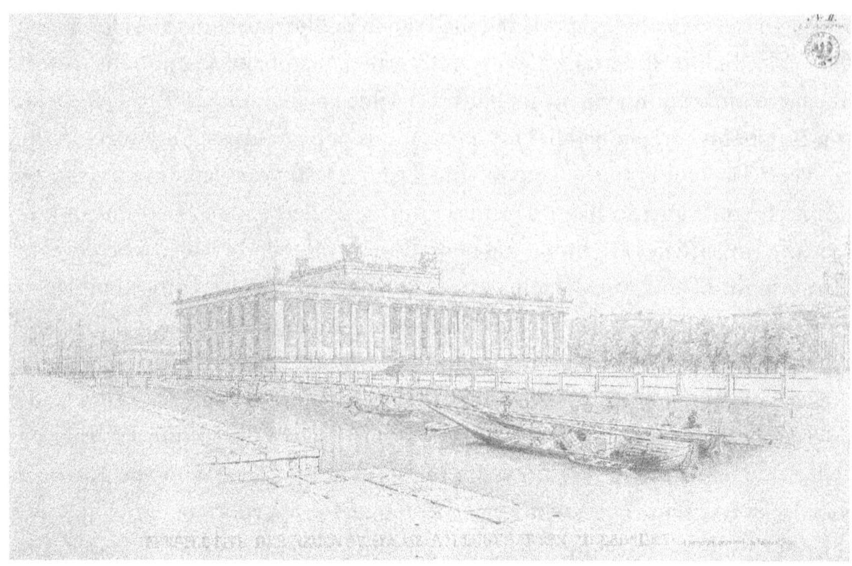

Figure 8 Karl Friedrich Schinkel (1781–1841). View of Schinkel's Museum at the Lustgarten, seen from the Castle Bridge in Berlin. Pen and brown ink on paper, 40.7 × 63.5 cm. Inv. SM 23b.44. This part of the island was reconfigured for what is today known as the Altes Museum. Kupferstichkabinett, Staatliche Museen zu Berlin.

aesthetic objects, Schinkel meant to inculcate visitors with a reverent, almost worshipful attitude toward art that had been so absent in the Parisian crowds. Deliberating how best to prepare the visitor for the experience of art, Schinkel consciously depicted the environment in which the museum would be placed (Fig. 8). Next to the cathedral and across from the royal palace, Schinkel seems to have wanted to set the museum into a symbolic relationship with surrounding buildings and institutions. At the same time, Schinkel also calculated how the museum beckoned visitors, shaping their expectations before they even gained entry. After approaching the museum from the Lustgarten, a space created as a space outside but leading into the museum, the visitor was supposed to move into the rotunda, which had statues placed at heights that encouraged awe in the spectator (Fig. 9). Such a strategy, according to Schinkel, would wipe clean the residue of everyday thought and make the spectator fertile for receiving the following experience of art.[26] As Schinkel put it, "The composition of such a powerful building as the museum . . . cannot in the end do without a dignified center. It must be the sanctuary in which the most precious objects will be enshrined. This place will be entered first when one comes in from the outer hall, and here the view of a beautiful and sublime room must make one receptive and create the mood for the enjoyment and the cognizance of that which the building preserves."[27] Thus cleansed, the visitor might walk into the classical collection on the ground

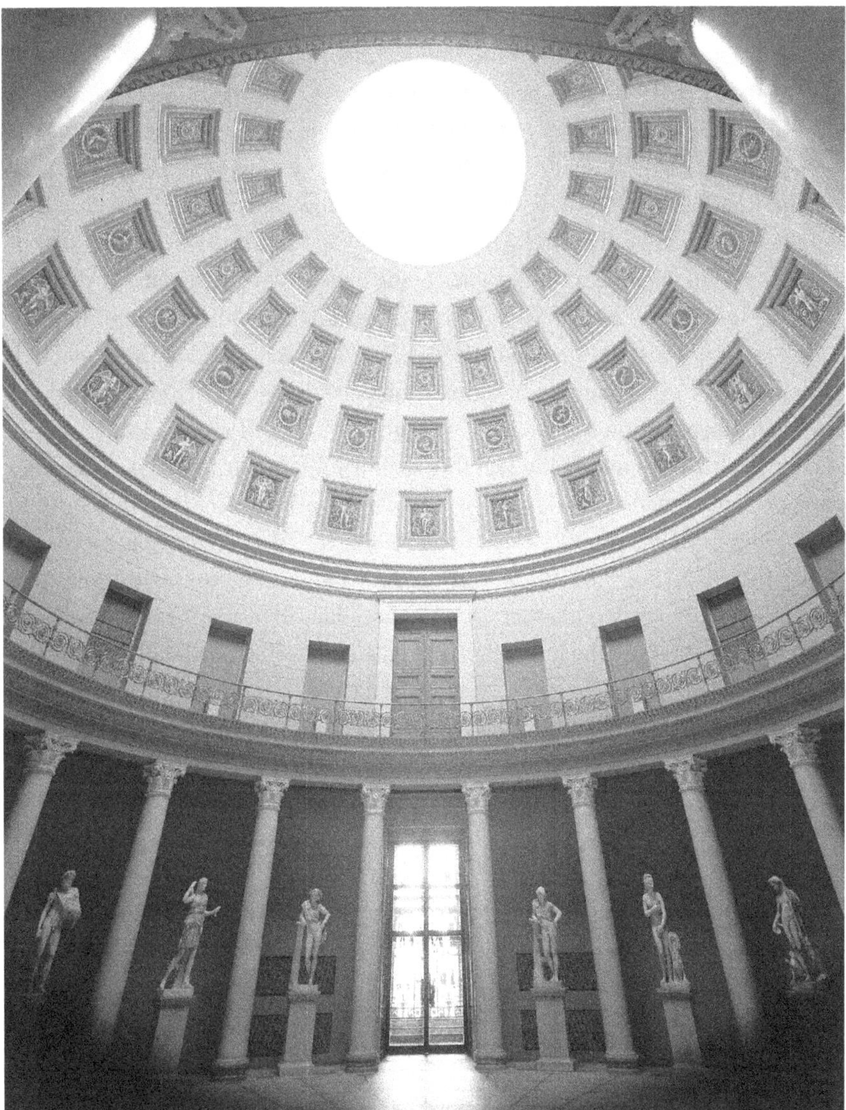

Figure 9 Karl Friedrich Schinkel (1781–1841). "Altes Museum," the Old Museum, Berlin, 1825. In this space, the statues were placed on high pedestals, which were intended to instill awe in visitors.

floor or move immediately to the staircases, which are dark at the bottom and illuminated at the top. The visitor who moves to the second floor to view European painting thus experiences a kind of "enlightenment" just by following the itinerary into the aesthetic surroundings of the collection. Yet as many commentators have stressed, pointing to Schinkel's labeling of the rotunda as a "sacred space," the entry is also inscribed as a ritual area that is captured in the designation "temple to art."[28] Thus Schinkel's museum is often thought to engender an experience in line with certain programmatic Romantic statements by Wackenroder, Tieck, and Novalis, in which deep reverence for art and its surroundings is instilled through an idealized experience of art galleries and their patrons.[29]

In Schinkel's gallery space, paintings and sculptures were to be placed so as to reinforce their aesthetic autonomy and to allow patterns to be recognized from one grouping to the next. These patterns were nothing less than a story of art history, with the Italian Renaissance being coded as the high point of Western painting. Indeed, a remarkable feature of its initial hang is its cosmopolitanism, for despite the museum's resonances with certain Romantic aesthetic conceptions, it makes practically no attempt to valorize German art. And finally, the knowledge production envisioned by Schinkel involved creation of dialogue, of narrative that bound people together over a contemplative experience of an artwork. Conceptual drawings he produced show patrons moving through the collections in small groups, clearly engrossed in interpreting some artwork before them (Fig. 10).[30] In this feature, Schinkel attempted to institutionalize a practice related to collecting that was commonplace in the age of Goethe, and in particular, one that Goethe himself practiced and described in detail. Indeed, the seminal text "Der Sammler und die Seinigen" (The Collector and His Circle) presents a typology and critique of the personalities who conduct social discourse while viewing collections. While Goethe himself never saw Schinkel's museum, he would have readily comprehended this aspect of his conception.[31]

Making art available to the public in this way was compelling because it seemed to offer a highly attractive possibility of molding political attitudes and behavior. As James J. Sheehan has argued, the availability of public art displays was expected to promote social cohesion through uplifting *Bildung*, thus working against the social tension and conflict that marked the German states in the decades following the French Revolution, the Napoleonic Wars, and the Restoration.[32] In these years, rulers and non-elites alike all across the German states were well aware that the public at large was a force to be reckoned with when it came to collections and museums. As the historical record demonstrates, public jubilation at recovering looted artworks, acquiring new artworks, or making holdings accessible was strong incentive to create public museums through reform.[33] Failure to institute reforms, particularly by not making holdings available, could also spark protest or revolution.[34] Such concerns were still pressing in 1830 just prior to the opening of Schinkel's museum, in no small part because of the revolution that had occurred in Paris that same year. Referring to the situation in Berlin at that time, Wilhelm von Humboldt wrote: "Nothing seemed so important to me as to transfer the museum . . . into public use . . . as quickly as at all possible."[35]

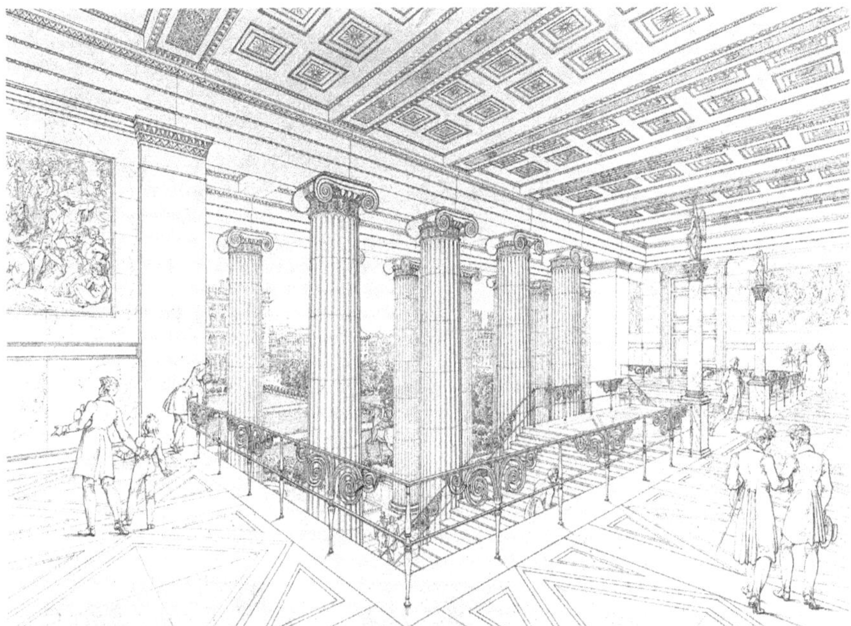

Figure 10 Karl Friedrich Schinkel (1781–1841). Perspective view of the upper vestibule, main staircase, and colonnade of Schinkel's Altes Museum in Berlin, with a view of the Lustgarten, 1829. Pen and black ink, 39.2 × 53.1 cm. Inv. SM 21b.54. Note the engaged conversations between these idealized museumgoers. Kupferstichkabinett, Staatliche Museen zu Berlin.

When the conditions were right, officials attempted to go beyond meeting public demands and in fact to shape the attitudes and behavior of the broad public through museal effects. As Theodore Ziolkowksi has cogently argued, the architectural strategies employed in the Berlin museum linked *Bildung* with a ritual recognition of the generosity and grandeur of the Prussian king Friedrich William III.[36] According to this argument, a subtle but unmistakable logic of exchange was inscribed into the museum: the experience of art history and the possibility of self-improvement were to be paid for through deference and respect to the king, attitudes that dovetailed with the reverence for art that display environments were intended to impart.

In this respect, it must be stressed that Schinkel's museum represented but one of many designs created to harness and direct the attitudes and behavior of the general public through museum reform. In Leo von Klenze's Pinakothek in Munich (1826–36), for instance, the desired impact was even more pronounced. As Klenze wrote: "A painting gallery ... should ... offer the visitor significant effects both outside and inside; effects that are suitable for putting the visitor into the appropriate mood: because such a collection needs and ought to be designated and designed more for the nation than for the artist, for whom this mood

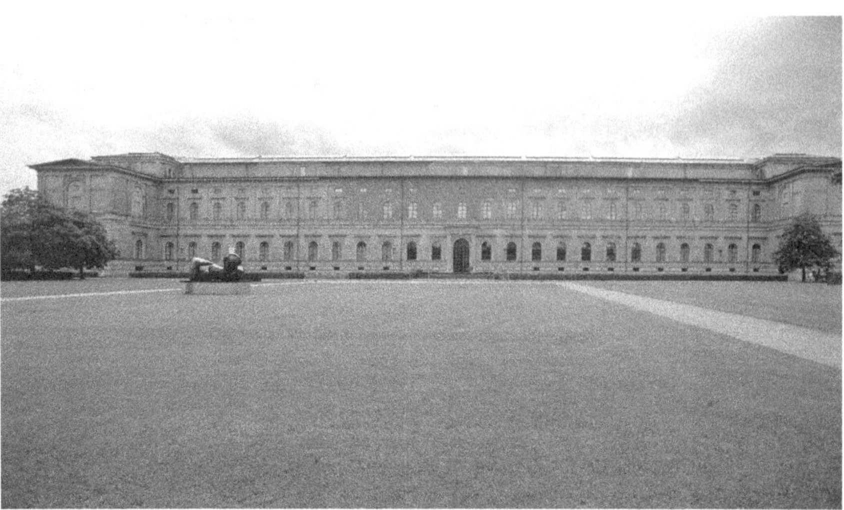

Figure 11 Leo von Klenze. Alte Pinakothek, Munich. Exterior view.

is already innate."[37] For Klenze, as for Schinkel, a significant aim of museum design was to enhance the ability of a collection to transport visitors into another space and to arouse in them an appropriate disposition. Yet it cannot be stressed enough that Klenze employed very different design features to impart those effects.[38] With a horizontal monumentality that seems to boggle the visitor's mind (Fig. 11), Klenze's façade in some sense sought to impress the viewer with the import of *Bildung* before even setting foot in the museum. Also notable was the fact that Klenze developed a sophisticated and unprecedented method of diffused overhead lighting—his project was the first to use this advantageous form of lighting—that greatly enhanced a painting's impact. The gallery's significant effects were intended to reinforce the fusion of people as nation in Klenze's concept, especially in that his political formulation exceeded the wishes and scope of his patron, Crown Prince Ludwig of Bavaria.[39]

Leading museum architects and planners in the first third of the nineteenth century thus were clear-minded in their expectation that an organized display environment could profoundly affect the attitudes and behavior of their visitors. The architects were also eager to employ those effects in the name of supporting particular social and political goals. To anticipate my argument with respect to the *Wahlverwandtschaften,* let us recall that in that text the characters experience altered mental states as a result of viewing the Architect's collections (366–68; 161–62). Moreover, the Architect convinces Charlotte to accept his proposal to renovate the chapel into "a monument to the taste of a bygone age" precisely when the effects of his displays are at their height (368; 162). The contours of the Architect's project suggest that beyond securing employment for himself, he aims to contribute to the Romantic reinvigoration of German culture by studying, recovering, and circulating certain monuments (*Denkmäler*) of its (Catholic) past. The practices employed by the fictional Architect are a direct expression of the prevailing tendencies of collecting and exhibiting in his time period. The same is true for the museums that would emerge in Berlin, Munich, and several other German cities. In other words, the museum function that gave rise to those manifestations in the museums also underlies the dynamics that are represented in Goethe's novel.

Outside Museum Walls: The Practices of Private Collectors

The first step in recognizing these common dynamics is to see that the museums I have been discussing were exceptional achievements representing the culmination of years of difficult debate and the coordination of resources. Museum sites are most often heavily contested and shaped in response to the exigencies, accidents, and demands of the specific local situation. The exceptional coherence of Schinkel's and von Klenze's museums, which permits us to read them as an attempt to transmit a particular ideology, should not cause us to overlook a certain hard reality. In the political and economic terrain in the respective German states, the consolidation of collections and other resources necessary for the viable construction of a public museum could often only be achieved at substantial financial and political cost. Popular protest erupted in Mannheim, for instance, when it became clear in 1802 that its collection of Palatinate masters was to be moved so as to expand the collection in Munich.[40] This was the case even though the ravages of war had left no secure place for the collection to be held in Mannheim.[41] In addition to revolt, for almost two decades Bavarian museum advocates also faced internal political struggles at the highest levels, which prevented the construction of a museum to hold the unified collection.[42] The erection of a walled institution was anything but a foregone conclusion in Munich. Munich's "museum" existed in paper form for many years before a building had any reality: it consisted of a systematic catalog of reproductions of the holdings strewn across the Bavarian lands.[43]

In Prussia, a different but thoroughly vexing set of constraints accompanied the first museum's construction. The Prussian kings had long wanted to integrate their own collections of paintings and sculpture, which were scattered among many different palaces, in order to compete with those of other European courts, especially France's.[44] These plans were delayed for decades because of the decimation of the collection by Napoleon, internal political struggles, and severe lack of funds for cultural administration. In the end, the same group of officials who linked the goals of national education reform to the enumeration and preservation of all cultural patrimony gained traction for the Prussian museum project by relating the museum to these projects.[45]

The scarcity of resources led, paradoxically, to a cautious improvement of the overall royal collection by forcing officials to implement strategies making the most of available resources and political conditions. While these strategies included the targeted purchases of private collections amassed by Edward Solly and Giustianni, they also required other innovative tactics, in part gleaned from private collectors, which saved funds, worked to preserve artifacts, and satisfied local political constituencies.[46] When deciding on methods for documenting and preserving artworks, artifacts, and other cultural patrimony in Prussia, officials such as Schinkel and Karl Freiherr von Stein zum Altenstein explicitly recommended against too zealously relocating artworks and artifacts to central collections. Their recommendations addressed a number of concerns and were intended to maximize the effectiveness of what resources were available. First, leaving old German artifacts in their traditional environment preserved local contexts and prevented the degradation of local culture.[47] This was a sore point precisely because Napoleon's looting had had devastating effects along these lines. Just as important, moving objects and providing appropriate shelter and care for them in a place such as Berlin was costly, if not impossible in many cases. Funds were so short that as late as 1845, inventories of important artworks, structures, and ruins in Prussia were still incomplete.[48]

As an alternative to these strategies, officials turned to a strategy of creating sketches, tracings, and other reproductions of important sites and objects to be compiled in a central location as the preferred approach to this problem. Not coincidentally, the production and organization of such renderings is a skill that the figure of the Architect in Goethe's novel is practiced at, and these reproductions form a significant portion of his holdings. Prussian officials saw in the techniques the same advantages as Goethe's Architect. Sketches and tracings were less expensive to produce and more mobile than most originals would be. Additionally, less damage was likely to be caused to the individual pieces as a result, and by leaving them in place, local resources, for instance, those of emerging *Geschichts-* and*Altertumsvereine* [Historical- and Antiquities Associations], could be enlisted to help with preservation costs.[49] Just as important, such methods of circulating reproductions permitted relatively cost-efficient dissemination of the holdings, thus promoting education. This strategy was especially effective because the circulation of sketches and copies was one of the most common means of encountering and experiencing pieces of art in the first half of the nineteenth century, whether as engraving, lithograph, or narrative rendition.

All types of reproductions were considered valuable, if not indispensable, means of experiencing art collections at this time in Germany. Many German collectors and even prestigious institutions were accustomed to displaying copies and reproductions of artworks in the same display environment as originals. This was a practice that would shift markedly only in the second half of the nineteenth century, with the ascendancy of professional curators trained in art history in major German cities, such as Wilhelm von Bode in Berlin. The Neues Museum in Berlin, for instance, contained significant numbers of casts and other reproductions of Egyptian art and classical sculpture that it was built to prominently house and display.[50]

In the first half of the nineteenth century, even seeing integrated collections of pictorial reproductions could be thrilling. According to Erich Trunz, one of the early authorities on collecting in Goethe's oeuvre and in the age of Goethe more generally, prior to the 1820s most books devoted to art were heavily narrative in form. Engravings and etchings, while prevalent, were seldom bound in book form and were comparatively rare.[51] Indeed, as Goethe himself noted: "The art aficionado does not always demand originals; if some remarkable image finds and moves him that cannot be possessed, then he rejoices in a copy. This is shown in the present time in the joy brought by old German art, that one demands and treasures reproductions of paintings of this kind."[52] While Goethe's reference to the old German masters is partly owing to the fact that he is discussing precisely that kind of art in his *Kunst und Altertum* [Art and Antiquity], the phenomenon is also crucial because the Architect's many originals and reproductions in the *Wahlverwandtschaften* are Germanic and old German in origin.

The ubiquity and success of this model of collecting and exhibiting was one of the signatures of German exhibition culture at this time. It marked private collectors at least as strongly as the collecting practices of public officials. Indeed, Schinkel and Stein zum Altenstein would not have made their recommendations if Romantic German collectors devoted to Germanic art, ruins, and manuscripts had not shown this method to be capable of captivating and educating a broader public, and in particular of winning support for preservation and restoration efforts.[53] Both Schinkel and Stein zum Altenstein responded in particular to the most striking and innovative practitioners of these methods, Sulpiz and Melchior Boisserée and their friend, Johann Bertram.[54] Guided foremost by a passion for medieval German and Dutch art, the Boiserées and Bertram began by salvaging medieval Dutch and German religious masterpieces from secularized churches, monasteries, and junk shops in the Rhineland from 1804 until 1808, in Heidelberg from 1808 until 1819, and in Stuttgart from 1819 until 1827, when Ludwig of Bavaria finally acquired their entire collection.

The impulse of the Boisserées to collect and exhibit was a response to many of the same formative experiences of museums that moved other leading German architects and intellectuals. Visiting the Louvre during their stay with Friedrich Schlegel in 1803, the Boisserées were stunned and inspired by the way the French museum combined "ancient and religious artworks" so as to provide an overview of Western art history and to offer a point at which French identity could crystallize.[55] Yet as with their compatriots, certain aspects of the French museum conflicted with their notions of the ideal museum and its cultural function, which they had been formulating before arriving in Paris.[56] Most lacking in the French galleries, and conversely what an eventual German museum most needed, was the transmission of art historical knowledge as it moved the (German) soul.[57] At once an expression of religious and patriotic fervor, reaching that German soul became at various times the life work of the three collectors, especially Sulpiz Boisserée. Each attempted not only to amass a remarkable collection of religious art, as important as this was, but to create an appropriate display environment and public interest for that collection. As time went on, architecture, exhibition, and the circulation of reproductions were all employed in innovative fashion in the name of achieving their goals.

The Boisserées' goals led primarily in two directions. One involved publicizing their collection so as to draw attention to its value and, it was hoped, ultimately to lead to its being converted into a state-supported national museum. Second, drawing on documents and artworks unearthed in the process of collecting, they wished to complete the Cologne cathedral, which lacked its characteristic towers well into the second half of the nineteenth century (Fig. 12). Both projects gained impetus when, in 1808, the brothers, frustrated by the indifference of Cologne city leaders to their plans, moved their holdings to Heidelberg. Beginning around 1810, when they had constructed an appropriately churchlike environment for their collection in Heidelberg, the brothers began luring prominent intellectuals to see their collection.[58] While Wilhelm and Caroline von Humboldt, Hegel, the brothers Grimm, Georg von Dillis, Carl Friedrich von Ruhmohr, Stein zum Altenstein, and Schinkel were all prominent visitors, highest on their list was in fact "the old heathen idol," Goethe.[59] Although they knew of Goethe's diverging religious views, Goethe was so prominent that they needed his endorsement. In spite of the enthusiastic support of Goethe and other intellectuals, the sale of the collection to an appropriate monarch and the cathedral project both stalled.

Revamping their strategies, the brothers moved their collections to Stuttgart and began to address the broad public with the dual purpose of pushing the value of the collection up and educating the public about their German heritage. To achieve these goals, they installed a lithographic shop in a Stuttgart gallery, which,

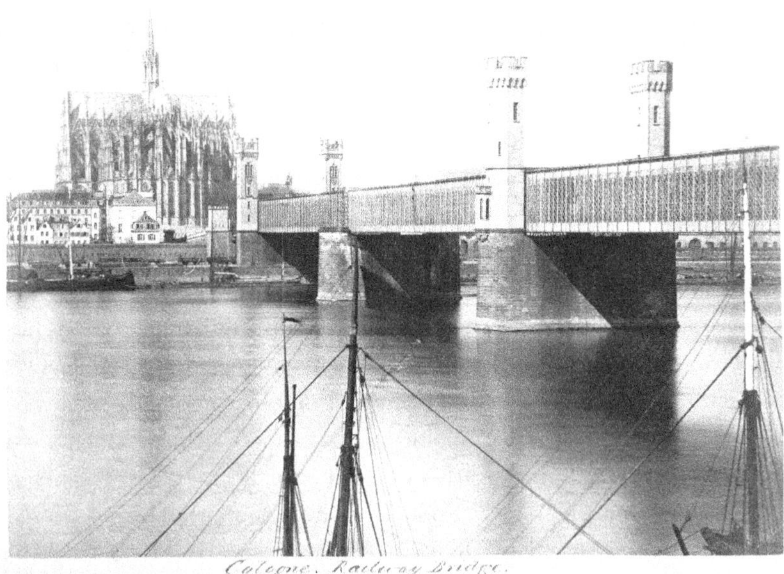

Figure 12 Cologne cathedral, ca. 1850. Though the cathedral is nearly unthinkable without its massive spires today, they were missing until well into the nineteenth century, despite efforts by the likes of the Boisserées to get the cathedral completed. 13.5 m high × 6.3 m wide. Library of Congress. LC-USZ62-108991, LOT 7738. In album: Athens, Egypt, Rhine, Switzerland, Tyrol, Salzburg, p. 28, upper left.

according to Valentin Scherer, was intended to seize public attention: "[T]he participation of the public was maintained by having the best pieces of the collection appear as reproductions after 1821. . . . The brothers had set up their own lithographic shop in the building that housed their collection in Stuttgart, with which they also contributed to the dissemination and perfection of this mode of reproduction."[60] Such a circulation of information could well increase the economic value of the holdings in question. Before the collection had been sold to King Ludwig of Bavaria for inclusion in the Pinakothek, competing bids came in from several German courts including Berlin, in no small part because such a purchase represented an instant rise in cultural cachet for the ruler who acquired it. The demonstrated ability to draw and influence an interested audience only enhanced the value of their collection, for the Boisserées as well as for the eventual royal purchaser.[61] Fundamentally, the techniques employed by the Boisserées aimed at achieving more than an increase in personal status and wealth. Such techniques effectively manifested how collecting and exhibiting, and the networks of circulation and reproduction inherent to them, could address issues such as public education, administration of cultural heritage, public control, and national identity.[62] This linkage of education, image control, and identity to collecting proved highly instructional to rulers and officials grappling with precisely these issues. The museum function of the private collector, therefore, can be seen to closely track that of the public museum; indeed, they were fundamentally interrelated.

The Museum Function of Goethe's *Wahlverwandtschaften*

The installation of the lithography shop in the Boisserées' Stuttgart gallery in 1821 was the culmination of a long process of experimentation with the circulation of objects and reproductions. For at least a decade, the brothers had consulted with publishers, artists, and other leading intellectuals in order to refine their techniques, and they tested various approaches of disseminating catalogs, price lists, and copies of their artworks. When Sulpiz Boisserée initiated contact with Goethe in 1810, it was in fact under the pretense of soliciting advice on how best to duplicate historical and contemporary perspectival drawings of the Cologne cathedral and, eventually, major artworks in their collection, which Boisserée intended to circulate widely in reproduced form in support of his proposals to complete the massive structure.[63] Boisserée was well aware that with such a monumental undertaking, potential supporters would need help in envisioning the completed Gothic forms. As an experienced exhibitor, he assembled a traveling display that would accomplish that task. The difficulty in this case was that Goethe was expected to disapprove of the ideas many of the artworks represented.

Convincing Goethe of the value of their project thus turned into an exercise in the persuasiveness of the traveling exhibit. After all, the Boisserées ultimately wanted much more than mere technical guidance from Goethe, however sincere their interest in Goethe's expertise in those matters. They were painfully aware of how tricky it would be to win Goethe's overall support in light of his skepticism of certain Romantic aesthetic, religious, and political claims. They were so concerned about Goethe's aversion to Schlegel's brand of Romanticism that they thought hard about how to avoid revealing their connections and intellectual debt to Schlegel. That they chose to emphasize particular cathedral images should, I think, be seen in this light—as images Goethe would least object to. Rather than initially confronting the man they recognized as "the old heathen idol" with medieval Catholic religious iconography, they selected a project and a mode of presentation whose contours they had surmised were familiar and acceptable to Goethe. The evidence for their belief was none other than the literary work that had appeared the previous year: *Die Wahlverwandtschaften.*

In *Die Wahlverwandtschaften,* four core characters, a newly married couple (Eduard and Charlotte) and two outsiders (Ottilie and the Captain), come to live in proximity on an estate over the span of several months. During this time, adulterous attractions being to form between Eduard and Ottilie on the one hand and Charlotte and the Captain on the other. With Eduard and Charlotte's pending breakup seemingly precipitated by the presence of the two outsiders, the characters' interactions stand in enigmatic relation with the notions expressed in the novel's title, which uses a contemporary theory of chemical bonding ("elective affinities") to explain how certain elements leave given pairings in favor of others. In the end, the chemical equation fails to predict outcomes in the social sphere, as Charlotte and the Captain renounce each other. Eduard pursues Ottilie, who, in spite of her love for him, cannot realize the bond, particularly after her negligence leads to the death of Eduard and Charlotte's son, Otto. Rather than marry Eduard, Ottilie starves herself to death and is eventually put on display in a glass coffin in the estate's renovated chapel, which is thronged with visitors wanting to see her supposedly beautiful, saintly body. This outcome connects to a powerful theme of the book, which is that the many measures the characters take to prevent accidents and improve the quality of life—for instance, by renovating the estate and chapel grounds—end up producing death. In the text, the renovation of the chapel is the pet project of a secondary but important figure, the Architect, who arrives to take the place of the Captain once he and Charlotte decide not to pursue a life together. Though I describe the chapel project in more detail in a moment, for now it suffices to point out that the Architect sees in the chapel the opportunity to transmit, using contemporary display strategies, the aesthetic values of the collected artworks from the past into the present.

As will be clear from my discussion of his projects, Boisserée proposed at core something remarkably similar. Moreover, Boisserée went about it in a way that allowed him to draw a subtle but explicit parallel between himself and the collector in Goethe's novel. This parallel was the thrust of the postscript of the first letter he sent to Goethe, along with original drawings for Goethe to review: "P.S. You will be so good as to return the drawings to Mr. Zimmer again upon his return, and you will not resent it if, in reminding you of the Architect in *Elective Affinities,* I request your particular attention to the careful packing up [of the drawings]."[64] By referring to his fictional counterpart in this manner, Boisserée intimates his estimation of Goethe through a careful reading of his novel. In that text, the Architect clearly articulates that he withholds access to his collections from most people because, in his experience, even civilized people (*Gebildete*) can act like "barbarians" toward priceless artworks (402). While Boisserée would probably not have greatly feared such behavior in Goethe, this allusion allows the former to drive home the points both that he had read Goethe's novel closely (something that would have greatly pleased Goethe) and that he is taking a risk by sending Goethe irreplaceable originals.[65] Significantly, this latter point was not lost on Goethe.

After confirming that the Architect was in a sense present during the packing up of Boisserée's "irreplaceable drawings," Goethe wrote: "[T]he trust with which you have sent us such precious work of many years of duration has increased our usual care in the display and otherwise as well."[66] More fundamentally, by identifying his situation with that of Goethe's collector, Boisserée was implicitly announcing his desire for an outcome with an uncanny resemblance to the one Goethe had himself devised in the *Wahlverwandtschaften:* that the immediate experience of Boisserée's artworks would produce a sympathetic endorsement of the proposal to renovate a ritual building.

It is unknown the extent to which Boisserée sought to create irony with his plan, in which the author was now handled in a manner befitting his literary characters. But two points are worth stressing. First, developments in the *Wahlverwandtschaften* were such that Boisserée could use them as a cipher for his own identity and ventures and as a means of communicating with Goethe about collecting and architecture. Second, Goethe's own account in several letters suggests that the immediate effects of Boisserée's drawings worked as Boisserée had hoped they would. In many respects, they seemed to work as Goethe had described them in his novel.[67] Though not every aspect of Goethe's imaginary world would necessarily translate into a testable or "real-life" experience, elements related to collecting and exhibiting in the text proved eminently capable of conforming to extraliterary "reality." Both of these points can be explained only by understanding that Goethe's text strikingly expresses and inflects the museum function of his day.[68]

That said, there is little evidence that Goethe necessarily sought to draw out collectors such as Boisserée.[69] So how is one to understand collecting and exhibiting in Goethe's novel? Rather than acting as a straightforward valorization of practices such as the Architect's, as Boisserée would seem to have it, Goethe's text, in my reading, reveals emerging practices of collecting and exhibiting to have potentially very troubling societal outcomes. Indeed, the novel's dynamics culminate in the morbid display of Ottilie as a cult object, as the expression of a society engaging in practices whose consequences it does not comprehend.

Such a critical perspective on collecting and exhibiting is consistent with the trajectory of Goethe's views from 1799 to 1814. Judging from recent critical work, by Harmut Böhme, Carrie Asman, and Elisabeth Décultot, on Goethe's collecting practices and attitudes toward exhibitory institutions, Goethe had concerns about the changes that were sweeping the world of collecting in the wake of the Revolution, secularization, and the Napoleonic wars.[70] Around 1799, Goethe was particularly anxious about the breakup of the cosmopolitan *Kunstkörper*—a notion that saw

European culture as a kind of body, in which artworks were rooted according to a quasi-organic logic.[71] As Asman has shown with respect to "Der Sammler und die Seinigen," part of what was at stake in this notion was a model of sociability and intersubjective creation of meaning through art.[72] Goethe's personal experiences in the *Tag- und Jahreshefte* [daily and yearly journals]—for instance, his lengthy interaction with the collector Hofrat Beireis—likewise show that the visitor to such private collections was practically required to interact with the owner of the collection, or at least to try to apprehend the personality of the collector in the holdings.[73] The advantage of the private collector in this respect emerges in his ability to rearrange the holdings at will and in order to address the interests of a particular visitor.[74] Such intercommunicative interaction, Goethe seems to have believed in 1799, would prevent objects in collections from suffering the deadening effects of musealization.[75] In contrast, state-run museums seemingly could not present an equivalent enlivening history and thus left their collected objects subject to potentially stultifying effects.[76] In these areas, Goethe's concerns bear a certain resemblance to Walter Benjamin's notion that only in the hands of a true private collector may aesthetic objects thrive in a condition of nurturing ownership.[77]

While Goethe remained concerned about the implications of improperly practiced collecting and exhibiting, his attitudes toward private collectors and public institutions shifted between 1799 and 1814. In these years, Goethe found reasons to support large public collections and reasons to be concerned about the actions of private collectors. In 1808, Goethe lobbied successfully for the creation of a state-run public museum in Weimar. By the time of his trip to the Rhineland in 1814, Goethe openly lamented the paucity of well-organized, universal public museums in the German states. At the same time, having observed the dynamics of secularization that had put so many artworks into circulation and exposed to an unknown future, Goethe realized that private ownership did not always guarantee proper treatment of art objects.[78] Thus Goethe worried about a whole range of issues, from the physical endangerment of the objects—which he observed might be risked if a collector were to move, have insufficient quarters, or even lose interest in the objects—to the questionable placement of the objects in private spaces.[79] As Goethe wrote about the lot of some of the secularized objects,

> [A]ll of those presentational and decorational [objects] dedicated to the worship of God, which have been removed from their sanctified places on account of the turbulent, fragmenting time, *do not quite seem to be in their places in private homes;* thus the cheerful inventive spirit of the owners and artists has thought of an appropriate environment in order to give back to taste what

> has been snatched away from devotion. Feigned house chapels have been conceived. . . . Colorful paned-glass has been copied to canvas in a deceptive manner; on the walls partially perspectival, partially upraised cloistral objects are depicted as real.[80]

Goethe's objection resides in the way in which an art form created for a communal purpose in a particular location and context is sequestered in the narrow confines of private homes. The creation of a seemingly appropriate display context in those confines does not fundamentally change the conditions of ownership, which might deny access to art lovers and artists. It merely masks it. Although "cheery" and, or perhaps rather because, no longer connected to religiosity, the spirit in which this development takes place nevertheless remains indebted to a fetishization of taste (*Geschmack*). This fetishization might in fact be possible only when the change of context inherent in all collecting is made to suppress its actual historical traces of an artwork.

Goethe's remedy to this problem was not to dispense with the pseudo-religious environment per se—this he recognizes as educationally beneficial, especially for those who lack much prior exposure—but instead to place it into a universal art museum (*ein allgemeines Museum*) where the art would be inscribed as a stage in a larger European cultural development.[81] Describing such a layout, Goethe writes,

> It is educational in a pleasant way, when sarcophagus, urns, and all the apparatus appropriate to death and burial are presented in imitation columbaria; when the Roman tombstone, age, and pedigree are enveloped with a decoration that reminds one of the Apian way; when the remains of the earlier Middle Ages are clad with ornaments of their kind in a harmonious way, just as with those of the later Middle Ages; when even natural realms are aided by copying of that which is absent.[82]

Even in Goethe's narrative proposal, he seems to envision a movement through history by stages, each of which, in the context of the other ages, prompts the viewer to reflect on the place of the individual piece in the whole. Unlike in the envisioned universal art museum, however, the viewer of the private pseudo-chapel is not prompted to reflect on what Benjamin would call the "total history of the object," even though the display was arranged by the private collector. What is denied through the simulation of older religious objects and architectural forms is in fact the materiality and historicity of the change of contexts wrought by collecting. The objects' own history is shorn from them, paradoxically enough, in order that they overcome a sense of separation between past and present. They are therefore denied the opportunity to enter into their own present where they can, in the words of Harmut Böhme, properly serve as a "medium for remembering."[83]

This dynamic is inscribed in *Die Wahlverwandtschaften.* Part of Goethe's critique in this era sought to reveal the problematic consequences of collecting and exhibiting. In the *Wahlverwandtschaften,* artifacts taken from burial sites constitute one of the Architect's most important collections. In their original context, these artifacts partook of Germanic death rituals and were meant to accompany the dead into the next life. In his possession, the Architect brings the objects into a new order made for viewing: "[The objects] had been cleaned and set out in portable drawers and compartments fixed to carved cloth-covered boards, so that these ancient, solemn objects had taken on a certain modishness, as if one were gazing upon the little boxes of a fashion salesman" (367; 162; translation modified). The apparent change in the character of the objects when rearranged in the little boxes is striking.[84] What was once old and grim now takes on the air of precious trinkets meant to provide viewing pleasure, precisely the pleasure, in fact, of looking over "the little boxes of a fashion salesman." Despite the apparent shift in character, a direct connection still persists with the cult value of the Germanic grave monuments, now expressed in terms of a modern commodity fetish.[85] I show later that the Architect wins approval for his plan for the chapel by showing his grave artifacts. The novel also ends with the statement that Ottilie and Eduard will one day awake in the chapel, making it and its objects functionally equivalent to the "grave mound" that accompanies them into the next life.[86] Art and fashion therefore retain an intrinsic and fundamental link to death in the *Wahlverwandtschaften,* but without immediately threatening the characters. Put differently, collecting under the sign of fashion appears to remove the threat of death, thus performing a kind of a talismanic function.[87]

In the Architect, the collector and fashion salesman are collapsed into one person. Oriented toward travel, the Architect's collections are compartmentalized and portable. The Architect's whole existence seems based on moving himself and his collections from one place to another. In view of the intense secularization that came about both in France after the Revolution, and later in some German cities close to France such as Cologne, the Architect indeed seems the contemporary of the many collectors and architects who circulated about the secularized remainders, finding new uses for the once religious buildings and salvaging the art they held.[88] The Architect in fact proposes to turn the estate chapel into a secular "monument to times past," albeit with a heavy heart, for "he could see that, the way things were going, his stay among such splendid society could not last for ever, but might perhaps even have to end quite soon" (368; 163). When the work is done, the Architect must move on. As the narrator reminds us, the Architect must sell his services to patrons in order to realize his projects and survive: "[T]he Architect did not find it difficult to extract from Charlotte a moderate sum, which he intended using to restore both the exterior and the interior to their original condition" (366; 161).

His collections play an important part in his obtaining his commission, and he shows them to Charlotte in a calculated presentation. He begins by showing "his collection of drawings and sketches of ancient tombs, monuments, urns, and other such objects" (366; 162). These pictures stimulate discussion of older monuments, at which point the Architect brings out the objects he found in Nordic grave sites (366; 162). The progression moves from picture to discussion to actual artifacts. Once having begun to show his collection, though, the Architect makes a point "[T]o appear every evening with some portion of his treasures" (367; 162). His relics of death entertain in the void of the characters' "solitude" (367; 162). The narrative slows down in a kind of ekphrasis as the Architect also slows. The reader receives meticulous detail about how the collection is ordered like the "little boxes of the fashion salesman" (367; 162), and is told about the objects as well: "[T]hey were mostly of German origin: old coins and seals and other objects of that kind" (367; 162). The effect of this narrative mode is to suggest that the reader is also viewing the presentation of the collection.

The effect of the presentation on the characters is clearly depicted. Like the pictures that initiate it, the objects organize the imagination: "[A]ll these things took the imagination back toward the more ancient times" (367; 162). So strong is the effect that the characters completely lose their sense of reality: "[T]hey had to ask themselves at length whether they were really living in modern times, or whether it was not a dream, and they were not dwelling among quite different costumes, habits, and ways of life" (367; 162). The collections have such a strong effect that the very solidity of contemporary culture—its habits, customs, ways of life, and ideas—can appear as no more than a dream. At this point the Architect applies his coup de grace: "Prepared for in such a fashion, a large portfolio which he brought out last of all had its maximum [best] effect" (367; 162). Coming last and underscored as the utmost through word choice ("best"), the "maximum effect" of the portfolio depends on what came before it.

Before moving on, it is worth pointing out that the effects of the collected objects on the imagination differ from those that arise from other archival instances in the novel. This issue surfaced in the first two chapters of this book, where I argue for the specificity of museum-related discourses. Early on in Goethe's text, the Captain helps Eduard put into practice a system of mapping and record keeping that is devised to modernize the estate's administration and free Eduard's energy for more interesting affairs (266; 46). Drawing up the map enchants Eduard and gives him a feeling of imaginary domination of the estate grounds: "It seemed to him that only now is he coming to know them [the grounds]; only now did they really belong to him" (261; 40). But insofar as the map increases Eduard's sense of control (however illusory), it works—in contrast to the effects of the Architect's portfolio as described by the narrator—to solidify the sense of the contemporary order. Edward's imagination seems similarly affected by the archival system for record keeping. Or rather, the implementation of the system produces a twofold sense of forgetting. Creating the system allows Eduard to employ an otherwise unproductive older man effectively and relieves Eduard of the problem of having to find appropriate work for him (267; 47). More important, the belief that his record-keeping system permits any past transaction to be recalled allows Eduard to file documents away and to forget about them until the necessary moment. As the narrator describes it, "[T]hey installed in the Captain's wing of the estate a registry for current documents, an archive for those no longer current. They collected together papers and reports which lay scattered in containers, rooms, cupboards, and boxes. With the greatest of speed the chaos was reduced to a gratifying order and lay categorized in designated receptacles" (267; 46; translation modified). The effect is described as a desirable splitting of Eduard's self, as something that allows him to separate past affairs from the joyous pursuits of the present (266; 46). Though potentially significant, such an impact seems to work counter to that of the Architect's collections, which structure the present in terms of the past. In any case, Goethe's novel focuses little attention on the effects of the archive in the subsequent course of developments. The Architect's collections and other related undertakings, in contrast, figure much more prominently, indeed as essential elements driving the action forward and structuring the present in terms of the past.

The effect of the Architect's presentation supports his ambition to add the renovation of the chapel to his other projects. Yet he does not immediately share his goal with the other characters ("for the moment he kept all this a secret from the others" [366; 162]), waiting instead to reveal his plan once his collections have had their "maximum effect." The narrator comments: "[A]fter [seeing the collections], it was impossible to resist the Architect's offer to paint the space between the pointed arches of the chapel after the model of these ancient pictures, and so preserve his memory in a place where things had gone so well for him" (368; 163). In addition to serving as models for the renovation, in the Architect's hands the ancient images induce the acceptance of his offer in the first place. It is hardly a coincidence that the characters willingly defer to the Architect after seeing countless pictures emphasizing religious veneration that translates into willing submission to authority: "[C]heerful composure, happy acknowledgment of one above us, silent submission in love and expectation . . . the character of each of the figures seemed to be fitted for an act of worship," as the narrator puts it (367; 163). This is, as I have been arguing, a tendency that private collectors and public institutions all tried to transmit to viewers in Goethe's age. The result is even more telling in that the characters feel transported into another world, the world of the aesthetic objects, before they see the pictures of religious deference. With their intensification of effect (the latter groupings have "the maximum effect"), the impact of that earlier world and its values is more powerful still. The Architect, then, exploits the fetish quality of the objects in his collections, not for worship of the divine, but rather for economic gain.

Like his collections, the Architect's tableaux vivants are equally part of his program of exhibition. They make up a series of pictures that are arranged to form an artistic program, but because they include people and put them on display, the tableaux can instill discipline to an even greater degree. They first appear in the text in connection with the visit Luciane, Charlotte's daughter, pays to her mother, during which she brings her fiancé and an entire entourage in tow. The focus for Luciane is the entertainment of the "society" accompanying her, to which she brings an impulsive, subversive, carnivalesque attitude toward life that turns everything on its head.[89] It is in this atmosphere of rambunctious amusement that a visitor, the Count, proposes to stage *lebende Bilder* [living pictures] as a means of matching Luciane's talents to the group's thirst for entertainment: "[T]he Count gave the Architect a few hints about how the tableaux ought to be mounted and the architect at once erected a stage for them and looked after the lighting that would be needed" (391–92; 190). The main tableaux are presented as a series of images reproduced from copper etchings: van Dyck's *Belisarius* (now thought to have been painted by Luciano Borzone), Poussin's *Ahasuerus and Esther*, and Terborch's *The Paternal Admonition*.

Norbert Puszkar has made the observation that the tableaux can be productively understood as a progression, in which the audience finds it increasingly difficult to discern "reality" and "illusion."[90] The first image succeeds in partially transporting the audience, which is troubled by a lingering perception: "The figures corresponded so well to their originals, the colors were so happily chosen, the lighting so artistic, you thought you had been transported to another world, the only disturbing factor being a sort of anxiety produced by the presence of real figures instead of painted ones" (391; 191). By the third image, in contrast, the audience has been so drawn in that it can no longer separate the image from reality. Significantly, this conflation of aesthetic illusion and reality recalls the effect of the Architect's collections on the other characters and marks an alteration in the perceptions of the characters in the audience.

This increasing conflation of reality and aesthetic illusion centers on a female character, Luciane. With each tableau having Luciane at its center, a narrative is created in which her person appears to be transformed. She begins as an active woman who is criticized by another woman for being outlandish (for donating too much money), changes to a woman fallen unconscious before the power of a man, and concludes as a young woman under the lecturing control of her father. In that transformation, the realm of male control over the female character expands. This is an important feature of these tableaux: the unexpectedly displayed reduction of a vibrant, uncontrolled woman to the status of a frozen, scolded girl. Accordingly, it is in the petrification of the tableaux that Luciane, who was previously criticized by the narrator for her restlessness, is suddenly seen positively by him. The narrator attributes the success of the second picture largely to Luciane's arrangement of herself so as to appear without agency: "[T]his time, Luciane had given herself a better role. In the figure of the unconscious swooning queen she was able to display all her attractions" (393; 191). Then, when Luciane reins herself in even more in the third image, the narrator expounds on her beauty: "[The third] picture was to be the occasion for Luciane to exhibit herself at her very best. Her braids and the shape of her head and neck were lovely beyond conception, and her figure, of which little was discernible under the mock classical dress worn by modern women, was wonderfully slim and dainty and light, and was shown to the greatest advantage in the older costume" (394; 192). In this third image, her frozen and speechless body is what is so attractive to the narrator. Here, in the climax to the Architect's collections, the narrative lingers on details with numerous superlatives. In a further parallel to his collections, his staging of the tableaux gains him additional employment: Luciane's fiancé asks him to accompany them to the city in order to restage them for other audiences (394; 193).

The aesthetic ideal in these pictures finds beauty in female silence and paralysis. As the narrator comments further: "Had she [Luciane] known that she looked more beautiful when she stood still than when she moved [*sich bewegt*] ... then she would have thrown herself into the preparation of the tableaux vivants with greater enthusiasm" (392; 190; translation modified). The reward for enacting the aesthetic program of the tableaux is to be called "beautiful." The tableaux succeed as entertainment precisely because Luciane embodies a "beautiful" femininity.

Historical practice of tableaux indicates that femininity and feminine desire were centrally important to their success. In their treatment of tableaux vivants, Dagmar von Hoff and Helga Meise argue that contemporary viewers believed that tableaux could make feminine desire visible and could represent its control. Hoff and Meise illustrate this by quoting a contemporary review of Henriette Hendel-Schütz, a renowned performer of tableaux:

> What is lost in terms of the perfection of the forms of visual arts she compensates for in her own way through unfolding and progression; for in visible transitions, in simple steps, that which we see in a painting as *completed,* isolated, and cut off, *appears* through her in a living context. The magic perfection in a painting may never be able to indicate that penetrating and heart-stopping something that mimicry paints of the inner conditions through ongoing pictures. Mimic performance contains the movements of the internal in a forward-moving manner, makes feelings visible with their struggling perceptions and indecisive resolutions.[91]

By setting up contexts and making transitions, the series of scenes usually performed in tableaux reveal "meaningful moments" that would otherwise be hidden or unsuspected. These moments occur between the frozen states. The transitions suggest a battle with desires that would then freeze into familiar scenes. Feminine desire would be briefly suggested, but would ultimately be trapped. Even more disturbing than the idea of finding beauty in a paralyzed, speechless female body is the notion that the transitions would represent a woman's body and her emotions being revealed and brought under control. One might refer to this latter idea as the "freezing of the feminine."

Yet in the scenes Luciane realizes, nothing is related of the movements between the scenes, even though contemporary viewers of tableaux found these movements important, and even titillating. Although the narrator's interest in her body is revealed through his lengthy description, there is no indication of Luciane's inner desires being contained, no evidence of how the tableaux affect her internally. The fact that Luciane does not explicitly know that silencing herself and staying still seem to make her seem beautiful is therefore important and revealing. Luciane *does not* internalize this aesthetic of paralysis, and she is expelled from the text soon after her performance. Tellingly, the narrator resumes his criticisms of her even after she has left the text (395; 193–94), and even after her betrothal (and social constraint through her husband) has been secured.

I suggest that in contrast to Luciane's tableaux, Ottilie's scenes expose her feelings and reinforce her tendency toward reticence in order to underscore the ideal she is performing. Ottilie's tableaux are also staged for entertainment: "[The Architect] did not want to leave them without expressing his gratitude by organizing to the honor of the one [Ottilie] and for the entertainment of the other [Charlotte] a far finer representation than the previous ones had been" (402; 201). A focus on Ottilie likewise preserves a narrative centering on a female persona, and an intended intensification of beauty emphasizes the aesthetic of female paralysis.

The difference that occurs in Ottilie's tableaux is that the narrative shows us the movement between the scenes. Ottilie's performance consists of two nativity scenes, a scene of "night and lowliness" that turns into a scene of "day and glory" (404; 201). In the first image, the narrator reports that Ottilie feels comfortable being identified with the Virgin Mary's humility and purity, in part because she believes only Charlotte and a few members of the household are watching her (404–5; 203). Between scenes, however, she realizes that an unexpected visitor has arrived, who disrupts her dubious identification with the Virgin Mary. When, during the second scene, Ottilie recognizes the voice of a surprise visitor as that of her former schoolmaster, she feels a burst of emotion: "The succession of joys and sorrows she had experienced passed like lightning through her soul and awoke in her the question whether she dared admit and confess it all to him. 'And how little worthy you are to appear before him in this sacred form,' she thought. 'And how strange it must be for him to see you thus disguised'" (405; 204). In contrast to Luciane, the full range of Ottilie's emotions are exposed between the pictures: the pleasures and sufferings that are connected with her illicit love for Charlotte's husband, Eduard; hence the words "admit" and "confess" and the gap between the Virgin's virtue and her guilt captured in her appearing in disguise. This flash of emotion has a powerful effect on her: "With a celerity with which nothing else can be compared, feeling and thought reacted against the other within her. Her heart beat fast and her eyes filled with tears, while she forced herself [*sich zwang*] to stay as still as a statue; and how glad she was when the boy began to stir and the artist found himself under the necessity of signaling for the curtain to be lowered" (405; 204; translation modified). The transition to this tableau enacts a "freezing of the feminine." Ottilie's body is forced to articulate her emotions, which she then contains by maintaining "the position." The outward sign of her pain, her tears, goes unheeded by the Architect, who stops the performance only once the baby moves.

The tableaux expose Ottilie's feelings and then teach her to respond to them by keeping them silent inside herself. But enduring the pain produces the feeling that she has done something wrong, for which she should also be ashamed. Ottilie has "a feeling of embarrassment" for not going immediately to the schoolmaster, upon which she feels "an even greater disconcertedness" (405; 204). Caught off guard in the clothes of the tableau, Ottilie cannot decide what to do. Characteristically, "she did not decide, and sought to get herself together, to calm herself down in the meantime" (405–6; 204). When she finally approaches the schoolmaster, there is no longer any mention of her confessing her feelings for Eduard. While the delay and reticence Ottilie employs can be interpreted as an attempt to create conditions in which she can make decisions, she seldom enjoys a greater set of options for her efforts. Indeed, Ottilie could use reticence as a means of ambivalence, which would force others to reveal their positions and put her in a position of control. But ambivalence carries with it the risk of conflict, which Ottilie strives to avoid. She instead learns to use her silence and restraint as a strategy of self-denial that implicitly limits her own growth and satisfaction.

It is important to acknowledge that in Goethe's aesthetics, Ottilie's attempts to reign in her body and passions are part of what makes her beautiful. Many critics have interpreted Ottilie's development in the text from a young girl to a religious icon in terms of Goethe's notion of intensification (*Steigerung*).[92] This term, which he develops primarily in his scientific writings, attempts to describe a tendency in some natural entities to transcend materiality. By denying her body, particularly by refusing to eat or drink, Ottilie follows an organic drive that moves her from the physical realm to the nonphysical realm. This transformation could, in Goethe's eyes, result only from Ottilie's setting her spiritual restraint against her bodily urges. In following Goethe's principles of polarity and compensation, the interaction of opposing bodily and spiritual realms in Ottilie's movement "upward" would be at once natural and beautiful.[93]

From the critical standpoint I am developing, however, it is possible to understand that Ottilie is not naturally saintly as the narrator often claims (368, 404, 490; 163, 203, 300), but must be taught through aesthetic mediation to take on that position. On one level, the reinforcement of a natural drive through aesthetic means is consistent with Geothe's aesthetics. As he writes in "Einfache Nachahmung der Natur, Manier, Styl" [Simple Imitation of Nature, Manner, Style], the artist will not succeed in capturing beauty without attaining "style," which is "based on the deepest foundations of insight, on the essence of things, insofar as we are able to recognize it in visible and manifest objects."[94] To cite Goethe's example, the artist who wishes to depict the "truth" of a plant must ideally possess the knowledge of a trained botanist. The reverse is also true for the scientist. In Goethe's writings, the scientist's eye is best schooled through the study of aesthetic objects, particularly ancient Greek art. This is so because the scientist strives to apprehend the general in the particular, a challenge nowhere better achieved than in the Greeks' aesthetic achievements. Nature and aesthetics are not, in the Goethean view, per se in conflict. What my discussion seeks to stress is that the Goethean terms, particularly if they are taken on a purely theoretical level, too easily elide the destruction of the female body through the aesthetic means I am linking to the practices of collecting and exhibiting.[95] The processes I discuss may well be unavoidable from the Goethean perspective, but this does not mean that a critic must necessarily ignore, let alone accept, the culturally derived details of their destructive impact.

In *Die Wahlverwandtschaften,* Ottilie's experience in the chapel is one of her first encounters with the text's dominant museal aesthetic, and just as with the tableaux vivants, it proves to be paralyzing to her there as well. When she sees the drawings of herself on the walls of the chapel, "she felt her existence and did not feel it; she felt that all this before her might vanish away and that she too might vanish away; and only when the sun ceased to illuminate the window did Ottilie come to herself and hurry back to the mansion" (374; 169). Only the lack of light frees her from this alienating paralysis prompted by the artwork, a specular loss of self that prefigures her dead body put to rest in the chapel; perhaps it is no accident that light is provided on the first night her corpse spends in the chapel (488; 296). But while Ottilie realizes that this experience comes the day before Eduard's birthday and she truly feels his absence in her life (374; 169), her temporary petrification in the chapel is only vaguely associated with her love for him. Through the tableaux, on the other hand, Ottilie's experience with aesthetic paralysis is brought into direct relation with her feelings for Eduard, and she practices restraining them in order to appear like the Virgin Mary. The tableaux therefore lay the groundwork for Ottilie's eventual refusal to speak and eat after little Otto's death, a decision to deny herself food that eventually brings about her own death. Ottilie's display in the glass-covered coffin at the end of the text is rehearsed in the tableaux, for they reinforce Ottilie's self-denial and motivate such behavior by valorizing it aesthetically.

The combination of a saintly ideal of self-denial represented in a beautiful way and the dynamics of the tableaux has a devastating effect on Ottilie. For Luciane the effect was negligible, despite the ideal of feminine paralysis at stake in the pictures she performed, since there was no exposure and containment of her desires. But what should be made of the fact that when the Architect comes to visit Ottilie's tomb, his experience of the tableaux has significantly altered his behavior, too? The Architect had performed in the first tableau, where he played a soldier mourning the dead Belisarius. Much later, when he approaches Ottilie's casket in the chapel, he strikes precisely the same pose: "Once before he had stood thus, in the tableau of Belisarius. Now he involuntarily adopted the same posture, and as the posture had then been a natural one, so it was now" (488; 296). The behavior the Architect has learned through the tableau is so strong that he executes it involuntarily, although it is certainly debatable how "natural" this behavior is, since it is based on a painting.

It is easier to see why the tableaux could also affect a man's behavior if one recalls that they seem to alter behavior by producing knowledge of a character's inner condition. With the narrative's focus on Luciane during the first set of tableaux, the reader is given too little information to know for certain which emotions are felt by the Architect while performing the Belisarius. In this role, he is in any case moved to tears when he poses before Ottilie's coffin: "[T]he young man stood in silence, and the girl too stayed silent for a long time; but when she saw tears flowing copiously from his eyes, when he seemed to be dissolving utterly in grief, she addressed him with such truth and force, with such kindness and certainty, that, astonished at her flow of speech, he was able to pull himself together" (489; 297). This response shows the Architect capable of an emotional reaction, and the possibility of his having an emotional response on stage cannot be ruled out.

What helps explain why the Architect does not end up behaving like Ottilie are the gender-specific cultural values transmitted by the tableaux. The narrator's description of the Architect's pose reveals that these ideals differ radically for men and women:

> Here too [at Ottilie's burial] something immeasurably fine had fallen from its heights; and if in the case of Belisarius, bravery, prudence, power, rank, and wealth combined in one man was mourned as irretrievably lost, if qualities indispensable for the nation and in times of crisis had, instead of being valued, been thrown aside and banished, so in the case of Ottilie many other quiet virtues not long since called forth by nature out of its capacious depths had quickly been obliterated again by its own indifferent hand: rare, beautiful virtues, whose peaceful influence on a needy world every age embraces with joy and satisfaction and longingly mourns for when it is gone. (488; 297)

Not only does art provide examples of the virtues categorized by the narrator, but these virtues are desirable because they are useful to the "Nation, the ruler" in the case of Belisarius, to the "needy world" in the case of Ottilie. This contrast in gender-based virtues shows how this social training engenders a social order extending to the state level, operating on the classical opposition of the daring, clever, active man and the quiet, unthinking, passive woman ("quiet virtues"). A successful transmission of the aesthetic values the narrator describes via tableaux vivants would therefore produce behavior in the Architect that differs from Ottilie's. Goethe's novel indicates that the impact of exhibitionary practices like tableaux vivants may not be limited to women, although that impact is potentially far more dangerous for them.

What also strikes me about this passage is that it associates nature with Ottilie's virtues, for it evokes contemporary discourses about femininity and beauty, including Goethe's own. The perceived ability of tableaux vivants to make feminine desires visible speaks to the need to answer these discourses' central questions with regard to "the interiority of woman," "the natural predisposition of woman," "her virtue."[96] The narrator of the *Wahlverwandtschaften* makes nature responsible for Ottilie's virtues—something he does not do for the figure of Belisarius. As I have discussed, this is in keeping with a Goethean aesthetic understanding. Yet I have also tried to show that collecting and exhibiting play a significant role in *naturalizing* those supposedly natural virtues. I also see the narrative trying to naturalize its own inordinate interest in Ottilie's interior, which both the tableaux and the inclusion of her diary are supposed to expose.[97] The culmination of the narrative with the permanent exposure of Ottilie might well be seen as a resolution of the enigmas Ottilie's desire (*Inneres*) presents the narrator. The drive to naturalize and aestheticize practices that aid his apprehension of feminine desire might not be fully conscious on the part of the narrator, though he seems more aware of the consequences of collecting and exhibiting than are the text's other characters.

That the Architect falls victim to the displays and exhibitions he himself arranges indicates that he lacks a full awareness of their consequences. Indeed, the Architect instrumentalizes collecting and exhibiting in order to better survive economically. A significant aim of his is to organize the objects for entertaining effects, for that is how they best support proposals like the chapel renovation. That he appears as a kind of fashion salesman reflects the inexperience most people, even educated people, had with collections at that time. As I have shown, the Architect acknowledges as much when he refuses to show his collections to Luciane's raucous entourage, for he fears their inexperience will destroy his objects.[98] But while the Architect affirms Ottilie's subsequent observation that "books of etiquette" should include "a really detailed one on how to act in art galleries and museums" (401; 199–200), his primary goal with his own collections is not acculturation per se. Moreover, the Architect seems unaware that the nativity scenes he stages contribute to Ottilie's death and to her becoming a cult object, even though the deadly effects emanating from the objects' ritual functions continue to organize the imagination.

I find a Benjaminian dialectic suggestive for understanding why Ottilie becomes a cult object and why collecting can bring about profound changes more generally, even when they are not explicitly sought. In Benjamin's theory of aura, the only true value a work of art can have (*Gebrauchswert*) arises from its use as a religious (cult) object.[99] Benjamin argues that when the dynamics of secularization and collecting bring objects into circulation, a new value he terms the exhibition value (*Austellungswert*) dialectically supplements, but does not replace, the original use value of the object.[100] Benjamin observes that where it was the uniqueness of the divine that prevailed in objects used for cult ritual, exhibited objects tend to foreground in the viewer's mind the authenticity of the artwork itself or the artist.[101] Remnants of the original aura, and the ritualistic function of the object, therefore always remain associated with it.[102] The collector is important for revealing this dialectic, particularly in that he remains in service to the fetish.[103] Benjamin in fact indicates that the collector is in a position to tap the cult power of his objects.

The Architect's collections of funerary objects and his portfolio in particular demonstrate that he participates in the fetish quality of his collections. Indeed, the Architect exploits his collections and his position in the service of the fetish in order to convince the other characters to support his plans for the chapel. One might also say that the chapel unwittingly becomes the epitome of his exhibitionary tendencies. The previous use of the chapel for religious ritual is augmented by the new aesthetic investment he gives it with his collection of medieval tracings and paintings of Ottilie. The new chapel thus emerges as a site dedicated to the worship of the new aesthetic, a dialectical combination of the old and new investments of the chapel.[104]

If one thinks of the chapel in this way, as a dialectical combining of cult and exhibition values, a cult value that needs consideration is death. The chapel is associated with death from the outset in the text because of its connection with a cemetery (366; 161). The chapel also takes on the function of a grave mound that will host Ottilie and Eduard until they wake up in the next life (490; 300). This is precisely the function of those sites where the Architect obtained these objects, objects that were, after all, involved in securing funding for the renovation in the first place. Friedrich Nemec has also pointed out that the Architect realizes his ideal of portraiture as monument to the dead in the chapel, referring to the fact that the Architect features Ottilie's face on the walls of the chapel (369–70; 166–67).[105] It is of course striking, however, that this aesthetic and the disciplinary practice of collecting also help produce a deceased.

In the chapel, then, Ottilie's body on display is therefore a medium through which the morbid and decorative converge, but where the morbid is no longer immediately perceived. Accordingly, Eduard insists that Ottilie should be treated "as a living person" (484; 293), dressed for burial as if for a wedding and placed on display in a glass coffin. Ottilie's servant, Nanny, likewise imagines the corpse to beckon, forgiving Nanny for having eaten that which Ottilie refused as she starved herself to death (486; 295). News of this "saintly act" inspires the masses of pilgrims who visit the beautiful and dead Ottilie, bestowing upon her the status of a fetish object. The enthusiasm of the pilgrims becomes so overwhelming that the chapel must be closed (486–87; 298). This dynamic bears some resemblance to the newly developing practice of museum going; Friedrich Schlegel, it might be recalled, complained when he visited the Louvre in 1803 that he could not see the paintings because of the masses crowding the spaces.[106]

I have tried to show that Goethe's novel manifests some of the same social dynamics that also produced a contemporary social institution, the museum. In particular, the collections arise from social dynamics devoted to entertainment and beautification (even beatification) that exert a disciplinary influence. This influence scripts the characters' behavior, blinding them to the destructive impulses inherent in these dynamics. One might see the extent to which the characters are (blissfully) unaware of these dynamics by questioning the narrator's assertion regarding "Ottilie's continuing beauty, and the state [that] resembled rather sleep than death" (488; 298), when she is placed on display in her glass coffin.[107] It is doubtful that this description can apply to the corpse of a woman who has starved to death. If Ottilie's display is seen as a premonition of a society that proceeds with collecting and exhibiting without fully understanding what it is doing—and I have shown just how closely the dynamics of Goethe's novel map onto the museum landscape of his day—then the future of museum-making seems to be ominous.

When later museum designers sought to exploit the organizing power of collected objects to their ends of civilizing their fellow citizens and molding them into a national community, they tapped much of the same ritual function that the Architect did without explicitly taking to heart the lessons of the *Wahlverwandtschaften.* Goethe's novel strongly suggests that Adorno's famous association of the words "museal" and "mausoleum" to highlight the stultifying effects of collecting might be more than just conceptual.[108] Part of what subsequent writers, especially those who look back to Goethe such as Adalbert Stifter, try to do is to dampen the potentially deadly effects of collecting and exhibiting. Just how a writer such as Stifter proposes to accomplish this, and whether such a program has any real chance to succeed, is taken up in the next chapter.

4

The Museum of *Bildung*: Collecting in Stifter's *Nachsommer*

The reader who reaches the final pages of Adalbert Stifter's *Bildungsroman Der Nachsommer* [Indian Summer] (1857) might well wonder, given the paucity of action in the text, what justifies its length of more than 800 pages. Whether in terms of the "Crown of Poland" offered by Friedrich Hebbel to the nonprofessional reader who staved off boredom long enough to verifiably finish the novel or the more appreciative and insightful assessments of a Friedrich Nietzsche, a Rainer Maria Rilke, or a Thomas Mann, *Der Nachsommer* has a notably massive and serene quality that, perhaps more than any other text in this study, justifies the term "museal."[1] Indeed, one of the more remarkable features of the novel is the amount of detailed narration—often describing the same houses and objects again and again—it takes to relate how Heinrich Drendorf meets and marries Natalie Tarona. As Heinrich explains of his accomplishment at the novel's end, "Whether I shall be able to accomplish anything in science—which I hope never to neglect—whether God will grant me the grace to be numbered among the greats in the field, I don't know; but one thing is certain: the pure family life that Risach was referring to has been founded. . . . I shall administer my property, shall be useful in other ways, and everything, including my scientific endeavors, has now gained significantly in clarity, solidity, and importance."[2] Lest there be any doubt that what matters most is taking a bride, Heinrich comes into a fortune of money and objects and the eventual rights to the estates of his father and the family friend Risach, precisely by establishing "pure family life." And with the closing of the text but a short time into his marriage, one is forced to conclude that nothing he may accomplish in the future will rival this accomplishment. But what takes Heinrich and Natalie so long to found this family? Why does Heinrich have to spend so much time learning about science, aesthetics, art, and philosophy if so little seems to be at stake in his amounting to anything as a scientist? And what does this tell us about the society to which the novel arguably has some identifiable, if complicated, relationship?

In this chapter, I claim that (1) the process of *Bildung,* like every other significant scientific, aesthetic, and social issue at stake in this novel, cannot be meaningfully separated from collecting and exhibiting, and (2) that an analysis of the dynamics of collecting and exhibiting operating in the novel can offer new and insightful answers to the questions stated previously. The kind of reading I have in mind examines the dynamics of collecting and exhibiting operating within this complex narrative construct by means of the narrator's museum function. The museum function is defined as the way objects are exchanged, collected, and given value in a particular society and historical period. As I argue in Chapter 1, the prevailing social impulses and exigencies that give rise to museums can also be detected in the behavior and activities of noninstitutional agents such as private collectors and in a variety of discourses circulating at the time. Devoting a portion of the argument in this chapter to Stifter's direct involvement in the management of museums in the cities of Linz and Vienna, I clarify how the imaginary world of a narrative can express and transform notions contained in related cultural discourses.

Examining the museum function sheds new light on the fact that, for men in this novel, reaching the top of the hierarchy of knowledge and beauty necessarily means attaining the pinnacle of identity (4.3:260; 465–66). In this cognitive quest, the maintenance of extensive and well-differentiated collections becomes synonymous with personal development and an ability to appreciate beauty. Learning to collect, exhibit, circulate, and exchange objects is therefore essential for Heinrich to move upward from scientific insight to profound literary and aesthetic comprehension and judgment. This in turn enables Heinrich to begin the process of recognizing the beauty and value of his future wife, Natalie. His esteem for Natalie also promotes certain modes of male-to-male, or homosocial, exchange between the elder Drendorf and Risach, which become increasingly entangled in Heinrich's wooing of Natalie.[3] That is to say, Heinrich's betrothal is itself revealed to be subject to dynamics of exchange and valuation constrained by collecting and exhibiting on the one hand and the dictates of heterosexual kinship structures on the other. As Gayle Rubin wrote in her essay, "The Traffic in Women," patriarchal kinship structures can be thought of as requiring the maintenance of a compulsory heterosexuality, in addition to an incest taboo, in order to be perpetuated.[4]

Collecting and the Path to *Bildung*

From the moment Heinrich leaves home at the age of 18 to study geology and biology in the field, he is involved with collecting samples of rocks and plants from regions outside Vienna. Heinrich proceeds by isolating objects with common physical features in order to classify them, which yields groups of objects by type:

grasses with grasses, trees with trees, and so on. Heinrich's endeavors are, generally speaking, taxonomic, aiming to arrange the samples to reveal the relationship of outer appearance to internal function and at the same time to elaborate what the place of those respective geological and biological samples might be in a larger natural historical hierarchy. While much more can be said about the scientific implications of Heinrich's collecting, for now I want to stress that Heinrich collects and arranges visible objects to glean information about invisible qualities and relationships. This collections-based practice is significant because it supplies a core paradigm for how Heinrich's *Bildung* proceeds.[5] At every stage, Heinrich must learn to view existing arrangements in order to apprehend the invisible logic(s) for the arrangement he finds before him. Once an arrangement has become "transparent," to use the term advanced by the theorist Tony Bennett to describe this process, Heinrich is able to decode other settings that employ similar display principles.[6]

A peculiar feature of many of the environments of *Der Nachsommer* is not only that they can be profitably approached in this manner, but also that they are often multiply encoded. Early in his study, Heinrich's work in the field is threatened by an impending thunderstorm, and he seeks shelter in Risach's nearby house. While being shown around the house by his host, Heinrich is struck by the rooms in the house that contain samples of many different kinds of wood and marble. While he initially understands the collections of wood and marble in taxonomic terms, that is, as scientific groupings based on similarities of structure or origin, the aesthetic principles Risach uses to arrange his marble deeply impress Heinrich (other items he is exposed to, for instance, the architectural drawings, similarly broaden his horizons). During his subsequent fieldwork, this new aesthetic awareness causes him to find a beautiful kind of marble Risach does not have (4.1:233–36; 135–37). Beyond taking samples of the stone for Risach's collection—an episode that reveals a great deal about the relationship of collecting to identity—Heinrich also begins to ponder how that marble might serve certain aesthetic purposes. Heinrich moves up the hierarchy from scientific knowledge production to art, literature, and philosophy because many of the settings he encounters lead him to discover overlapping (scientific and aesthetic) regimes of knowledge supported by the arrangements of his discoveries.

Enabling this movement is the marked tendency for Heinrich to encounter many of the same objects again and again (which is not without its implications for the reader as well). In his first visit to Risach's library, Heinrich is invited to use the collection. He laments,

> They were almost exclusively works of literature. I found a volume by Herder, Lessing, Goethe, Schiller; translations of Shakespeare

> by Schlegel and Tieck; the Odyssey in the original Greek; in addition, there were also Ritter's description of the Earth, Johannes Mueller's history of mankind, and works by Alexander and Wilhelm Humboldt. I put the poets aside and selected Alexander Humboldt's *Journey in the Tropical Countries,* which, to be sure, I was already familiar with but still liked to read. (4.1:57; 37; translation modified)

Finding "almost exclusively works of literature" is quite a disappointment for Heinrich, so much so that he would rather read a scientific text (albeit one that deploys an aesthetic program in support of its scientific aims) he already knows than discover an unknown literary work. Later, when Heinrich's scientific explorations unleash a long series of disturbing metaphysical questions about the geological constitution of the Earth, his unexpected response is: "From such questions I fled to the poets" (4.2:33; 193; translation modified). On subsequent visits, the *Odyssey* becomes the text he reads again and again. While both Humboldt's travel narrative and Homer's epic involve long trips in exotic lands, Heinrich's attitude has clearly shifted. Moreover, the same change in attitude that appears with literature can be observed in Heinrich's experience of his father's Greek stones, paintings, jewels, architecture, music, and, eventually, of Natalie. For this to happen to Heinrich (and for us to register this as readers), Heinrich must be able to access the objects repeatedly. Heinrich makes it a point to return to "catalogued" objects upon each return to a house, since he habitually tours a house whenever he visits it, in order to see objects he knows are there (4.1:121–29, 4.3:126–30; 48–60, 383–93). The rigid sense of order reigning in each household Heinrich frequents thus serves a particular purpose, but what is crucial is that this order is encoded with meaning(s). One result of this principle is that an object of a certain type can easily be located once the underlying principle of organization has been comprehended, in other words, has become legible and transparent. A significant portion of Heinrich's *Bildung* consists in learning to apprehend these invisible principles of organization (the reader who realizes this performs an analogous feat, having built a mental museum that grows with each set of comments Heinrich makes, and is able to recognize crucial moments on the path to *Bildung*).

Heinrich's *Bildung* fundamentally depends on the way the respective estates exhibit their objects. Seen this way, each of the houses, gardens, and even the Alps becomes a kind of extended exhibition, a collection of collections that Heinrich visits again and again. With respect to *Der Nachsommer,* I use the term "itinerary" to mean that the path Heinrich takes contains certain localizable events that culminate in his attaining a highly developed identity and founding a family as a (re)productive member of bourgeois society, although the itinerary may not be comprehensible as such while it is in process. As I will show, it is highly productive to analyze several crucial junctures in Heinrich's meandering but steady progression toward a *gebildete* identity in terms of how the junctures operate according to museal techniques. First, however, I want to consider the notions prominent nineteenth-century museum architects thought they could support with particular museum layouts, before arguing that Stifter's familiarity with the concerns of museums of his day makes it highly plausible that the appearance of museal techniques in his novel is calculated.

Museum Itineraries and Stifter's Museal World

In terms of museum organization, encoding a route through an exhibition to have a particular meaning is an extremely common, conscious practice; in many ways it inheres in the practices of organization and display.[7] Very often that route culminates in a high point or finale, toward which all previous developments on the route progress. That high point is usually demarcated by a semiotic encoding that emphasizes a particular object, room, or concept being represented. Highly valued objects might be set off from other objects spatially or with special lighting, placed in the largest room, or put at the end of a path. Likewise, interpretive markers and texts reinforce the semiotic encoding, thus further heightening the sense of having reached a culmination. Many museums and exhibitions from the nineteenth century onward have offered inexpensive catalogs to guide visitors through the collections. These catalogs were often simultaneously intended to educate their users.[8] Many museums have also provided signs to show the visitor to the next room when the architectural structure does not explicitly designate the possible path. It is nevertheless important to see that the concept of the museum itinerary need not be simplistic or even linear. In fact, one of the challenges of museum studies is to do justice to the multiple visual and bodily effects an exhibition can produce, even when visitors behave in ways not predicted by museum designers.

German museums, such as Schinkel's museum in Berlin, employed this kind of "scripting" as a point of their construction. Examining the plans and writings that reveal the dominant functions Schinkel hoped his museum layout would achieve is instructive for three reasons. Schinkel is unmistakably clear in his attention to the meanings he thought his building's structures could impart to its visitors.[9] Just as important, however, the influence of Schinkel's conceptions was very quickly felt in other cities, particularly Vienna, a museum landscape Stifter was familiar with. Finally, the notions of *Bildung* attached to particular architectural features resonate powerfully with those at stake in Heinrich's development. Understanding them helps us delineate the conceptions operating in Stifter's novel.

As I discuss in Chapter 3, Schinkel designed his museum with certain visitor pathways in mind. The rotunda, it might be recalled, contained only a few sculptures, placed at a height that discouraged contemplation and instilled awe (Fig. 9).[10] Once made receptive (*empfänglich*)—a word that recalls Humboldtian ideas of *Bildung* even as it brings to mind associations of feminine fertility and penetration[11]—visitors could enter the rooms of classical sculpture or ascend the staircases to paintings, arranged by historical hang.[12] To heighten the effect of ascending from daily life into the arts, the bottom of the staircase remained in darkness and opened into light on the first floor, so that visitors were at least illuminated if not "enlightened" by following this path.[13] Within the painting galleries, the rhetorical emphasis fell on Renaissance Italian painting, housed in the largest room.

The Berlin museum can thus be seen as employing several strategies that constitute an educational scheme, laid out in spatial terms: by dispensing with the visitor's everyday thoughts, the exhibition could more easily impart the effect of its iconographic program on the viewer. This program was to convey a sense of the historical development of art through the conscious organization of objects by school and period, the logic of which was to appear transparent to the visitor.[14] In combination with the frescos, the historical layout of objects demonstrated the progressive victory of culture over barbarism and the forces of nature.[15] According to the emphases of the galleries, the Italian Renaissance represented a high point in that victory. The viewer who completed the itinerary through the museum emerged ideally as someone who could carry this inheritance into the present-day, quotidian reality. Understood in this way, *Bildung* can be seen as converging in the structure and encoding of the Berlin museum.

Even though it is not known whether Stifter knew Schinkel's design, he was familiar with many of the notions that informed it. Discussing Stifter's lifetime desire to envision ideal houses for a life of beauty, Walther Rehm observes that in his younger years, Stifter's house plans closely resemble "those great edifices that recalled Schinkel's southern architectural dreams, with the noble family of white, slender columns."[16] Although Rehm does not elaborate on this claim, the classicism of Schinkel's museum is often remarked, so that one might certainly extend Rehm's observation to it. Moreover, the design of Schinkel's museum had a large architectural impact outside Berlin. Leo von Klenze, whose Glyptothek and Pinakothek in Munich were roughly contemporaneous with Schinkel's design, was acutely aware of the developments in Berlin even as he strove to supply his own unique structures that surpassed Schinkel's in the areas of lighting and preservation. Like Schinkel, von Klenze believed that a museum structure should be monumental and historically organized.[17] It can be said with respect to the Pinakothek that von Klenze implemented a more rigorously historical and chronological hang than did Schinkel, with precisely the idea of transmitting a sense of the power of art to the visitor.[18] According to James Sheehan, "[H]ere, too, everything was done to produce the proper conditions under which art's power could be felt: both the interior and the exterior of the Pinakothek, Klenze wrote, were designed 'to put the viewer's soul in an appropriate mood' to appreciate beauty."[19] Munich, which Stifter visited in the late 1840s, can therefore also be seen as a place where museum design and the project of *Bildung* powerfully converged.

Also highly aware of Schinkel's projects was the Danish architect Theophil Hansen. While Hansen is best known as a chief architect of Vienna's Ringstrasse and the designer of the Parliament building there, he had practiced historicist techniques years earlier as the architect of the first purpose-built public museum in Vienna, the Austrian Heeresmuseum.[20] In preparing his museum layout, Hansen studied many of the features of Schinkel's temple of art, which he adapted to his needs in Vienna. As in Berlin, the core of the Heeresmuseum resembles a consecrated space, with the visitor entering a vaulted room holding fifty-six statues, on high pedestals, representing Austria-Hungary's greatest military commanders. After proceeding through what is accordingly termed the *Feldherrenhalle,* the visitor advances up a grand staircase and moves into the so-called *Ruhmeshalle,* a frescoed, monumental space created for ceremonies and representation of Austrian military glory. Many of Schinkel's elements reappear in Hansen's design (albeit in rearranged form), especially the imposing statues, the evocation of consecrated space, and the preparing of the visitor for the rest of the museum by passing through these ritual spaces before entering the exhibition galleries.

Stifter likely knew about the planning of the Heeresmuseum, since it was being constructed in the 1850s, precisely the years when he was writing the *Nachsommer.* It has been documented that Stifter avidly visited museums in Munich and Vienna on his travels, and some critics have plausibly claimed that several of the art objects represented in the *Nachsommer* hail from the royal collections in Vienna.[21] Moreover, Stifter had more than passing awareness of the museum world of Vienna, Linz, and Munich, and his behind-the-scenes involvement with museums and officials in Linz and Vienna could well have familiarized him with the design issues being worked out as the public museum was being invented. In particular, Stifter was deeply involved in the operations of the Överösterreichisches Landesmuseum in Linz, where he served as a *Kunstreferent,* member of the museum board, and expert restorer of medieval and Baroque objects both in the museum and in Upper Austrian churches such as Kefermarkt and Saint Wolfgang (Figs. 13 and 14, respectively, both of which are alluded to in the novel).[22] In these capacities, Stifter evaluated potential museum acquisitions and provided reports on several of the archaeological digs taking place in Upper Austria at that time, including the excavation of Roman artifacts at Lauriacum, Wels, and Linz and the discovery of Celtic graves at Hallstatt (see Chapter 5). These tasks placed Stifter in regular correspondence with officials administering the royal collections and required him to have knowledge of the plans and operations of the museums in Vienna, in part because he sometimes had to report to the officials there about the work he was doing, and in part because he negotiated with them while exchanging objects that were considered duplicates in Linz's holdings. Additionally, it is due to Stifter's skills and knowledge of the movements of the international museum market that Johann Kain's collections of Roman artifacts and certain of Johann Ramsauer's collections of Celtic objects from Hallstatt ended up in Linz, and not in Vienna or Russia.[23]

Stifter furthermore contributed to the museum landscape in his founding of the Oberösterreichische Landesgalerie in his native Linz, which within his lifetime went from a private experiment to a state-endowed institution.[24] Here Stifter's professional occupation as a public educator and his interest in exhibition converged, for he was a published pedagogue with strong views on reform—he proceeded "in order to make the viewing of good, serious artworks as the best educational and ennobling material possible for the public at all times."[25] To support the regular exchange of artworks between local artists and those as far as away as Munich and Düsseldorf, Stifter helped publicize the regular shows at the gallery by publishing reports in the Linz newspaper. His involvement on so many levels in the Oberösterreicher Verein and the Landesmuseum in Linz gave him detailed experience with techniques of exhibition.[26] Finally, as the appointed Kunstconservator of the State of Upper Austria, Stifter was charged with identifying and rescuing objects at risk of being plundered, illicitly sold, or destroyed by neglect, such as church altars, old pieces of furniture, and churches themselves.[27] In this capacity, Stifter was carrying forth the original mission of the Landesmuseum, which was founded in 1883 by Anton Ritter von Spaun, to promote the study of ruins, historical objects, and documents that might bear witness to the cultural and historical past of the Germanic peoples.[28] The Linz group Stifter was associated with sought no less than to awaken in the general populace an appreciation of German art and culture by means of preserving monuments (*Denkmäler*).[29] The Landesmuseum was accordingly charged with preserving cultural artifacts for the public and with making those objects accessible for the purposes of *Bildung*.

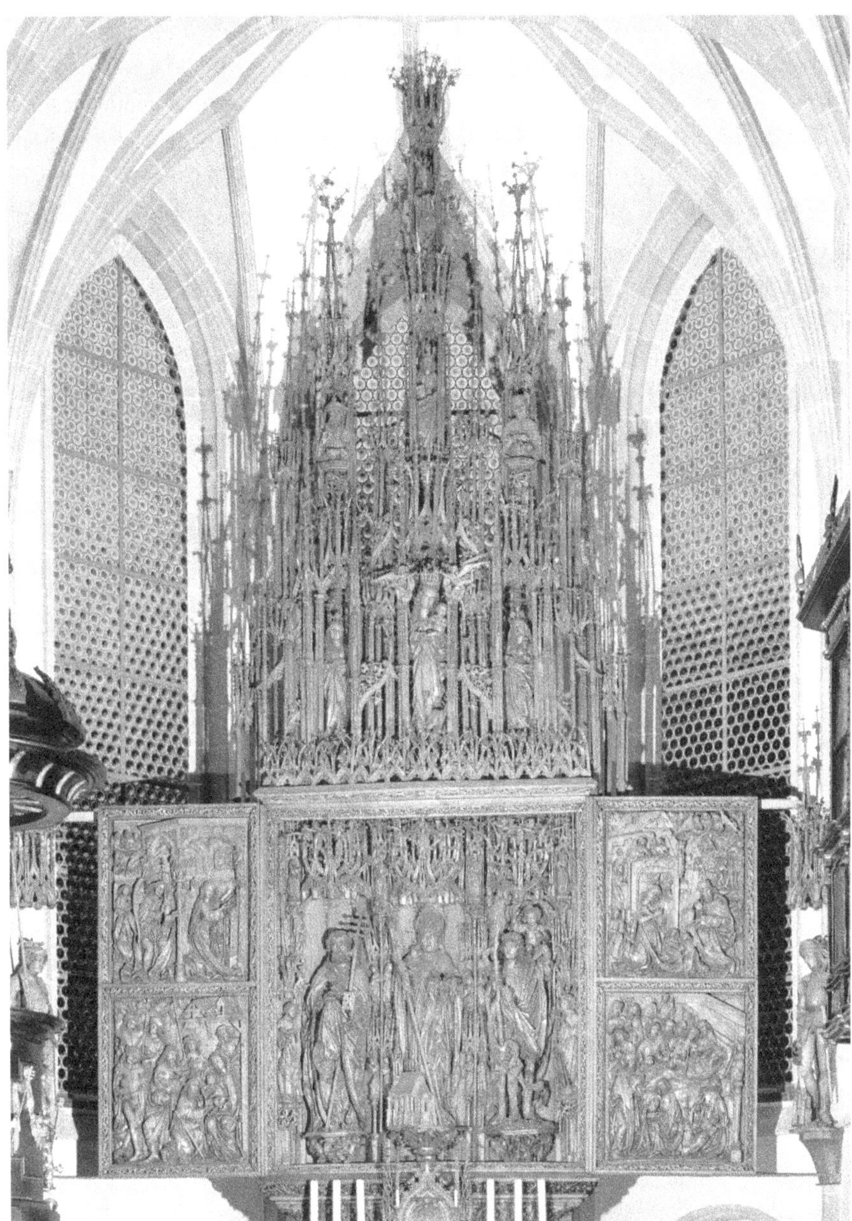

Figure 13 Anonymous, fifteenth century. The altarpiece of the Parish Church of Kefermarkt, Austria. Stifter had an instrumental role in saving this Gothic altarpiece, which is alluded to in his novel *Der Nachsommer*. Carved wood, total height 13.5 m. Parish Church, Kefermarkt, Austria.

Stifter shared these views and the belief that museums could effectively contribute to public *Bildung*. As he wrote in the essay "Über die Schule" [About Education], art should no longer be "the property of individuals, but rather that of the state. Arrangements should be made so that whenever possible [art's] graceful appearance *be accessible to everyone* and affect everyone with its beneficence."[30] Stifter's endorsement of the public functions of museums here again meshes well with his vocation as a professional pedagogue and his drive for school reform in Upper Austria. Stifter's high reverence for figures such as Wilhelm von Humboldt, whose writings are mentioned in the *Nachsommer* (4.1:57; 37), might have made him familiar with the views expressed in Humboldt's report concerning the installation of Schinkel's museum in Berlin and its design intended to increase *Bildung*.[31]

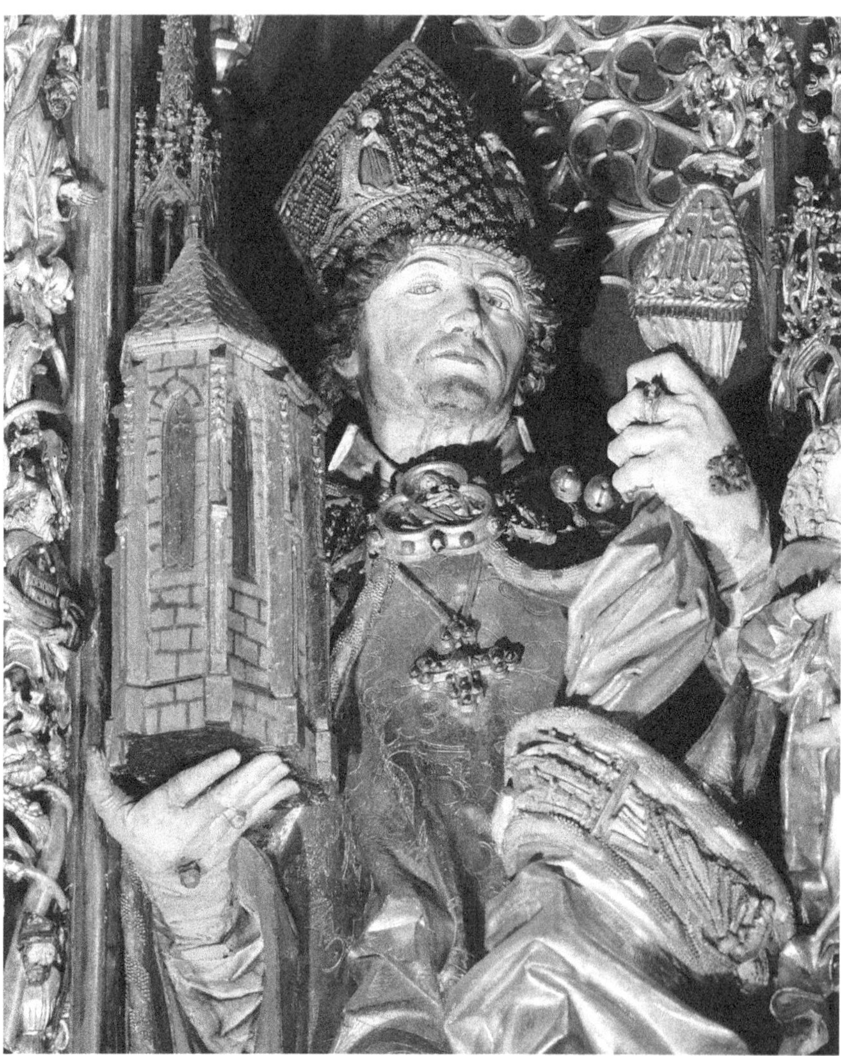

Figure 14 Michael Pacher (ca. 1434–98). Saint Wolfgang holding a model of the church of Saint Wolfgang. As with the Kefermarkt altar, Stifter had an instrumental role in saving this Gothic altarpiece. Carved and painted wood (1475–81), 100 cm × 75 cm (reproduced section); total height 12.16 m. Saint Wolfgang Church, Saint Wolfgang, Austria.

The Museum Itinerary and *Bildung* in Stifter's *Nachsommer*

Given Stifter's deep and varied experience with museums and their functions, it should not come as a surprise that many of the features I have been describing appear in the novel as an itinerary that underpins the process of *Bildung*. In the following section, I examine those manifestations in the text. I also take up the question of why Stifter, despite his highly visible engagement with public museums and *Vereine*, chose to deemphasize their educational impact in the novel, instead placing the onus on interactions with private collectors and their holdings.

Although the terms of her argument are different, Margrit Wyder demonstrates that the first seven lines of Stifter's *Nachsommer* have a static rigidity that forces the reader to abandon any preconceived notions when approaching the text: "If for Stifter it is the mark of an artwork 'that it suspends all moods in the reader in order to create its own,' then the conscious formalization of the opening of the narrative perhaps has to a certain extent the purpose of producing in the reader a mental tabula rasa, a condition of complete sobriety, upon which the following text then is able to develop the desired effect."[32] This mental tabula rasa banishes all that is unclean and improper from what Wyder calls the *Vorhof zum Tempel* [courtyard of the temple] and prepares the reader to receive the lessons that then follow.

The functional similarities of the opening of the *Nachsommer* to the rotunda of Schinkel's museum are too striking to ignore. They operate on the presumption that a structurally instilled sobriety and awe increase the potential of the art that follows to impress itself on the reader. In order to explain the near-absence of references to commerce in the novel, Wyder employs the word *temple* in terms of the biblical story of Jesus casting out the moneychangers; yet no contradiction emerges in considering this *Vorhof* as a museal structure.[33] Indeed, Heinrich Reitzenbeck employed precisely this terminology in his characterization of Stifter in 1853: "[Stifter] hates more than anything the saucy and boorish intruders into the temple of art, who want to spread out with their rags, their mess, and their pitiful purpose. 'Chase the buyers and the sellers out from the temple'—Stifter calls out—'this temple is a house of prayer and the highest art, like the highest love is worship'—from this it follows how much he loves art as something divine."[34] If Reitzenbeck is right in his depiction of Stifter's views, Stifter may well have constructed this museal text as a kind of temple to art. The characters in Stifter's novel discourage the use of a room for any purpose other than what it was explicitly intended for, which lends a sacral quality to the rooms that display art. Heinrich even remarks that the way a Greek statue is displayed suggests it is part of a temple. *Der Nachsommer* deploys precisely the same features, and is indebted to the same values, as the museum layouts of its day. Schinkel wanted his museum to be a secular temple, a sacred space for art; a banning of pedestrian business activity from it would align well with his intentions.[35] What makes Stifter's text so fascinating is that these principles form the core of its functioning as a literary text, allowing Stifter's *Bildungsroman* to be seen as performative for the reader.

The reader's itinerary follows the one that Heinrich traces out, with Risach's estate figuring as the place where many pivotal events in Heinrich's *Bildung* take place. This is fitting, since Risach in fact seems to have constructed his entire house according to museum techniques then being experimented with throughout Europe in order to achieve calculated aesthetic effect. Most often, that effect is one based on the overall impact of the collection as a whole, as can be seen in the way Risach has arranged his paintings. He creates frames to suit each picture and its place in the larger order (4.2:112; 236), and as he explains to Heinrich, "We have also carried out serious consultations and many experiments as to which color we ought to give the walls. We arrived at the powerful red that you still see in the painting room" (4.2:112; 236). Risach's expertise and taste would have suited him for work in the Berlin museum; Schinkel chose a powerful red for the paintings there.[36] As in his other rooms, the effect of the collection as a whole is also an important consideration for Risach. As he explains of a Madonna with Child in his collection, "The picture no longer hangs where it originally was. We have rehung the pictures several times, and it produces a particular pleasure to see whether the effect of the whole is not a better one in another arrangement" (4.2:112; 236). The collector can control and manipulate art to produce effects, which adds an individual, creative potential to both acquiring and owning the artwork, each of which has its narrative. This potential produces the pleasure of rearranging. Risach then claims that the whole of a collection can produce as much of an impact as any singular piece of art.

The principle of overall effect operates throughout his house. The floor of the marble room, for instance, is inlaid according to the design of a medieval church window that also shows off the dazzling array of Risach's marble. Moreover, the delicate nature of the floor as exhibit piece diminishes its functional value. Felt shoes must be worn while walking across it, and Risach no longer uses the space as the entrance to his home (4.1:52). Literally a place from which most pedestrian affairs are banished, the space becomes consecrated (the wedding banquet, itself a ritual ceremony, is the only "event" that takes place there). These measures simultaneously conserve the aesthetic array and ensure that visitors' attention is focused on those aesthetic elements that are supposed to be regarded devotionally. As previously observed, leading museum architects in Berlin (Schinkel), Munich (von Klenze), and Vienna (Hansen) conceived of a variety of designs, typically as a space entered at the start of a museum visit, that attempted to instill just this sense of awe and receptivity to art in the museum goer.[37] The marble room prompts Heinrich to take aesthetic considerations into account, with the display techniques promoting (and signaling) this growing awareness.

In other rooms, notably those where Heinrich experiences epiphanies in his *Bildung,* Risach has expended considerable thought and energy on intensifying the effects of his best objects. Risach's placement of a statue of Nausikaa in the stairwell entails carefully measuring its size and constructing a small pedestal that raises the sculpture to a height appropriate to the architectonic form of the room (4.2:84–85; 220–21). Such an approach seems to anticipate aesthetic concerns prevailing in major museums built in Berlin, Munich, and Vienna between 1830 and 1860, where diverging approaches were taken in the quest for the optimal display of sculpture.[38] And as he explains to Heinrich, "I am so happy that I had the marble corridor and stairway done as I did. Even at the time I was thinking a statue of white marble would be put on the stairway; *best of all the light would come down from above,* and the surrounding walls as well as the floor must have a darker gentle color" (4.2:87; 222; my emphasis). As in von Klenze's Pinakothek in Munich, which was one of the first museums to experiment with the technique, Risach knows that overhead lighting can be an advantageous way to illuminate artworks. The overhead lighting not only enhances the statue's whiteness against the darker floor and background (4.2:87; 222); the glass also allows lightning flashes to illuminate the statue in the dark: "Whenever the lightning flashed, a pink light flowed down it; then the previous color was there again. It seemed appropriate that they had not put this figure in a room where there were windows, where ordinary things could gaze in, where a confusion of light would be streaming in; rather, they had put it in a space all its own, lighted from above, surrounding it with the light of a temple" (4.2:74–75; 215). Because the glass roof provides the sole source of light, the lightning flashes flow across the statue in undiminished clarity. As a result of this movement of light, Heinrich thinks the statue has come alive in a Pygmalion-like manner: "I had a feeling as if I were standing beside a silent living being and almost shuddered to think that the maiden might move at any moment" (4.2:75; 215). The overhead lighting, the background, the whole mode of display produce this enlivening effect, which marks the strongest epiphany Heinrich experiences. This revelation occurs in the central chapter of the book, making it a structural and conceptual turning point in the novel. Here Heinrich discovers the power of (Greek) art and becomes capable of recognizing Natalie as the living embodiment and descendent of ancient Greece (4.2:86–87; 222–23). Thus Heinrich's first aesthetic impressions in Risach's marble room later bear fruit, after several detours, in the neighboring stairwell (and still later, as will be seen, in Heinrich's garden and Natalie's private chambers, before concluding at the wedding banquet in the marble room).

The overhead lighting underscores the on-going connection of the sculpture to its provenance in that it maintains an important continuity with the environment in which Risach found it. During a trip to Italy, Risach came upon the statue in a roofless shed that left the statue open to the sky (4.2:76–77; 216). When Risach brought the figure to Austria, he eventually placed it in the marble staircase next to the marble room, into which the entire southern sky gazed (4.2:73; 214–15; 221). The glass roof in the stairwell preserved a direct relationship of the statue to that sky, albeit protected from the harsher Austrian weather by the glass. Besides providing optimal lighting conditions for the statue, the overhead glass upheld a continuity that normally gets lost when objects are circulated from one context to another. This episode is a good example of a piece of collected art deriving part of its cultural meaning and value through the maintenance of a connection to its earlier context(s) of display.

The connection to the sun proves vital for other unusual and prized objects on Risach's estate, namely, the exotic plants in the greenhouse. In the Austrian climate, a greenhouse provides the only way for these plants to survive. But in addition to sheltering them, the glass also encapsulates them. They are kept next to, but separated from, the native Austrian plants. Like the statue of Nausikaa, these plants were imported from distant lands and brought together in Austria. This dynamic of circulation culturally centers Austria relative to other cultures and regions, inscribing the exotic into the narrative of that which is "native Austrian."[39] The containment of the foreign and exotic within Austria scripts Austria as superior to non-European cultures and regions; Austrians can, after all, appropriate objects from these cultures and make them articulate Austrian cultural values. In Stifter's *Nachsommer,* the exotic plants are deployed to underscore particular concepts of aesthetic beauty, for it is precisely on Heinrich's and Natalie's wedding day that the *Cereus peruvianus,* a flowering cactus, is made to bloom (4.3:271; 472). Stifter's novel can be seen participating in the cultural discourse that produced the fairs and the World Expositions of the nineteenth century and that went so far as to include animals and even people of other ethnic origins in the anthropological narrative of central European cultural superiority.[40] This is, in other words, a budding Euro- or even Germanocentrism.

Both the revelation of the statue's beauty and its cultural significance depend fundamentally on the sophisticated modes of exhibition that Risach employs. In explaining the beauty of the Greek statue to Heinrich, Risach articulates an aesthetic principle he sees in all art: "That's the nature of the best works of ancient art and, in my opinion, of the best art in general: you can't ascertain particular parts or plans about which you can say, that is the most beautiful; rather, the whole is beautiful; you might say of the whole: it is the ultimate in beauty, but its parts are merely natural" (4.2:87; 222). To Risach it is paramount that the components betray no intentionality or dominance over one another; rather they should combine with their neighbors and the environment to produce an entity that feels "natural." Put another way, the components' arrangement reveals a certain *transparency* of function. This fidelity to natural states is, as I discuss in Chapter 3, an aesthetic criterion that harkens back to Goethean aesthetics. In that view, beauty can be revealed by the artist only when he selects and depicts elements in line with an object's or organism's dynamic existence in nature.

What collecting and the stories attached to it reveal are the complex mechanisms that go into the selection of appropriate elements and the securing of an aesthetic illusion as natural. In Stifter's text, the configuration of aesthetic objects springs from what seems to be an inner logic, so that it seems readily intelligible why they appear the way these objects do. This goal can be supported by collecting and exhibiting, for instance, in that the careful arrangements of parts can construct a coherent whole on one level even as undesirable elements can be rendered invisible.[41] Risach's exhibitions behave according to such a logic, since he also tries to create an effective whole from individual artworks that comply with his idea of beauty (4.2:87; 222). When Risach rearranges his paintings over and over, gives them special frames and a particular background color, this transparency of arrangement is what he is trying to achieve in order to get the "effect of the whole." The same can be said of the display of the statue, which so well blends with its surroundings that Heinrich remarks that it looks as if the girl stepped up onto the stand to have a look around (4.2:73; 214–15).

According to Risach, the naturalness of true art impresses itself upon both educated and uneducated people. Risach recounts a tale of peasants in a museum tiptoeing up to a statue of a sleeping boy as support for his view:

> Once I was in a gallery of ancient statues where there was a white marble statue of a sleeping youth who was seated and leaning back. Country folk came into the gallery who, judging from their native costumes, lived in a very remote part of the country. They wore long skirts, and the dust of a journey perhaps just completed that very morning still lay on their buckle shoes. When they approached the sleeping youth, they did so carefully, on tiptoes. An artist rarely receives such a direct and deep appreciation of his work. (4.2:87–88; 222–23)

Taken by Risach to be an expression of awe, the people's tiptoeing would seem to result from their thinking the statue is so true to nature as to be alive.

But more than mimesis comes into play in securing such fidelity to nature.

Like the statue in his home, the display in the public museum is produced by a complex, yet almost invisible environment that surrounds objects deemed to be aesthetic with appropriate amounts of space, proper lighting, sumptuous materials, and so on. Moreover, Risach's account depends on a mythic narrative that, though it seeks to ground his claims about the objects' mimetic qualities, depends on a number of interpretive assumptions in order to be true. Risach assumes the people are peasants by their long coats and buckled shoes, which is plausible, as clothing became a marker of social class in the bourgeois social rise of the nineteenth century.[42] More contentious is that the peasants' clothing alone can indicate their level of education and insight into artworks. For Risach, the peasants' clothing guarantees that their response is somehow more "natural" and authentic than his, with their tiptoeing indicating an unmediated and deep recognition of the artist's talent.

Yet as uninitiated and uninvested in culture as they allegedly are, these peasants have indeed come a great distance on foot to visit such a cultural institution as the museum. But most important, the practice of the public museum was extremely new in the 1820s, the decade in which the novel was set. Even then it was unlikely for peasants to enter collections in the German-speaking countries. The royal decree of 1792 opening the imperial collections to the public in Vienna specifically called for clean shoes, which these peasants do not have.[43] The peasants' shoes instead invite us to recall that the novel was written after the 1848 revolution, when true public access to Viennese museums was made possible as part of the reforms introduced to quell the possibility of further rebellion. As I have mentioned, Stifter himself was an advocate for universal access to museum spaces. The appearance of these dusty-shoed peasants in a museum before it was historically probable is perhaps a case of after-the-fact revisionism that was trying to suggest a retrospective corrective to a society that had been badly shaken by its inability to educate and provide for its masses.

But since peasants would most likely have been just as unfamiliar with museum going and museum etiquette in the 1850s as they would have in the 1820s, it is plausible that they might tiptoe in the museum because of the overwhelmingly monumental character of the building and the exhibition. Architects like Klenze, Schinkel, and Hansen clearly designed their structures to instill awe and reverence in their visitors, especially the *Ungebildeten.* It is equally plausible that the peasants tiptoe because they know someone like Risach is watching them. Museum going represents one of the earliest modes of "see-and-be-seen" public culture, where individual members observe and "police" one another's behavior.[44] According to discourses of the period, one task that public culture was to achieve was to mix the middle and working classes, so as to expose and incite the working classes to "proper" modes of behavior, which required the polite regulation of one's gaze.[45]

The ease with which Risach moves between the art in his home and the art in museums to make his argument about the peasants illustrates another feature of his techniques of display. Risach employs several techniques of exhibition that the architects Schinkel, Hansen, and Klenze use in their museum construction. While the parallels indicate that Risach finds agreement with the cultural currents of the 1820s, they also reveal that as a private collector, Risach largely endorses the interests of the state. The issue comes up subtly when Risach discusses the possibility of collecting silk: "A collection of such material would be most remarkable; however, he could not do it since it would entail journeys through all Europe and considerable parts of Asia and Africa; the project would probably exceed the powers of a single man. Societies or the state could set up such collections for comparisons, for edification, even for the enrichment of history itself" (4.3:133–34; 395). For Risach, only the scope of their ambitions and their budgets differentiates the aims of the state and museum societies, and those of private collectors. In particular, Risach regards the tasks of collecting to educate and relate history as domains of the state and museum societies.

Risach's lumping of the museum societies and the state together reflects certain historical trends. Without wanting to reduce Risach's position to an autobiographical expression of Stifter's background, I would nevertheless like to recall that Stifter had considerable experience with the private Art Association (*Kunstverein*) of Linz and the state museums in Vienna. Additionally, it is commonly argued that Stifter freely placed objects held in state collections such as the Gemma Augustea into the private holdings of Heinrich's father.[46]

While it is essential to regard private collectors, museum societies such as *Museumsgesellschaften* and *Kunstvereine,* and state-founded museums as separate entities whose goals and politics do not necessarily coincide, Gudrun Calov demonstrates that the museum societies at times played pivotal roles in founding museums in nineteenth-century Germany.[47] This certainly can be said of Stifter's personal activities in both state and private organizations in Linz as well as in more general terms. Historically, too, museum societies were founded primarily by bourgeois private collectors who sought to establish publicly accessible art collections. In cities such as Hamburg, Leipzig, and Braunschweig, the societies proved adept in convincing the local governments to collaborate with them.[48] This development is not surprising, since, as David Blackbourn has argued, members of museum societies often presided over business empires and had connections to government officials, which allowed them to influence government actions without taking official responsibility.[49] Even in the comparative position of the newly unified German empire, museum directors such as Wilhelm Bode found it advantageous to create private bodies such as the Kaiser-Friedrich-Association, to raise funds and to collect items the state could not afford.

Walter Benjamin points out that this allegiance need not take shape in this way. On the model of the collector Eduard Fuchs, Benjamin argues for a private collector who operates in opposition to the "continuum of history" that the state assembles to legitimize itself.[50] The private collector can rupture this continuum by assembling artifacts that represent another history. Eduard Fuchs collects political caricatures, pornography, and Tang sculpture, all of which were neglected by state collections in the second half of the nineteenth-century. Such cultural "scraps" are unlikely to be included in a traditional history, yet they are telling of a historical dimension denied.[51] In contrast, Risach as a private collector in no way undertakes to undermine the "official" art and social history that a public collection might perpetuate in Austria. Risach and his collections serve instead as perhaps more rarefied versions of many of the same values the state would ideally transmit.

Exhibiting as an Index of the Educated Personality

Part of what Heinrich learns on his path is that making and maintaining collections is the way to express and relate his identity through collected objects. Previously I noted that Heinrich's budding aesthetic sense leads him to detect a gap in Risach's collection of marble, which he determines to fill with a gift. However, after acknowledging that the gift is inordinately precious, Risach says of Heinrich's find, "I do not have [this marble] at all in my collection; also the slab seems to be thick and faultless enough so that a clean cut would be possible. I am very happy to own such a piece and thank you very much for it. However, it can't become part of my house collection since I only have pieces that I have collected personally. Because I enjoy this sort of collecting and categorizing so very much I won't depart from this principle now or in the future" (4.1:235–36; 137). Despite the ideal fit the marble would make, Risach refuses even to place it in the house, solely on the grounds that he has not discovered it himself (see also 4.1:127; 76–77). In this way, Risach inscribes the collections, and as a result the house and gardens as well, into his narrative of self. It is a mode of collecting memorably described by Walter Benjamin when he writes, reflecting on his own experience as a book collector, "[F]or inside [the collector] there are spirits, or at least little genii, which have seen to it that for a collector—and I mean a real collector, a collector as he ought to be—ownership is the most intimate relationship that one can have to objects. Not that they come alive in him; it is he who lives in them."[52]

In like fashion, Risach finds himself in the objects he arranges. Rehanging his paintings for the whole grouping to achieve a maximum effect is an activity that Risach enjoys immensely, yet it is one that he has stopped doing because he has finally grown accustomed to the current hang: "I won't make any more changes. The present arrangement of the paintings has become a habit with me; I have grown to like it and wouldn't like to see it changed. It has become a joy for me, a flower in my old age" (4.2:112; 236). Part of Risach's satisfaction with the arrangement has to do with the way it represents a particular version of his own personal history and presents his life with a narrative stabilized by habitual order.[53] As Walter Benjamin notes in the *Arcades Project,* the collecting of teacups in the Biedermeier period served this kind of function: "The mania of teacups ... is characteristic for the Biedermeier. Parents, children, friends, relatives, bosses, and underlings expressed their feelings through teacups ... as Friedrich Wilhelm III filled his study with pyramids of porcelain teacups, so too the bourgeois collected in his serving room memories of the most important events, the most valuable hours of his life."[54] Risach makes much the same point when he reflects on the function of his paintings: "The acquisition of paintings ... which was not always easy, represents a special path in the course of my life, a path that has seen some happy and some melancholy memories" (4.2:112; 236; translation modified). Each picture relates for Risach a particular set of experiences, which is an intertwining of the picture's history, how it was acquired, and the correlated events of Risach's life (4.2:112; 236). The final instance of the way that all these paintings came to enjoy their current context is Risach. This particular arrangement of paintings constitutes part of the manner in which Risach has come to understand himself and to structure his identity. The display might be said to constitute a visual memoir. In the way that Risach, Heinrich's father, and Heinrich himself all engage in encoding multiple rooms of their homes with practically all the objects they collect and arrange—and not only cups—this principle is pushed to its extreme. To miss this point is to miss a central, essential feature of *Der Nachsommer.*

The construction of identity in this novel thus involves appropriating available objects, rearranging the appealing parts, and quietly discarding those elements that are unsightly or unacceptable. This latter aspect should not be overlooked, for as most theories of exhibition observe, no exhibit can exist without its material somehow having been selected and without privileging what it displays over what it hides. When the maintenance of collections has such a strong inflection to the creation and representation of identity as it does in this novel, the destruction and more generally the hiding of "inappropriate" material can be likened to a representation, perhaps also a mechanism, of psychological suppression.[55]

For instance, when Risach receives sets of copper etchings to evaluate, Heinrich immediately passes moral judgment on the deceased collector to whom the etchings had belonged and on his whole family simply by looking at the arrangement of his copper etchings (4.3:131–32; 393–94). Indeed, it is not merely that that collector liked different art than did Risach and Heinrich, but that he lacked the good sense to keep his predilections hidden. Moreover, he failed to realize that allowing this kind of art to exist can have bad effects on *Ungebildete precisely* because its reproducibility allows wide dissemination (4.3:132; 394).[56] Because Risach claims to know better in every respect, he decides to buy the entire collection so that he can destroy those pieces deemed to be inferior. Only then will they properly represent him and simultaneously fulfill the public moral function of "good" art.

The wall of roses at Risach's estate provides another poignant example of this encoding of self. For one thing, Risach systematically removes plants and sprigs that are sick, dead, or unsightly in order to preserve the visual perfection of the roses on display (4.1:146; 88–95). Indeed, the roses initially appear as a particularly lavish part of the gardens, whose blooming each spring is the basis of a celebration (4.1:258–69; 154). This blooming is a public event with a public significance. Not only do Natalie's mother Mathilde, Natalie, and Heinrich usually join Risach at this time of year, but friends, servants, local farmers, the pastor of Rohrberg, and others come by to view the roses at their peak (4.1:266–69; 154–56). These visitors are also shown whatever other part of the house and grounds they want to see at this time (4.1:267; 154). At the height of their blooming, Heinrich notes that the roses have considerable effect as a whole, much like Risach's paintings, and there is also discussion as to whether arranging the roses in another way might further heighten their effect (4.1:259; 150). Given the personal importance the roses have, it seems unlikely that, even if the group viewing the blooming roses had wanted another arrangement, Risach would oblige them, since their current ordering simultaneously serves an entirely different, personal function for him and Mathilde. Displayed this way outside his house, the roses relate a most intimate side of Risach that he normally conceals (4.1:147; 87–88). As the reader eventually learns, the roses link Risach to the time in his youth when his passion for Mathilde caused him to overstep the bounds of bourgeois propriety, an act that condemned Mathilde and Risach to years of painful separation (4.3:197–219). Since the roses are an index of Risach's love and penance, it is not surprising that Mathilde inspects the plants carefully to make sure that nothing has changed from the previous year (4.1:259; 150).

But in that the personal encoding is the same as the public encoding of the roses, the novel anticipates Nietzsche's observation that notions of personal style and character are essentially public and subject to approval from the outside.[57] That Risach allows the group of visitors to consider rearranging the roses shows that his unity of self is made manifest by the group. According to Nietzsche, this unity fails to exist, except when observed by others.[58] Any opposition between the public and private realms dissolves with this model of identity (arguably one reason that all of Heinrich's collections and drawings are to be made accessible to others, especially to his mentors, at all times). Risach's enormous personal stake in public perusal and verification of his representation of self finally makes his outlandish efforts to maintain the roses in flawless condition (purging the display of "unsightly" sprigs, having a "rose hospital" for sick plants, installing a special shower system, and luring birds to eat pests, 4.1:144–52; 87–94) more comprehensible.

His behavior appears especially obsessive and uncompromising in the context of his personal history. The particular fact that the roses bloom regularly every spring, and that Risach needs to maintain their level of perfection each year, strengthens the suspicion of a repetition compulsion existing in the wake of the trauma of his past separation from Mathilde. The semiotic encoding of the roses, which the ekphrastic text registers without explicit commentary, allows past and present to be connected in a way that confirms this suspicion. Though the group viewing the roses perceives their arrangement as pleasing because of its "charming randomness" (4.1:259; 150), Heinrich reports that a certain order can be perceived in the display: "The roses moved across the surface, going in color from the purest white into a yellowish white into yellow into pale red into fiery rosy-red into purple into violet into dark red" (4.1:266–67; 154).

The colors of the roses roughly follow the order of a rainbow, an ordering that, in addition to recalling the visible spectrum, has another meaning. The house where Risach once worked as a tutor and where he met his love Mathilde had a similar array of roses (4.3:174–75; 417). Upon Risach's arrival there, Alfred, Mathilde's younger brother, shows him the house: "Since it was then the time when the roses bloom, and since these roses were also blooming in an extraordinarily rich way, so it seemed as if a temple of roses were standing there . . . all the colors were present, from the darkest red, at the same time violet-blue, through the rosy-red and yellow until white" (4.3:175; 417). At Mathilde's house, the roses appeared in the same order, but starting from the opposite end of the spectrum. A close match materializes between the way Heinrich presents the roses and the way Risach remembers his *Urrosen.* This match leaves no doubt that Risach's ordering of the roses is supposed to recreate the conditions with which he associated his love for Mathilde before their misunderstanding and long separation. When Risach sees Mathilde again after many years, it is at her house in front of the roses

(4.3:217; 441–42), which represent both a "punishment" for their youthful transgression and a sign of his love for her (4.3;219; 443). Risach similarly considers the roses "that marker of our separation and unification" (4.3:222–23; 444).Thus the semiotic encoding of the surroundings, which the text leaves to the reader to discover, expresses the behavior and desires of the characters in ways that their verbal expressions do not. The presentation of emotion through the display of objects needs to be stressed. *Der Nachsommer* has been seen by many critics as a novel so repressed as to obliterate any trace of personality or meaningful interaction.[59] While it is true that few if any overtly subjective verbal statements are made in the novel, the encoding of the various displayed objects, rooms, houses, and gardens serves to represent personality and to enable communication.[60]

I connect this communicative strategy with Benjamin's observation that Stifter's writing is characterized by a visual hypertrophy marked by the absence of practically all acoustic sensation and therefore of the possibility of liberating expression. To Benjamin, Stifter's style represents a metaphysically dangerous deception by passing off historically and ideologically bound conditions as simple descriptions of natural laws and human nature. Benjamin argues that the dominance of the visual in Stifter's style occurs at the expense of the acoustic, so that speech between characters becomes nothing more than ostentatious display. The result is Stifter's characteristic, well-ordered "peacefulness." While I agree with the thrust and the implications of Benjamin's argument, it is important to note that the visual is semiotically encoded, so that communication of emotion is filtered through the register of the display. It is perhaps not surprising that *Nachsommer* appears so static and emotionless, with so much *Ruhe* [peacefulness], in the words of Walter Benjamin.

An additional dimension to the development and communication of personality through collecting and exhibiting is related to the strict separation of rooms according to function and meaning in the novel.[61] In Risach's house, the marble room contains only samples of marble, the wood room only wood; the paintings are hung in a painting room, and the wall of roses consists only of roses—the list could be expanded considerably. Risach's organizational regime is so extreme that the library houses only books, so that reading must occur either in the reading room or in one's apartment in the house and books must be returned to the library when they are not being read (4.1:58, 93; 37, 57).

The same conditions exist in the homes Heinrich has grown up in, where a revealing transition has occurred.[62] When Heinrich was a boy, Heinrich's father conducted his business in part of the house, making the house a place for both residence and economic transactions. This house was small, so that the children had to do homework and sleep in the same space and to play in their mother's room (incidentally, the mother is the only person who does not have her own space).[63] The mixing of functions in a room is particularly abhorred by Heinrich's father: "The room's function should also be obvious. He couldn't stand 'mixed rooms' as he called them—rooms that were used for several things, such as a combination bedroom-playroom or the like" (4.1: 11; 11). When the family moves from the dark, crowded house in the city to the light, roomy house in the suburbs, "great joy" (*grosse Freude* [4.1:13; 12]) is created by the clearer separation of rooms and the disappearance of certain functions. The children receive more rooms for themselves in the new house, and Heinrich's father is able to devote rooms solely to his respective collections of sculpture, weapons, and paintings. At the same time, business is no longer transacted at home (4.1:13; 13), allowing a clear demarcation between the realms of economics and living. Just as crucially, one room that simply disappears in the transition is the parents' bedroom. In the old house, the parents' bedroom represented a sexuality that made it taboo for the children to enter it (4.1:11; 11). In the new house, the bedroom seems to have utterly vanished, especially since the "elderly maid" charged with its maintenance (4.1:11; 11) is no longer mentioned (4.1:13; 13–14).[64] To the extent that the move to the new house signifies progressive human development, this move seems to go hand in hand with the increasing dissociation of economics and sexuality from the immediacy of bourgeois family life (as well as a typically museal need for more space: it is a truism that museums seldom, if ever, have enough space to display all their holdings).

The same mastery of economic and sexual realms is produced in the course of Heinrich's *Bildung,* which is inflected by subtle modes of surveillance and discipline. From a very early age, Heinrich is required to keep financial records, with his father increasing his available resources upon demonstration of his ability to manage them responsibly and to document his pursuits in writing and displays (4.1:24–26; 18–19). Heinrich's father's endorsement of his collecting explorations seems designed to minimize conflict and to encourage the young man to return home at regular intervals. Yet during his second summer in the field, Heinrich is allowed to stay much farther from the city, and he can visit his parents only once (4.1:28; 20). He subsequently finds that he must compensate for the lack of visits with lengthy descriptions and reports of what he sees and does. What makes this method of instruction so effective is that the pupil is made to regulate him- or herself. Risach's foster son Gustav learns by reporting what he has read or seen because he is required to. In contrast, Heinrich seems to do this voluntarily, at his own speed. When Heinrich finally apprehends the beauty of Risach's Greek statue, he suddenly realizes that Risach has long seen this beauty but has withheld it from him:

"If you had told me it earlier, I would have known it sooner," I replied.

"Telling someone that something is beautiful," [Risach] answered, "doesn't always mean giving him possession of its beauty. In many cases he might only believe it. That way you would certainly spoil his possession of beauty which would have come anyway of its own initiative. I presupposed this of you and gladly waited." (4.2:76; 216)

According to Risach, often the best way to indoctrinate people is to let them indoctrinate themselves. Significantly, this act of learning is an act of appropriation ("the possession of beauty"). Rarely does Risach step in overtly to direct Heinrich's learning, and when he does it is simply to suggest that Heinrich should spend a summer developing his abilities outside geology (4.2:44; 199). Since Heinrich is the proper type, and the environment around him has been properly arranged, the danger of "losing" the person by letting him or her wander seems small.

Risach must wait for Heinrich because Heinrich must make a succession of discoveries before he can apprehend the beauty of the statue. This process is described in terms of the path of Heinrich's *Bildung,* following a hierarchy that begins with the sciences, leads to literature and art, and finally culminates in his recognition of Natalie as the ultimate desirable object. Heinrich's first experience with this procedure occurs in the name of science. At the same time that Heinrich starts to arrange and order his observations for his letters home, he begins "to deal with natural history" (4.1:29–31; 20–22). "To do this," Heinrich explains, "I went out in all directions, and tried to become acquainted with the location and method of growing various plants, and tried to collect a specimen of all types" (4.1:32; 22). Collecting in this instance can mean more than the amassing of actual objects: "I took back to my room the ones that I could carry and could preserve in some fashion. I made descriptions of those I couldn't move from their places—trees in particular belonged to this category—and also added these notes to my collection" (4.1:32; 22). By creating a representation of the objects in question, here primarily trees, Heinrich can bring the objects into circulation and thus effect different arrangements. With these different arrangements, the scientific endeavor consists of identifying the characteristics common to groups of plants: "It seemed that the botanists made the categories according to just one or a few characteristics as, for instance, the cotelydon or flowering parts; as a result, plants were in one group that were quite different in their whole form and the majority of their characteristics" (4.1:32; 22; translation modified). The isolation of a few identifying structures in taxonomy facilitates the naming of families and species whose members may in fact otherwise have little in common. Thus the mammals, from the platypus to the bat to the human being, for all their outward differences, possess a few defining features in common: they are warm-blooded and have hair and mammary glands.

This taxonomic practice of finding similarities in structure or origin, which emphasizes not the unusual and unique properties of things, but seeks instead to apprehend the small details that are common to diverse groups of things, can be seen as an expression of Stifter's *sanftes Gesetz* [the gentle law]. *Das sanfte Gesetz* valorizes these commonalities as the true expression or essence (*Wesenheit*) of the qualities of things, for although they are small individually, they take on great proportions when found to link whole groups of things.[65] This "secret" greatness Stifter takes as the expression of the divine and beautiful in things and beings.[66] Collecting and displaying, then, serve the apprehension of the divine, and in Stifter's understanding, these acts endow life with unity and cohesion.[67] It is thus not surprising to find collecting and displaying employed as pedagogy explicitly for the training of young individuals.

It is important that Heinrich recreates those groupings of plants that others have established as meaningful, even as manifestations of "natural law"; he prefers to make his own orderings to gain insights into the qualities of the objects he studies. Interestingly enough, in the plant example Heinrich cites, prevailing biological theory leads him to focus on precisely the reproductive organs of the plants, whose sexual functions a figure such as Goethe, in his essay and poem the "Metamorphosis of Plants," had unabashedly identified as central to the purpose of life (and not only for plants). Heinrich, in contrast, seems led to consider these parts of the plants only by dint of biological theory, and he appears squeamish about granting much authority to such a sexual view of the world. "I retained the conventional categories but also put my own descriptions beside them. In these descriptions the plants were arranged according to obvious lines, according to, if I may use the term, their mode of construction" (4.1:32; 22). To Heinrich his ordering is "meaningful" and as legitimate as the established system, because to him this system captures more features of the plants and makes their characteristics more legible to him, and because his system can skirt the whole issue of sex and sexual function.

In each instance of Heinrich's scientific experiments, the same feature appears as in Risach's collections: an arrangement of material is made in agreement with a general principle of public discourse, but in the service of a personal goal or need. However, Heinrich is less of a scientific dilettante than might appear at first glance. Because he applies the same principle of analysis and legibility as the established scientist, his ordering could in fact become accepted as "natural law," provided it supplied a more useful and experimentally valid explanation than that which came before. Risach asserts that Heinrich's collecting of plants and rocks is advanced science, saying,

> "I think," replied my companion, "that the science we are now discussing is in its collecting stage. The distant future will build something out of all this material, something we can't even imagine. Collection always precedes science; that isn't at all remarkable; it must be so; however, what is remarkable is that this urge to collect comes into various minds and hearts almost simultaneously, even if they still don't know what this new science will actually be." (4.1:76–77; 76)

Heinrich's endeavors reflect the cutting-edge of science in the first half of the nineteenth century. Charles Darwin and Alfred Russel Wallace spent many years traveling the world and collecting a range of species broad enough for them to respectively devise a theory of evolution. The theory, based on the principle of natural selection, provided an overarching criterion for relating and ordering plants and animals into a grand master narrative.[68] Before the twentieth-century acceptance of Darwin's theory in the "modern synthesis" eliminated competing explanations—and one would do well to note that Darwin's and Wallace's first papers were published only after *Der Nachsommer,* in 1858, with the *Origin of Species* following in 1859—the existence and potential legitimacy of alternative orderings and explanations hardly seem preposterous.[69]

Although Heinrich manages to develop an alternative taxonomy for plants in order to obscure the operations of sexuality in nature, his aesthetic development eventually requires him to represent the human form. Learning how to draw women in particular forces him to confront in a more protracted manner the way that his gaze and lack of skill reveal his desires. The more Heinrich draws, the more he thinks aesthetically in order to find the object most suitable for drawing. Heinrich is fully aware that societal conventions regulate how drawings of women are interpreted when he concludes that the figure of one of Risach's friends has "still had all the freshness and health of a beautiful lady whose figure was just a bit too ample to serve as a model for a drawing, at least as they usually portray beautiful women in drawings" (4.1:262; 152).

At the same time, Heinrich is tellingly "ashamed" (*beschämt*) when it is pointed out to him that he seems oddly fixated on drawing the heads of young girls (already a metonymic substitution that takes his gaze off their bodies) (4.1: 201; 117). Given the relationship of elision and psychic suppression in *Der Nachsommer,*

Heinrich's mental separation of the heads of living women from their bodies appears as a strategy to deny the sexuality represented in those bodies, which the novel in general and Heinrich in particular seem ill-equipped to accept. These drawings appear sexually charged when it is recalled that Heinrich nervously disavows even having looked at his sister as he does other young women, let alone having thought of drawing her head. "It was strange," Heinrich proclaims, "that I never happened upon the idea of observing my sister to see if her features weren't suitable for drawing" (4.1:201; 117; translation modified). Strange, indeed: as in all disavowal, Heinrich must have had the thought in order to claim he never had it. Heinrich averts his painterly gaze from his sister for another reason: "I never dared to" (4.1:201; 117), he later confesses. Instead, the thought often comes to Heinrich, "[N]o one in the world could be so beautiful or pure as Klothilde" (4.1:201; 117). Taken as an expression of inadmissible desire, her "purity" exposes the relation between the gaze, drawing and representation, and desire for Heinrich. No wonder he never has the courage to survey his sister: doing so might reveal the fragility or even the violation of the incest taboo, one of the cornerstones of the compulsory heterosexual matrix being constructed in this novel.

When Heinrich also admits that he would have to be much more aesthetically developed to approach Natalie this way (4.1:201, 4.3:37; 117, 341), this admission again underscores that the advance of aesthetic insight signifies increased control of desire. At one point, Heinrich focuses on Natalie after having observed and labeled the appearance of the daughters of a friend of Risach's: "Natalie—I don't know—was her beauty infinitely greater or did she have a totally different nature—I had not yet been able to fathom this nature even to a slight degree since she had spoken to me so little, I hadn't been able to judge her walk or movements since I didn't dare to look at her as you would a drawing" (4.1:261–62; 151). Afraid to consider his desire for her, Heinrich declines to treat her like a drawing. Unlike with his sister, Heinrich hints that this reluctance arises, not because drawing her is an intractable problem, but because he still needs to develop his aesthetic categories. The need for these categories is clear: with them Heinrich can recognize and understand Natalie's beauty and put a fix on her being. As becomes clear, this fix comes in the form of representational appropriation, which Heinrich can integrate into his own identity like a new painting into a standing collection. This appropriation also represents Heinrich's ability to recognize value and to regulate his own desire.

In concert with his growing control over finances and sexuality, Heinrich's apartments in both his father's and Risach's homes undergo significant expansions, so that he can differentiate his activities, lay out his possessions in a highly organized fashion, and maintain a visual overview of all the areas he has already developed.[70] The point is that Heinrich and Natalie start their lives together having mastered the emotional predicaments and pitfalls that complicated the lives of their parents' generation. Yet underwriting the concept of bourgeois development with the collections-based mechanisms simultaneously suppresses the economic and procreative impulses necessary to perpetuate bourgeois existence over generations. The possibility arises that the museal achievement of a highly developed identity and a highly differentiated living space might therefore bring the bourgeois order to extinction.

Collecting, Exchange, and the Family

I have until now considered Heinrich's *Bildung* in terms of a museum itinerary and making of collections, but now take into account ways in which collecting structures social relationships by means of fostering the exchange of objects and information and thereby affecting individual perceptions and behavior. After his epiphany in Risach's stairwell, Heinrich intensively undertakes the study of art, and particularly oil painting, in order to develop aesthetically. Heinrich's paintings appropriate and bring into circulation objects that are otherwise inaccessible, functioning in the manner of postcards of collected artworks that can be purchased from museum gift shops. A powerful upshot of this multivalent practice is that it facilitates bonds between members of his and Natalie's family even as it shapes his personality and his ultimate ability to appreciate Natalie's value in several crucial stages.

One way that Heinrich helps ensure his father's esteem of Risach, and thus of his bride to be (and vice versa), is by relating the objects Risach owns (for instance, 4.2:43, 48–49; 185–87, 258). Heinrich secures Risach's esteem for his father by telling Risach about his father's collections (4.1:87–88; 54). As such, one function of Heinrich's paintings, reports, and letters is to supply a medium of a male-to-male, or homosocial, exchange that cements a bond between the elder Drendorf and Risach as Heinrich nears initiation into their ranks.[71] In the various critiques of Levi-Strauss's work on exchange in kinship relations, homosocial exchange is typically considered to emerge in heterosexual regimes in which most male expressions of intimacy for other men, including but not limited to homoerotic desire, are taboo.[72] This principle, which may not be universal, can be shown to operate in *Die Nachsommer.* This part of my argument turns on the notion that male-to-male desire of a variety of forms is expressed indirectly through mediation or exchange of information, objects, or women. The copies of Risach's objects that Heinrich circulates greatly stimulate his father's desire to see the objects owned by Risach, so much so that the planning for the visit is accelerated considerably (4.2:50; 202). As Heinrich's mother quickly grasps and articulates, meeting Risach is precisely what is at stake in the visit (4.2:49–50; 201–2). But her bringing this into the open only causes Heinrich's father forcefully and abruptly to break off the discussion of his travel plans. "The floors must be magnificent!' he exclaimed" (4.2:50; 202). Shifting attention away from the man, the elder Drendorf insists that only art objects such as Risach's marble floors are germane. The practice of collecting in *Der Nachsommer* is crucial because the mechanisms that foster the formation of Heinrich's collection also bring men together through the medium of art. Men can have close contact through the exchange of art without requiring them to acknowledge that part of what they seek is the company of other men.

At the same time Heinrich is trapped in a disciplinary game between two men because of his mediating role. In analogy to Risach's modes of collecting, Heinrich submits his drawings and paintings for viewing, and Risach, and occasionally other men, critique them. The regular probing into Heinrich's painting constitutes the most invasive intervention in Heinrich's development in the novel, where painting and drawing are significant ways to appropriate objects for collection. This intervention is all the more effective in that it appears under a different guise. Throughout his *Bildung,* Heinrich has repeatedly reported his actions to his father in letters and descriptions of what he has seen, and he has received critical feedback (for instance, 4.1:24–26, 28–29, 88; 4.2:51–52; 20–22, 23–24, 54, 203). Pictorial representations are an escalation of Heinrich's communicative experience. Artistic "corrections" that others make should thus be understood as attempts to alter Heinrich's sense of self. As such, the paintings form part of a process in which Heinrich practices collecting objects. Because the accuracy of his paintings conveys how well he understands the world, it also shows where Heinrich's development needs further refinement. Since aesthetic development is so closely related to the development of identity in this text, the process of improving Heinrich's ability to represent the world aesthetically likewise serves to cultivate his identity.

Once aesthetic matters predominate, Heinrich's identity is constrained in another way as well. His aesthetic experience derives almost exclusively from the nearly identical collections of his father and Risach. The few visits to public museums alter this situation little, since Risach's collections differ primarily in scale from public collections in the text, not in kind (4.3:134; 395). Moreover, the collections of the Sternenhof, Mathilde's estate, are also monitored by Risach. At one point, Heinrich feverishly and repeatedly rearranges Risach's copper etchings, seeking to find the arrangement that optimally expresses his insights. This can be seen as an attempt to represent and constitute a new identity. But since Risach has already destroyed etchings that might produce an undesirable effect, only certain outcomes are possible. This implicit, a priori control over the product of *Bildung* allows Heinrich to wander through the collections unguided and still to internalize Risach's concept of beauty. When Heinrich finally stumbles on the statue of Nausikaa and is able to comprehend it, he learns that the (expected) effect is much stronger because he feels as though he has discovered its beauty himself (4.2:75–76; 215). So personal and intimate is the sensation that it seems like an awakening of supreme beauty.

As important as the recognition of the supremacy of the beauty of Greek sculpture is, Heinrich in fact begins to comprehend Natalie's value only by seeing that same beauty in her and noting the way that others esteem it. Perhaps his earliest moment of insight into what Natalie embodies occurs after Natalie returns to her mother from a walk in Risach's garden and finds Heinrich there. Natalie is shocked, and her blushing face momentarily turns pale (4.2:193–94; 281). The flash of white and red across her face recalls the effect of lightning on the statue of Nausikaa (4.2:74; 215), leading Heinrich to another epiphany: "Not until now did I realize why she had always seemed so remarkable; I realized it only after I had examined my father's cut stones [Greek sculptures]. It seemed Natalie's was like the faces I had seen on the stones" (4.2:196; 283). In his thinking, Natalie's features replace the Greek stones as that which is "most beautiful" in his mental framework, and he concludes that her family genealogy must reach back to the ancients (4.2:196; 283). This coming to life of Greek culture through Natalie is one indication that collecting in the novel operates in the belief that it can not only conserve, but also awaken, the spirit of past cultures in a dialectical movement that recalls the collecting efforts of nineteenth-century, German-speaking *Denkmalpfleger*.[73]

A crucial point to grasp is that Natalie's behavior regularly contributes to Heinrich's recognition of her beauty and its ultimate valorization. Alarmed by the redness of her daughter's face, a color traditionally associated with passion and the abandonment of bodily control, Mathilde interrogates her daughter as to what she has been up to. While Natalie insists on her right and need to walk around as she pleases, she also creates as she talks a new bouquet from the flowers she had picked. Heinrich's commentary is revealing:

> She continued arranging her flowers; she kept taking one after the other from the larger bouquet and putting it into the smaller until the smaller bouquet became the larger and the larger constantly diminished. She didn't discard a single flower; she didn't even throw away a blade of grass; it seemed she was less making a selection of the flowers than giving the old bouquet a new form. This was the case since finally the old bouquet disappeared and the new one lay finished on the table. (4.2:198; 284)

Natalie's arranging of the flowers occurs when she has been startled by Heinrich and is not as calm as she would like to be. Heinrich comments on her face as if she were an extension of the bouquet—"the red blossomed [*blühte*] like a clear shimmer of gentle light on her cheeks" (4.2:197–98; 283–84). At once producing a more pleasing presentation of the flowers and a more beautiful representation of her self, Natalie presents her identity in ways similar to those of Heinrich. His approach differs from hers not in principle, but rather in the elements they respectively employ in their displays. Most women in the novel are relegated to collecting dainty, perishable objects like flowers. As can be seen with respect to Heinrich's sister, Klotilde, it is acceptable in his family for young women to engage in some of the same pursuits as men, such as learning to manage money, practice sports, speak Spanish, and draw, with the important caveat that, as her mother expresses, these pursuits never interfere with womanly duties in the home (4.1:22–23, 26, 4.2:54; 19, 24, 207–8). Women tend to learn and collect less then men, not because they are constitutionally inferior, but instead because of an underlying need for clearly differentiated gender roles that support traditional kinship structures.[74]

An important difference between male and female roles is the person for whom the arrangement of self is made. Men such as Heinrich collect and display the objects primarily for themselves and to a lesser extent as a stand-in mode of communication with others. Natalie, on the other hand, seems to present herself to be viewed. She produces a new, more beautiful "bouquet" directly in front of Heinrich, signaling her disciplinary compliance with the demand that she embody an aesthetic value. Often, in fact, Heinrich tends to regard Natalie as if she were displaying herself for him. After the two have revealed their feelings for each other, for instance, they must follow various protocols in order to gain permission for their betrothal. Since Natalie first approaches her mother to obtain assent, and the order of the house calls for a time and a place for all exchanges to take place, Heinrich must wait to hear the news. In what would be a critical time to respect the order of the house, Heinrich tries to slip out unnoticed to take a walk (4.3:13; 328). Oddly enough, his chosen corridor leads directly past the private rooms occupied by Natalie and her mother (4.3:13; 328). This seems to be a dangerous place to be should he be discovered, and yet Heinrich looks in when he passes an open door. Failing to perceive his own voyeurism, he goes on to describe Natalie's body and dress, using his knowledge of "statuesque" aesthetics as a hermeneutic:

> But I could see not only into the antechamber, but also into another adjoining room which was connected to the antechamber by a glass door that was standing half opened. Natalie was standing in

> this room. Exquisite medieval cabinets were by the walls behind her. She was standing almost in the middle of the room in front of a table covered by a very expensive old tablecloth that had two zithers resting on it. Save for a hat she was completely dressed, as if she were just about to go out. Her beautiful locks were swept back somewhat toward the back of her head and held in place by some type of ribbon. As usual, her dress came up to her throat and was closed there without any additional adornment. Again it was made of light gray silk but had very fine bright red stripes. It was close fitting around the hips and extended to the floor in rich folds. The sleeves were narrow and extended to the wrists; the entire sleeve had dark horizontal stripes that were closed like armbands. Natalie was standing erect; actually, the upper part of her body was even bent back a bit. Her left arm was outstretched with her hand resting on a book that was standing upright on the table. Her right hand was resting lightly on her left forearm. (4.3:13–34; 328–29; translation modified)

Not only is Natalie motionless; her posture is unusual and picturesque. Together with the colors and form of her dress, Natalie's pose matches so well with the surroundings that one seems to be witnessing yet another critical moment of Risach's museal staging. Her clothing has the same characteristics that Heinrich has noticed in his father's Greek stones (4.2:156; 261–62), and the red and light gray of the dress are the same as when lightning played across Nausikaa and over Natalie's face in the garden, although now the stripes are extremely constrained. The sense of the statuesque is deepened when Heinrich remarks, "Her indescribably beautiful face was peaceful [*in Ruhe*]" (4.3:14; 329), evoking an earlier discussion with Risach of Lessing's term *Ruhe in Bewegung* as a criterion for beauty in art (4.2:89; 223). But what is most critical is that Heinrich locates a certain "spirituality" in her features that reliably signifies something for him. Heinrich may not know her thoughts when he remarks that Natalie stood there "as if her eyes were cast down and she were meditating" (4.3:14; 329). Yet he can nevertheless conclude that, because she resembles a piece of art, her posture can represent only her blissful acceptance of their betrothal ("it has come to pass!" [4.3:14; 329]), an interpretation all the more "true to her being" for its having been viewed (illicitly) in private space and not as part of an interactive, verbal exchange. The impression Natalie gives through her statue-like pose helps confirm Heinrich's perception of her as an embodied representation of what he has learned about beauty: "I could hardly comprehend that I was the one for whom this figure that expressed the most beautiful things I had up until now known . . . had sunk into such a deeply reflective state" (4.3:14–15; my translation). Moreover, Heinrich is thrilled by the narcissistic implications of Natalie's beauty; the thought that he can enrapture this beautiful "figure," and that she is his as a result, is the exciting prospect in his relationship with her. She serves as a marker that he has attained a high level of *Bildung*.

But despite Heinrich's belief that he grasps the deep, intrinsic worth of Natalie, a consequence of his coming to comprehend her value through collecting is that she seems to be subject to dynamics of exchange. Her "value" can therefore be determined by "market forces" like supply and demand, and thus it can become volatile (for example, a comment by Risach, 4.2:83; 220). Heinrich's *Bildung* cannot be complete until those values are stabilized through interactions that likewise cement family ties. The characters in the novel address this problem of value not by removing objects from the "market" or from display, but rather by taking measures designed to bring exchange values into line with aesthetic values that ostensibly express the intrinsic worth of the person or object.

When Risach first buys the statue of Nausikaa in Italy, he pays a high price based on the beauty of the statue, even though he thinks it made only of plaster (4.2:78; 217). Once the plaster is stripped away and it is discovered that the statue is marble, Risach considers it his only after he has traveled again to Italy and renegotiated the purchase, which this time is a "considerable sum" (4.2:83; 220). Not an arbitrarily set, one-time exchange between buyer and seller, proper possession in *Nachsommer* rests on a trade value bridled by an aesthetic value taken to express the intrinsic value of the artwork. Many of the efforts of characters in the *Nachsommer* to restore and research the history of aesthetic objects are mobilized in order to discover and give expression to aesthetic values, such as that of an Italian Madonna with Child that Risach owns (4.2:109–11; 235–36). If the properties of the object change as a result of research or other insights, the novel's law of exchange value requires additional compensation to make that value "real."

At the same time, the care and involvement of possession require an on-going commitment to the valued object, part of which means attention to proper care and maintenance of the most appropriate display environment that can be achieved. This commitment is not surprising given that identities in this novel are constituted through processes of collecting and exhibiting. It is not only the case that the collector's relationship to his objects is such that he feels he lives in them. True collectors also endeavor to possess their objects in accordance with the objects' perceived "fate" (*Schicksal*), in the present and with respect to the future.[75] With regard to Heinrich's feelings for Natalie, his sense of self-worth is increased by the value of what he possesses, so that protection of the "object" is an investment in the male self. Indeed, as Benjamin observes, "true freedom" exists only for objects that the collector has in his possession.[76] From the standpoint of the collector, a mutually beneficial relation seems to result from Heinrich and Natalie's pairing. As the most cherished of all that Heinrich possesses, Natalie is too valuable to him and his identity to neglect or destroy; in turn, Heinrich gains in narcissistic echoes from whatever care he directs at Natalie. The critical point, of course, is that Natalie must in some sense be willing to accept being possessed by Heinrich. This in turn means that she must permit her autonomy to be constrained, and she must maintain an appropriate appearance. As I have shown, a dictate for clear gender roles requires that women collect and display in a way other than men. These issues are most at stake in the final stages of Heinrich's *Bildung,* which involve the consolidation of his ownership and the stabilizing of Natalie's particular value.

Crucially, questions of ownership and Natalie's value turn on transactions between the father figures and other forms of exchange. On the one hand, the notion of transactional exchange on a familial level is firmly in the foreground from the wedding on. Indeed, one reads nothing of the vows in the church (4.3:261; 466), but at least three times the relevant "papers" legalizing the marriage and the rights to property and estates are mentioned (4.3:261, 265, 279; 466, 468, 477). At the wedding banquet, Risach reveals to Natalie that from the moment he met Heinrich, he was thinking of deal-making possibilities: "'Didn't I do well, Natalie,' my former host said, 'in finding the right husband for you? You always thought I didn't know anything about such things, but I could tell at the first glance. The eye for business [*Geschäftsblick*] is, like love, as fast as lightning'" (4.3:265; 469; translation modified). But if love and the eye for business operate in similar fashion (a point Russell Berman underscores by arguing that Risach's interest requires his "seduction" of Heinrich in the name of Natalie),[77] most of the details of the "deal" that Risach has been arranging ultimately get worked out between the two father figures without input from Heinrich and Natalie. Not only does Heinrich leave the room with Natalie when the papers are being prepared (4.3:261; 466), but he looks at the documents only many days after the wedding, discovering then his material reward for having fused the two families (4.3:279; 477).

In the meantime, other male-to-male exchanges such as the "jewelry war" impress Natalie's value upon Heinrich, particularly her willingness to comply with the social order. At the wedding banquet, the elder Drendorf reminds Natalie of a gift he had given her some time prior to the wedding. He tells Heinrich in Natalie's presence:

> "In addition to her other virtues, I have discovered one very good quality in your wife," my father continued, "she isn't curious; or, dear daughter, have you already opened the package I gave you?"

> "No, father, I was waiting for you to tell me," Natalie answered. (4.3:266; 469)

Publicly adding a virtue to Natalie's image, Drendorf shows that Natalie has self-restraint and willingly conforms to male requests. The jewels are to be opened only on the wedding day, to verify their aesthetic superiority; otherwise, Natalie's wearing them could be attributed to her wanting to satisfy her father-in-law at the cost of other, more beautiful jewels (4.3:267; 470). Revealed in this way, the jewels signify both absolute aesthetic beauty and the moral values of restraint, lack of curiosity, and authenticity. The jewelry functions as part of the novel's rescripting of women's relationship to curiosity, which, since the biblical story of Eve, has typically been regarded as dangerous in Western society. Before the equation of the jewels with restrained curiosity can be established, though, the jewels given by Heinrich's father must be shown not only to surpass all the others Natalie possesses, particularly those given by Risach, but they must be shown on her:

> "Jewelry in a box," a voice said, "is like a painting without its frame, or even more like a frame without its painting."
>
> "That's so," Risach replied, "you can only judge a thing in its appropriate place and since my friend has appeared as a rival, it wouldn't be a bad idea. . . . Natalie, are you my loving child?"
>
> "Father, I'd love to!" she answered. (4.3:268; 470; original ellipsis)

After she changes into suitable clothes, Heinrich reports: "The diamonds and rubies came first. How splendid Natalie was, and the contention that jewelry was really only the frame proved more than correct" (4.3:268–69; 470). In his own oddly objectifying idiom, Heinrich reveals his sense that Natalie's beauty (and all that it represents) cannot be surpassed by even the most precious stones. Shown to others, Natalie's value increases through the male-to-male exchange of the two art warriors ("The expression of admiration was general," 4.3:269; 471). In keeping with the novel's general endorsement of constraint, this exhibition occurs only within the context of marriage. Unlike Lily Bart's appearance in a tableau vivant in Edith Wharton's *The House of Mirth,* which spawns an excess of speculation on her beauty and social position largely because of the ambiguity of her being unwed and unpossessed, Natalie, as a married woman, is not an enigma.[78] Her value goes up, but speculation on her desirability leads back to the man who possesses her, stabilizing her value and increasing his status.

Such an increase in status is precisely what happens when Heinrich and Natalie make the social rounds in the city following their wedding. "I learned," Heinrich states, "that my marriage to Natalie Tarona had caused a bit of commotion" (4.3:277; 475). Heinrich's marriage draws attention in part because many young men have been watching Natalie. One of these men, a jeweler who is Heinrich's friend, has always wanted to show Heinrich the "beautiful Tarona" (4.2:181; 274). Natalie's significance relates directly to the desires of other men, who find it incomprehensible that Natalie has decided on Heinrich (4.3:277; 476). Heinrich has also found Natalie's feelings difficult to fathom before others acknowledged it. As Heinrich puts it, "To me, Natalie's love for me had always been an unexpected gift and thus was incomprehensible; but when these people put it into words, I suddenly saw it wasn't so incomprehensible after all" (4.3:277; 477; translation modified). Only with other men commenting can Heinrich conceive of the reality, and the social implications, of his relationship with Natalie. In some sense, Natalie's intrinsic value can be fully grasped in this novel only when it is verified externally through others. Accordingly, his feeling that her affection represents a gift is transformed once her value has been expressed as a public exchange value. But making the public rounds after the wedding at the end of the novel not only puts Heinrich's self on display for public confirmation in the Nietzschean sense; the visits also ask that the public reconfirm the status of Mathilde, Risach, and Heinrich's father through the sound mentoring they have performed. In this scheme, the family is constituted as an expansion of the public display of the individual self (that of Heinrich) extended to all its members. It takes so long to bring the families together in this text because it is not only Heinrich who must discover his identity and that of his wife-to-be; the father figures must also deploy *him* and *each other* within their respective frameworks. Thus the jewelry contest also functions as a culminating and transformative moment in the homosocial exchanges between Risach and Heinrich's father that Heinrich had once initiated. From this point forward, the two men can interact without Heinrich's mediation, needing only the buffer of artistic exchange and the mild antagonism of their competition, as they strive to outdo each other in beautifying their respective estates (4.3:270; 471).

Heinrich's interactions with other men following his wedding reveal that he has quietly been following the proper path to *Bildung* by means of collecting and exhibiting, while others languish in traditional career paths without comparable means to form extensive family ties. The novel endorses collecting as a master passion that is capable of imposing order and manageability even on unacceptable desires. However, collecting also exacts a high cost on those who would increase their acceptability. It is not merely that the personal and social discipline—understood as control of both male and female desire as well as male control of women—necessary to make the model operate is staggering. One might even wonder whether Heinrich and Natalie lack the passion necessary for procreation and hence perpetuation of the system. With the novel ending so soon after their wedding, there is no robust confirmation that their relationship flourishes (reproductively). The elaborate imaginary world of *Der Nachsommer* might advance a vision of serenity and might propose mechanisms for the attainment of an apparent social harmony, but its victories over chaos, contingency, and the irrational might be Pyrrhic. And as tempting as it might be—thinking of the line of criticism that harkens back to Hebbel—to dismiss *Der Nachsommer* as a utopia gone boringly awry, the techniques of exhibition carefully deployed in the novel are fundamentally related to those at work in contemporary and subsequent museums in Berlin, Munich, Vienna, and other German-speaking cities. Historically, these real, established collections were heavily invested with, and justified by, the intention of educating and forming identity through the program of acculturation known as *Bildung.* It is worthwhile to take a closer look at the values and identities these collections, and their literary counterparts, have been transmitting since the nineteenth century.

3

Acculturation, Commodification, and the Nation

5

Archaeology, Exhibition, and Tourism:
Raabe's "Keltische Knochen"

Unlike Goethe's *Wahlverwandtschaften* [Elective Affinities] and Stifter's *Nachsommer* [Indian Summer], Wilhelm Raabe's "Keltische Knochen" [Celtic Bones] (1863) is a novella known for much of the twentieth century mostly by experts in nineteenth-century German prose. In the nineteenth century, in contrast, this fascinating literary text had a wide readership that recognized the text's ties to a spectacular nexus of collecting, cultural preservation, and museal knowledge production that has since faded from cultural awareness. As in the case of Goethe and Stifter, the appearance of these themes has something to do with the proclivities of its author, who has been shown by recent scholarship to have been generally interested in issues of archaeology, paleontology, and preservation of ancient artifacts. Indeed, as early scholarship on "Keltische Knochen" evidences in particular, the basic aspects of the story can be related to Raabe's experiences as a tourist in Vienna, Linz, and the Hallstatt region. But whereas that scholarship attempted to use this text to illuminate its author and his views, an approach that focuses instead on the text's museum function reveals a great deal about two things: first, workings of the text that cannot be explicitly linked to Raabe's experiences, and second, the wild events and contexts to which this underappreciated and quirkily humorous story refer. Indeed, because the story appeared in a popular illustrated middle-class periodical, the Raabe text is well suited to give access to the role of collecting within the rising constellation of mass tourism, archaeology, and the notion of the German nation.[1]

In the contexts surrounding Goethe's *Wahlverwandtschaften* and Stifter's *Nachsommer,* a significant dimension of collecting and exhibiting was devoted to recovering, preserving, and presenting past artifacts so that they might bear on cultural developments in the present. But if the discoveries, practices, and sensations linked to early archaeology are any indication, the past had truly become "up for grabs" by the middle of the nineteenth century in Central Europe.

That archaeological past was in fact becoming increasingly interpreted by wider segments of the population through the advent of the mass press and practices such as mass tourism, with knowledge of those discoveries representing part of what defined the community of "educated" (*gebildete*) people. This occurred in part because, in the century of its disciplinary formation, archaeology unearthed astonishing objects whose origins were mysterious; the objects were at times beautiful and often inexplicable in terms of prevailing modes of learned thought. From bog men to Neanderthals, from Germanic grave mounds to Slavic ceramics, from the Celtic graves at Hallstatt to the Trojan treasure of Priam, to name a few, archaeology grappled with material remains that raised questions as charged as the creation of humankind, the factual status of founding national and religious texts, and the identities of prehistoric predecessors to modern Europeans. These topics were particularly dramatic and resonant ones, as many of the pressing religious, cultural, and political debates of the nineteenth century seemed to turn on wringing increased knowledge from the past.[2] With archaeology's reliance on concrete objects lending its arguments an air of accessibility and incontrovertibility (despite the actual complexities in interpreting those objects), this discipline was uniquely positioned to contribute to these debates, which with the rise of newspapers and other mass communications increasingly involved large audiences. In important ways, the questions and concerns of archaeology were shared by large segments of the literate population.

Recent scholarship on German archaeology has shown its widespread appeal to be indispensable in accounting for the ways in which it shaped Germans' conceptions of their perceived cultural heritage.[3] With classical archaeology dominating in museums and universities, prehistoric and Germanic archaeology were particularly shaped by extraacademic efforts, especially those of bourgeois *Vereine* and local *Heimat* museums, to excavate and preserve objects from relevant sites.[4] Many of these excavations were conducted by amateurs, so that it is possible to speak of a division of labor in which the collection of artifacts fell to amateurs and the interpretation to scholars trained in philosophy and philology.[5] Still, even many pre-1900 professional expeditions exploited sites primarily for large museum pieces and failed to painstakingly document a dig and its contents.[6] Systematic stratigraphy, field surveying, and intrinsic description of found material—hallmarks of contemporary conceptions of "archaeology"—were the exception rather than the rule for most professional excavations before the twentieth century.[7]

Wilhelm Raabe's novella "Keltische Knochen" is a rich vehicle for exploring these issues. In this work, two credentialed scholars attempt to steal bones and funerary objects from the Hallstatt graves in order to support their rival contentions about whether the objects represent Celtic and Germanic cultures. But *why* is it that these professors are so keen on stealing the bones, and *why* did Raabe choose this particular situation as the core for his humorous novella? With the assistance of archaeological accounts, travel guides, and contemporary magazine articles, looking at "Keltische Knochen" as part of a network of collecting, exhibiting, reproduction, and circulation of archaeological information can help answer these questions. Two paradigmatic figures are important here: the collector as *Fetischdiener* [fetishist] and what I call the "ritual tourist." "Keltische Knochen" makes clear that the collector and the ritual tourist differ foremost in their positionality, that is, in their ownership and control of the objects in a particular collection. These concepts, in historical context and in the material record of the Hallstatt dig, help explain the scholars' desires to make off with the bones of the past and to reverse the asymmetrical power divide that the museum upholds. Yet those unruly desires also tell a great deal about how tourism, gender, and commercialism intersected in Raabe's time.

Hallstatt: An Archealogical Sensation

Excavated by Johann Ramsauer from 1846 until 1863, the upper Austrian village of Hallstatt gained archaeological significance when roughly one thousand Bronze and Early Iron Age graves were found, lying some 400 meters above the village located on the Salzburg mountain. The graves held skeletal remains and burial objects.[8] The first discovery of what was later concluded to be Celtic culture in Central Europe, Hallstatt became a sensation, both as a news story and as a source of mass tourism that coincided with burgeoning efforts to attract visitors to southern Germany and Austria.[9] From the mid-nineteenth century onward, travel guides in both German and English described Hallstatt, the graves, and the museum in the *Rudolfsturm* as worthwhile excursions from the nearby imperial spa of Ischl.[10] A particular attraction for travelers, especially those of wealth or high social standing, was the opportunity to participate in the digs and to take home the souvenirs they unearthed. The story goes that Ramsauer, originally a mining engineer with twenty-two children to feed, sought financial backing to cover the cost of excavation and potentially even a buyer for his private collection. Although not a free-for-all, Hallstatt was a place where the rules of access and compensation were still being determined. Notable "guests" treated to this privilege included the Princes of Bavaria Ludwig and Leopold, the Hofrath Az, and the Duke of Meingingen.[11] The archaeologist Adolf Meyer reported that, in addition to upper-class souvenir seeking, outright plunder also occurred prior to a museum being built on site. Even for those who could not travel to the site, Hallstatt was news and "on the tips of everyone's tongues." Largely responsible for its sensational status were its scale, the exotic quality of the objects unearthed

(Figs. 15 and 16), and the questions it raised about the origins of the people currently living in Austria and Central Europe. Indeed, one of the most hotly debated topics was whether the site represented Germanic or Celtic people, and the extent to which the find could therefore be used to magnify historical claims to geographical and ethnic unity in the then-splintered German-speaking territories.[12] The confusion is expressed, for instance, in Hallstatt's Celtic objects finding their way into designs of Germanic costumes created by the Duke of Meiningen for the Meiningen Court Theater. The costumes for Richard Wagner's operas at Bayreuth likewise fancifully mixed objects derived from various regions and people.[13] There has been long-standing debate about whether the Duke of Meiningen had stolen the objects whose designs he used or whether the designs were culled from illustrated catalogs of Hallstatt objects that had been published in Paris, London, and Germany and were available to him.[14] Either way, objects *and* reproductions were in circulation and can account for the creation of Wagner's costumes. Incidents like this indicate the compelling need to account for the ways that archaeological objects *and* their reproductions circulate to a collection, if Hallstatt's cultural significance is to be understood in relation to processes of collecting and exhibiting, tourism, and commercialization.

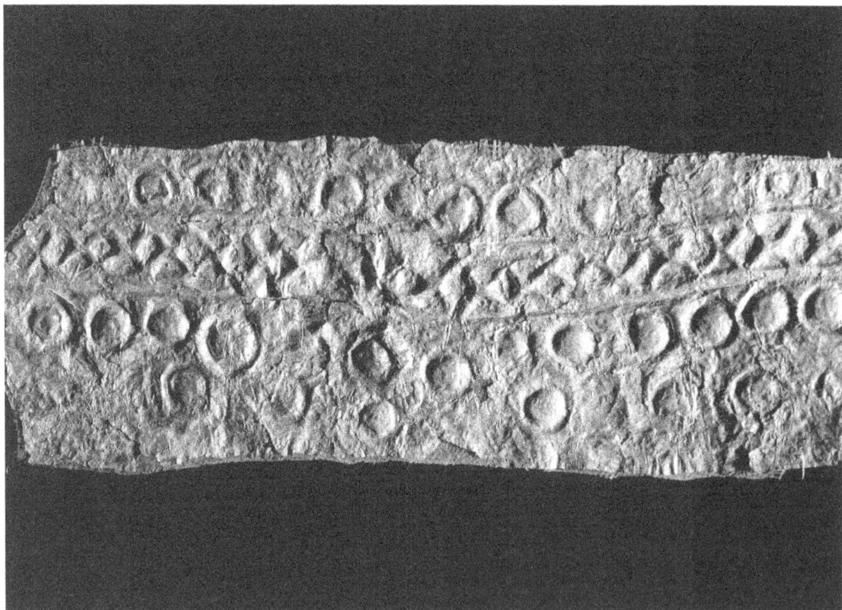

Figure 15 Detail of a chased gold belt with hook, from a grave at Hallstatt, Austria. Items such as these fascinated the general public in the nineteenth century.

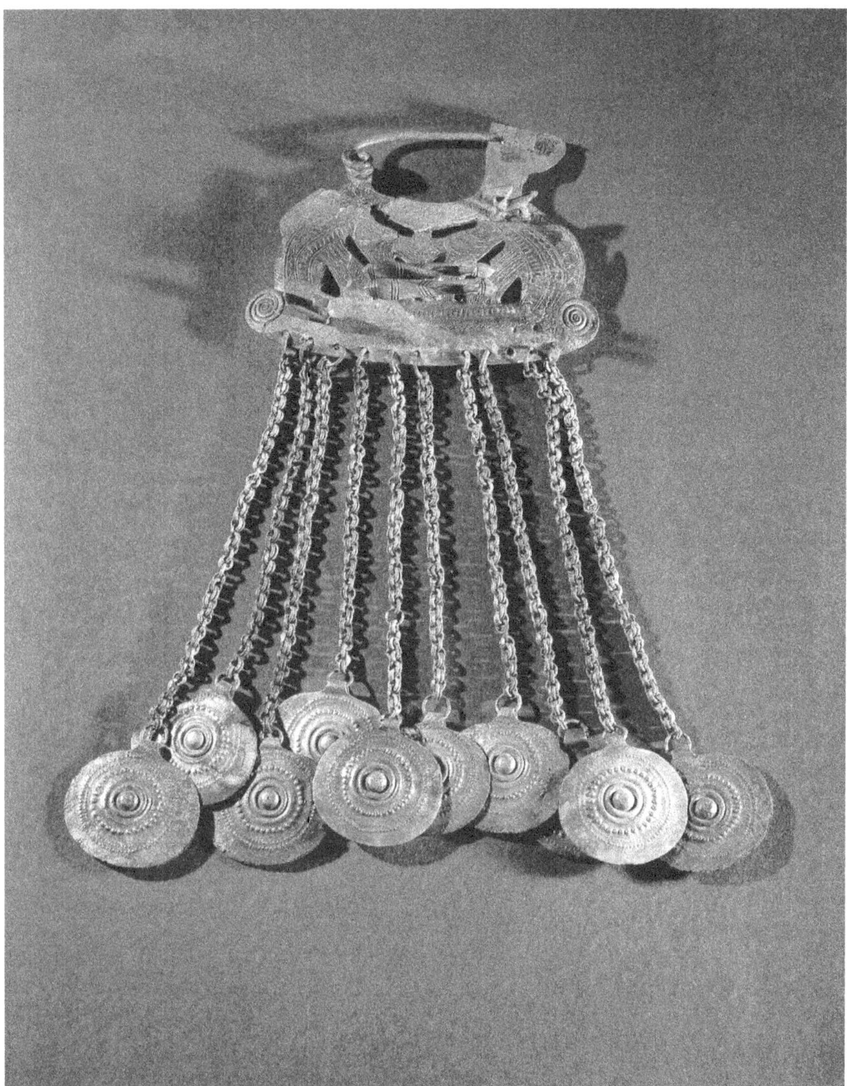

Figure 16 Large bronze fibula, probably worn as a pectoral, from the necropolis in Hallstatt, Austria.

Archaeology and the Museum in the "Keltische Knochen"

Many features from the then-current archaeological context can be encountered in Raabe's story. The text makes much of a vehement scholarly debate on the supposed ethnic identity of the bones, which, together with the shared goal of Zuckriegl and Steinbüchse to steal bones and objects from the cemetery, drives the plot and provides a physical humor bordering on slapstick.[15] Over and over, the two scholars nearly come to blows on the question of whether the bones are

"Celtic" or "Germanic," and their antagonism of course eventually foils their thievery (213).

The humor and plot take off in the text when Zuckriegel and Steinbüchse are presented as mirror images of each other. Returning from a brief walk in the rain, the narrator enters the inn to hear two men screaming. He goes on to write, "In the Viennese Prater I saw a magician who grabbed a live rabbit by the hind legs, tore it down the middle, and presented the astonished and enthusiastic public henceforth in either hand a blithely fidgeting little animal. A similar experiment seemed to have taken place with the prosector Zuckriegl—he was present a second time in Seebauer's inn and—he was arguing most violently with his doppelganger" (212). Evoking the low-culture entertainment value of the spectacle before the narrator, the violent debate recalls a sensationalized touristic atmosphere as might be found in a sideshow in the Wiener Prater (Fig. 17). Driving home the freakishness of the episode are descriptions emphasizing strange bodily behavior and appearance, as when "Zuckriegl shot up and down like a jack-in-the-box, his neck developing a horrifying elasticity" (212). In the context of each scholar appearing to be a magically produced double of the other, the seriousness of the debate between the two scholars appears comic in itself.[16] Moreover, as nearly identical copies, neither, it seems, has any claim to originality or truth. This is especially true in that neither of them has examined the bones in question, as the narrator learns when he tries to restore peace:

> "Stop, stop, stop, gentlemen!" I also screamed at the top of my lungs. "No new breach of the peace! No unnecessary salaciousness! No learned rhetorical figures! Please, professor, are you just now returning from the bones in question?"
>
> "I am on my way to them."
>
> "Thus you have not yet seen the bones at all?"
>
> "Only in the medium of the public papers."
>
> "And you, too, have not been up at the Rudolfsturm, Mr. Zuckriegl?"
>
> "In this weather? I'd have to be a fool!" (213)

If comments like "no learned rhetorical figures" indicate hostility on the part of the narrator toward scholarly discourse and behavior, these characters clearly deserve it. Zuckriegel, after all, applies his intellectual gifts to studying the *Geschichte des deutschen Gaunertums* [The History of German Rapscallionism]

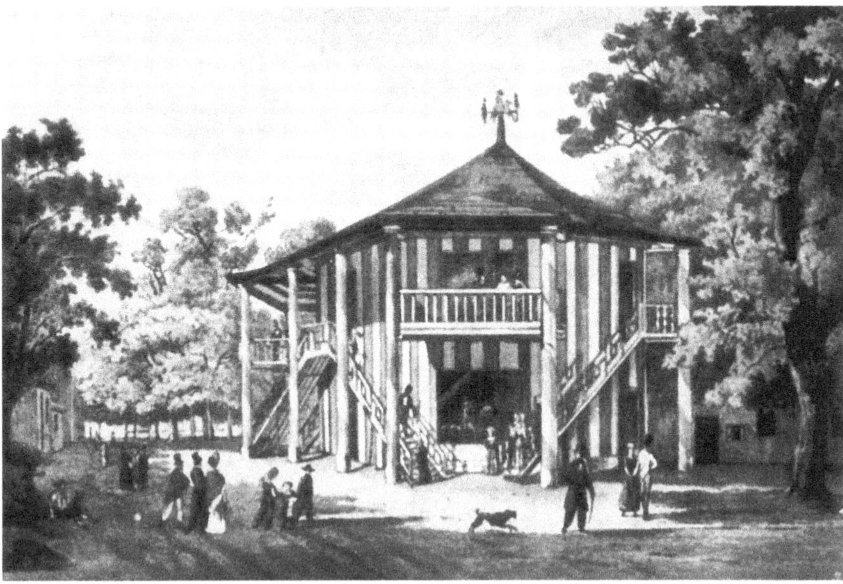

Figure 17 Jakob Hyrtl. Ringelspiel im Prater, one of the many institutions of entertainment in the mid-nineteenth-century Viennese Prater. Colored engraving, 22 × 27 cm (Blatt) bzw. 17.8 × 22.6 cm (Kupferplatte). Inv. no. 173.302. Reproduced courtesy of the Museum der Stadt Wien.

while plotting to steal the bones, and neither of these learned men has yet to submit his contentions to the least scientific scrutiny. Each instead relies solely on the "public papers," mass-consumption newspaper and magazine articles that presented the debates about the origins of the finds in terms of concerns about national identity. With this gesture, Raabe's text seems to aim to underscore the ridiculousness of this kind of archaeological struggle and to turn learned culture on its head.

Such a gesture of inversion is, of course, one of the identifying features of the carnivalesque, a privileged mode this narrative makes little effort to hide.[17] Characteristic of the carnivalesque turning of the serious world on its head, the language of the text is generally hybridized, combining high and low cultural forms. The narrator displays a remarkable sophistication in expressing himself not only through high literary and rhetorical structures but also with scientific terminology. While phrases like "No unnecessary salaciousness! No learned rhetorical figures!" are meant to communicate a simple desire (stop making fools of yourselves!), the narrator nevertheless has formed them spontaneously and wittily. Later in the text, he fully understands spoken Latin phrases, and when he is arrested as an accomplice to a heist, he speaks to the Salzinspektor in discourse sprinkled with words such as "antediluvian" and "osteology." From the first page, moreover, the text contains numerous foreign words and high cultural literary

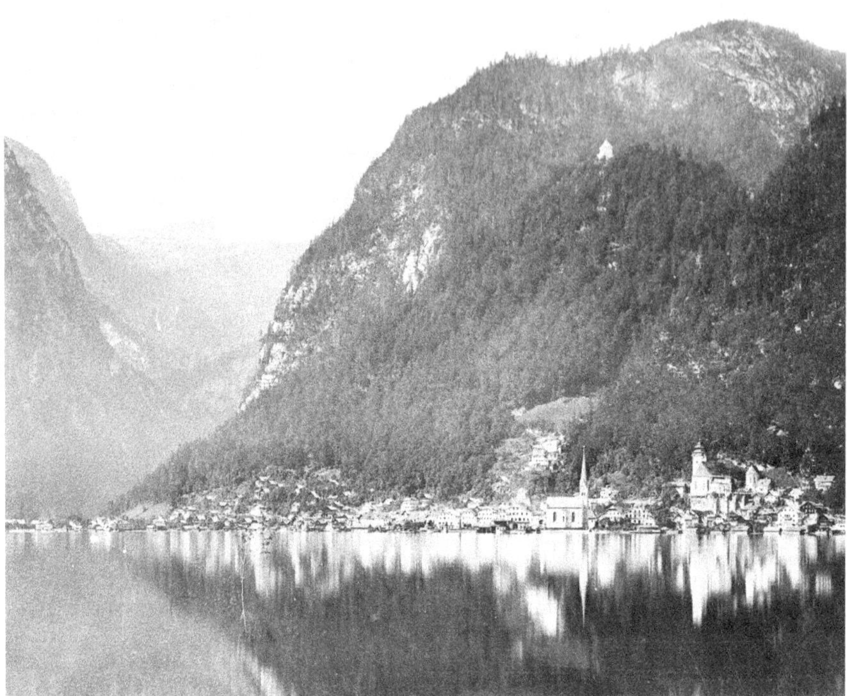

Figure 18 Hallstadt (Hallstatt), ca. 1860. This photograph taken shortly after Raabe's visit shows the typical approach to the village, across the lake. From the distance, the village seems to cling to the surrounding cliffs. Photographic print, albumen. In album: Prague, Innsbruck, Munich, Nuremberg, Dresden, Berlin, Hombourg, Edinburgh, opposite p. 157. No. R24. Library of Congress: LC-USZ62-109014. LOT 7739.

references and quotes. The boat passage to Hallstatt—an inhabitation known for its seeming to cling to the cliffs surrounding the eponymous lake (Fig. 18)—invokes multiple Western treatments of the underworld going back to Greek and Roman myth ("a female Charon"), Virgil and Dante, and Mephistopheles. These notions were consonant with prevailing notions of archaeology, since following the discovery of Pompeii, archaeology was thought to be concerned with certain notions of the classical world, the pornographic, and the obscene.[18] Understood as a folk symbol of the underworld, and in particular the place where the dead gather before descending into it, the inn in the text is likewise a crucial site linking the carnivalesque and learned conceptions of the afterlife.[19] The evocation of Hades/hell in "Keltische Knochen" in fact echoes Mikhail Bakhtin's point that "in the Rabelaisian system of images the underworld is the junction where the main lines of this system cross each other: carnivals, banquets, fights, beatings, abuses, and curses."[20] In addition to the grotesque bodily images, fights, abuses, and curses abounding in this text, a further feature of the carnivalesque world is manifested through the behavior of another character, the poet Roderich, who is visiting the dig. While waiting for the weather to clear, Roderich changes into the suit of a fool and thus becomes a carnivalesque figure. Recalling Bakhtin's repeated point about the propensity for the carnivalesque to renew the sense of the world (and recalling that for Benjamin, collectors, too, accomplish this), I want to keep the question of this text's function in the present in mind.

One clue to this text's renewal of the past in the present comes from the mention of the public papers during the narrator's intervention in the scholarly "debate." The "public papers" reference is important, since Raabe wrote the "Keltische Knochen" for one of them, the *Westermann's Illustrirte deutsche Monatshefte* [Westerman's Illustrated German Monthly] in 1864–65, after a visit to the Hallstatt site in 1859.[21] Drawing on reader reception theory and scholarship on nineteenth-century middle-class periodicals shows that Raabe's novella would require an ideal reader familiar with Hallstatt's graves, the scholarly and nationalistic debates surrounding them, and the practices of tourism to have its full impact. A regular reader of *Westermann's* would have been exposed to these topics, in that the magazine itself had carried an extensive, well-illustrated report on the excavations in Hallstatt and its tourist-friendly environs prior to Raabe's text (Figs. 19 and 20).[22] Countless other reports on digs and other travelogues and ethnographic reports from near and distant lands indicate that at least one type of typical reader would have been familiar with the prevailing issues in archaeology and stories of travel.[23]

Although not directly engaged in what might be called "Germanic archaeology," Heinrich Schliemann perhaps best exemplifies the German-speaking archaeologist with one foot in the public sphere, concerned with educating a broad public. Renown among the middle classes was in fact a necessity for him, since he lacked traditional academic credentials and faced scorn and rejection from colleagues. It is no accident that it was to newspapers and magazines like the *Augsburger Allgemeine,* the *Vossische Zeitung,* and the *Gartenlaube* that he and his champions, notable among them Rudolf Virchow, turned to force acknowledgment of his achievements.[24] These were made by appealing to the cultural "glue" of *Bildung.* That the educated public considered archaeology a kind of extended review session of their basic *Bildung* can be seen, for instance, when on 17 June 1870, editors of the widely read *Gartenlaube* asked Schliemann whether he would be willing to expand on his discoveries, given that, in their view, "the subject that initially pertained to the scholar of antiquity now, through Homer, belongs to every educated [*gebildet*] person: could [that subject] not be given a treatment that would make it a pleasantly stimulating lesson for the large and varied readership of the

516 Illustrirte Deutsche Monatshefte.

Thon, sind große und kleinere Schüsseln, Becken, Schalen und Töpfe von nicht immer zu errathender Bestimmung. Doch scheinen die aus Bronze jedenfalls mehr dem Prunke oder irgend welchen religiösen Zwecken, die aus Thon dem täglichen Bedarfe gedient zu haben. Die bronzenen überdies als Kessel von 20—30 Zoll Umfang, dann als verschieden geformte Vasen und Schalen kommen ausschließlich bei Leichenbränden vor; die thönernen dagegen in jedem Grabe und zum öftern mit Thierknochen gefüllt, — vielleicht den Resten von den Leichen in's Grab mitgegebener Speisen und Opfer.

Unter den Geräthschaften und Werkzeugen aus Bronze, zum kleinen Theil auch aus Eisen, finden sich Meißel, Beile und Spaten, Feilen, pincettenförmige Zängelchen und Fischangeln, die letztern ganz von der noch heutzutage üblichen Größe und Form; unter den Bruchstücken einzelne, von welchen nicht gezweifelt werden kann, daß sie von Werkzeugen, ähnlich unsern Meißeln und Brecheisen, herrühren. Sie zeugen von den friedlichen Beschäftigungen ihrer Eigenthümer.

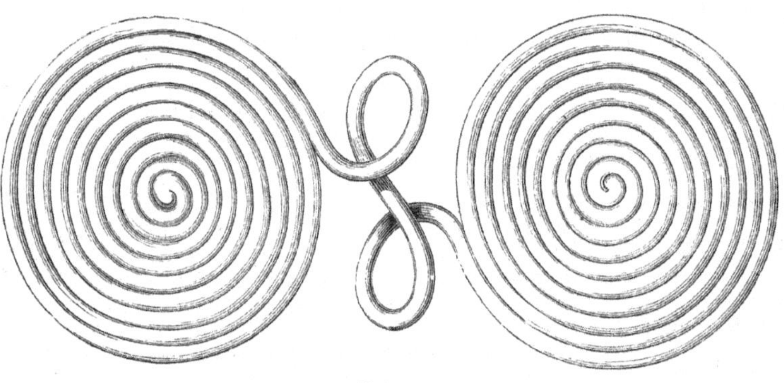

Spange.

Aber auch von nicht geringer Geschicklichkeit und verhältnißmäßig nicht unausgebildetem Geschmacke zeugen diese Gegenstände. Für die Güte der Bronze spricht der Widerstand, den sie den Einflüssen der Zeit und des Bodens nicht nur in compacten Stücken, sondern selbst in den feinsten Drähtchen und Plättchen entgegengesetzt. Eine nur dünne Schicht bald hellerer, bald dunklerer Patina hat sich an sie angelegt, indeß das Eisen oft bis auf den Kern vor den verzehrenden Gewalten des Wassers und der Kohlensäure geschwunden. Die Lamellen, aus denen die Gürtel, Wehrgehänge, Brustschilder und Gefäße zusammengenietet sind, sind oft bis zur Dünne eines Papierblattes ausgearbeitet und haben bis zur Stunde ihre Elasticität bewahrt. Die vielen Kettchen, Ringlein und Gehängsel, welche, wahrscheinlich des Geklirres wegen, an Schmuckstücken sowohl wie an Gefäßen eine Hauptrolle spielen, sind oft auf's Feinste und Sinnreichste geschlungen und erinnern nicht selten an die subtilste Filigranarbeit.

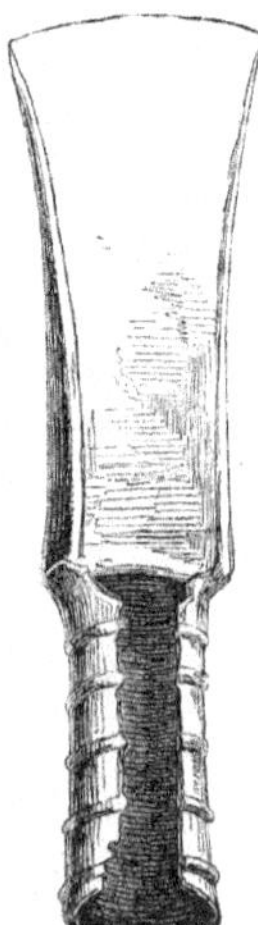

Meißel.

In den Formen herrscht sichtlich das Streben nach dem Schlanken und Ebenmäßigen und begegnet das Auge nicht leicht etwas Plumpem oder Eckigem. Seltsam zwar, doch nicht unschön sind die Handgriffe mancher Waffenstücke, nicht ohne Anmuth manche Gefäße gestaltet. Als besondere Eigenthümlichkeit erscheinen die flachen Spiralen aus Bronzedraht, welche als Schmuck und Zierath sich mannigfach angewendet finden.

Bemerkenswerth ferner sind die Verzierungen an den verschiedenen, namentlich plattenförmigen Gegenständen, wie Schüsseln, Schalen, Gürteln, Halsbändern u. dgl. Sie sind getriebene Arbeit und von der einfachsten Erfindung: gerade Linien, die sich auf verschiedene Art zu Zacken, fortlaufenden Rauten oder Gittern verbinden, einfache oder gruppirte Punkte, einfache oder concentrische Kreise, allein, oder mit dazwischen eingereihten primitiven Darstellungen menschlicher Figuren und eben solchen Abbildungen von Rossen und gekrönten oder ungekrönten Schwänen. Alles das vereinzelt und ohne irgend welchen inhaltlichen Bezug auf einander. Nicht ohne symbolische Beziehung scheint jedoch der Schwan, der so zu sagen das hauptsächlichste Motiv aller Verzierungen bildet und fast nirgend

Figure 19 Reproductions of Hallstatt objects in circulation in nineteenth-century periodicals. Reproduced courtesy of Duke University Libraries.

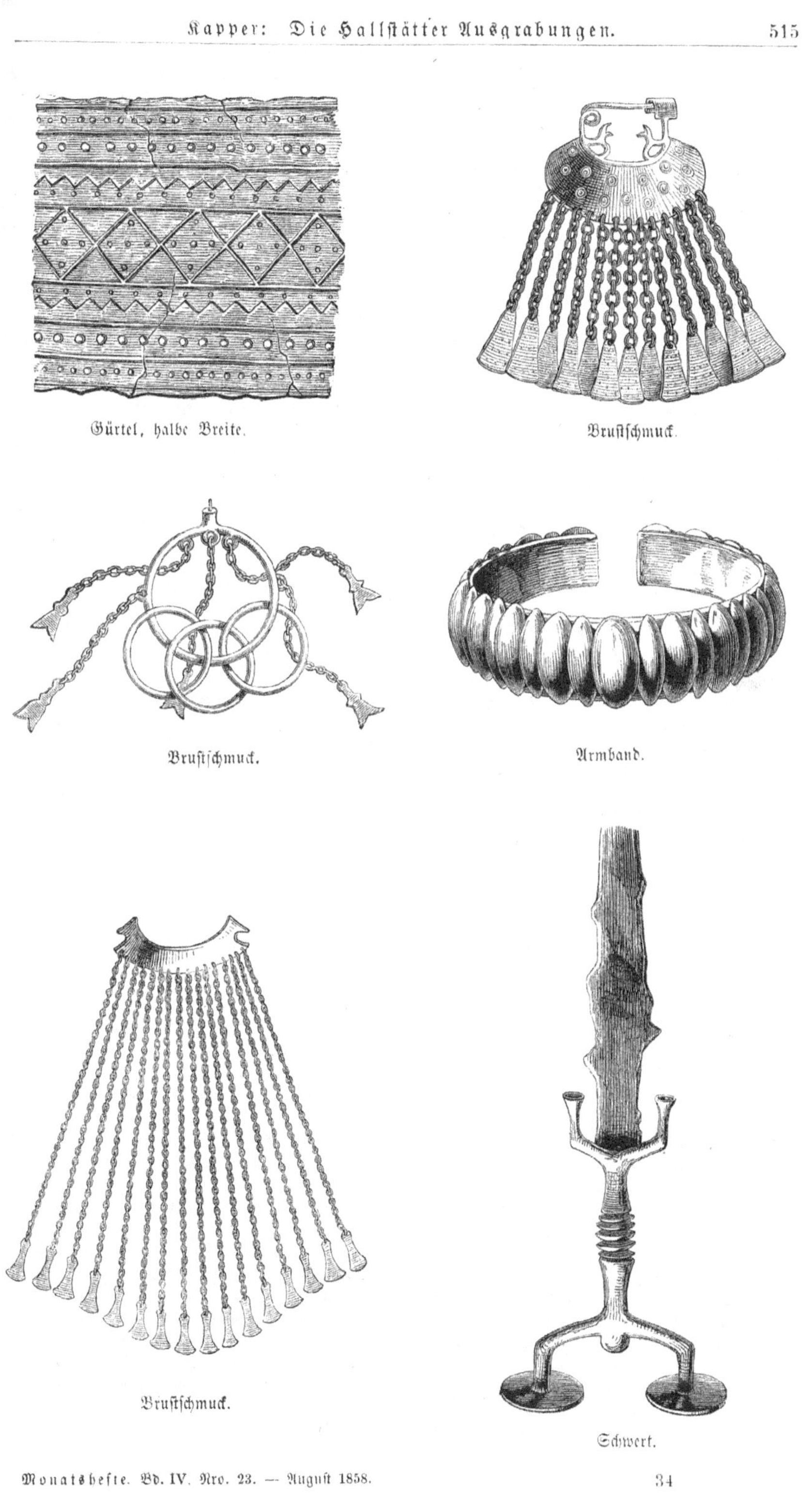

Kapper: Die Hallstätter Ausgrabungen. 515

Gürtel, halbe Breite.

Brustschmuck.

Brustschmuck.

Armband.

Brustschmuck.

Schwert.

Monatshefte. Bd. IV. Nro. 23. — August 1858. 34

Figure 20 Reproductions of Hallstatt objects in circulation in nineteenth-century periodicals. Reproduced courtesy of Duke University Libraries.

Gartenlaube?"[25] Since the editors also asked for copious illustrations of Schliemann's find, the prospect of witnessing material evidence that Homer's Troy might have existed would have stoked public interest in Schliemann's claims.[26] For Schliemann himself, bearing witness to authentic and authenticated objects as educational project takes on religious dimensions when he writes: "May this holy, sublime monument of Greece's heroism henceforth . . . become a pilgrimage site for the inquisitive youth of all future generations, and may it make them enthusiastic for scholarly knowledge [*Wissenschaft*], especially for the magnificent Greek language and literature."[27] Worth mentioning here is the modern subtext propagating a different cultural myth: that the task of renewing the greatness of the Greeks falls to the (equally great) nineteenth-century Germans. Moreover, for nineteenth-century archaeologists of the German tradition, the same tendency existed, substituting "Germanic heroism" and "the marvelous German language and literature" for "Greek." It perhaps also goes without saying that Schliemann would achieve mythic status if his hopes of linking the power of auratic art and a priestly function came true.

Archaeology also mounted its truth claims by means of a process of witnessing predicated on collecting and exhibiting practices that were related to religious ritual. This, it seems, is part of the point made by Theodor Fontane in *Vor dem Sturm* [Before the Storm], a historical novel about rising German nationalism in response to the wars of liberation. In that context, an archaeological debate—there turning on identification of Slavic versus Germanic objects—is carried out between a pastor (Seidentopf) and a learned Justizrat Turgeny. Undercutting his passionate insistence that his Germanic objects can be interpreted only one way (something the text explicitly questions with the debate on "Odin's Wagon"),[28] Seidentopf reveals his project of German national identity to be ritualistic and irrational. On the one hand, the pastor maintains a collection of strange objects whose centerpiece—a stuffed alligator hanging from the ceiling—recalls an early modern Wunderkammer (84–85; see Fig. 6). Viewed on one level as marking Seidentopf as a "passionate collector" who collects in strict adherence to an idea (84; 86), the perceived disorder of such a collection evokes, from the standpoint of the late nineteenth century, a sense of antiquated, nonscientific irrationality. On the other hand, Seidentopf's collecting and religious practices collapse into each other, so that the pastor is known to unwittingly confuse his collector's-edition Luther Bible with his collector's-edition archaeological source (85). With religious doctrine and a one-sided collector's passion becoming interchangeable, the notion that Seidentopf's collection can prove his belief that the Mark Brandenburg "had not only always been a German land from the earliest times, it had *remained* German over the centuries" (86) becomes intelligible as an article of faith that the rituals of collecting help to buttress.

A Benjaminian framework helps to understand that in each of these cases (Schliemann, Fontane, and Raabe), collecting and ritual are fundamentally linked. Recalling that Schliemann describes his site as "this holy, sublime monument . . . a pilgrimage site," I find a divine, unapproachable quality that resembles Benjamin's familiar conception of aura, which is defined as "a unique appearance of distance, however close it may be." But Benjamin conceives of aura dialectically. In Benjamin's "Work of Art" essay, he explains that the only true value a work of art can have (*Gebrauchswert*) arises from its use as a religious or cult object. Benjamin argues that when the dynamics of secularization and collecting bring artifacts into circulation, a new value he terms the exhibition value (*Ausstellungswert*) dialectically supplements, but does not replace, its original use value. In terms of Benjamin's dialectic, collections of auratic art remain bound to a sense of ritual even if not brought together for religious purposes. The dialectic also reveals that all collecting, including that done by public museums, has from the outset been embedded in a process of circulation that transfers objects from an original, cult context into a new context dictated by a collector. Benjamin sees the collector as participating in the divine qualities of the collection and accordingly labels him a *Fetischdiener* [fetishist].

Benjamin mobilizes and valorizes this nexus of circulation and collecting outside the socially stratified Wilhemine museum for materialist purposes in his essay on Eduard Fuchs. Fuchs, it will be recalled, was a private collector of political caricature, erotic art, and Tang sculpture, art forms that were largely ignored by public collections at the end of the nineteenth century. In Fuchs the private collector, Benjamin locates a political potential that can oppose the "cultural history" promoted by public museum displays. As Fuchs puts it, "cultural history" in the public museum shows "culture in its Sunday best," ignoring the majority of everyday events that make up life and its triumphs and tragedies. Crucial to Fuchs's collecting was that he not only wrested objects from a nearly forgotten historical context and saved them from oblivion, but that he gave them their due in the present by reproducing and circulating them as books outside the museum, *in place of* his collections.

By combining Benjamin's observations in his two essays, it can be realized that art and cult objects are necessarily enmeshed in a dialectic of circulation and reproduction. Reproducible etchings and engravings were essential to art education well into the nineteenth century, since contact with originals was impractical for most people. This practice is expressed in André Malraux's twentieth-century idea of *le musée imaginaire* (translated into English as "the museum without walls"). Malraux advanced the notion that photographic reproductions of artworks enable one to supplant the Grand Tour of the nineteenth century and to create "museums" unencumbered by the walls of official institutions.[29] Consider also the role of exhibition catalogs, museum shop postcards, and other kinds of reproductions that circulate outside the museum in place of the works inside, and yet refer to the originals back in the museum. Without catalogs and price lists, moreover, it is otherwise hard to see how collectors and dealers operate. This dynamic affects the exhibition and exchange value of the objects on display.

Archaeology at Hallstatt was bound up in this dynamic. Beyond permitting wealthy personages the opportunity to dig up objects, Johann Ramsauer also attempted to profit commercially by having Isidor Engel illustrate a rich grave-by-grave catalog, containing watercolor renderings of the nearly one thousand graves at Hallstatt (Figs. 21–23). Ramsauer was so driven that even when he could not find a publisher he produced several scribal copies of the text by hand, which he then sent out to potential patrons, some of whom had participated in the digs and who had other forms of "souvenirs." The protocols were designed to increase the value of the objects Ramsauer had unearthed, by convincing the recipient either of the worthiness of the undertaking or to purchase objects that Ramsauer considered part of his personal collection. Already by 1850, he started to see results from this strategy. In one letter, Ramsauer's friend Simony, a geographer and alpine researcher who was the first to chart the Hallstatt region (he was also a friend of Adalbert Stifter), advised him of the interest of the Geological Institute, which wanted to begin an ethnographic museum with the objects.[30] Simony wrote: "I believe, dear friend, you should not delay in selling your beautiful collection for the simple reason that sooner or later some busy bureaucrat could figure out that the entire collection by right of God and law actually belongs to the state and that you at most have a claim to compensation and indeed only really to a letter of commendation."[31] Although it would take us too far afield to explicate the legal basis of Simony's reasoning, he can clearly see that any chance Ramsauer has in converting the display value of his "beautiful collection" into a usable form of compensation rests on his asserting ownership more quickly than the state. Here I see the hand-produced quality of the protocol enhancing this claim, since, in a sense, it represents the labor that was invested in unearthing the objects and his personal knowledge of them.[32] As Simony also intimates, control of these unique objects is a crucial factor in extracting value from them.

Simony's letter is particularly interesting because it leaves no doubt that museums of the time were hotly competitive. The potent appeal that "patriotic archaeology" offered as a tourist attraction in fact led to a popular excavation boom throughout the German-speaking countries, creating a frenzy of dilettant-

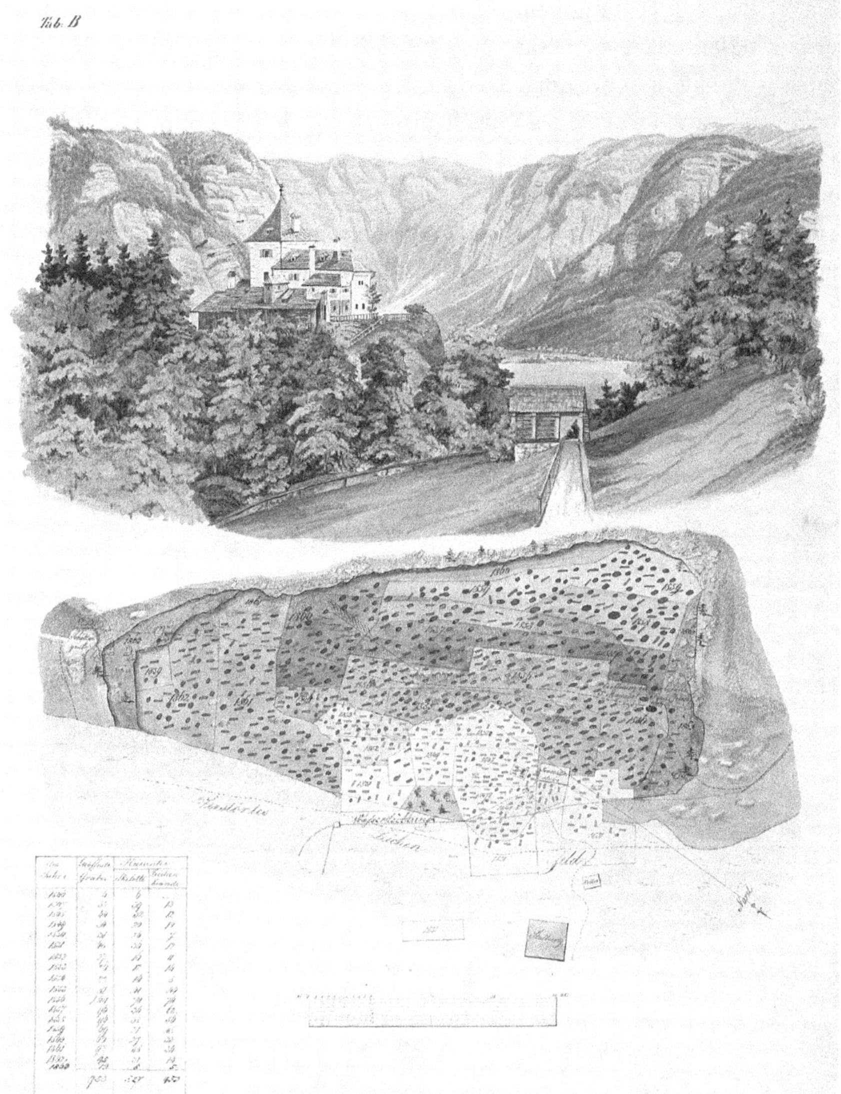

Figure 21 Watercolor drawing of the tomb-site at Hallstatt, Austria, by Isidor Engel, 18 × 8 cm. Engel was employed by Johann Ramsauer. Naturhistorisches Museum, Vienna.

ish plundering of sites and the selling of their artifacts.[33] Large museums heated up this market as they jockeyed for the control of objects, for the ability to command the attention of researchers, tourists, and foreign powers was at stake.[34] In this environment, the formation of a museum at Hallstatt was designed to achieve the most basic level of control: that is, to prevent the theft of the grave objects and bones. The nineteenth-century archaeologist Adolph Meyer recalls this to have been a common problem: "Since a museum association has recently formed in Hallstatt, it will in time become difficult if not impossible to add . . . the remains still lying in the grave field to already extant collections."[35] For Meyer, the on-site museum provides a mechanism by which items remain at Hallstatt, which meant that collections existing elsewhere would no longer be expanded and would remain fragmentary. To examine the artifacts, tourists and researchers would have to travel to the site.[36] With not only nationalistic debates but careers on the line, access to and control of objects of study became an increasingly

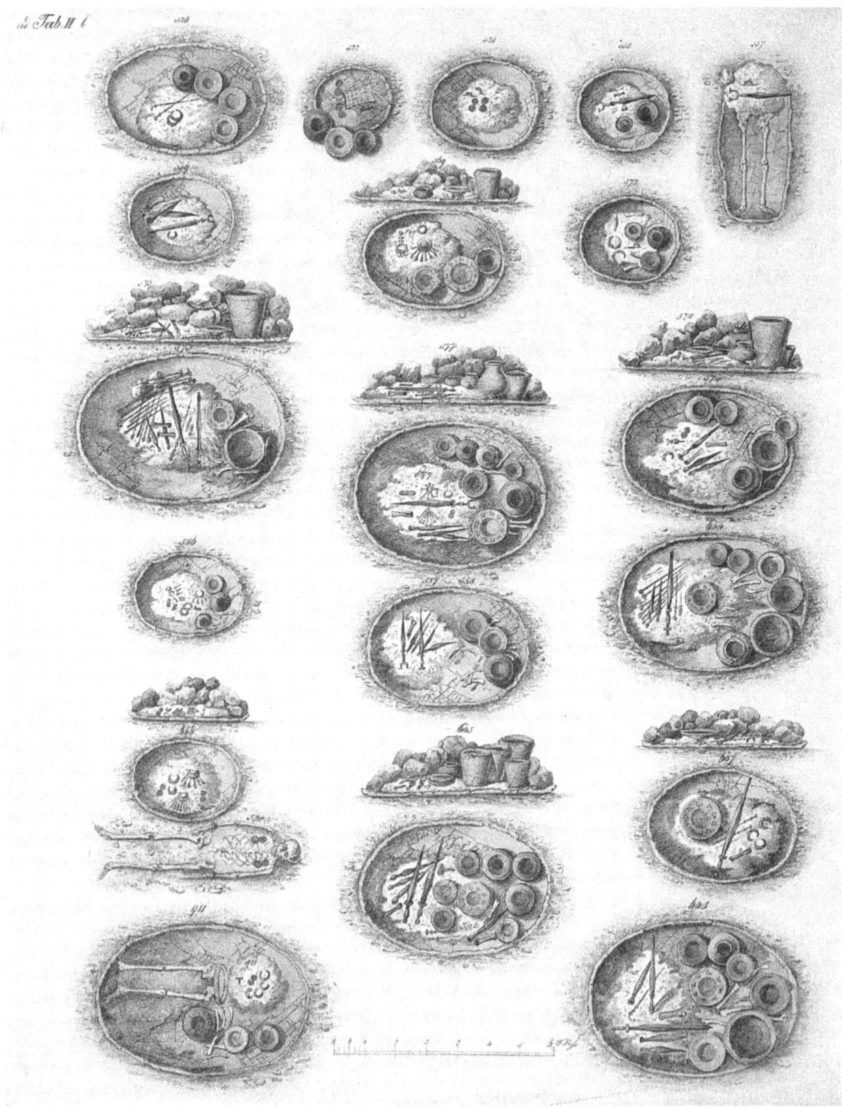

Figure 22 Twenty-seven graves found at Hallstatt burial site, from a collection of nineteenth-century watercolors painted on the site by Isidor Engel in 1878. These images represent only a small fraction of the watercolor protocols of the Hallstatt excavations demanded by Johann Ramsauer.

important criterion for professional advancement. In "Keltische Knochen," the drive of both Zuckriegel and Steinbüchse to steal the bones of the past must be seen in this larger context of collecting and exhibiting.

In the text, the issue of who controls the objects and their potential conversion into various forms of value looms large, and as far as I can tell, this fact has gone undetected by Raabe scholars. It is a museum guard who sounds the alarm when the scholars make a grab for the bones, and the community at large responds in a way that confirms its awareness of the value of keeping the objects in Hallstatt.

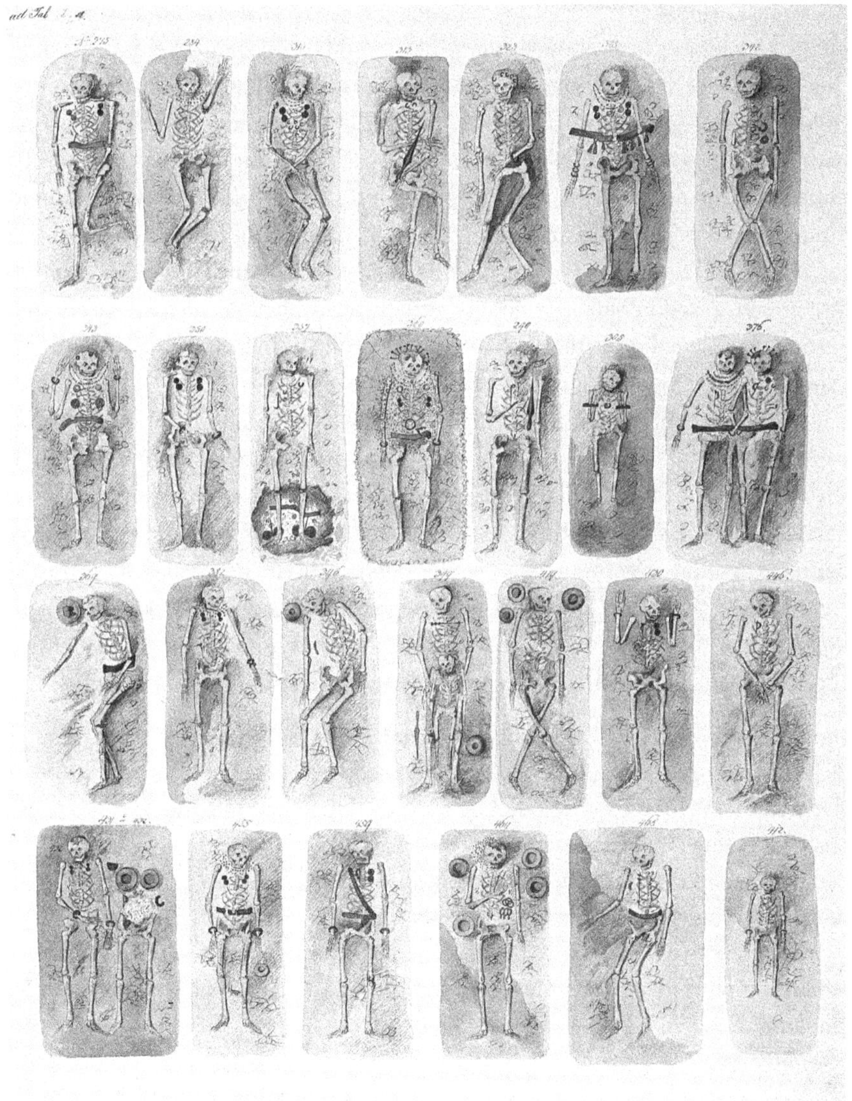

Figure 23 Clay tubs where bodies and offerings were placed at burial, as painted by Isidor Engel, 18 × 8 cm. In many cases, images such as these are important for reconstructing the provenance of burial objects. Naturhistorisches Museum, Vienna.

But when the narrator is arrested for his role in the crime, it is his subtle argument that provides insight. Addressing the inspector in a professional idiom, he pleads, "Esteemed sir, your antediluvian cemetery seems to be quite extensive; have another *ur*-German dug up and have your box with lid, lock, and key put over it. How important is any one Celt to you? That you would be performing a perhaps infinite service to science, to osteology, and to archaeology through your calm acceptance must otherwise offer you comfort" (237–38). In the narrator's eyes, the remaining number of gravesites and the thought of the enormous scientific insights that might result from calm acceptance (*ruhiges Nachsehen*) of this theft would provide sufficient compensation for the lost bones. Simony mentions a letter of commendation, which would be this kind of compensation, and the inspector rejects the idea. By making this argument, the narrator presents museum control of the site and scientific advancement as being in tension with each other and potentially incompatible. The conflict the narrator points to turns on the museum's tacit preference for tourism and its material compensation over service to the archaeological profession. Otherwise, the narrator's strategy would not rely on reminding the inspector with professionally colored discourse ("antediluvian," "osteology") that the inspector's allegiances should perhaps be placed with the archaeological professionals and not focused on exploiting the site for economic purposes.

In emphasizing economic exploitation of the site, I refer not only to the ways the museum frames the burial objects in order to extract tips and sell small stones and other objects in the museum (points I discuss shortly). Rather, the narrator at three different times mentions that tourists to Hallstatt might leave behind personal effects—glasses, wigs, handkerchiefs, umbrellas, snuffboxes, and the like—after they have seen the bones (235, 237, 238). The first scenario of these forgotten tourist objects arises after the narrator envisions the skeletons coming to life and exacting revenge on those who have opened the graves:

> These poor dead warriors, women, youths, and maidens! It is not pleasant to be awakened after so many centuries of undisturbed sleep and to have to be gawked at by such a warped and atrophied tribe. How would it be if suddenly such a thousand-year-old decayed skeleton pulled itself together with a clatter, stood up, rubbed the sleep from its empty eye sockets, and angrily grabbed for its bronze sword in order to descend on the hemorrhoid sufferers, the crinolines, the professors, and the yawning tourist laggards?

> That would turn into a frolicking running and leaping down the mountain; and what would the nineteenth century not lose on the twisting paths along the way down to Hallstatt! What would that old Celt or Germanic tribesman be able to snap up by way of glasses, wigs, snuffboxes, parasols and umbrellas, galoshes, plaid blankets, and opera glasses! (235)

The narrator's blasting of his fellow tourists and his century illustrates one function of the abandoned personal objects: to reverse the ethnographic gaze that tourists typically direct at the host culture they are visiting. Indeed, an old Celt or Germanic person might be fascinated with the culture of nineteenth-century Europeans.

But if the tourist's encounter always has the potential to raise awareness of himself and his culture as an "other" might see it, Raabe's text illustrates that the more typical pattern precludes this potential. Instead, the tourist proceeds by converting exchange value into memory value. In the narrator's imagined scenario, tourists are most likely to think of the event as a kind of mental souvenir linked to the lost objects. As the narrator writes, "Hussa, what a souvenir that would be, my gentlemen and ladies, when one *is again sitting safe* on the train or at home, thinking of the prehistoric spook!" (235; my emphasis). The narrative juxtaposition of lost objects and travel memory suggests an equation and a conversion of valuable object into authenticated experience.

Furthermore, the tourist crosses boundaries as a means of this exchange. If the tourist on the train or at home is "again safe" (*wieder sicher*), there is an interval between arrival and departure that is ostensibly unsafe and unusual and that can be made memorable. Raabe's text suggests that going home with a memorable experience derives in no small way from having discerned the "truth markers" at the boundaries when they are crossed.[37] This process is ritualized in the text, for example, when Krautworst suggests that certain sites must be witnessed and converted to memory if he and the narrator are not to be laughed at upon return home (229). "Keltische Knochen," then, impels the reader to consider tourism in terms of a semiotic and a framing of experience that relate economics, techniques of display, and, as will become clear, gender.

The narrator's impulse to go to Hallstatt arose from a desire to flee the denial of political reality and oppression in the Hapsburg capital, where he was already a tourist observing the widespread poverty and the promotion of a dynastic war. In spite of that miserable situation, at the start of his visit to Hallstatt, the narrator crosses not from the underworld but into it. When he finally reaches tranquility in the Hallstatt church, a begging woman forces him to acknowledge that the dialectics of tourism prevent any real escape. "Now I suddenly knew again," he writes, "that I had left Vienna and fled into the mountains only in order to get the misery out of my mind for at least a couple of hours" (215). By taking to tourism as a flight from Vienna's "misery," the narrator finds himself unexpectedly face to face with precisely that miserable situation that he sought to avoid, inscribing tourist practices dialectically into the text. This occurs in part because of tourism's thriving in conditions of economic despair, for why else would people be begging, and why would secondhand personal items like toupées and glasses be considered valuable compensation?

In this context of war and poverty, the narrator's repeated focus on women in positions connected to tourism comes into sharper relief. Although men appear in the Hallstatt environment, it is first of all notable that they are either young boys or imperial bureaucrats. Men of military utility are absent. But then there is *ein weiblicher Kellner* [literally "a feminine waiter"], which has been rendered by one translator as "waitress" but which could also mean "an effeminate waiter." Since Raabe later refers to waitresses clearly as *Kellnerinnen* [waitresses], this deliberate phrase, together with the "fat maiden" in the ferry, the waitress, and the young museum guard, leads us to suspect that the absence of military-age men should prompt consideration of the ways tourism feminizes those in its "front lines." Beyond mentioning that each of the men in his own way singles out women in a voyeuristic fashion, the narrator seems very sensitive to the ways in which the tourist's experience in the Hallstatt area is marked by the convergence of desire, commercialism, and display.

With respect to the latter, the narrator draws explicit attention to the dual function of the devices used to cover the opened graves, observing that "one had rigged up a peculiar device in order to preserve the opened graves with their skeletons and to be able to show them to a curious or inquisitive public for a tip" (235). The locking covers allow the conversion of curiosity into currency by controlling and channeling the spectator's gaze. For the visitors, moving from grave to grave involves delayed gratification and a building of tension in a way reminiscent of a peepshow. When the young female museum guard finally opens the grave to be robbed, the built-up desire is expressed in a sexual idiom: "[T]he lock now opened with a crash; the girl pushed the lid of the box back, and the two learned men shot forward, with greedily flashing gazes—there lay the Celt or Germanic tribesman well preserved, peaceful, and comfortable on his left side. . . . It was as if a sly grin were wrapped around the bare mouth of the skeleton, an expression like 'come and kiss me!' Zuckriegl would have done the latter in ecstasy" (236). Although the emotional tension of the men is related to their readiness to steal the bones, the words used to describe the men have a sexual edge to them: they shoot forward with greedily sparkling eyes as the skeleton beckons them slyly and seductively. Zuckriegel, it is said, would be ecstatic to succumb, and what follows is a male animal scream that blurs conquest and sexuality: "[W]ith a scream that seemed to stem from the animal realm, Zuckriegl and Steinbüchse rushed onto the Celt and started grabbing" (236). This passionate animal cry is an important moment, for the scholars' loss of control foils both the theft and still another scene of desire and attempted conquest.

Lest it be forgotten, the metaphorically sexualized theft was to coincide with an actual act of seduction that has significance for the economy of artifacts, narratives, and belonging in the text. Zuckriegel's strategy turns on the narrator's distracting the young guard and extracting (at least) a kiss from her, which he does not resist doing: "[T]he greed of the two scientific body snatchers did not permit me to pursue my promise of getting the attention of the maiden through tender affections" (236). This seduction is described as sacrificing the narrator in the name of another's desire, namely Zuckriegel's "scientific urges, [his] wild craving." Everything was going according to plan when the scholars' unforeseen cry interrupted the seduction and prevented the guard from becoming totally immersed in bodily pleasure (235). With the reader presumably to believe that the seduction would have otherwise succeeded were it not for the perverse excess of scholarly desire, the point is not merely that certain conventional narratives about the easy sexual touch of peasant women might have been confirmed. Rather, this implied outcome shows that the narrator is also a tourist and "one of the boys," but "one of the boys" in a clearly delineated way. By means of this heterosexual subplot, the narrator can share in the scholars' quest to indulge their desires without overstepping the tightly regulated bounds of homosociality. That is to say, male-to-male bonding—recalling my argument toward the end of the last chapter—must be channeled into certain acceptable modes of male-to-male exchange. By conspiring to direct his potency to a feminine object in collaboration with other men, the narrator manages to belong to the masculine conquest without sharing the scholars' specific proclivities—in this case the unusual desire for conquest of dead bodies and burial artifacts, which in themselves in some sense inflect the desires that run between the two scholars. A similar point might be made with regard to the other features of the text, particularly the use of irony and carnivalesque elements to disrupt the sense that the narrator belongs to the scholars' educational, if not social, class, as betrayed by his use of elevated language. On the level of desire and language, the narrator as tourist perhaps has more in common with the raiding scholars than might, at first glance, meet the eye.

By developing an understanding of nineteenth-century archaeology in a context of burgeoning nationalism, commercialism, and tourism, I have suggested that this text forms part of the same network of collecting, circulation, and reproduction that it can be shown to describe. My reading shows the thrust of Raabe's text to be partly an admonition—that archaeology's intense study of the past should not distract people from realizing the complexity and problematic nature of archaeology's "work" in, and in the service of, the present. This ritual mobilization of the past in the present is portrayed critically by means of two idioms recognizable for their ability to renew the past in the present: collecting and the carnivalesque. Part of what this text locates are the contradictions in the discourses accompanying nineteenth-century archaeology; these contradictions help to reveal how the interests of the mid-nineteenth century selected and arranged physical evidence in order to make meaning and money out of the past.

6

Flâneur Optical, Collector Tactile:

Rilke's *Neue Gedichte* as Imaginary Museum Landscape

In the nearly forty years after Adalbert Stifter published his *Bildungsroman Der Nachsommer* [Indian Summer] and Wilhelm Raabe wrote "Keltische Knochen" [Celtic Bones], the dynamics of collecting and exhibiting in European society underwent extensive change. Stifter's novel reflected many of the practices of collecting and exhibiting of the time, as I showed by referring to those employed at Schinkel's museum in Berlin, von Klenze's museum in Munich, the emerging museums of Vienna, and the galleries of Linz, where Stifter himself worked. For Stifter, the museum was commonplace enough not to need much justification; a simple mention that Heinrich visits public collections in Vienna suffices for the reader. At the same time, the lion's share of the project of *Bildung* in *Der Nachsommer* does not take place in a public realm. In the 1850s and 1860s, the discourses of public collecting were still becoming ingrained in the public sphere, so that Stifter could plausibly place these discourses in the private realm, creating an imaginary world in which he could explore the educational purposes implicit in the practices of collecting.

In Wilhelm Raabe's "Keltische Knochen," museums and collections were being discovered and pitched as tourist destinations. During the next several decades, public museums flourished and diversified to such an extent that they started to crowd the cultural landscape. Indeed, the museum landscape had become so monumentally omnipresent that by the 1880s and 1890s, various strains of oppositional museum critique, for instance, those of Nietzsche, Eduard Fuchs, and the modernist avant-garde, began to be formulated, in the hopes of challenging the institution's dominance.[1] By Rilke's time at the turn of the century, the museum had become so entrenched in the cultural mainstream as cultural bastion, educational institution, and tourist destination, that it could to some extent be taken for granted. This is as true of Germany as it is for France.

When Rilke first arrives in Paris in 1902, he makes the rounds of the larger museums, sending his wife, Clara, a catalog of his experiences:

> Yesterday I was in the Louvre: the only thing that seemed completely great was Leonardo. Medieval sculpture: the eight nuns with the seneschal . . . (it is painted stone!). In one room, where the new acquisitions are, I discovered small clay (or plasticine) sketches of Carpeaux. . . . I have also seen Notre-Dame de Paris. . . .
>
> This morning was the Musée du Luxembourg: odd, odd, to see all of this for the first time, and yet to see it again. Disappointments are so blended with surprises that they cannot be separated. . . . Now all that remains for me, spread over the next few days: the Musée Cluny, which is my neighbor, the Musée Gustave Moreau, . . . and then only Rodin remains.[2]

Rilke's agenda includes such diverse spaces as the Louvre, Notre-Dame, the Musées du Luxembourg and Cluny, Gustave Moreau's museum, and Rodin's studios, and yet he has hardly exhausted the range of museum options available in Paris at the turn of the century. Since the time of Raabe and Stifter, museums had not only become common; they had exploded in number and kind. In some ways, all of Paris, several times organized as the site of Universal Exhibitions, could be considered an extended museum space. The same can be said of other major European cities, including Berlin, where entire museum complexes such as the Museum Island emerged to hold and display the world's art and artifacts. In this environment it is necessary to think not of individual museums, but of an exhibitionary complex, to use Tony Bennett's formulation, in which the cultural "work" done by individual institutions depends on their position among and differentiation from other museal institutions.[3]

As a former art history student and an art critic, Rilke has expectations of what museums have to offer, and he makes a point of visiting them time and again, even when they disappoint him. Rilke's statement underscores the unquestioning normalcy of museum going for him, a normalcy to be expected then among those intellectuals familiar with the concepts of art and art history, and nowadays familiar to almost anyone, even those who do not live in major metropolitan areas. Tourists to London, Paris, or Berlin today might well choose not to visit institutions such as the British Museum, the Louvre, or the Museum Island, but they would no doubt have to decide not to do so and might be ready to explain their decision.

Given Rilke's enthusiasm for museum experiences, critics might want to investigate the ways they shed light on his poetic production. Yet this task is not a simple one, insofar as the poetic form Rilke perfected in the *Neue Gedichte*—the *Dinggedicht*—seldom exists in a straightforward relationship to a single object or museum setting, thus rebuffing interpretations dependent on an alignment of his writing with a single biographical experience.[4] Moreover, as Judith Ryan has recently stressed, a number of poems in the *Neue Gedichte* seem to have derived from "imaginary paintings," or what John Hollander terms "notional ekphrasis."[5] Emerging from the complex network of spatial experiences and mental processes behind Rilke's writing—with the final composition of a poem sometimes coming up to a year after a visit to a site and combining elements from other experiences and thoughts—the many poetic "objects" evoked by Rilke's *Dinggedichte* cannot exist anywhere but in the mind's eye. As flexible as the imagination may be, however, the ability of a poem to bring to mind not only the sense of the physicality of objects, but also their placement in a rarified spatial environment, is structured by the metaphorical regime regulated by museum discourses. As such, Rilke's *Neue Gedichte* must be considered not merely as a kind of imaginary museum, but as an illumination of the public museum's imaginary regime in the years around 1900. Such an imaginary museum would have an identifiable, if complex, relationship to the museum landscape of the day, making it "legible" to its creator and to readers familiar with museums, and yet not constrained in crucial ways by the physical limits of built museum spaces.

This chapter approaches this problem by means of the studio-museums operated by Auguste Rodin, the sculptor and artist whose relationship with Rilke proved to be pivotal in the poet's artistic development. Much can be gained by revisiting Rilke's Parisian context with a dynamic and rigorously historicized conception of museums and display environments. Rilke's descriptions of how he came to appreciate art in a way that sustained his own artistic productivity suggest that he was adapting a peculiarly museal gaze in order to gain artistic stability. Part of what Rilke's poetry clarifies is Walter Benjamin's phrase, "flâneur optical, collector tactile," a notion that describes the transformation in tactile and visual perception occurring around 1900, owing in part to photography and other modes of reproduction bringing objects into increased circulation and new, unusual contexts. In the manner of a Benjaminian collector, Rilke proves capable of isolating objects spatially and also temporally so that they exist for him in a rarified perceptual realm of his making. Applied to objects whose aesthetic status is constructed by normally unperceived museal operations, Rilke's peculiar museal gaze leads to a reworking of turn-of-the-century museum discourses in imaginary registers, challenging traditional subject-object relations on the one hand

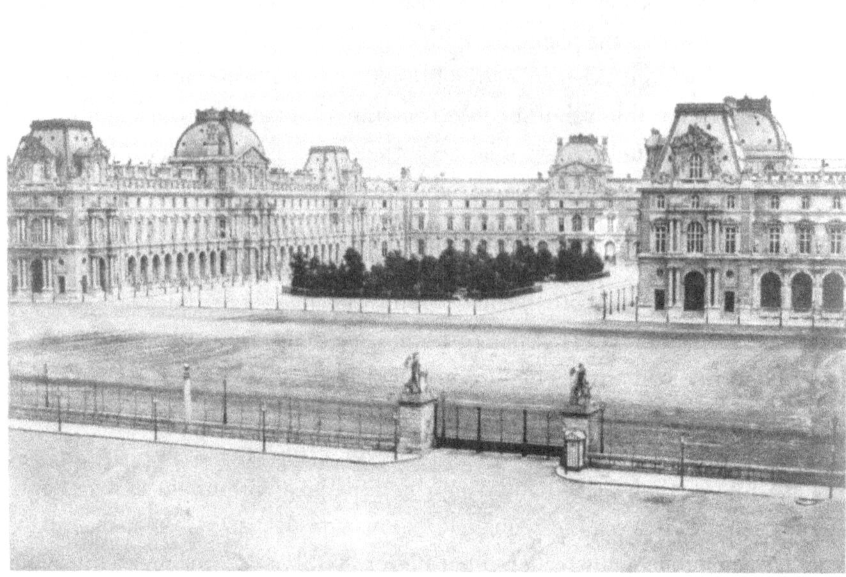

Figure 24 E. Baldus. Paris, Louvre. This image shows the Louvre in the second half of the nineteenth century. Photographic print: albumen, gold toned. In album: Paris et ses environs en photographies, p. 15. No. 11. Library of Congress, reproduction number: LC-USZ62-17876 (b&w film copy neg.). LOT 7743.

and exposing the museum's role in constructing heterosexual masculinity and femininity on the other.

Rodin's Studio-Museums: Re-Learning How to See

The designation "studio-museum" for Rodin's studios tells us a great deal about the cultural valences of museums in the late nineteenth and early twentieth centuries. In the list of museums Rilke attentively visits upon his arrival in Paris in 1902, many spaces vie for the title and function of art museum. The Louvre, often known as a "universal survey museum" for its broad scope, depicting the development of art and culture for its people, still dominates the museum landscape (Fig. 24). In some photographs of the time, it serves as the vantage point for viewing the rest of the city's venerable landmarks (Fig. 25), and Rilke, too, locates it as the center of his Paris. As he puts it, "[E]verything will relate to [the Louvre] and surround it."[6] Yet there is also the Musée du Luxembourg, an institution for contemporary art, the Musée Cluny, devoted to medieval art, and the cathedral Notre-Dame de Paris, which contains medieval sculpture in a layout that, since the advent of museums, is also read as a kind of exhibitory space. Later, Rilke also speaks of the interior decoration in the Panthéon and his intention to visit the artist museums

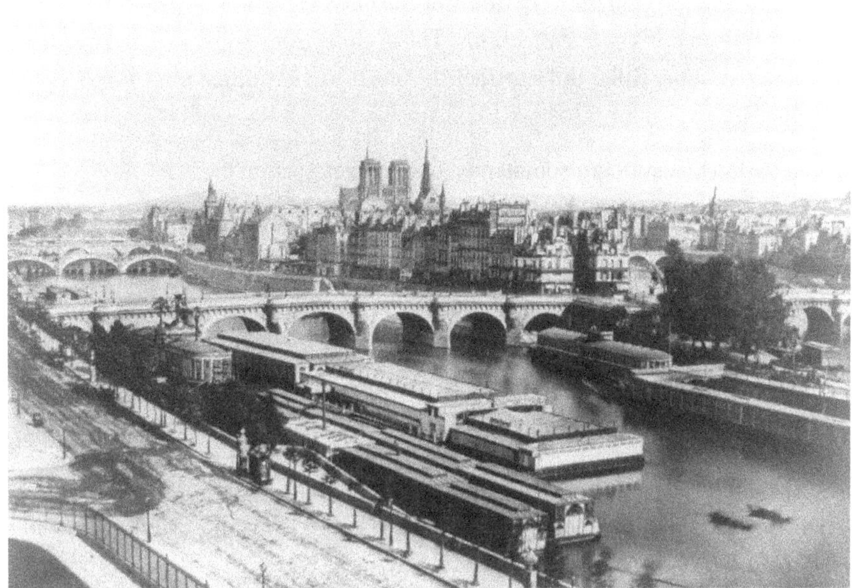

Figure 25 E. Baldus. Paris, Panorama. This image shows Paris from the vantage point of the Louvre, a view of the city that anticipates Rilke's own idealized sense of the city. Photographic print: albumen, gold toned. In album: Paris et ses environs en photographies, p. 15. No. 52. Library of Congress, reproduction number: LC-USZ62-17875 (b&w film copy neg.), LOT 7743.

of Gustave Moreau and Auguste Rodin. The list could be extended still further within the realm of "high art," judging from turn-of-the-century guidebooks to Paris.[7] The types of "low art" or spectacle also available in exhibition spaces like the Musée Grevin (a wax museum) and the Morgue (which Rilke presents in at least two poems in the collection) would make that list even longer.

In major European metropolises and certainly in Paris, art museums represented the dominant paradigm for the definition and reception of art at the turn of the century. But while museums were unparalleled in determining what could be counted as "art," the explosion of competing institutions and museal permutations shows the dispersion of the museum within the era's cultural space. This very diversity of institutions laying claim to the name *museum* makes a specific definition of such an ideal museal institution increasingly elusive. As Tony Bennett has stressed by coining the term "exhibitionary complex," the stability of the term relied on pressures from the place of each institution in relation to its respective high- and low-culture neighbors such as World Expositions and the fair.[8]

In this museum "landscape," Rodin's studio-museums appear as a significant variation of the art museum. Beyond the sense of self-importance and prestige that the designation "studio-museum" surely brought to Rodin, there are good reasons for this designation. In addition to his own sculpture, Rodin's studio-museums housed his own collections. These collections were so extensive that, in Rodin's studios, Rilke did not feel the need to visit other museums. As he described his experiences to his wife, Clara:

> I yearn for the Luxembourg sometimes, but I do not get into the city at all and also I have everything here in fact, complete fullness. . . . [Rodin's] great joy is to buy beautiful pieces of antiquity; there is an abundance of gorgeous things, of fragmented stones in Meudon, in the garden, in the house, in all the rooms and studios and work rooms: vitrines with small Egyptian objects, with sitting, wonderful cats, birds of prey, and lizards, and then all these dear little fragments that recover around him.[9]

Just like public museums, Rodin's studios employed methods of exhibition like showcases to display his pieces (Figs. 26 and 27).[10] In Rilke's description, they fill every conceivable room whether used for living or working. The spaces were so rich in number and scope that they more than make up for Rilke's not being able to visit traditional museums such as the Musée du Luxembourg.

Underscoring his observation that all museums in Paris are ultimately related to the Louvre, Rilke testifies to the seriousness of Rodin's collections by comparing some of the pieces favorably with what could be found there. Containing

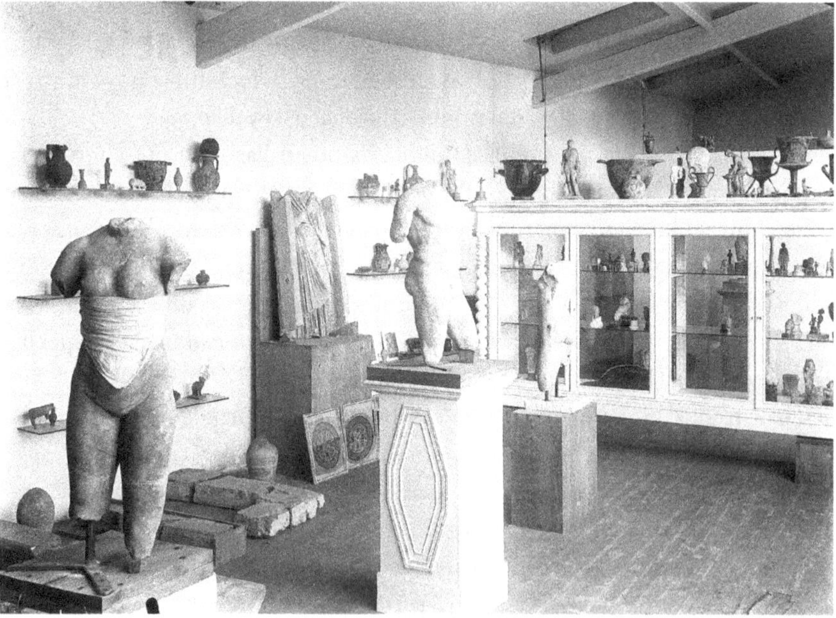

Figure 26 A portion of the collection of antiquities owned by Rodin at his Meudon studio, ca. December 1906. For Rilke, the quality of Rodin's collection saved him from many trips to institutions such as the Louvre. Francoise Antoine Vizzavona (1876–1961). 13 × 18 cm. Fonds Druet-Vizzavona.

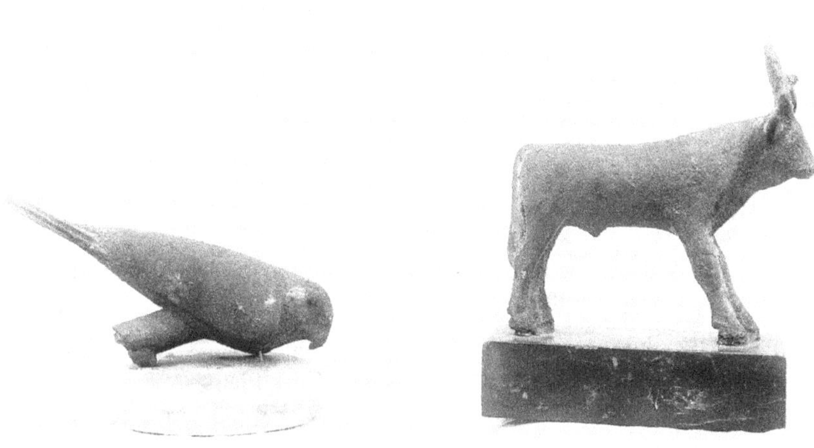

Figure 27 Sparrowhawk and bull. Bronze and plaster, 13 × 18 cm. From the Egyptian collection of Rodin, which Rilke greatly admired and which he credited with helping him understand the plastic arts. Fonds Druet-Vizzavona.

"works of Greek and Egyptian provenance of which some would get noticed in the rooms of the Louvre," the "Musée Rodin," then, could be seen as "a very personally selected museum of statues of antiquity and fragments."[11] Photographs of his studio-museums confirm Rilke's perspective. In a strict sense, and independent of the studio facet of Rodin's home, it can be argued that Rodin's studio-museums deserved their designation "art museum," since they exhibited collections of art objects in a traditional manner.

It is well known that Rodin had Rilke practice viewing and interpreting art in a variety of museal environments. What is less clear is that Rodin's work—at least the work known by Rilke—must be seen as embedded in a particular physical environment governed by the dynamics of collecting, which Rilke learned to exploit. Starting with his studio-museums, Rodin took Rilke through his own collections of Greek and Egyptian art, which Rilke identified as extremely important for his making connections to earlier artistic traditions. As Rilke put it to Lou Andreas-Salomé, "Rodin's body of work, through which I have walked deeply and patiently, connected me with them [that is, the small objects of antiquity] and the gothic sculptures."[12]

Making connections in this manner lies at the heart of museum culture. No matter how it is theorized, collecting involves the movement of objects from one context to another. As with the concept of montage, the juxtaposition of objects in particular arrangements permits similarities and relations to be uncovered, creating conditions for new configurations of thought. The proximity of Rodin's art to traditions reaching back to ancient Greece and Egypt enabled Rilke to interpret Rodin's artistic production within the context of the studio-museum's collections.[13] Viewed in a display environment, moreover, the collections taught Rilke to structure artistic creation through a dialogue with remnants from earlier artistic traditions brought into the artist's present spatial environment. Depending on a process of bringing objects into one's life in the proper way, this dialogue is, as becomes clear, a Benjaminian process.

Having internalized the display techniques and the mode of organization of Rodin's studio-museum, Rilke found himself increasingly able to decode objects on display in the museums of the Cluny, the Luxembourg, and the Louvre, as well as the Notre-Dame and the animals in the Jardin des Plantes.[14] Expanding his ability to work outward from the studio-museum coincided with Rilke's particular attempts to overcome problems he faced as a poet. One of the fundamental problems he faced in his creative efforts, now often associated with his personal and poetic crises beginning to take hold in 1902, was his inability to comprehend and control the images he encountered.[15] Cars seemed to race right through him, and people, living in abject poverty, seemed capable of crossing into his person.[16] This involuntary loss of boundaries, in particular, which represented Rilke's comprehension of the plight of the underclass as well as his fear that he might belong to it, disquiets Rilke both personally and creatively.

One way of reading his *Neue Gedichte* is to see them as responses to these devastating incursions, with the poems representing Rilke's gradually increasing ability to employ aesthetic craftsmanship to address his emotional responses to the world around him.[17] Rilke's gains are fragile, however, and he remains susceptible to moments when his environment seems to take him over.[18] Breakdowns could happen even in familiar museums, as he reports about a 1906 trip he made to the Louvre. For that entire visit, the huge number of paintings and the bustle of other visitors disturbed him, and he felt that "there were only images and many too many images, and everywhere someone was standing, and everything was irritating. And I asked myself: Why is it different today. Was I fatigued? Yes. But what did this fatigue consist in? By my allowing everything to cross my mind; by having everything pass through me like water through a mirror image, dissolving my contours into something flowing and in flux."[19] Recalling his complaints about cars and indigent people violating his sense of boundaries some four years earlier, Rilke sees that in this museum images and people pass through him, dissolving his sense of self. Such breakdowns in his sense of personal and artistic integrity, while not occurring during every museum visit, could take place even in a comparatively rarified space like the Louvre. Though able to bring art into his own space, as it were, Rilke cannot keep the art where he would like it once it is there.

What is fascinating about this particular incident, and what informs my approach to the *Neue Gedichte,* is that Rilke responds by increasing his concentration and by perceiving himself as if he, too, were an artwork on display: "And I said to myself: I do not want to be the mirror image any more, but rather the image that is right-side up. And I rotated myself so that I no longer stood on my head, and I closed my eyes for a short moment, collecting myself and tightening my contours the way one tightens a violin string until it feels solid and resonant. Suddenly I felt like I had the outline of a Dürer drawing, and so I stepped before the *Mona Lisa* and she was incomparable."[20] Putting an end to objects and people invading his being by attaining a state of concentration (a condition he termed *Gesammeltsein* and that he linked to Rodin's work ethic), Rilke is suddenly able to apprehend the beauty of the famous painting. He thereby addresses a difficulty he had also had in approaching the *Mona Lisa* five weeks before, when he described the painting as "unapproachable in her haughtiness."[21]

Crucially, this mode of concentrated museum gazing matches a later, more detailed description of looking that Rilke continues to develop with Rodin and with his encounter with Cézanne's painting. As Rilke writes to Clara in 1907,

> Looking is such a marvelous thing, of which we know but little; through it, we are turned absolutely toward the outside, but when we are most of all so, things happen in us that have waited longingly to be observed, and while they reach completion in us, intact and curiously anonymous, *without our aid*—their significance grows up in the object outside: a powerful, persuasive name, the only name these inner events could possibly have, a name in which we joyfully and reverently recognize the happenings within us, a name we ourselves do not touch, only apprehending it very gently, from a distance, under the similitude of a thing that, a moment ago, was strange to us, and the next moment will be estranged anew.[22]

Turning absolutely to the outside is an instance of what Rilke called *Gesammeltsein,* a condition he describes in the Louvre as taking on the contours of a Dürer drawing.[23] During that state of outward concentration, his internal state becomes able to respond to the condition outside in such a way that, for a brief moment, he overcomes the strangeness of the external object. In this state, the things internal remain intact and untouched and the object outside is apprehended gently from a distance. The ability to apprehend specific objects results from the inside and outside achieving a kind of resonance condition in which, rather than collapse into each other, inside and outside correspond with each other in a way that causes both to separate from their respective contexts.

In the museum, Rilke stabilizes his sense of self and his ability to perceive beauty not merely by emulating a Dürer drawing, which in turn establishes a particular, purified context for himself and the painting. Rilke in some sense joins the ranks of the paintings he wishes to appreciate—in this case the *Mona Lisa*—by rendering the plethora of overwhelming images invisible. This practice is significant because the demarcation that results from the creation of a particular display context can be described precisely as the effect of a museal gaze, made to operate in a particular museum environment. It is a peculiar but highly revealing mode of bringing objects into one's present context that becomes possible at a point in history when capitalism and the new media are giving rise to a "dialectical transformation of tactility" that likewise reconfigures the operation of the optical.[24]

Part of this process can be explicated in terms of modern museum display. In his critique of Lacan's "The Split Between the Eye and the Gaze," Norman Bryson shows that the practice of modern museum display creates entities by way of a decontextualized, well-demarcated separation between an object and its context.[25] As Bryson states: "Stabilizing the entity as a fixed Form, with a bounded outline, is possible only if the universe surrounding the entity is screened out and the entity withdrawn from the universal field of transformations. The concept of the entity can be preserved only by an optic that casts around each entity a perceptual frame that makes a cut from the field and immobilizes the cut within the static framework."[26] Bryson's optic is one that applies to the display of aesthetic objects in the manner that is decisively in place in the museum culture of the early twentieth century. This is precisely what happens, nearly down to the level of word choice, when Rilke directs the optic at himself in order to gain artistic stability. Until Rilke establishes boundaries around himself and becomes an entity, his subject status is relinquished to nihility, a vacuum of meaning that, giving rise to a core personal and artistic problem, allows the objects around him to merge with him.[27] With Rilke emulating an aesthetic object in order to establish contexts for approaching other objects, it is no wonder that the *Dinggedichte* (thing poems) of his making are routinely described in terms of a withdrawal of the experiential poetic voice as it was known in nineteenth-century poetic tradition of *Erlebnislyrik*. Indeed, as Rilke articulated it, achieving the "objective speaking" (*sachliches Sagen*) of the *Neue Gedichte* meant abandoning the notion that the poem expressed the feelings and experiences of the poet.[28]

What this moment of museal reification suggests is a severe but also highly specific sense of alienation. Notably, the crises in Rilke's mode of vision occur in indoor and exterior spaces. With the street in fact becoming an extended exhibition space at the turn of the century, it makes sense that the street scenes of Paris disturbed his sense of self as much as the experience in the Louvre. The street becomes an extended exhibition space approachable like an interior, so that it makes sense to think of Rilke as a kind of *flâneur*, albeit not one in the mode of Baudelaire.[29] In this state, Rilke embodies a condition Walter Benjamin describes in the *Arcades Project* as emerging around 1900: "[W]ith the turn away from naturalism of late the primacy of the optical that dominated in the nineteenth century is ending." He then goes on to add, "*flâneur* optical, collector tactile [*taktisch*]."[30] While the practice of *flânerie* is still possible, the objective distance the *flâneur* is reputed to have once enjoyed can, by 1900, no longer be easily maintained. At the same time, according to Benjamin, the new rhythm of experience and perception changes so that objects seem to impinge on us. "If we responded to certain things in a more leisurely manner and to others more quickly, one might say if we lived according to another rhythm, then there would be nothing 'lasting' for us, but rather everything would happen before our eyes, everything would befall us."[31] As Norbert Bolz shows, Benjamin elsewhere speaks of these effects as "objects coming dangerously close" to us, as objects that "have attacked . . . human society."[32] This phenomenon has a particular resonance in Rilke's alienated experience that this opposition of the "*flâneur* optical, collector tactile" seems to capture.

Yet in two ways, Rilke's experience complicates and deepens our understanding of this opposition. In the Louvre, Rilke restores the idealized museal quality to the environment, isolating the painting spatially and also temporally so that it exists for him in a rarified perceptual realm of his making. This process resembles what Benjamin generally describes as the collector's approach to thinking about things in modernity: "The true method of making things present is to represent them in our space (not to represent ourselves in their space). (The collector does just this, and so does the anecdote). Thus represented, the things allow no mediating construction made of 'large contexts.' . . . We don't displace our being into theirs; they step into our life."[33] Viewed from this standpoint, Rilke is capable not only of accessing and selecting scenes from museums, an artist's studio, or a city slum, but also of creating the proper conditions for the objects to enter his life. The objects become present to him (*gegenwärtig*) in spatial and temporal terms, giving the impression of being subject to no mediation other than his own. The effect that it brings about on the objects is marked and forces commonplaces of Rilke scholarship to be rethought. The poems demonstrating the Rilkean "learning to see" problematize subject-object relations because they unravel the once "transparent" museal operations that enabled categories such as autonomous art.

At the same time, and this is the second complicating factor, Rilke's internal realization of this mode of vision fails to retain the objective distance between himself and his objects that the traditional *flâneur* seeks to preserve. If distanced *flânerie* is understood to be a typically masculine activity, then one can see that Rilke's *flânerie* offers a potential gender transgression for its inability to maintain distance at all times.[34] Rilke's vision has the potential, then, to make visible a kind of gendered cityscape that the masculine *flâneur* is supposed to render invisible. I want to read this shift in gendered effects as directly resulting from the museum method Rilke developed in response to his encounters with Rodin and the metropolis.

It might be expected that if Rilke has learned how to place any object into a personal museal space, a "notional museum," as it were, he becomes aware of both the contingent quality of the modern subject and also a resulting transformed perception of the object.[35] Instability appears, for example, in the claim that every point of the appropriately observed surface "looks" back at you. The poem "Archaïscher Torso Apollos" has a well-known phrasing of this quality of surface: "[F]or there is no point, / that does not look at you. You must change your life" (13–14; 557). Though the poem's warning addresses the challenge that the object, particularly the modernist object, poses to the modern subject's stability, perhaps even more revealing are the ways in which Rilke's application of the museal gaze affects other objects he views. The eyes of the cadavers on public display in the poem "Morgue" have literally turned around. They were washed so as not to disgust "those who gawk," but then "Behind their lids the eyes [of the corpses] / have turned around and now peer inward" (13–14; 503).

His poems "Der Panther" and "Der Hund" [The Dog] comment on this process, too. Like Rilke's gaze in the Louvre, the caged panther's gaze has become tired and overstimulated and, like Rilke in the Louvre, can no longer hold onto anything: "From the passing of the bars his gaze has / become so tired that it holds nothing more" (1–2; 505). Also, when the panther opens his eyes, "Then an image goes inside, / moves through the tense silence of the organs / and ceases to exist in his heart" (10–12; 505). As a wild animal, the panther has no knowledge of self, and without this the images enter and course through his body unimpeded.[36] Unlike Rilke, the panther cannot marshal the concentration to draw boundaries in order to create a museal context with which he can defend himself; only shutting his eyes protects him. Being locked up and put on display has numbed his great will (8; 505), and the occasional image that reaches his heart dies there.

As a creature to which Rilke ascribed a special position between human existence and that of other animals, in the poem "Der Hund" the dog has a gaze that exists "completely beneath" that of the human world but that "sometimes" succeeds in penetrating the "image that is constantly renewed by the gazes of the world above" (1–2).[37] Thus the dog has experiences in which a thing (a *Ding* in the Rilkean sense) can "come and place itself next to him" (3–4), allowing a meaningful context to exist for the dog and the object as it would for the Rilkean poet. Yet the dog's curious condition between banishment and integration into the human world causes the dog to give his reality to the image, forgetting it in the doubt of his existence (12). Thus if the poet is to retain an image, he must also doubt in his existence as little as possible. It is the dual crisis of artistic vision and existential mean that concentrated looking in the museal mode hopes to resolve.

"The Panther" is interesting because it exemplifies the condensation of studies of objects from several venues into a single *Dinggedicht.*[38] The original impulse for the poem came from a small plaster cast that Rodin owned, the original of which was displayed by the Bibliothèque Nationale.[39] This object attracted Rilke's attention because its surface was similar to that which he describes in the "Archaïscher Torso Apollos" and sees in Rodin's sculpture: "[T]his small thing has ... a hundred thousand points that are all alive, in movement, and different from each other."[40] In the Rodin monograph, Rilke speaks of the plaster cast's supple-powerful paws that evoke the "supple powerful gait" (5; 505) of the panther in the poem.[41] But the label affixed to the poem further complicates the situation by referring to two different display environments. While it recalls the conventions of naming sculpture, it simultaneously locates the panther in the Jardin des Plantes, a setting consistent with the cat's cage and bored resignation. These features resonate with the continuities in other poems written on confinement (e.g., the Africans on display in the Jardin d'Acclimation in Paris in "The Aschantis," the prose poem "The Lion's Cage").[42] As these cases show, the *Dinggedicht* is derived from Rilke's particular method of applying museal vision to individual objects, sites, and even thoughts, so that any final poetic product might conflate features of varying provenance. The result is a mental image of objects and spatial environments that can exist nowhere but in the imagination.

This combinatorial logic can be accounted for by realizing that Rilke's method of visual collecting places all manifestations into an unmediated present context of his making. Yet, for the notional object to appear convincingly tangible, it coheres in the mind's eye only by respecting the prevailing conventions of display. In light of existing Rilke scholarship, I want to stress that the linguistic regime Rilke seeks to exploit is structured not just linguistically, but also by the museal discourses constructing the objects he encounters. To be sure, combing dictionaries to learn the expressive possibilities of individual words and phrases was crucial, but overcoming the troubled state in which boundaries dissolve entailed learning how to concentrate in a way that meant that expressive possibilities were also fundamentally structured by existing museal institutions and practices. These were in fact beginning to undergo significant shifts that Rilke's poetry is one of the first to explore.

In the first decade of the twentieth century, the imaginary regime at stake in these explorations ran the gamut not only of exhibitionary institutions in European metropolises and tourist destinations, for instance, cities such as Venice, Rome, and Bruges, but also of the circulation of photographic reproductions for the purposes of exposure and sales—the beginnings of the culture industry. The growing circulation of photographic reproductions would eventually inspire André Malraux's 1930s theorization of *le musée imaginaire*. On the literal level, Malraux understood the imaginary museum to consist of individuals assembling photographs and copies into their personal museums, following individual desires and preferences.[43] Developed in dialogue with Walter Benjamin's notions of how photography would alter art and politics, this principle has not made museums obsolete.[44] Malraux's argument, in the minds of some commentators, presages an "indefinite expansion" or even a recuperation of the museum following the ravages of mechanical reproduction.[45] Beyond this, the ability to remake the museum outside its walls, as Rosalind Krauss has argued, also alters the conceptual framework that visitors can bring to bear in existing institutions. One result is a greater propensity for museal processes and dynamics to pass into everyday life, supplying in particular a means for creating one's own story in terms of humanity's past and present culture and styles. As interventions in and exploitations of those discourses, Rilke's poetry captures the shifts beginning to occur with the explosion in exhibitionary venues and the rise of photography.

Shifts in the Museum's Imaginary Regime Around 1900: Prestige, Commodities, and Photography

While Rilke was certainly a privileged visitor to Rodin's studio-museums, particularly when he worked as Rodin's secretary and lived in Meudon, Rodin was motivated to encourage many visitors to visit his studio-museums. Turn-of-the-century guidebooks list Saturday as the day Rodin typically opened his spaces to callers, and it was considered an honor to be received by him.[46] But prestige is only part of the story. Since art dealers usually did not negotiate with Rodin, he used his studio-museums to sell his pieces directly to collectors.[47] The open declaration of sculpture's dual nature as commodity and aesthetic object made by this use of Rodin's studio-museum is by no means unprecedented; Charles

Baudelaire had identified it as a problem of modern sculpture in his 1846 essay "Why Sculpture Is Boring."[48] Rather, what warrants attention here is the way that Rodin's mode of production was influenced by this duality through exploiting the potentials of exhibition.

Rodin's use of his studios as a point of sale must be seen in the context of the nexus of production, display, and commerce heavily influenced by the Paris Salons, the Musée du Luxembourg, the Universal Exhibitions, and governmental commissions. In the late nineteenth and early twentieth centuries Paris was a hotbed of artistic activity, with fierce competition among artists. Sculptors had greater difficulty than painters in getting art dealers to buy and show their works. The Salons provided an avenue for crucial recognition and exposure that could lead to purchases and commissions. Indeed, the majority of art produced in Paris at the end of the nineteenth century was made directly for exhibition in the Salons or museums. But with the crush of artists entering works, there could be no guarantee of favorable conditions of display. While Rodin succeeded in getting his sculpture placed in advantageous ways, public scandal often accompanied his entries to the Salons and jeopardized his commissions.[49]

In an attempt to shore up his reputation and establish himself as a star of the French scene, Rodin borrowed money to stage his own exhibition in a special pavilion at the Universal Exhibition of 1900.[50] During this Exhibition, Rodin netted more than 200,000 francs in sales and solidified his international standing.[51] Already a fashionable place to visit prior to 1890, his studio-museum got a big boost from this success, particularly after the pavilion was moved to Meudon after the Exhibition ended.[52] The throngs of visitors (some 32 million came to the 1900 Universal Exposition) allowed him to recoup some of the studio's costs.[53] It is nearly impossible to imagine Rodin's success as an artist without his skilled use of direct exhibition to promote his own work.

Still, direct exhibition had its limits. Rodin also used photography as a way to increase exposure of his works in ways that direct exhibition could never achieve.[54] Exploiting the possibilities of photography and the circulation of reproductions like few artists before him, Rodin worked with a number of well-known photographers, including J. E. Bulloz, Eugène Druet, and Edward Steichen, to make reproductions of his art as it appeared in his studio-museums. Carefully placing his signature upon prints as a means of establishing "originality," or at least "authenticity,"[55] he sought to maintain the status of the original artwork while garnering worldwide exposure. In 1898 Rodin "could exhibit his proposed monument to Balzac and know that in a matter of weeks it would be reproduced photographically in Tokyo, Hanoi, London, New York, Algiers, Berlin, Stockholm, Prague, Buenos Aires, and Milwaukee."[56] This network of exposure increased attention, buyers, artists, and photographers, allowing Rodin to tap the fast-growing art markets in the Americas and Germany.[57]

Rilke also actively and consciously extended Rodin's network in a way that complemented Rodin's other efforts. His Rodin monograph supplied photographs of Rodin's sculpture and eventually drawings, and Rodin gave him slides for his lectures in Germany and Austria.[58] Moreover, in the preface to the lecture that Rilke eventually included in the Rodin monograph, Rilke acknowledges that the entire relationship of the public to contemporary art is changing because of the increased accessibility of artists in their studios and the growing ability of technologized art criticism to keep pace with artistic advances. But if Rilke understands this changing relationship to be partly expressed through the greater public interest in art and the art market, his lectures are motivated by the claim that the conventional art market is prone to undervalue art such as Rodin's. As Rilke writes,

> The studios have become more accessible and also more involved with an art criticism that can no longer be accused of being antiquated; the art market itself has availed itself of these advantages and . . . placed itself at the forefront of this development in which the public can now easily participate: with its criticism and its desire to acquire art. However, this attitude (as pleasing and progressive as it may be) passes a work like Rodin's by; it skips over it, failing to touch it.[59]

By suggesting that reproduction and commodification fail to capture the significance of Rodin's art, Rilke is not implying that Rodin should not employ these methods. Rather, additional, auratic means of mediation are necessary for the public to appreciate his art.

But if Rilke formulated his promotional strategy based on his understanding of the role of reproduction and circulation in the burgeoning art market, he believed it would help to insert himself into the process as a kind of auraticizing element. As a witness to Rodin's process and his confidant, he presented Rodin's work with a first-hand knowledge and intimacy that aimed to circulate a positive depiction of him and his art. Yet Rilke seemed to think that his own poetic voice could help supply a suitably rarified context. During his Rodin lecture tour, for instance, in Vienna, Rilke read from his own work in addition to presenting slides of Rodin's pieces.[60] Rilke allowed Rodin's art to pass through him and next to his art as a strategy designed to reach audiences in the desired way.

Rilke's helping Rodin was not entirely "selfless," but seems designed in some sense to channel desire through the medium of art. In this period of their relationship, Rilke seemed to have identified with Rodin in ways that made Rilke's engagement with Rodin's art always seem to be also about Rilke—both in the sense that Rilke wished himself to be as "great" as that art and in the sense that he wished for Rodin to take notice of, and perhaps reciprocate, his admiration. In these ways, then, Rilke seems to have regarded the promotion of Rodin's art as an opportunity to engage with, and to construct an exchange with, the artist. In other chapters I have used Eve Sedgewick's term "homosocial" to describe exchanges between men that are conducted either through the exchange of art, women, or both. It appears that there is a homosocial dimension in the Rodin book and lectures, though in some ways Rilke seems to appear both as exchanger and as medium. This peculiar feature raises the question of gender both within the relationship of the two men to each other and with respect to Rilke's own methods of artistic creation. This terrain will be explored in the next section.

Rodin and Rilke in the Museal Landscape: Contrasting Views of Gender, Sexuality, and Creativity

Rodin's savvy use of direct exhibition and photography to increase his exposure, and of course his income, is directly responsible for his success as an artist. Rodin and Rilke alike seem to have realized that the potential of the new technologies for unlimited reproducibility, and the increased speed with which reproductions could be distributed worldwide, turned the world into a kind of extended museum space that in turn altered the way that museum spaces could be conceived of and approached. Photography radically expanded the scope of exhibitionary potential already made possible by engraving and lithography.[61] It would be but a short time until André Malraux would consolidate these developments into his famous formulation that circulating photographic reproductions enabled the making of "imaginary museums," that is, of museums defined not by institutional walls, but rather by the exigencies of the art lover assembling the images. At the same time, though, such wide dispersion of exhibitions made them more commonplace, more ordinary. As the world became an extended museum space, everyday movement in urban spaces increasingly verged on a processional spectatorship, presaged by the Universal Exhibitions of the late nineteenth century.[62]

Paradoxically, while Rodin attempted to retain an auratic authenticity of his works by imposing his signature on photographs of them, part of his intention in having his studio-museum photographed was to dispel the aura of the artist's studio as a place of magical inspiration and instead to depict it as a place of incessant work.[63] From Rilke and other contemporaries all the way through to recent Rodin criticism, the image persists of Rodin as a humble man made famous by hard work as much as by genius.[64] The constant stream of circulating photographs fed this reputation, especially those that show a studio space overflowing with many of his famous sculptures, and several in the midst of production.

Hard work and ceaseless toil are but one feature of Rodin's reputation. The sculptor was also linked with unbridled sexuality and the notion of artistic creation as a manifestation of male potency. Female models were asked to perform sexual acts for and with him, from which Rodin produced quick clay modeling and countless sketches known as "instantaneous drawings."[65] Rilke emulated this process to some extent when he studied objects, although it must also be said that Rilke most often avoided using human beings as models.[66] For some commentators, the image of Rodin as the sober worker who sacrificed for his art tended to counter his satyric image.[67] Rilke, in his Rodin monograph, in particular presented an image of Rodin as a ceaseless, isolated worker. But rather than see the hard-working male artist in opposition to the creative sexual predator, I suggest that the two are fundamentally interconnected in the fin-de-siècle concept of (male) artist. "Rodin's genius (his genius as a preeminently male attribute)," writes Anne M. Wagner, "his representations of women, and even the tattle about his goat-like behavior, were necessary and mutually consistent components of the public phenomenon that was Rodin."[68]

If situated in the context of early modernism, the conventions operating both in his art and in his society are more readily noticed. In the accounts of proponents and detractors alike, the dominant assumption of creativity and art understood them to be founded in a sexual truth telling, a revealing of the supposed "reality" of heterosexual male and female desire.[69] Time and again Rodin draws and sculpts women's genitalia as the center of femininity, as a synecdoche for the female body and an icon of feminine desire.[70] The statues *L'Ecclesiaste, L'Avarice et la luxure,* and *Iris, Messenger of the Gods* all prominently expose female genitalia (see Fig. 28).[71] Moreover, women's genitalia in Rodin's work most often appear inseparable from representations of feminine pleasure, depicted either by showing the women engaged in sexual acts, as in *The Kiss* or *L'Avarice et la luxure,* or in the symbolism of a pose. The figures in *L'Ecclesiaste* and *Iris,* for instance, all grasp their feet, shorthand in the French tradition for women's orgasm, while others, like the *Torso d'Adèle* [Torso of Adèle], focus on an arched back suggesting ecstasy.[72] Of course, the unpolished, marred surfaces of these sculptures, as well as their isolation of sexual features, make it clear that while they are modeled on women's bodies, they are not completely mimetic. This foregrounding of the constructedness of the object breaks with the neo-Classical and Naturalist traditions in sculpting prevalent in France up until the late nineteenth century, yet not enough to lose fully the claim to scientific truth found in Naturalist art.[73] Crucially, in their departure from pure mimesis they bear foremost the mark of the man who created them.

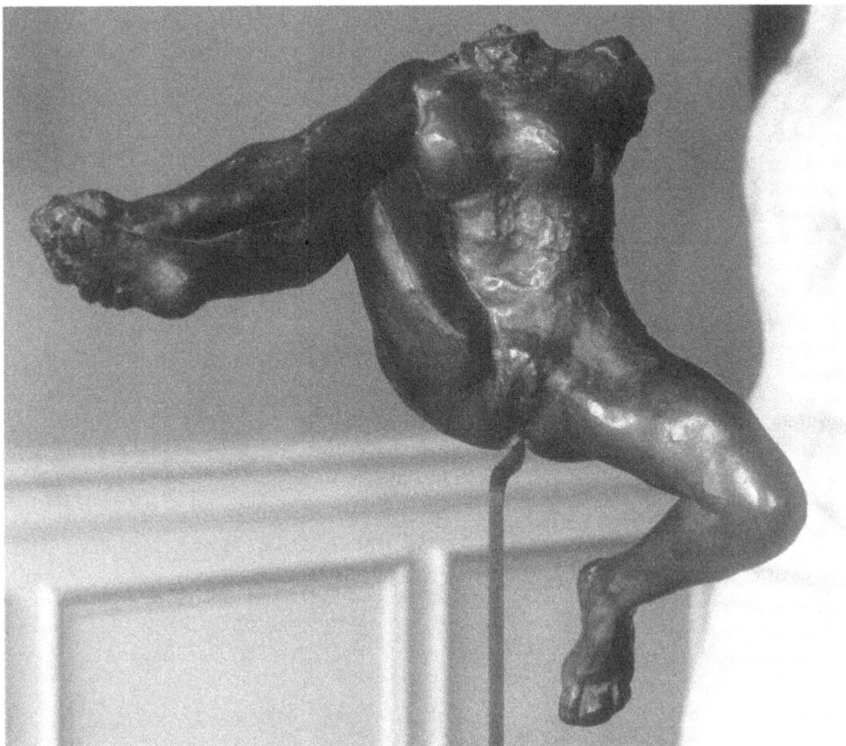

Figure 28 Auguste Rodin (1840–1917). Iris, messenger of the gods, 1890–91, bronze, 82.7 × 69 × 63 cm. Musée Rodin, Paris.

Like the new "science" of psychoanalysis, Rodin's art was often understood as a kind of sexual truth telling, capable of revealing "reality" and "truth" in a way that expressed the sensibilities and maladies of "modern" society. This is not to say that Rodin did not sculpt male bodies or ever engage directly with male sexuality (of course, Freud also addressed masculinity in his way). Yet when Rodin sculpted men, the terms were different than they were for women. Rilke depicts the differential succinctly in the Rodin monograph, where he claims that when Rodin created images of women it was

> as if Rodin most preferred to experience the face of the woman as a part of his beautiful body, as if he wanted to have his eyes be the eyes of the body and his mouth the mouth of the body. . . .
>
> It is different with the male figures. The essence of a man can be conceived more easily in a condensed manner in the space of his face.[74]

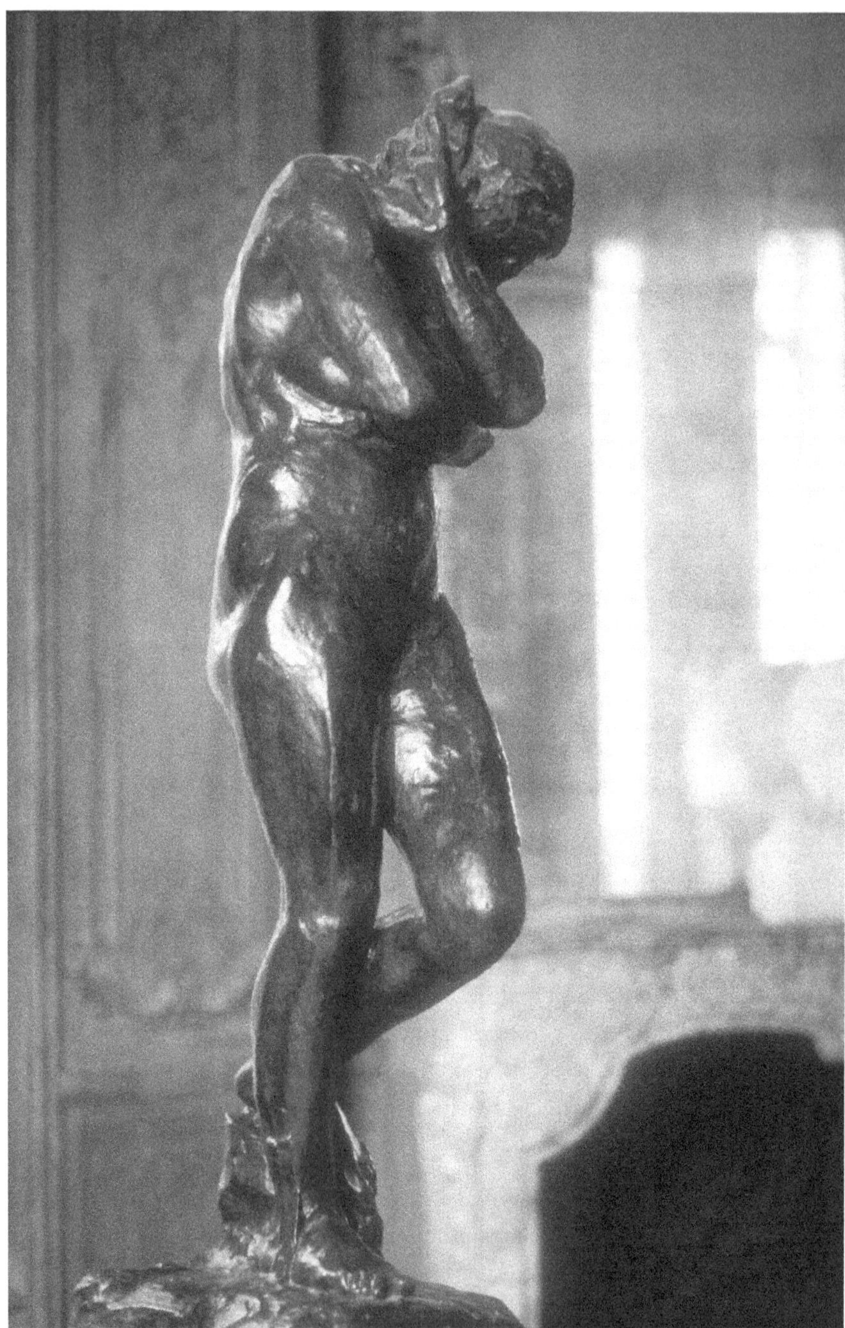

Figure 29 Auguste Rodin (1840–1917). Eve, 1881, bronze, 174 × 533 × 61 cm. This sculpture supposedly depicts the model in the early stages of pregnancy. Musée Rodin, Paris.

According to Rilke's description, Rodin not only locates the important qualities of a woman in her body; he fragments that body to correspond with Rodin's face, eyes, mouth, and so on. Remade through the context of Rodin's features, the woman's cohere as part of Rodin's own, now "beautiful body." In contrast, the male body retains its autonomy and fixity of reference in relation to Rodin, enjoying an illusory wholeness that, unlike the female body, pretends that it need not be made ancillary to the body of the male artist. Though Rilke seems to approve of Rodin's distinctive treatment of male and female bodies, his explanation of Rodin's method captures the relational quality of masculinity and femininity in it.

Rodin's *Adam* and *Eve* enact a scenario of this kind of sexual differentiation. Rodin's figures both retain their similarity to the human beings who modeled for them. His *Adam* was based on a strongman in a fair and clearly shows the hard, rippling muscles that stand for masculinity, as in the similarly muscular man in *The Kiss.*[75] Showing Adam immediately after the fall from grace, the pose signals masculine strength despite the suffering caused by the "original sin." In contrast, *Eve* manifests not just the rounded features that represent femininity in Rodin's oeuvre (Fig. 29). Indeed, the figure was carefully designed to reflect the fact that the model had become pregnant in the course of her posing. As Rodin reported to Dujardin-Beaumetz: "The contours of her belly had hardly changed; but you can see with what sincerity I copied nature in looking at the muscles of the loins and sides. It certainly hadn't occurred to me to take a pregnant woman as my model for Eve; an accident—a fortunate one for me—gave her to me, and it added to the character of the figure singularly."[76] Liking the implications of Eve as a pregnant woman, Rodin makes sure his sculpture demonstrates this fact. It is known from Rilke's description of this figure in the Rodin monograph that Rilke, too, was aware of the pregnancy and appreciated its effect; for him she is "bent as if listening over her own body, in which a foreign future is beginning to stir. And it is as if the gravity of this future were acting on the woman's senses, pulling her down into the deep humble servitude of motherhood."[77]

To be sure, the idea of pregnancy is hardly foreign to the story of Eve, but Rodin's emphasis is nonetheless telling. One way to understand the lack of an apple motif is in terms of the traditional exegesis of the biblical story, according to which Eve becomes pregnant after eating of the tree of knowledge causes Adam and Eve to recognize their nakedness (and difference). It is part of Eve's punishment upon banishment from the garden that she should desire her husband despite being cursed with pain in childbirth.[78] Rodin's figure distills these cultural myths of creation (and their traditions of misogynist interpretation) into a bodily cipher for the recognition and functioning of sexual difference. As a pregnant figure, she not only presents the outcome of female desire, but also confirms paternity and becomes a signifier for the "phallus."[79] What's more, except for the title, this figure could stand for any woman. No wonder Rodin found pregnancy a singular contribution to this *Eve.*

Given Rilke's dependence on the museum culture of his day, it is remarkable that, precisely during this time, he increasingly shows a sense of gendered being very different from Rodin's. Rilke's early writing deploys gender constructs quite similar to prevailing late nineteenth-century gender conventions.[80] Many Rilkean male figures of this period are clearly strong, masculine, and "hard" like Rodin's *Adam,* whereas the female figures tend to be ethereal and frail.[81] Yet by the time the *Neue Gedichte* and *Malte* are being completed, the gender constructs in Rilke's writing shift in complex and fascinating ways. From 1903 on, Rilke's fiction, poetry, and letters show him questioning strict heterosexual binaries in favor of a model of creativity predicated on a male appreciation and appropriation of certain traditionally feminine characteristics such as selflessness and renunciation, exemplified for Rilke by figures such as Gaspara Stampa, Mariana Alcoforado, Louise Labé, Bettina Brentano, and Sappho.[82]

Particularly in his novel *Malte,* Rilke explores whether a male identification with the feminine can achieve a new language that holds out the promise of transcending the fragmentation and loss of meaning in modern life. Recent readings have argued that Rilke's novelistic exploration is valuable, paradoxically, for its ultimate inability to achieve its transcendent goal and reveals in the process how even an apparently appreciative male appropriation of femininity fails to address the problems of creativity and meaning in modernity.[83] Indeed, by the end of the novel, Malte abandons his identification with the feminine and rewrites the biblical parable of the prodigal son as the one who loves but is not loved. This rewriting shifts Malte's identification from a female voice back to a male voice, exposing a crisis of modern masculinity behind the aesthetic deployment of femininity.[84] In his treatment of Rodin's female and male figures, Rilke tends to present gender relationally, complicating essentialist notions of gender and sexuality that Rodin's sculpture seems to support.

The interest in Rilke's exposure of the relational operations of gender lies primarily in showing that it can be explained in terms of the museal imaginary. There has been considerable documentation of the relationship between Rilke's (gendered) experience of the modern cityscape and his growing divergence from Rodin and other contemporaries on questions of gender,[85] and this work is valuable because it leaves little doubt as to how indispensable gendered categories are for illuminating the particularity of Rilke's writing in this period. I wish to highlight two aspects that enable us to deepen the understanding of the relationship of gender to Rilke's museal gaze, especially the ability of gender to engage with processes of fragmentation.

One thing that stands out about Rilke is that, as a male artist, he is able to have uncomplicated access to public spaces of exhibition and the street that women artists who moved in the same artistic circles as Rilke, for instance, Gwen John and Marie Bashkirtseff, could not visit alone without being harassed and challenged.[86] Yet Rilke's ability to act as a male *flâneur* seems to have been compromised by neuroses and personal exigencies that, in all probability, were related to a life history of gender ambiguity going all the way back to his having spent his formative years dressing as a girl named Sophie.[87] Constantly reflecting on what thoughts and fragile acts of looking were necessary to keep people and objects from becoming uncontrollably close and menacing, Rilke described the streets and other public spaces as depicting a male gaze turned upon itself in an effort to create nonthreatening conditions.

As a means of clarifying how that inwardly turned gaze operates, it can be said that attaining these nonthreatening conditions means that Rilke and his fictional alter-ego Malte must attempt to come to terms with a childhood that was never resolved, by using techniques practiced in Rodin's Paris. As Andreas Huyssen has perceptively argued, Malte's fragmenting experience of Paris and its people (the woman whose face comes off in her hands, the recognition of the wall of a demolished house, the trams driving over and through him in his bed) can be seen as triggering recollections of a childhood full of fragmentation.[88] The well-known scenes of the hand coming out of the wall as Malte seeks his pencil, his dressing up before the mirror, and Malte's diseases, among others, involve a fragmenting and deformation of the male body that Malte rediscovers under the pressures of modernity. These perceptions of a fragmenting world affect not only Malte's experience of himself, but also his view of others with significance in his life. Indeed, relatives and strangers alike seem to be going to pieces all around Malte.[89] An especially revealing case appears when Malte suddenly dredges up a fragment of his past by reassembling the features of his deceased mother's face in the face of his mother's cousin, Mathilde Brahe:

> The longer I observed [Mathilde Brahe], the more I found all the fine features in her face that I had been unable to remember since the death of my mother. Only now, since I have seen Mathilde Brahe daily, did I know again how the deceased woman looked; indeed, I knew it for the first time. Only now did an image of the dead woman compose itself in me, that image that accompanies me everywhere, made up of hundreds and hundreds of details [*Einzelheiten*]. It later became clear to me that all the details that

> defined my mother's face were really there in Miss Brahe's face, only they seemed as if a foreign face had pushed itself between them, pushing them apart so that they were no longer in contact with each other.[90]

In this representative scene, a process of fragmentation and combination provides the means by which Malte constitutes the memory of his mother's face for the first time since her passing. Crucially, the memory of his dead mother is constituted in Malte as a backward temporal projection as a function of his looking. The projection comes into being by fragmenting the body of another and recognizing a coherent pattern that is presumed to be prior (thus the foreign face distorts the integrity of the "original" face). Though it is produced in the present, the story that emerges from this recognition takes the form of a "retrospective prophecy" or "just so" story, in which the present very often feels like the necessary outcome of past conditions.[91]

The operations of fragmentation and backtelling are what warrant discussion of this and similar scenes in *Malte* most at this point, particularly since Huyssen supplies an excellent overall analysis of how Malte's artistic strategies pursue the illusion of overcoming the splits and ruptures of modern (masculine) existence.[92] It remains an unanswered question, however, as to why Malte's memory techniques represent an important variation of an aesthetic method whose contours bear the same shape as the modern museum's imaginary.[93] Indeed, Malte's memory emerges within him in the manner one would expect from an application of Rilke's museum gaze, with his memory becoming recognizable as conditions are recognized in the external object. What is the relationship of the fragmenting gaze and backward temporal projection to the museum gaze discussed earlier? And how does the museum gaze figure in Rilkean projects of transcending the crisis of fragmented male identity?

To illuminate how Rilke's techniques of fragmentation and backward projection exploit museum discourses, it is productive to revisit Rodin's studio-museums, where fragmentation features as a privileged mode in the artistic process. Previous analyses of Rilke's understanding of Rodin's process of fragmentation have ignored its dependence on "retrospective prophecies" or "backtelling" regulated by a museal dialectic of petrification and reanimation. I see this dynamic corresponding to the dialectic described in Adorno's memorable essay, "Valéry Proust Museum." For Adorno, art museums in the early twentieth century represent the place where art, severed from the fabric of human society by the effects of exchange value and circulation, loses organic meaning and dies for humanity.

At the same time, art museums, by virtue of being rarified spaces removed from a world increasingly dominated by commodities, remain practically the only places in capitalistic society that permit humanity the kind of interaction that brings the autonomous artwork back to life, at least for the individual viewer. I see the latter, backtelling, as an invention of a post hoc "just so" story that specifies the conditions that seem to account for the past and present relationships between a set of objects or fragments.[94] In light of these museum dynamics, certain features of Rilke's thinking and poetry become more comprehensible, including the ability of his poetry to provide, as he once expressed to Lou Andreas-Salomé, a reality that was more real and more preferable than unmediated experience.[95] As a meaningful expression of the museum function of Rilke's day, it makes sense that the *Neue Gedichte* would operate as a precise analog to actual museum spaces.

In Rilke's encounters with Rodin and the studio-museums, there is a constant sense that Rilke paid particular attention to Rodin's ability to produce huge numbers of works by breaking up the bodies of whole figures and reassembling the fragments in new works that isolated the body's parts. In his day Rodin enjoyed a reputation for sadism, for his figures retain the marks of his sawing and chopping off limbs, heads, and other vital organs. Albert Elsen quotes an account of one incident that Ambrose Vollard observed during a visit to Rodin's studio:

> Standing outside the atelier door, he heard a woman's voice imploring Rodin to "have mercy for such a charming head." . . . Rodin opened the door. "He had a large saber in his hand. On the floor, in the studio one saw the debris of statues, hands, decapitated heads. . . . Rodin spied one of the statues, the only one that remained intact. . . . He wielded his sword. The head fell." One of the assembled guests picked up a fallen head, and Rodin took it in his own hands: "How beautiful it is without the body!"[96]

Rodin clearly made little effort to obscure his particularly violent method from his guests. The incident described above was staged for public consumption, to demonstrate his belief that violence, linked to the female body, could yield something beautiful. A plethora of Rodin's female figures betray mutilation, leaving no doubt as to the sculptor's linking of violence, aesthetics, and female sexuality. His *Figure Volante* [Flying Figure], conceptionally similar to *Iris* with its spread legs and exposed genitalia, had its limbs hacked off and its back "brutally sawed away by a wire."[97] The plaster of *La Voix Interieur* [The Interior Voice] has clearly been mangled.[98]

In order to make them productive, Rodin kept the fragments he created on constant display in his studio-museums, along with versions of his completed works.

As Rilke describes this situation to his wife, Clara: "What all is there—everything, everything. The marble of *La Prière:* plaster casts of almost everything.—Like the work of a century... an army of work. There are giant vitrines completely full of fragments of the *Gates of Hell.* It cannot be described. For meters and meters there are nothing but fragments, one after the other."[99] Photographs of Rodin's studios show that Rilke in fact describes the studio spaces accurately. In one photograph, Rodin stands among completed busts and a sculpture of Balzac, with arms, hands, and other limbs strewn about on the floor.[100]

While the practice of display served in part to receive visitors who came to the studio-museum, it was most important for the artist himself, for his method of work depended on its dynamics. As Albert Elsen points out: "By seeing sculptures juxtaposed in the studio, we are reminded of how Rodin's art helped to breed itself. He may have spent as much if not more time manipulating his plasters, seeking their fruitful friction or effecting new grafts of limbs and bodies, as he did in working directly from the model."[101] Rodin produces art in the traditional way by copying models, but also by rearranging pieces he had already produced. The piles of figures lying around at all times were essential to a significant aspect of Rodin's production.[102]

I draw attention here to two museum features operating in Rodin's method. Museums, of course, contain large quantities of objects; this is a seemingly inescapable condition of collecting. The museum renders each object, regardless of age, origin, or genre, as present and visually accessible as any other.[103] What results can be called simultaneity. That Rodin keeps parts of his former figures

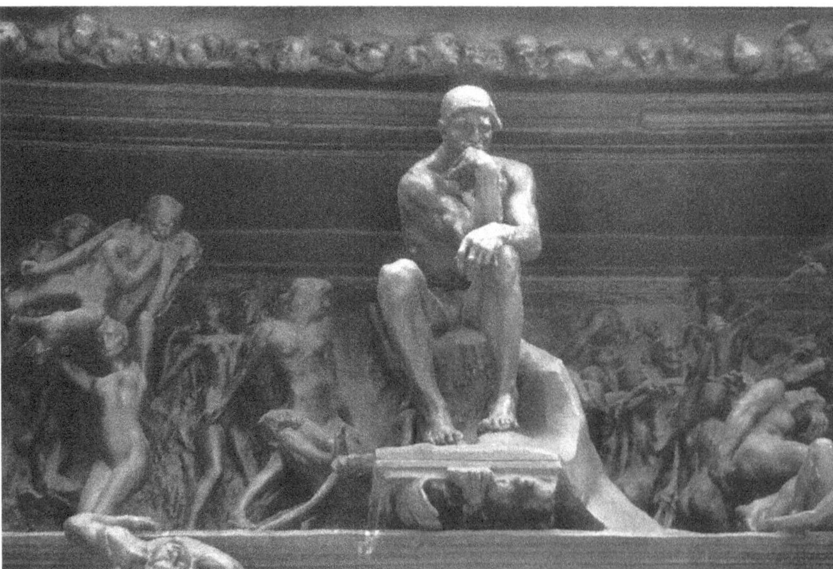

Figure 30 Auguste Rodin (1840–1917). The Thinker, detail from Porte de l'Enfer, 1880–1917. 71.5 × 40.58 cm. One of Rodin's most famous pieces, it existed as part of the Gates of Hell, as well as in multiple copies sold around the world. Musée Rodin, Paris.

and other objects lying around makes them continuously present to his creative process. He puts this simultaneity to extreme use by working on several pieces at once. "Old prints," Elsen writes, "that conjoin two or more sculptures in process, like *The Porte de l'Enfer* and *Eternal Spring, Faun and Satyr,* and a *Burgher of Calais,* bring home the simultaneity of his creative efforts that account for a productivity which many still find hard to believe."[104] By working on several sculptures at once, composing them from many of the same broken-up sources, Rodin made fragmentation a condition of production. Indeed, a key element in his work is the way he incorporates images of fragments preserved in museums

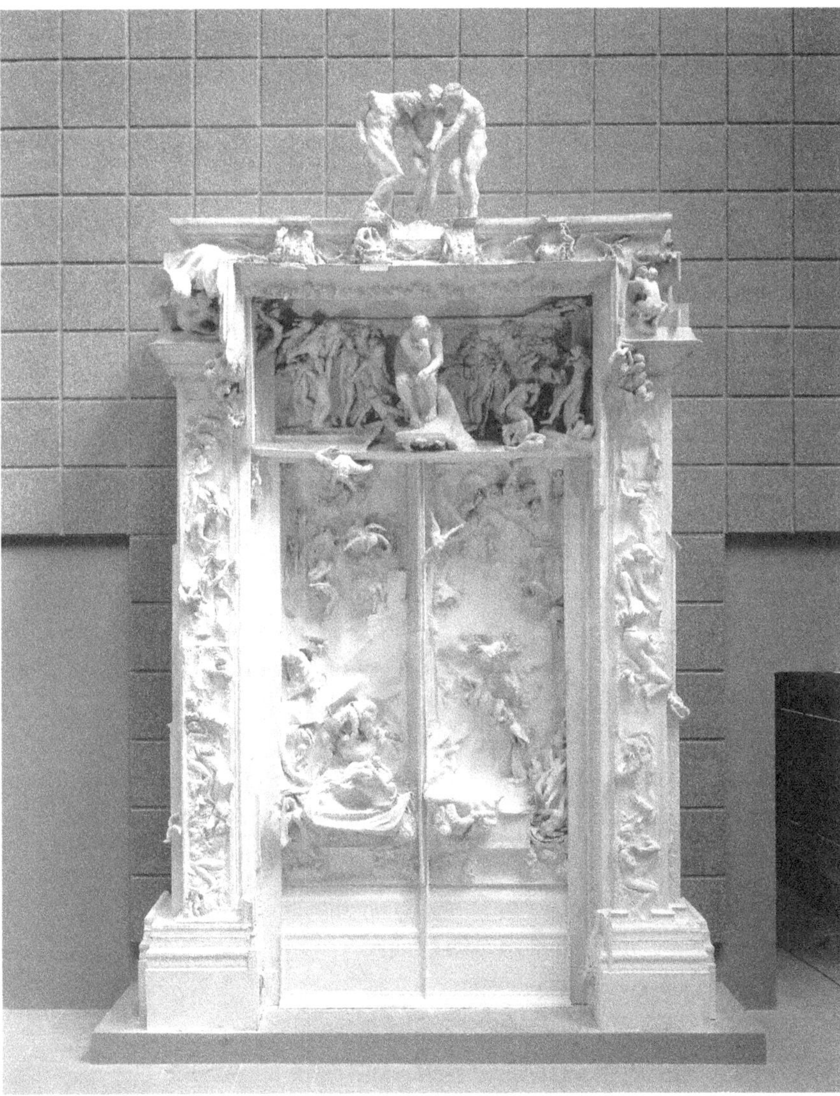

Figure 31 Auguste Rodin (1840–1917). The Gates of Hell, 1880–88. Plaster, 552 × 400 × 94 cm. DO 1986-4. Musée d'Orsay, Paris.

as the chance effects of weather, time, and "history." Moreover, these fragmentary sculptures often belong to groups like the *Gates of Hell,* a collection of individual figures organized to stand together but whose separate figures—like *Le Penseur* [*The Thinker*]—can be copied, circulated, and sold independently of the whole (Figs. 30 and 31).[105] In this way Rodin reinforced the heavy circulation of photographic reproductions of his work outside his studio-museums with casts and easily made copies of his own works, with photography also used to identify ways in which pieces could be combined, and where cutting had to take place. He was a master at scaling his works, altering them in various media and making new sculptures by combining portions of already existing ones. Given that he trained himself by observing and replicating fragmented museum pieces,[106] his art betrays a reification predicated on and supported by museum display.

The process of grafting and combining various bodies and parts particularly impresses Rilke, because such a method of composition allows endless variation and great productivity. In a letter to his wife, Rilke explains: "One often sees only part of an arm, part of a leg as they walk together, and the accompanying piece of the body that is quite close to it. At one point, the torso of one figure is pressed together with the head of another and the arm of a third ... as if an unspeakable storm, an incomparable destruction had passed over this work. And yet, the closer one looks the more deeply one senses that all of this would be much less if the individual bodies were whole."[107] Rodin's artistic process astonishes Rilke because it produces composite figures that seem more whole than the ones that contributed individual parts. At the same time, Rilke recognizes full well the violent dismembering that produces the new forms: it is likened to "an unspeakable storm, an incomparable destruction." Higher artistic achievement and a previously unknown aesthetic experience result from this violence in Rodin's studio. The individual parts appear as if they are broken out of their limiting surroundings. New connections can be made by collecting parts and recombining them. Artistic creation appears as collections within collections.

The violence that Rilke senses in Rodin's process of fragmenting and combining is an integral and constitutive part of Rilke's poems. A powerful storm sets the scene in the poem "L'Ange du Meridien," one of the first of several cathedral poems. Rilke writes:

In the storm that pitches around the strong cathedral
like some negator's [*Verneiners*] endless thought
one suddenly feels more tenderly
drawn to you by your smile:

> Smiling angel, feeling figure,
> your mouth fashioned from a hundred mouths:
> are you not at all aware of how our hours slide off your full sundial,
>
> on which the day's entire sum at once,
> completely real, stands in deep equilibrium,
> as if all hours were ripe and rich?
>
> What do you know, stone creature, of our life?
> and is your face perhaps more blessed [*seligrem*] still
> when you hold your tablet out into the night? (497)[108]

By virtue of its negating violence, the storm draws attention to the angel figure in the first stanza, breaking the angel out of its cathedral surroundings just as in Rodin's studio the individual body parts are broken free of the "bodies" to which they belong. The enjambment between the two quatrains duplicates this action, disrupting the flow of the sentence and placing emphasis on the angel that appears in the first line of the second quatrain.

At the same time, the angel figure itself is a concatenation of other parts. Following Rilke's vision, one is made to see that the smiling angel "has one mouth, fashioned from a hundred mouths:" (6, 497), so that just one fragment of the angel, the mouth, coalesces out of many mouths. Similarly, one sentence runs through the two quatrains and the first tercet of the sonnet, which grammatically pulls together sections that are traditionally self-enclosed. So "L'Ange du Meridien" shows both sides of the compositional process that Rilke learns from Rodin, worked out in terms of his linguistic medium.[109] The enjambment and the storm break apart contexts otherwise experienced as continuities, a grammatical sentence and the cathedral environment. In tension with this breaking apart, the figure of the angel and the grammar show a (re)assembling of individual parts. The breaking out of traditional forms like the sonnet receives greater weight, though, insofar as the last tercet ends with questions whose answers the poem cannot contain.

It is possible to read this and the other cathedral poems as a commentary on the poet's learning to see as a search for meaning, starting with the fact that the cathedral formed a privileged site for Rodin's tutelage of Rilke. As Rilke reported to his wife, Rodin was explaining Gothic art to Rilke as they walked through the town of Chartres on the way to the cathedral that seemed to grow from its midst (Fig. 32):

> When, however, we reached the cathedral, a wind came unexpectedly around . . . the corner of the angels and bitterly cut through

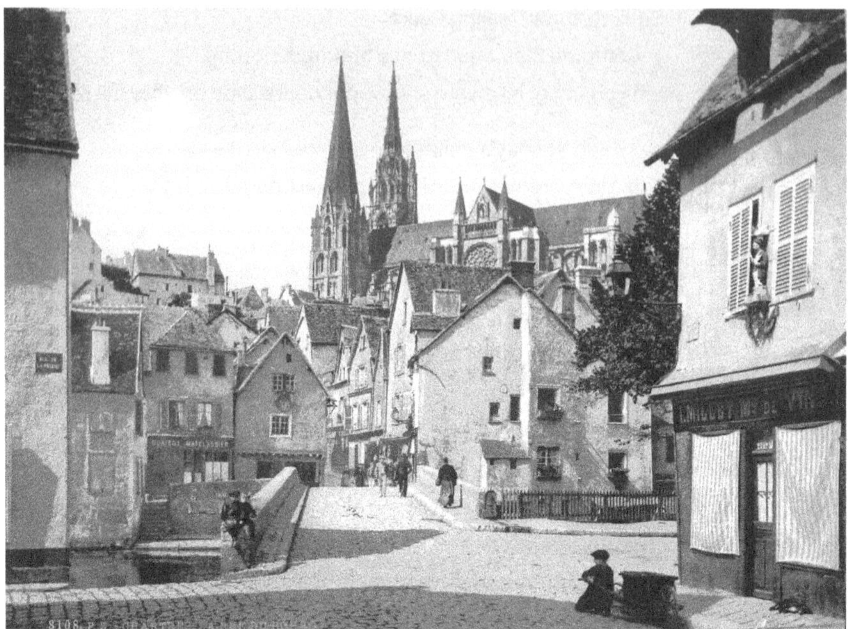

Figure 32 The market street, Chartres, France, ca. 1890–1900. The cathedral seemed to emerge organically from the small town of Chartres. Photomechanical print: photochrome, color. Title from the Detroit Publishing Co., Catalogue J—foreign section, Detroit: Detroit Publishing Company, 1905. Print no. "8108." Library of Congress: LC-DIG-ppmsc-04994, LOT 13418, no. 088.

> us. "Oh," I said, "a storm is coming." "But you just do not know," the master said, "there is always wind blowing around the great cathedrals. They are always accompanied by bad and agitated gusts that are tormented by the [architectural] grandeur. It is the air that drops down the contreforts, and it drops from such height and all around the cathedral."[110]

The effect of the cathedral architecture on the airflow is explained in front of the angel. Just as in Rilke's poem (3–4; 497), in this letter the air drops around the cathedral. Attention is drawn to the angel: "[A]nd in this errant wind we stood like the damned in comparison to the angel, who held his face to the sun that he always saw."[111] In the poem, moreover, the contrast between damned mortals and the immortal sculpture is maintained, even though the terms are redeployed (sun becomes night) as the angel is queried about the modern human condition: "[W]hat do you know, stone creature, of our life? / and is your face perhaps more blessed [*seligrem*] still / when you hold your tablet into the night" (497, 14).[112] The unusual comparative "more blessed" creates a feeling of unease that is not present in the letter. The anxiety of the "nighttime" modern condition is further underscored when the poem asks whether the angel, secure in its immortality, would appear even more blessed when peering into mortal existence.

Rilke's turning to the cathedral and its past for answers about the anguished and increasingly fragmented human present is itself one of the lessons he learned. For Rilke, the cathedral and its sculptures made the anxieties created by the coherent medieval belief system visible.[113] Forming the basis of a common system of reference, the hypostatization of these anxieties was believed to further community and belonging. With no recourse to a coherent belief system and few possibilities for materializing contemporary anxieties, urbanized modernity faced a vacuum of meaning, or nihility, that acutely plagued Rilke. The description of Rilke's experience in the Louvre is a vivid example of the effect of this void on Rilke's sense of self, as are the many neurotic episodes triggered by the urban environment in *Malte.*

According to Rilke, Rodin had discovered a law by which artists could find an organic necessity and make modern anxieties visible. This process revealed this meaning in the bare human form: "Here there was no disguising it, here it went unguarded where it was remiss, behind the backdrop of clothing. Here he found the world of his time as he had recognized that of the medieval world in its cathedrals: collected around a mysterious darkness, held together by an organism, adapted and made serviceable to it."[114] Like his use of the Dürer drawing in the Louvre to stand in for the bounded self, Rilke sees the human form in analogy to the cathedral, as a collection constituted by an organic principle of meaning. Rilke pushes his analogy so far as to claim that "the human being had become a church, and there were thousands and thousands of churches, none like the other and each alive. The task was to show that they were all of one God."[115]

By declaring the human being a church, Rilke seems to invest the human body with a divine presence (an aura) as a manifestation of life. But this divine investment does not unify the human subject and the world in the sense of Stifter's *sanftes Gesetz* (gentle law)—far from it. Here the countless manifestations of unique human subjectivity confound anything like a universal expression of human experience. Rather, only at the level of separate parts of the body can one ascertain a law (*Gesetz*) that applies to all animate and inanimate things. This law is a quality of surface (*Oberfläche* or *modelé*) that allows "infinitely many intersections of light with the object."[116] When the surface allows this play of light, no matter how small or fragmentary, the object has *Leben* [life].[117] This is the quality of surface seen in the poem "Archaïscher Torso Apollos" [Archaic Torso of Apollo] and "Der Panther" [The Panther]. In his Rodin monograph Rilke justifies the fragment as follows: "Rodin knows that the body consists of nothing but scenes of life, of life that at every point can become individual and great. Rodin has the power to give any independence and fullness of a whole thing to one part of this wide resonating surface."[118] This focus on surfaces bursts the bounds of sculpture traditionally imposed by the human body by ascribing wholeness to its fragments.[119] If Rodin's fragments make the modern condition visible, as Rilke claims, then they can be seen in relation to a fundamentally fragmented, decentered sense of self. To use the words of Georg Simmel, the reassembled fragments are the dynamic mirror of modern society.

The conception of self related through the physical surface indicates that perceived boundaries are transmutable so long as the viewer can detect what has "life." Justified only by the "life" of the surface, entities formally "outside" the body proper can merge meaningfully with those "inside," and by the same token, individual parts can stand on their own: "As the human body represents an entity for Rodin only as long as a common movement (internal or external) holds all of its parts and forces in array, thus in contrast other parts of different bodies that, due to an internal necessity, cling together can also be integrated into one organism. A hand that lies on the shoulder or thigh of another no longer completely belongs to the body from which it came."[120] Rilke practices a mode of vision that transfers the hand of one body to the shoulder of another in order to make sense of the arrangement. By reconstituting the hand and shoulder as "belonging" together, Rilke differentiates them from the bodies deemed no longer to be integral, despite their biological connectedness. Crucially, it is the viewer and creator of the fusions who finds the proper context for perceiving the life latent in the various objects.

The activity of the Rilkean viewer reanimates reified fragments by establishing the proper context for the elements that belong together. Thus while the initial stages of Rilke's method are dependent on reification—for example, when he takes the Dürer drawing to constitute his self or when the human body is taken to have metaphysical properties—the fragmentation and drawing of boundaries prepare the ground for the moment when the objects can enter our lives and live in our context. When the *Neue Gedichte* capture these moments of fragmentation and reanimation, they precisely portray the kind of dialectic of petrification and reanimation Adorno saw as the hallmark of the early twentieth-century art museum. What is remarkable about these poems is not merely that they function as a museum in this fashion, but that, as an imaginary regime, they also provide the requisite space set aside from the swirl of modern quotidian existence in which meaning suddenly and fleetingly seems capable of materializing.

Part of what accompanies the finding of meaning in this manner is the ability to construct a form of "retrospective prophecy" for the constellations that emerge in the contexts of the imaginary museum. Backward projections in Rilke's writing can be seen as a kind of backtelling, which is a direct outcome of his taking museum practices as the basis for his poetic project. As Tony Bennett has argued, backtelling forms an integral part of the museum's narrative machinery at the end of the nineteenth century.[121] Based on a particular display, these narratives supply post facto rationales for the historical origins of the objects, trading on the physical presence of the objects as a vouchsafe for their importance. While museal backtelling can be tautological and problematic for reducing the complexity of past events, what it ensures for Rilke's poetry is a means of transmitting past constellations, with traces of human use and thought, into the present.

There is, in many poems, a fascination with settings in which unknown historical processes have largely done the work of arranging the objects in a way that makes them ominous or significant for the present, tempting the viewer to reconstruct conditions that relate the past and present post hoc. Some of the more interesting instances are poems such as the morgue poems ("Morgue, "Leichenwäscherei" [Corpse-Washing]), and the "Hetären-Gräber" [Tombs of the Hetaerae]. In the latter poem, the bones in the tombs have, over time, become mixed up with funerary objects placed near the bodies at burial (1–36; 540–41). The organic necessity of the extant arrangement in the tomb coincides with the unknown vicissitudes of intervening historical events, with the women's bodies coming to hold "all that was tossed into them" (36; 541; 36; 169). But rather than rearrange these fragments, in this case the first stanza of the poem merely surveys them, producing a palpable sensation of their on-going condition with present-tense verbs and describing the static sense of their presentation with highly ornamented adjectival phrases arrayed without verbs of action (1–33; 540–41). Coming to life before the mind's eye, the objects demand a past, which they receive from the perspective of the viewer. Indeed, the poem closes by relating the fateful existence of these women whose major life purpose was to channel the pleasure of men and boys, thereby giving their lives depth and meaning (38–53; 541).

On the one hand, the shift to past tense for the invented past in the third and fourth stanzas neatly supports the arc of backtelling (38; 541), with the poem's depiction of the social function of the Heterae explaining why they were buried the way they were. Together with the reanimation of the first stanza, the emulation of museal backtelling reinforces the poem's sense of objective reality. On the other hand, the shift to the preterite can be read as being too abrupt and grammatically emphatic to escape notice: "And they *were* riverbeds" (38; 541; 38, 169; translator's emphasis). The shift exposes the museal machinery operating in the background, prodding the reader to recognize that past not as pre-existing the display, but being invented on the spot. The exposing of the museal machinery amounts to the museal gaze being turned on itself. It coincides, moreover, with the creation of a gendered story of male and female sexuality that, in all probability, resonates more with the anxieties and conventions of Rilke's age than the lives of the Heterae. Whether or not this occurred by conscious design, this constellation of past and present captured in the museal imaginary seems to prompt the reader to reflect on the artistic and institutional conventions that seem to shore up identity, even as the feeling is produced that the traces of these past lives need to be activated in the present.

In thinking and writing in this manner, Rilke turns the fin-de-siècle museum function on itself, revealing the extent to which museum practices permeated all public spaces and everyday life. Rilke's writing operates within the dialectics of display, reproduction, and circulation that were then being (re)formulated through exhibitions and media like photography. But if at times the *Neue Gedichte* represent a rarified reality to be retreated into as an evasion of the shocks that can trigger existential crises, they likewise provide respite and transmit instances of meaning. In Rilke's poetry, this meaning emerges as the poetic voice constructs notional objects and environments with traces of past human use and thought ("life," in Rilkean parlance), constructing fragile moments when experience in the Benjaminian sense *feels* as if it is accessible at a dialectical remove from the crush of images and urban life. In this, Rilke's poetry anticipates some of the thinking of Durs Grünbein, who more openly valorizes museums for enabling meaning to be found in an era when those images are becoming digital. Finally, Rilke's poetry marks a juncture at which musealization was becoming increasingly naturalized, constructing culture in the background, out of sight but not out of mind. From this point forward, as the writing of Ingeborg Bachmann (Chapter 7) and Siegfried Lenz (Chapter 8) demonstrates, the literary imagination is concerned with reversing this trend as it intervenes in the museal construction of inventoried consciousness.

4

Narrative Interventions in the Museal Abuse of Culture

7

"Quiet Violence": The Army Museum in Ingeborg Bachmann's *Malina*

Ingeborg Bachmann's 1971 novel *Malina* ends with an urgent cry: "It was murder."[1] It is a difficult ending to a challenging text, presented from the viewpoint of a voice, the *Ich* [I], who the reader knows is female and conflicted but who is never known by name. On one level, the *Ich* is the lover and housemate of the novel's namesake, Malina; both are caught in a love triangle with their neighbor, Ivan. On another level, the *Ich* and Malina are best understood as part of a psyche undergoing a dialectical process of gendered identity formation that is necessary to produce literary prose.[2] On either level, the bizarre mode in which the narrator is murdered defies simple explanation: the text matter-of-factly states that she disappears into a crack in the wall, after which time Malina discards everything having to do with her. Though the reader must ponder what this act of killing means, the text leaves no doubt that Malina is unequivocally implicated in it.

For all the effort that has rightly gone into interpreting this puzzling conclusion, at least one level of this mystery has escaped scholarly notice. Such a lack of critical attention is remarkable because the first page of the novel, where Malina's main features are outlined in the style of dramatis personae, identifies him with the museum. Following the entries for Ivan and his children Béla and András, Malina's entry reads:

> Malina Age indeterminate according to appearance, turned forty years old today, the author of an "Apocrypha" that can no longer be obtained in bookstores and of which several copies were sold in the 1950s. Appointed for reasons of disguise to the Austrian Army Museum as a Class A Civil Servant, where a completed degree of history (major) and art history (minor) enabled him to be accommodated and to assume a favorable position where he advances without moving, without drawing notice to himself by

> intervening, showing ambition, making demands or unfair proposals for improvement in the procedures between the Ministry of Defense on the Franz-Josefs-Kai and the museum in the Arsenal, a museum that belongs to the strangest institutions of our city without attracting particular attention. (11–12)

In this crucial segment of the text, half of Malina's "statement" involves the museum and its peculiar mode of operation. This and other elements of the novel such as verbatim quotes from the museum's published catalog and its location in the same Viennese district as the narrator's "Ungargassenland" erase any doubt that the critic can declare the museum to be irrelevant to this important postwar novel. On the basis of the text's constitution, the critic must interpret the novel's association of Malina with the Austrian Army Museum if he or she wishes to comprehend the text and its complicated relationship to postwar Austrian culture.

I argue in this chapter that allowing the museum to be ignored in this novel would perpetuate a state of consciousness that Bachmann's text sought to diagnose and correct, namely, that Austrian society remained in a permanent state of gendered war.[3] For Bachmann, the virulent violence of the Austrian past, including but not limited to its manifestations in fascism, had yet to be eliminated in postwar Austria. Bachmann's text couples this diagnosis with insights into museum displays that transmit cultural myths into personal memory and consciousness. As becomes clear, her narrative layers events from the collective past in a Benjaminian "topography of memory" (Weigel). Through the example of the Army Museum, the text leads the reader to discover how, in spite of being officially disavowed, objects and anecdotes from Austria's violent past go underground, continuing to structure consciousness.

The Museum, Memory, and Consciousness in *Malina*

Critics' oversight of the Army Museum on the novel's opening pages is striking, not least because the language used to describe the institution resonates with both Malina's personality traits and the museum's material record. While some allowance might be made for the fact that the official postwar name of the Austrian Army Museum is now the awkward Heeresgeschichtliches Museum [Military History Museum], the other defining information in the passage, such as its location in the Arsenal and its administration by the Ministry of Defense, identifies the museum. The narrative's persistence in using the old name in spite of denazification resonates with Bachmann's description of the Heeresgeschichtliches Museum as an "anachronistic museum" and with her remarks about Malina being decisively out of step with the trends of the time.[4] Appointed to this anachronistic museum "for reasons of disguise," Malina succeeds by manifesting a quiet professionalism and not questioning the status quo. Such behavior, the narrative suggests, suits this museum as a whole in that it attracts disproportionately little attention, despite the fact that it is appropriate for "one of the strangest institutions in the city." Bachmann carefully chose the museum and the way its material record was introduced into the text.

Part of what makes the Army Museum difficult to appreciate is that it impacts the narrator and her thinking in spite of her not setting foot in it. The museum's impact largely derives from items, notions, and practices associated with the war museum—from catalogs to Malina's attitudes—being transported into the narrator's home environment. In one crucial passage, an emotional crisis prompts the narrator to abort her vacation in the Salzkammergut and return home. Much of what she desires is simply to be at home with Malina. He cannot meet her at the train station, however, since he is where he often is in times of crisis: on emergency duty in the museum.

Frustrated and feeling, when she arrives home, as though her distress matters little compared with the needs of an impersonal institution, the narrator attempts to conjure up Malina's presence by understanding why anyone would visit the museum at all, let alone be as devoted to it as Malina is. She wanders through the rooms in the house with the museum's catalog in hand, asking herself angrily, "Who in this day still wants to see that cursed automobile in which Archduke Franz Ferdinand was murdered in Sarajevo, and that bloody military cloak?" (170–71). This statement is curious. Even though the narrator thinks about the museum in terms of highly specific artifacts and even knows that the cloak is bloody—the most salient details in the museum's material record, as it turns out—she cannot recall the display's details: "Just one time, I have to look it up in Malina's books" (171). Her willingness to take this step "just one time" makes the reader privy to an extraordinary instance when she forces herself to think in detail about the museum's contents (when she tells Malina she was reading the catalog because her interest in the museum was growing, Malina quips, "[Y]ou don't believe that yourself," to which she says, "[Y]ou're right," 172). The museum display represents not unknown territory for the narrator, but rather something she prefers not to think about consciously. Her knowledge of the museum is suppressed, that is, mentally present but consciously inaccessible under normal circumstances.

Bachmann's narrative captures the mental process the narrator goes through as she forces herself to recall her suppressed knowledge by means of specific narrative techniques. One technique consists of introducing minute variations into a verbatim quote from the museum's 1960 catalog. Walking through the rooms of her apartment, the narrator reads about Franz Ferdinand's car:

Automobile of the make Graef and Stift, License number AIII-118. (Model: Double-Open-Coach-Body, 4 cylinders, bore 115mm, stroke 140, 28/32 horsepower, engine number 287). The rear panel shows damage by shrapnel from the first assassination attempt (by a bomb). On the right panel the hole of the shot is visible that led to the death of the duchess. The Duke's standard that was used on the 28th of June has been mounted near the windshield on the left . . . (171; ellipsis in original)

Careful comparison between the source text and *Malina* reveals that the only difference is the concluding ellipsis. The ellipsis represents a crucial alteration with respect to both the text's genesis and its final form. In both cases, the ellipsis works as a textual mechanism that indicates how knowledge of the museum and its past remain suppressed but operative in the narrator's psyche.

Reconstructions of the major stages in *Malina*'s creation reveal that the ellipsis replaces a second passage from the museum catalog that had appeared in the manuscript's first four drafts. The earlier drafts read: "I also know, I know, the automobile was placed on view between 1914 and 1944 in the Feldherrenhalle and, at the end of the Second World War, it suffered damage on the upholstery and on the tires that could be repaired. I know indeed, I know."[5] In the original catalog, this passage does not immediately follow the one that remained in the manuscript. Bachmann was not only aware of the automobile's presence in the museum during two world wars, but the information she cut also produced a stronger sense of temporal continuity between the past and present contexts. In her draft, the narrative moved more seamlessly from the contemporary display and the car's career prior to 1945. Actually connecting the sections, in both narrative and cognitive terms, is the phrasing, "I also know, I know." Later varied as, "I know indeed, I know," both phrases make it clear that the narrator is not discovering this information for the first time. Rather, reading the catalog triggers memories of information with which she is all too familiar, even if that information most often remains just beyond her conscious grasp.

The text Bachmann ultimately published takes a different, subtler path to depicting the relationship of the museum to both the novel and the narrator's psyche. Such quotation with careful variation represents an exemplary narrative strategy that can sensitize the reader to the narrative's general construction of presences, absences, and traces.[6] In this sense, the ellipsis represents a form of "looking away" from high culture that the narrator recommends in an interview with Herr Mühlbauer, a journalist for a major Viennese publication, whose patience is tried by the narrator's unorthodox views. Rather than embrace Austria's cultural achievements, she recommends putting an end to the celebration of Austria's music and museums in order that they may be viewed as institutions that erase the violence present in Austrian culture. It also anticipates later textual moments such as the crack in the wall into which the narrator disappears. As Jost Schneider observes, Bachmann aimed to teach the reader how to pay attention to "particularly quiet speaking," that is, how to discern and follow up on the signals given by small textual cues. Replacing the second passage with the ellipsis imparts a sense that the quoted narrative is cut off in midstream. The ellipsis continues to refer to the 1960 catalog, but now in its entirety. Pursuing this intertext leads the reader to discover not only the one passage Bachmann considered including, but also others that, for instance, reconstruct the paths of the bullets and Ferdinand's blood, and sections that reveal the National Socialists' role in saving the museum from dissolution after the Anschluss in 1938 (to be discussed in a moment). Beyond potentially propelling the reader to figure out how that narrative stream continued, cutting off the narrative flow with the ellipsis represents the interaction of the museum with the narrator's thought processes, as if the narrator's consciousness had deflected information that she cannot bear to think about.

Significantly, the Army Museum becomes an encoded absence in the narrator's "topography of memory," to use Sigrid Weigel's term.[7] With this term, Weigel refers to Bachmann's engagement with the relationship between language, memory, and cityscape that Benjamin elaborates in the "Berliner Chronik" [A Berlin Chronicle]. There, Benjamin writes that "language shows clearly that memory is not an instrument for the investigation of the past but its theater. It is the medium in which dead cities lie interred."[8] For Bachmann, Vienna represented a "dead city" insofar as she could best approach it not by living in it, but by exploring it in memory while living and writing in Rome. As she stated in an interview, "[W]hat is hard to explain is that I indeed live in Rome, but I lead a double life, for from the moment I enter my study I am in Vienna and not in Rome. . . . But I am better [situated mentally] in Vienna because I am in Rome, for without this distance I could not imagine it [Vienna] for my work. And I travel once in a while to Vienna to see how it has changed, to see to what extent it no longer corresponds with the Vienna of five or ten years ago."[9] Bachmann could not write about Vienna, though it is not a wholly imaginary construct, without conjuring it first in her mind. This is true especially of the Ungargassenland, the imaginary territory in Vienna's third district that Bachmann developed from maps, memories, occasional visits, and other materials such as the Army Museum's catalog, before making it the center of *Malina*. As Weigel aptly puts it, "[T]his imaginary topography comes into being beyond the opposition of real and fictional space, from the transformation of concrete places and place names into images and sites of memory."[10] By means of such a narrative strategy, personal experiences and historical anecdotes can be woven together into a complex but coherently layered tapestry shaping the meaning of a particular site.

Though her narrator cannot share Bachmann's exact relationship to the city, the narrator clearly inhabits as much a mental as a physical environment in her Ungargassenland. In thinking about why the third district draws her in like a magnet wherever she is in the city, the narrator reflects, "No one has ever claimed that the Ungargasse was beautiful, or that the intersection Invalidenstrasse-Ungargasse had enchanted him or made him speechless. I therefore don't even want to start erecting unjustifiable claims about my street, our street; rather I ought to look for my bonds with the Ungargasse *in myself, because it only makes its arch in me*" (16; emphasis added). In this internal topography, the narrator's desires, needs, and experiences shape what she sees and remembers from the area's past. The narrator is decidedly oriented toward Vienna's first district, the central area where she often shops, walks, or visits cafés, and her stated awareness of her environment falls off as she moves beyond her street or toward the third district's periphery (15–17). The narrator offers deeper, more impersonal knowledge of the third district when she portrays how a tourist might approach and regard her street (15). And she seems to know more than she cares to admit about painful aspects of the third district's past when she says, contrary to her initial assertions, that the building she lives in was not in fact "reconstructed" (*wiederaufgebaut*) in the years following the destruction of World War II, but was only "patched up" (*zusammengeflickt*) (17). The fact that she lived only around the corner in the Beatrixgasse during these years makes her claim that she knows "next to nothing about such things" happening in the neighboring street (17) seem implausible. That proximity, together with the knowledge she inadvertently betrays, indicates a selective consciousness at work.

A still more pronounced case of knowledge suppressed from consciousness surrounds the Army Museum, which, as I have discussed, figures as a prominent, but negatively charged site in her topography of memory. Such a negative valence makes sense geographically, in that the Army Museum lies at the edge of the third district, even farther away from the Ungargasse than the nearly disavowed Belvedere Palace (15). That Bachmann worked so carefully to introduce the museum's material record into her narrator's consciousness also makes sense on another level. From a Benjaminian standpoint, museum spaces are privileged in their relationship to consciousness and memory. In the same passage where Benjamin speaks about language being the "medium in which dead cities lie interred," he goes on to write, "[F]or the matter itself is only a deposit, a stratum, which yields only to the most meticulous examination what constitutes the real treasure hidden within the earth: the images, severed from all earlier associations, that stand—like precious fragments or torsos in a collector's gallery—in the prosaic rooms of our later understanding."[11] For reading a text in dialogue with Benjaminian thinking on memory and consciousness, the idea that memory images reside in the mind as do objects in gallery space casts museum space in a tantalizing light (it is tempting to think that Benjaminian thinking might have even motivated Bachmann's decision to introduce the museum).

As I discussed in Chapter 2 with respect to Durs Grünbein's use of the diorama as a means of collecting and organizing childhood memories, Benjaminian thinking clarifies how mental inventories of dream images can be produced by means of three-dimensional display techniques. As I have argued in several chapters in this book, *only* a museum—and not some other form of archival institution—can fully support the relationship between telling stories with objects and consciousness and memory. As in the other narratives in this study, Bachmann's novel needs to be approached with the same specificity in mind.[12] With respect to dream images, Grünbein and Bachmann's narrator differ perhaps most in their interest and willingness to call these images into consciousness. Whereas Grünbein approaches the diorama purposefully as a productive, if ritual, means of converting lived experience to "true" experience (*Erfahrung*), Bachmann's narrator has difficulty coping with her traumatic, Nazi-era dream images such as those that surface in the novel's second chapter.

Presumably, the narrator cannot address those traumas so long as they remain suppressed. Yet recollecting them is not a straightforward function of developing the proper ritual for accessing lived experiences, in part owing to the problematic cultural mechanisms such as high-culture museum display that structure the suppression and deprive sufferers of an appropriate discourse for exploring those traumas. Diagnosing this condition becomes possible through the ability of museum spaces to construct personal and collective memory at one and the same time. For the reader, literary writing provides a discursive way of "looking away" from traditional museum culture in the manner recommended by the narrator in her interview with Herr Mühlbauer. One way of understanding why a museum figures at all in Bachmann's text has furthermore to do with the ability of literary discourses to intervene in inventoried consciousness as constructed by museum culture.

Yet certain questions remain about the particular museum Bachmann chose for her novel. The third district's Belvedere Palace houses the Austrian National Gallery, a museum with a long history and cultural pedigree that Bachmann might have chosen to use to explore Austrian consciousness but did not (Fig. 33).

Indeed, it is worth noting that the Belvedere was the site where Austria's Second Republic was declared in 1955, an event that made that museum an icon for popular imaginings of the Second Republic and what it could and could not represent. By turning to the Army Museum's material record, it is possible to explicate the peculiar relevance of this museum—in particular its curious, bloody remains from Franz Ferdinand's assassination—to Bachmann's "Death Styles" project.

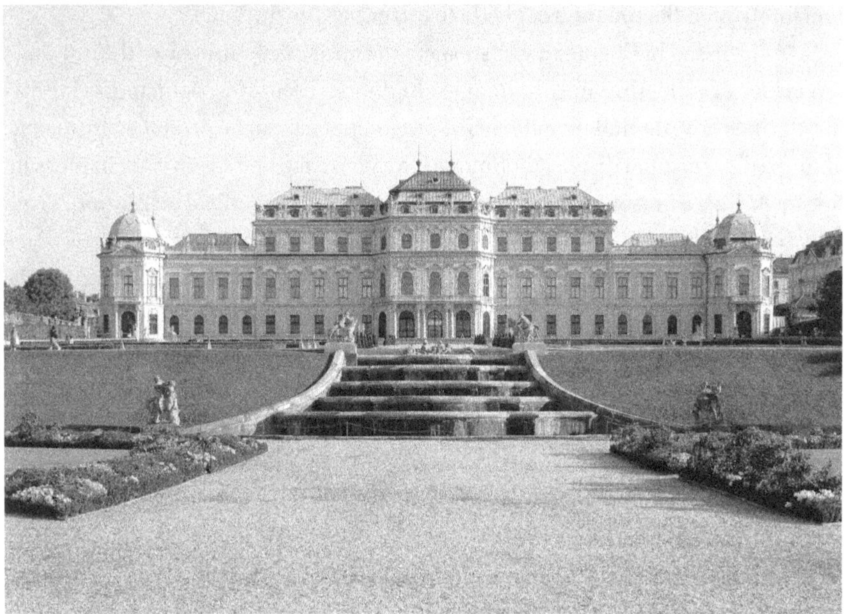

Figure 33 Belvedere Palace, Vienna, Austria. The Second Republic was declared from the balconies in 1955, making it an icon for Austrian democracy. Built 1721–23, using designs of Johann Lukas von Hildebrandt (1668–1745).

One of the Strangest Institutions in the City

The Army Museum has always linked politics, aesthetics, history, and the military. It was the first purpose-built museum in Austria, designed to bolster historical awareness and pride in the Austrian Army, which was demoralized following the Army's having to fire on fellow Austrians in the 1848 revolution. Forming an integral part of the transformation of Vienna from a medieval fortress to a modern city ruled by the principle of mobility, the Arsenal emerged as a huge defensive complex with its own church, barracks, armaments manufacture, and museum (Fig. 34). As a major staging area for the immediate deployment into the city center, the Arsenal and its museum took shape militarily and culturally in lockstep with the nineteenth-century urban transformation more typically thought of in

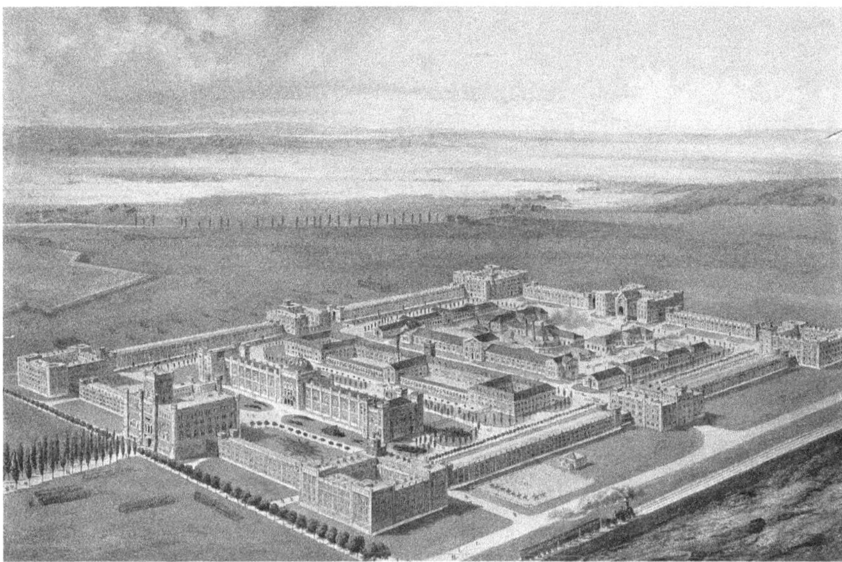

Figure 34 The Arsenal barracks, Vienna. This massive complex was created to bolster the military's ability to respond to internal disturbances and uprisings by fellow Austrians. Nineteenth century. Heeresgeschichtliches Museum, Vienna.

terms of the Ringstrasse.[13] This is not merely because the Arsenal provided the new base where troops would live and train (Fig. 35) and from which troops could sweep onto the Ringstrasse in times of emergency. Rather, the buildings of the Arsenal provided a testing ground for some of the architects who later built the historicist monumental buildings on the Ringstrasse.[14] Indeed, the designer of Austria's neo-classicist parliament building, Theophil Hansen, pioneered a Byzantine historicist idiom as lead architect of the Army Museum (Fig. 36). While the museum emerged from the same cultural and political nexus as the Ringstrasse, the military has exercised direct control over it for nearly all its existence. Only between 1945 and 1955 was the Army Museum administered in a manner more like other Austrian museums of its day,[15] that is, through the Ministry of Education, Science, and Culture.

It might not come as a surprise that the ten years following the Holocaust (1945–55) turn out to be critical for understanding Bachmann's decision to depict Malina as a murderer who has gone "underground" in the Army Museum. The museum was "denazified" in these years, to be sure, but as accounts such as Gerhard Roth's 1991 essay on the museum have suggested, the museum has failed to come to full grips with the Army's questionable role in events such as Hitler's Anschluss and the atrocities of the Second World War and the Holocaust. But as critical as the insufficiencies of denazification are for my analysis, the question of

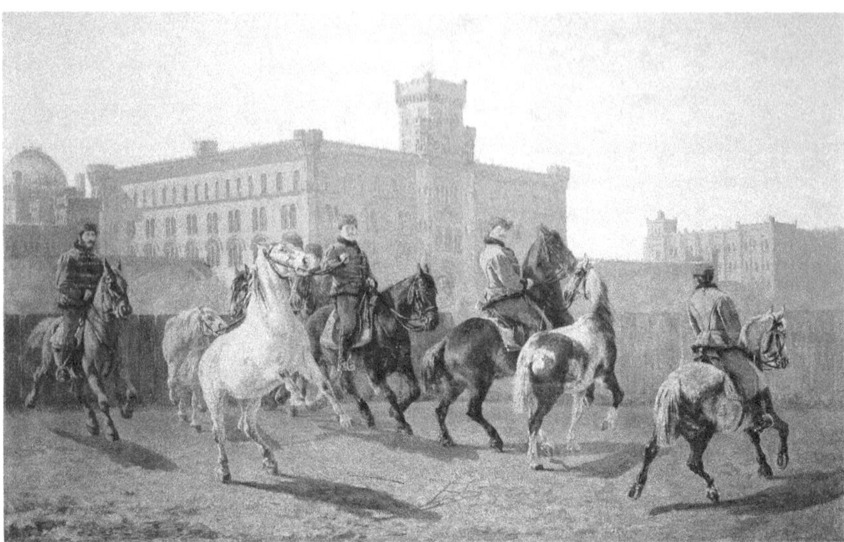

Figure 35 Training of cavalry horses in front of the Vienna Arsenal barracks. Heeresgeschichtliches Museum, Vienna.

violence in Austrian society is by no means limited to a discussion of fascism in Austrian history. Rather than invent new traditions, National Socialists in Austria continued older practices of aestheticizing violence in existing cultural institutions. The "removal" of fascist cultural markers in the museum's denazification therefore left Austrian heritage cleansed of overt references to fascism, without addressing longer standing cultures of aestheticized violence.

Roth offers an instructive discussion of violence in Austrian history and culture, particularly in that he mounts it in reference to the cultural mode presented in the Army Museum. "Austrian history is violent," Roth writes,

> even when it appears not to be, when everything is transfigured and offered in waltz rhythms or, if that is not possible, then fragmented into twelve-tone chamber music and intoned in atonal opera arias. The violence of Austrian history, and may it be that of a bureaucrat army that waged war with sharp fountain pens and blue-blooded, black, and later brown ink, has been registered in the country's ledgers. This is so even if so many accounts have been forged, made invisible through a kind of killing accomplished on the level of writing, as a kind of erasure.[16]

Roth's metaphors of book-keeping in blue-blooded, black, and brown ink are meant to indicate that before fascism took hold in Austria (brown ink), earlier regimes were not only bloody and oppressive, but they also employed bureaucratic means of carrying out violence under the guise of civility and cultural refinement. Over and again in Austrian history, victims were written out of existence, or, when that would not work, the traces of crimes were at least obfuscated. Roth's notion of violence obscured in the name of cultural niceties echoes the paradigm Bachmann presented some two decades earlier by means of the same institution, the Army Museum.

In the Austrian Army Museum, fascist agents mobilized Austrians' heritage for their own ends, making Nazism appear to emerge as the natural culmination of centuries of Austrian culture. The fascist impact on the Army Museum and its holdings was, however, anything but superficial.

Were it not for the National Socialists, the Army Museum would likely not exist at all in its present form or location. After the First World War and the end of the Hapsburg monarchy, the museum faced severe difficulties. In addition to lacking funds, plans existed to create a new museum devoted to the First World War in the Neue Hofburg on the centrally located Heldenplatz.[17] The completion of such a topical museum would have split up the Army Museum's holdings, and the new museum would likely have eclipsed the old one in prominence because of its connection to recent events and its central location. Work on this new museum stopped permanently in 1938 with the Anschluss of Austria.[18] A 1960 catalog, edited by the museum director Heinz Zatschek (himself with a past as a high-ranking Nazi), accordingly credits the Nazis with preserving the original building as the sole institution dedicated to displaying the history of the Army in Austria when he writes, "[T]here is also no doubt that an ideal solution (*Ideallösung*) would not have been realized without the Germans marching in."[19]

Traditionally, the Viennese Museum had had a direct administrative relationship with the Army and the Ministry of Defense. When Austria was absorbed into Nazi Germany in 1938, control of the Army Museum was transferred to the Wehrmacht in Berlin. This did not mean, however, that the museum had become the tool of a foreign power and that Austrians had no say in the museum's future directions. National Socialist museum policies were more complex, less centrally coordinated, and more attuned to local conditions than is often recognized. In taking control, authorities in Berlin preserved the relationship of the Viennese Museum with the Army, creating a new administrative position called the *Chef der Heeresmuseen* [Chief of Army Museums] that would allow the museum to retain a direct connection to the Wehrmacht.[20] The new arrangement seemed to please Hitler, who demanded in 1938 that *all* other army museums that had been controlled by the Reich's Ministry for Science and National Education (REM) likewise be taken over by the Wehrmacht and follow the naming convention of the

Heeresmuseum Wien [Army Museum Vienna].[21] While this order took more than a year to implement, it shows that features of the Vienna Museum offered a useful paradigm and exerted influence on other National Socialist institutions. (As an aside: such "model behavior" for the refining of Nazi ideas and goals seems not to be isolated. Vienna's eager approach to "Aryanization," including the expropriation of Jewish property, likewise served as a kind of model in many other parts of the Reich.)[22]

Beyond the exportation of its administrative model throughout the Reich, the Viennese Army Museum cannot be thought of as having been forced to "follow orders." Local museum directors and staff retained a certain amount of autonomy over their holdings and the way they were used to support National Socialist goals.[23] Quoting a newspaper interview with the acting "Chief of Army Museums," Lars-H. Thümmler claims that the function of that office was primarily to advise and coordinate, especially to distribute material captured from the various fronts to the appropriate museums.[24] That office did not, apparently, dictate that museums exchange objects or use their holdings in any particular way, only that they pursue similar overall goals with the means available to them.[25] Personnel in Vienna determined the directions taken by the Viennese museum according to their resources and local needs.

Most postwar accounts of the museum in the Nazi era pay attention primarily to four temporary exhibitions and give the role of the permanent collection only passing notice.[26] Yet the National Socialist impact on the Viennese Army Museum went beyond the temporary exhibitions, so that the museum as a whole functioned in two interrelated ways. First, the museum provided a setting in which individual temporary exhibitions could be mounted, and second, it structured a stand-alone collection whose coherence meant that it could be visited independent of any particular temporary exhibition. Important about the overall context is that it seemed neutral and familiar, because it contained historical objects that made reference to events and people that had always been at the heart of Austrian historical self-understanding. Framed in this way, specific National Socialist tenets and objectives could seem much more like an outgrowth of local conditions.

When museum staff in Vienna set out to follow Berlin's recommendations to inspire the local populace to contribute to and support the war effort,[27] they mounted exhibitions tracking the movements and triumphs of the Wehrmacht in areas deemed to be of special interest to Austrians. This special emphasis is shown in the titles and content of these shows. In 1941, "Deutsche Soldaten und ihre Gegner" [German Soldiers and Their Opponents] introduced Austrians to the specific enemies that Austrian soldiers would be facing in the east and south.

Later that same year, the installations "Sonderschau Sowjetrussischer Beute" [Special Show of Soviet-Russian Booty] and "Griechenland und Kreta 1941: Bild und Beute" [Greece and Crete 1941: Images and Booty] looked more closely at the regions and people that Austrian soldiers, as a continuation of past conflicts, were again facing. And finally in 1944, "Kampfraum Südost" [South-Eastern Battle Area] presented the military campaigns in an area part of which had belonged to

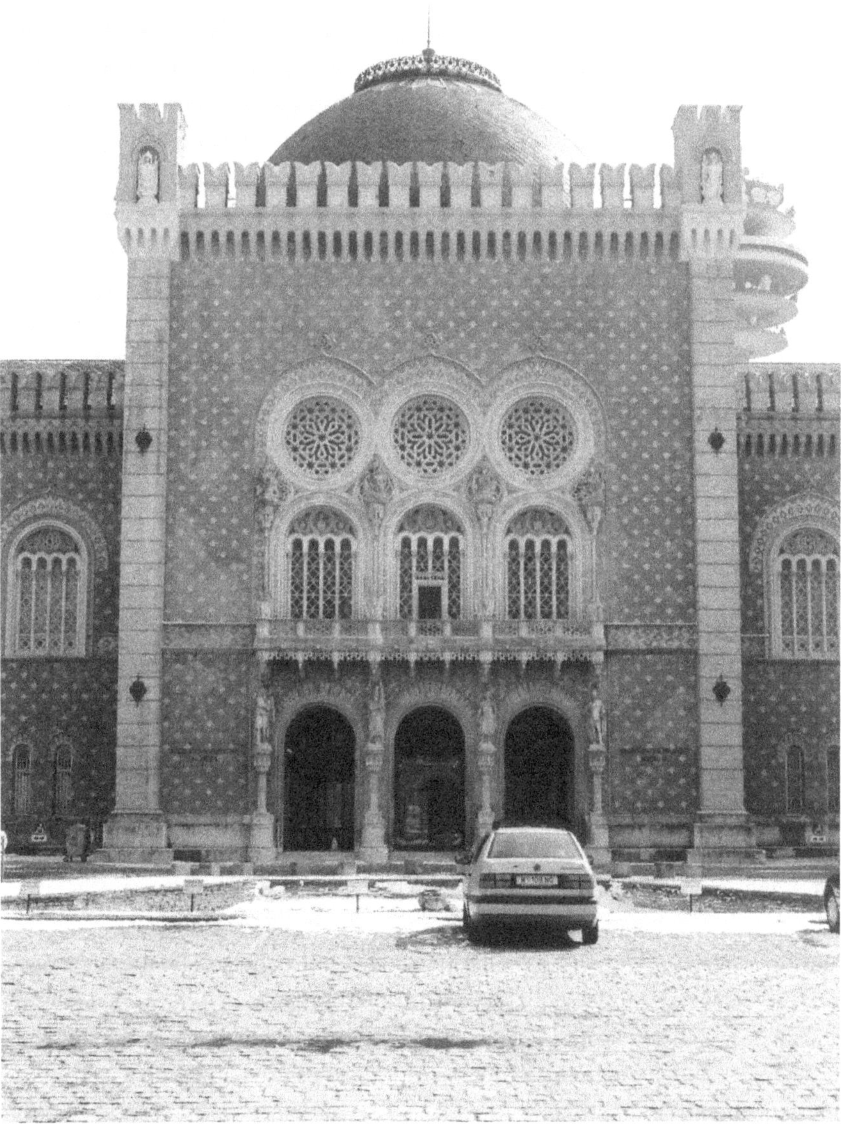

Figure 36 Façade of the Heeresgeschichtliches Museum, as reconstructed following the designs of Theophil Hansen.

the Austrian-Hungarian empire. These propagandistic shows focused on areas of ethnic and geographic conflict that had long had a place in Austrian hearts and minds—and in the museum.[28] In contrast, comparatively little stress is placed on relatively remote foes such as England, France, and the United States.

The shows reflect general Nazi exhibition practices as a function of local conditions and audiences. Recent analyses of Nazi propaganda exhibitions indicate that they seldom took place without being embedded in a framework that constructed "enemies" in opposition to Germans and their culture, according to what Gerhard Paul and Christoph Zuschlag have termed an "antithetical exhibition principle."[29] Perhaps most clearly exemplified in notorious Nazi exhibitions such as "Entartete Kunst" [Degenerate Art] and "Der ewige Jude" [The Eternal Jew], but detectable in almost every other show, these techniques oppose realms depicted in tension with each other so as to frustrate any possible reconciliation between the two (Fig. 37). In "Degenerate Art," German art and its qualities were set off against art regarded as sick, immoral, Jewish, bolshevist, and so on. Similar, and to some extent related, points were made in "The Eternal Jew" by constructing and then contrasting "German" and "Jewish" categories. By intensifying existing prejudices, these exhibitions served to prepare or justify violence against those elements designed to be utterly incompatible with what it meant to be "German." What is staged in representational terms as deserving of elimination stands in direct relation to actual acts of destruction and annihilation, not only of artworks but also of people.

Exhibitions such as "The Eternal Jew" prefigured and prepared the way for the Shoah, although recent work on the massive expansion of the Jewish Museum of Prague under the Schutzstaffel (SS)—today one of the largest Judaica collections in the world—has revealed that a consistent museal logic and dynamic of collecting inform National Socialist genocide all the way up to Auschwitz.[30] The existence and contours of the Prague museum, which was not open to the public and did not resemble more commonly known anti-Jewish propaganda, is partially attributable to the fact that some SS leaders were able to act on their desire to preserve artifacts, objects, and documents of Jewish life as the Shoah was carried out. The creation of collections on this scale was possible only in the wake of annihilation brought about by the Shoah. According to the historian Dirk Rupnow, the investment of energy and resources stems in part from the perception that, for a variety of reasons, National Socialist identity and culture might one day need to recall and represent its "enemy" "after Auschwitz."[31] Before and after the Shoah, National Socialist identity required a constant shoring up and stabilizing at the expense of a number of "others." Museums offered one way of impacting consciousness in this way.

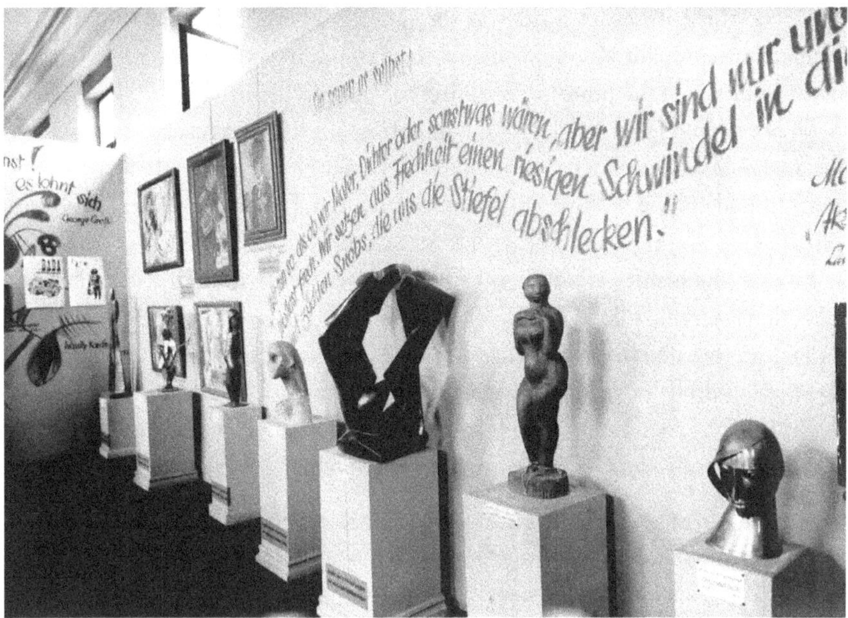

Figure 37 Image from the third room, right wall, upper level of the exhibition "Entartete Kunst" (Degenerate Art), Munich 1937. This image depicts the technique of labeling "enemy" art and culture with derogatory slogans.

The first show mounted in the Viennese Army Museum, "German Soldiers and their Opponents," followed this model very closely. It culled many paintings of and by Austrians and other objects from the museum's collections, setting off in order to set contemporary images of Austrians against anticipated and actual foes.[32] This exhibition was less convincing than desired, so that another, subtler approach to framing was taken in subsequent shows.

The next show, devoted to captured Soviet equipment, demonstrated the firepower that had to be overcome by the Wehrmacht, thereby boosting the sense of German superiority by highlighting the strength of the antagonist.[33] As the catalog stressed, this was "firepower" that the Austrians had encountered before in their history. References were made, for instance, to machine guns that Austrian soldiers had seen in the years "1914–1918."[34] By the time of the "South-Eastern Realm of Battle" exhibition (1944), additional artifacts from past shows, particularly "Greece and Crete," also become embedded into a historical framework where blood and history have the greatest purchase: "The south-east region, soil that has been drenched in blood for centuries, has been linked to the history of German warfare for a long time. Prince Eugene gained his immortal fame here. Generations of border troops have protected Central Europe from Oriental incursions.

The First World War, 1914–1918, was set in motion here."[35] In depicting Austria-Hungary's perpetually bloody struggles, this temporary exhibition draws heavily on the holdings of the museum reaching back to the Turkish wars.[36] History and metaphors of blood are used with the intention of fortifying resolve, making the National Socialist cause a function of past military glory and conquest. Used as a frame, the historical holdings function as an integral part of the Nazi appropriation of the museum.

By 1941, the historical holdings of the Army Museum formed a "stand-alone" collection referring to any number of "enemies." To the greatest extent possible, a context was created that made current Nazi conflicts nothing less than the fulfillment of hundreds of years of Austro-Hungarian history. As with the temporary exhibitions, the shedding of blood is used to reinforce allegiances. Thus, a lengthy but central passage on the programmatic function of the museum reads,

> After the return of the partial state into the German Reich in July 1938, the Army Museum was transferred into the administrative control of the German armed forces. . . .
>
> In this union, it is incumbent on the museum above all else to exemplify the imperial army of the first empire, which collapsed in the fall of 1918 after several transformations in state form and after 300 years of glorious, continued existence as the cumulative armed forces of the Austrian-Hungarian monarchy.
>
> Defender of the borders of the German Reich to the east, west, and south, colonizer of the soil of south-eastern Europe, pioneer of German language and culture—this threefold function is represented on the shield of honor of the old-Austrian army—it carried out this function . . . until its final pulse: until the last beat of that heart that forms the core German lands of the Babenbergs and the Danube monarchy with its Sudeten German influx. The Army Museum of Vienna is the site dedicated to its memory and consecration.
>
> Brought home into the Reich, into *his* Reich by the Führer, the great son of this German land, soldiers of the erstwhile [Austro-Hungarian] army have renewed their old glory under new banners and have reaped new laurels with their young comrades to such an extent that the heroic song of the most distant future times will still tell of these deeds which are hardly comprehensible in their immensity.[37]

National Socialists sought to depict themselves as inheritors of the traditions and history of the Babenberg and Hapsburg rulers, thus laying a claim of continuity going back to the "first empire." In keeping with fascist corporatism, the dual monarchy is envisioned as a vividly living body: blood pulsed through its veins until the last beat of its heart, and it begot Hitler as its son. A similar point, tracing the course of Austro-Hungarian history to the Nazi era, is expressed in a 1943 guidebook.[38] Then as now, the guidebook's narrative begins with the Thirty Years' War.[39] The Nazis made ready use of the historical sweep of the museum's itinerary because it suited their purposes with minimal alteration.

The most virulent National Socialist appropriations of Austrian history were expressed in the layout of the museum's ceremonial spaces. Most visitors enter the museum through the Feldherrenhalle [Hall of Leaders], a room with 56 solemn statues of Austria's military greats, from which they can ascend a grand staircase adorned with a seated Lady Austria, before passing into the Ruhmeshalle. In the Nazi era, visitors encountered a number of important micronarratives when passing through these rooms. One micronarrative is inscribed in these two rooms through the placement of the car and uniform of Franz Ferdinand, the figure whose assassination precipitated World War I and the downfall of the Austro-Hungarian empire. Visitors encountered the car immediately in the Feldherrenhalle, which in the 1941 guide is framed with this narrative: "Automobile, in which the heir Archduke Franz Ferdinand and his wife Sophie Duchess of Honeberg were murdered on the 28th of June in Sarajevo. (At the rear of the car, traces of the first unsuccessful assassination attempt, near the car door on the right, the hole from the shot that killed the Duchess)."[40] The text leads visitors to bear witness to the events of 28 June 1914, first stating the outcome and then pointing to verifiable evidence on the car. Leaving this room, the visitor climbs the staircase and encounters Hitler's bust and Franz Ferdinand's uniform (Fig. 38). By ascending through past Austrian leaders to Hitler (whose bust stood "on a high pedestal with the inscription: 'Creator—Leader—Enhancer of the Empire'"), visitors see Austrian military history figured as a precursor to the Nazi era.[41] This point is reinforced by the inflection of the blood on Franz Ferdinand's uniform: "The blood-drenched uniform of the Cavalry, of the Admiral and General Inspector of all the Armed Forces Arch Duke Franz Ferdinand who was murdered on June 28, 1914—the shot penetrated between both lower collars and the blue material at the gold braid—we are literally standing before the source of the streams of blood that have been shed since then."[42] By repeating date, place, and name of the archduke, this text links the uniform to information provided about the car and attacks. The reconstruction of the bullets' path asks the visitor to bear witness to past and present Austrian suffering. That is, the uniform stands in as the source of all blood and suffering that occurred not only in World War I, but also in the name of the Nazi cause. Surrounded by the busts of fallen World War I leaders, the car and uniform become ritual objects at a crucial ideological pivot point, where the fall of Austria-Hungary is conjoined with Nazism using the metaphor of blood. These points are reiterated in the subsequent 1943 guide, with blood again serving as a symbol uniting Austrian past and German present.[43] Requiring little alteration to shape the display as an illustration of propagandistic history, the symbols of Austrian history could be used as rallying points for the Nazi cause.

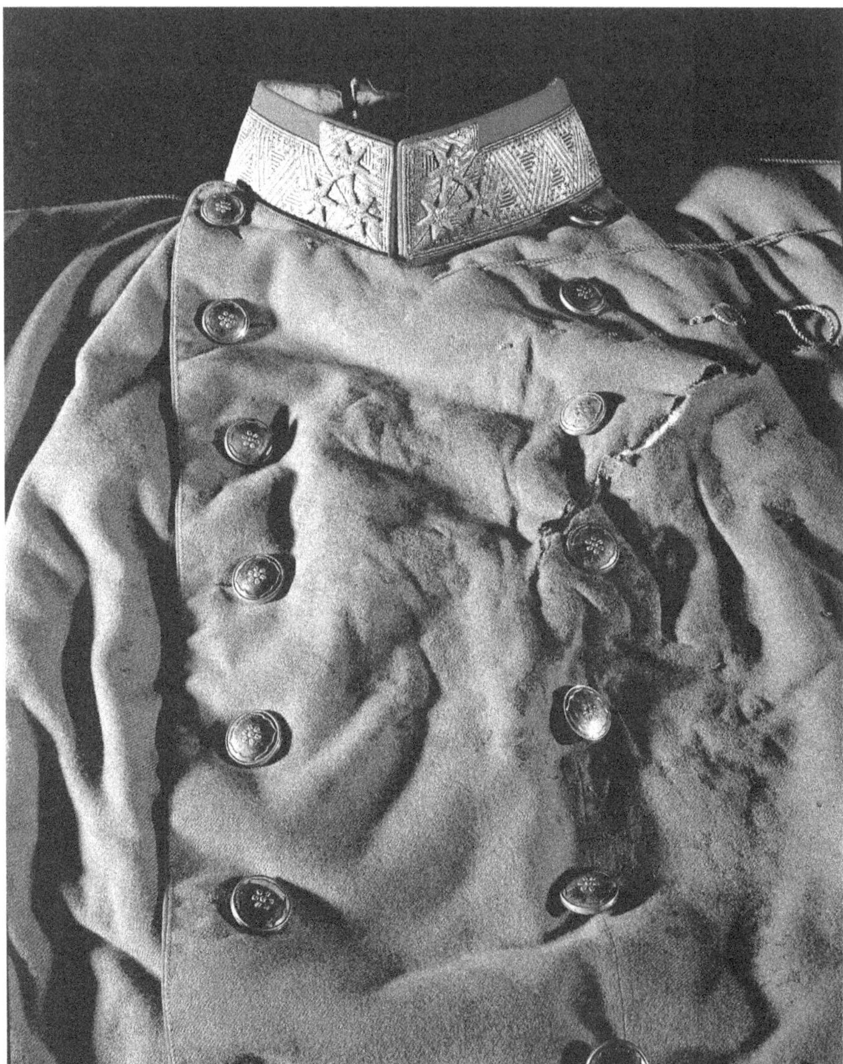

Figure 38 Uniform coat worn by Archduke Franz Ferdinand on the day of his assassination in Sarajevo, June 28, 1914. Note the carefully preserved traces of blood and the areas where the uniform was cut open by doctors trying to save the archduke. Heeresgeschichtliches Museum, Vienna.

What is remarkable about the car and uniform is that, so far as I can tell, they did not become significant to the museum's collection until the Nazi era. Although car and uniform entered the museum immediately after the shooting in 1914, they could not have been seen publicly until 1920, for the museum was closed during the war. By all accounts, the financial and planning difficulties prevented World War I material from being rapidly assimilated into the previous holdings, although a few rooms were eventually opened (a painting gallery in 1923, World War I ordinance in 1934, and a special exhibit about Franz Josef in 1937).[44] Yet while pathos and even nationalism are present in these evocations of the First World War and what its outcome portended for interwar Austria, no extant catalog from this period mentions the car or uniform. While it is possible that the car and uniform were displayed similarly in the pre-Nazi and Nazi eras, there is no evidence for this. Moreover, the Franz Josef exhibition was held in the Feldherrenhalle and the Ruhmeshalle. Only in later accounts, for instance, the 1960 catalog, does the car receive mention as resting in Feldherrenhalle from 1914 to 1944.[45] Whatever feelings might have been stimulated for visitors by the car and uniform, curators seem not to have explicitly elicited reactions to these objects prior to 1938. Only in the Nazi era, when they formed the ritual core of the museum, did these objects begin to symbolize particular sentiments and worldviews.

The career of these artifacts has not abated to this day, with guides and museum directors alike still referring to them as a "high point of any museum tour." In Gerhard Roth's 1991 account, for instance, museum guides still attempt to bring the flow of Ferdinand's blood to life in the mind's eye:

> "The first shot penetrated the right side wall [of the car] and killed the wife of the heir to the throne. . . . Immediately, however, the crack of the second shot was heard that hit the heir in the throat and ripped his artery to shreds. Using your own imagination you can imagine what the first shot brought about. . . . We will now look for the trace of the second shot on the uniform, the shot that killed the heir. . . . Following the tip of my pointer please look at the uniform . . . you will see there, under the right collar point, a quite small entry hole. The deadly projectile penetrated the body there. Blood ran out of the wound in a thin stream downwards from right to left under the uniform; it pooled under the left side of the chest, in a completely different place [from the actual wound] and where it colored the uniform a dark red. . . . The general's hat has been badly damaged by souvenir hunters—the uniform is still markedly stained with blood."[46]

In summer 1999, advertisements for the museum in Vienna pictured the car and uniform with the text, "Wir haben das Original!" [We have the original or real thing!]. In June 2004, Ferdinand's bloodied undershirt and the possible murder weapon were added to the collection, with DNA testing to be used to ensure the authenticity of the blood and thus the items. [47] Even though the exhibits can change, meaning continues to turn on the status of blood.

The place of the car and uniform in the present-day museum cannot be separated from events at the conclusion of the war and the process of denazification. In his account of this period, Kaindl has explained that in the postwar Heeresgeschichtliches Museum, military emphases were in fact toned down in favor of a view of the cultural-historical role of the Austrian Army. Overt traces of the Nazis, especially the bust of Hitler, were removed from the museum. "That this documentation is strictly ordered by historical period, is not politically tendentious, and is free of emotions," Kaindl wrote, "probably does not need special emphasis."[48] This scheme represents the Nazi period as a "caesura" in Austrian history, "the most decisive caesura in the history of our museum," according to Kaindl.[49] According to Heinz Zatschek, the destruction of the war helped create this sense: "It again proved to be true that everything has two sides. The good one with respect to the destruction and the salvage was that one did not have to connect up with just anywhere, but rather we could start in a completely new manner."[50] Radical changes might be expected given the emphasis on "new beginnings."

More continuity than radical change can be found. Following the war, the museum's overall structure and layout, with the exception of the floor of the Ruhmeshalle, were returned to their pre-destruction state. Franz Ferdinand's car and uniform were assembled in their own room. Earlier, in discussing the use of the museum's catalog in *Malina,* I presented a key description of the car, uniform, and its sober reconstruction of the violent events. Yet, it bears keeping in mind, the Nazi description of the car was also free of emotions. In fact, the core of the 1960 passage contains mostly slight re-phrasings of the Nazi designations. The description of the uniform likewise retains certain elements of the Nazi description:

> The deadly projectile from the assassin Gavrilo Princip's 9mm Browning pistol penetrated the seam of the collar below the row of general's stars on the right; it ripped the jugular apart and damaged the windpipe. The cuts on the left portion of the chest of the top, on the left sleeve, and from the back of the collar to the waist stem from the medical attempts to save the dying heir to the throne. The top is drenched on the interior and on the front; bloodstains can also be seen on the pants.

The main difference between this text and those of the Nazi era resided in the explicit attribution that the visitor was standing before the source of all the bloodshed in World Wars I and II. The rephrasing still presents in gruesome detail the effects of the bullet and where to locate the traces of blood. Its stress is, moreover, remarkably consistent with the museum guide's recreation of the blood's path in Gerhard Roth's 1991 account. Blood was the key metaphor the Nazis privileged in their mobilization of Austrian history in the name of fascism, and in 1961 and 1991, blood remains the narrative's most important element. Neither Zatschek's claim that denazification offered the possibility of radical new departures, nor Kaindl's assertion that the representation is less "tendentious" than in the Nazi era, obtains.

A continuity of this kind likely motivated Bachmann to single out the museum and indeed these particular objects, in part because such a continuity is not so easily explained away. These objects were never overlooked, as museum staff has consistently promoted the objects as the most historically significant in the museum. A special ceremony was in fact held when the room renovated especially for them was opened in 1957, some two years after much of the museum had reopened in 1955. Even if museum staff had begun work on these objects only in 1955, it seems that a couple of completely new paragraphs could have been drafted for the catalog in the intervening two years. Moreover, on the face of it, the minimal paring down of the Nazi catalog entries does not represent the most obvious way of supporting the museum's official postwar mission, which aimed at seeing the history of the multinational Hapsburg state as a potential model for a new, peaceful Europe. If the museum's commitment to this goal was and is in fact sincere, it seems that its catalogs and labeling could reflect this goal more effectively and openly.[51]

More than a paired-down version of the Nazi text would have been required for the visitor to understand the museum's objects as an argument for a new model of European cooperation and understanding. This is apparent in part from the fact that the Nazis had to make practically no special mention in their catalogs for the visitor to understand how Hapsburg history meshed with Nazi plans. It therefore does not stand to reason that any Austrian knowledgeable of Hapsburg Austria's past would leap unaided to the conclusion that its most important development was the accidental emergence of a multiethnic state. At the same time, a visitor aware of the socio-political context could not assume the museum had made a radical cultural departure because the administration of the museum also had significant continuities with the Austro-fascist and Nazi eras.

During Allied occupation (1945–55), the museum found itself under the administrative control of Heinrich Drimmel, a prominent conservative Austrian

People's Party (ÖVP) politician who served as Austria's Education Minister. Drimmel, it was known, remained unapologetic in his support of Austro-fascism, that phase of government from 1934 to 1938 in which reactionary forces outlawed the Socialist and Communist parties and by some accounts prepared the ground for the National Socialist takeover of Austria in 1938.[52] Drimmel also directly profited from "Aryanization" following the Anschluss, in that he was able to live at Grosse Schiffsgasse 24 in the second district after more than two-thirds of its Jewish inhabitants lost their apartments.[53] As a plaque in the museum and a 2005 catalog on the museum from 1945 to 1955 make clear, Drimmel considered the reconstruction of the museum "his" special project.[54] Having played a prominent role in press coverage of the rededication ceremonies, Drimmel would have been associated with the museum by the public.

Heinz Zatschek's direction of the museum, from 1957 until 1965, might have also prompted suspicion that the postwar Vienna museum harbored recidivist views. Born in Vienna in 1901, Zatschek was a prolific historian who wrote on topics such as medieval history and diplomacy, the history of the Sudeten Germans, and enemies of the Reich such as England. "A long-term supporter of Nazism," as the Archive of the Czech Academy of Sciences described him, Zatschek was in charge of the Philosophical Faculty of the Prague University and its Research Libraries until Nazi defeat in 1945, when he was forced to return to Vienna.[55] Though denazification there stripped Zatschek of his academic credentials, he nevertheless regained Austrian citizenship in 1950, and in 1955 the university rehabilitated him on the grounds that he had continued to publish "as a distinguished scholar" after the war. By the time of his appointment as "Kustos 1. Klasse" [Curator First Class] to be director of the Heeresgeschichtliches Museum in 1957, Zatschek had returned to giving lectures at universities and associations on the Sudeten Germans and their history.

It is difficult to imagine figures such as Drimmel and Zatschek taking bold steps to shed vestiges of the Nazi past and foster critical engagement with Austrian history in light of political, bureaucratic, and military contexts maintaining a decorous silence with respect to the past. As Wolfgang Kos and Oliver Rathkolb have argued about the bureaucracies established in the Nazi era, the dismissal of a large number of civil servants from them did not change the structures themselves.[56] And as Anton Pelinka has demonstrated in analyzing Austrian politics, most National Socialists in Austria were permitted full participation in the political process by 1949.[57] By 1955, the year that Austria regained full sovereignty under the condition of neutrality, once prominent members of the National Socialist party were completely reintegrated politically.[58] Paradoxically, the fact that Austria had established a parliamentary system reinforced this restorative tendency.

On the one hand, Austrian political parties subsequently went out of their way to avoid engaging the Nazi past so as not to scare off potential voters.[59] On the other hand, the formation of the Socialist Party of Austria-Austrian People's Party (SPÖ-ÖVP) Great Coalitions (the dominant postwar governmental mode) managed to achieve political stability in part on the basis of a de facto anticommunist consensus held over from the Austro-Fascist (1934–38) and National Socialist (1938–45) eras.[60] Though in some ways the maintenance of consensus promoted the survival of Austria's democratic institutions, this consensus also posed barriers to posing questions about the fascist past.[61]

The tendency to promote continuity manifested itself in military matters as well, which is significant in that the military's direct administrative relationship to the Heeresgeschichtliches Museum was reinstated in 1955. Crucial for understanding the Heeresgeschichtliches Museum and its continuities with the past is Austria's official military neutrality. Though neutrality became a core component of postwar Austrian identity, the concept represents much less of a rupture than often believed. For one thing, neutrality translated into the need for a strong national defense capability and a relatively strong military.[62] Contrary to a prevailing postwar myth, moreover, the "new" Austrian Army was not constituted the moment that Austria regained sovereignty in 1955. The units that eventually became the core of the Bundesheer had grown out of the Alarmbataillone [alarm battalions] and B-Gendarmerie, which were armed and trained in secret.[63] According to recent scholarship, the secret forces maintained substantial continuities in conception and personnel with earlier eras. Over time, Wehrmacht officers were increasingly reintegrated into the command structures, while fighters who had resisted Austro-fascism and Nazism were turned away.[64] At the same time, a model for the "new" sense of democratic military duty was formulated in terms of authoritarian allegiances; some leaders instructed their soldiers to think of their loyalties in a democracy as equivalent to a soldier's obligations to the Kaiser in the Austro-Hungarian empire.[65] And while all this was occurring, certain foundational discourses of postwar Austrian identity, such as Austria's status as fascism's first victim, its lack of culpability for war crimes, and especially the notion of a "clean Wehrmacht" (*saubere Wehrmacht*) were established in the media.[66] Discourses about Austria's status as a victim of the Allied bombing also took hold in these years. These discourses were conducive to an uncritical conservation of past military traditions, and impulses to break away from or critique these traditions seem improbable, particularly in an institution run by the military such as the Heeresgeschichtliches Museum.

Malina's Museum Landscape and Austrian Identity

Under these circumstances, continuities with Nazi cultural programs in institutions and bureaucracies probably seemed to be indications that National Socialist militarization of Austrian culture and history had not totally disappeared, but rather had gone underground. Examining the museum function of the novel, I now show that the museal processes operating in the Army Museum also operate in the novel. The novel's engagement with the cultural nexus surrounding the War Museum makes visible hidden agendas and ideologies, namely, the perpetuation of violence from Austria's past into the present day.

The Austrian Army Museum and its operations permeate *Malina,* but they are only part of a larger cultural landscape that operates by similar principles. The narrative registers the Army Museum with a high degree of resolution in the cultural and political landscape. Malina works as a "Class A State Civil Servant," carrying out the orders of the Ministry of Defense on the Franz Josef Quay (11–12); these words, as I have shown, capture the particularity of the museum's administrative reality as a department of the Ministry of Defense. Yet the narrative refuses to refer to the museum with its official postwar name, the Heeresgeschichtliches Museum, and instead refers to it with the designation it held during its administration by the Wehrmacht, the Army Museum (11). The retention of the old name resonates with Malina's rootedness in old ways of doing things, as Bachmann writes: "Malina is not à la page, he is not up to date; he lets his work in his anachronistic museum take care of everything."[67] What might appear to be a small equivocation or avoidance of an awkward word (*heeresgeschichtlich,* history of the army) in fact draws out the continuity between the museum's pre-1945 and post-1955 forms. The anachronistic existence of the museum has an edge to it.

As befits his professional surroundings, Malina maintains iron discipline in carrying out his duties. Strictly regulated by the clock and by the hierarchical chain of command in the museum, Malina scrupulously avoids entanglement with his partner's emotional needs. Even when a love triangle comes into being through the narrator's love affair with Ivan, the narrator fully expects, and on some level desires, Malina to confront her. Instead, as a measure of how he "tortures her with his impeccable control" (87), he gives her only the full details of his schedule and duties at the museum:

> There is filming today in the Ruhmeshalle, he has talks with the weapons expert, the uniform expert, and the medals expert, the director is out of town giving a lecture in London, and as a result he has to go to an auction of weapons and pictures alone, but he will not decide anything, the young man from the Montenuovo

> family will get his definitive lifetime appointment (*Pragmatisierung*), Malina has duty (*Dienst*) this Saturday and Sunday. (88)

This passage characterizes Malina's approach and mindset. Though he consults with the respective experts before going to the auction in place of his superior, he refuses any course of action that might represent a challenge. Rather than despair that he can and will decide nothing himself, he rigidly follows his schedule. His thinking is articulated in bureaucratic and military jargon. A word used only in Austria, *Pragmatisierung* refers to the process that confirms that a civil servant has been retained for life. The word "duty" (*Dienst*) connotes service in both a civilian and a strong military sense, as befits the employee of an institution where the state administration and the military converge. Yet Malina's discipline is perhaps best expressed not merely in his zeal for serving on weekends, but in how he perceives the world around him. As the narrator continues: "I forgot it was his turn to work [the weekend shift] again this week, and Malina has to notice that I have forgotten, for I have misspoken and shown my surprise too blatantly, but he continues to deceive himself as if there was not anyone or anything else there, as if only he and I were there. As if I were thinking about him—as always" (87–88). Malina's discipline transforms his environment so that he registers neither the unpleasantness of the narrator's memory slip, nor what she deems to be the palpable presence of his lover. Malina's sense of order and commitment to the smooth operation of the Military Museum displace all other needs and demands.

The filmmaking in the grandiose Ruhmeshalle and the auction at the Dorotheum also reveal the placement and normalization of the museum within a larger cultural landscape that the narrator regales as detrimental to life in the present. Placing higher regard for life in the past than the present, Viennese culture ritualizes the past in a peculiarly museal mode. As the narrator quips to Herr Mühlbauer: "We have already begun with the palaces, the castles, and museums, our necropolis has been researched, labeled, and described down to the last detail on the enamel signs" (98).

On the decorative signs, specific historical details get inscribed into the very buildings of the city (98), turning the entire city into an exhibition space that signifies on multiple levels. One effect of these signs is the increased "readability" of the buildings. As the narrator ironically puts it:

> Before, you could never be completely sure which was the Trautson palace, which was the Strozzi palace, and where the Trinity Hospital was, and what history each had, but now everyone can get by without special knowledge, also without a guide, and the intimate connections that would have been necessary to gain

> access to the Palffy palace or the Leopoldinischer Trakt in the Hofburg are no longer necessary; one ought to strengthen the [cultural] administrations. (98)

These architectural signs supposedly enable anyone to comprehend events long gone without any guide whatsoever and also signal a shift toward democratic principles over aristocratic privilege. The meaning of such a transformation is entwined with the history, symbolism, and cultural function of the public museum. After the French Revolution, the conversion of aristocratic spaces into public museums such as the Louvre remained a key gesture signifying progress toward equal rights and cultural enrichment. As the art historian Carol Duncan has pointed out in her analysis of the Louvre and other public museum spaces, the progressive rhetorical meaning of these spaces was supported by what she calls "civilizing rituals."[68] Such rituals define community by addressing those who theoretically and practically have the right to pass through the museum spaces and thus partake in the "ownership" of the spaces and their objects. By the end of the nineteenth century, as the museum theorist Tony Bennett argues, these rituals had expanded beyond individual museums into entire European cityscapes, working in much the same way as in individual museums. In these spaces, according to Bennett, the public should *feel* able to recognize itself as the republic's proprietors of power, since, by being able to monitor who can access its public venues, the public can view itself as part of the city on display.[69] Open to all, the Viennese cityscape is passed off as an arena devoted to the enlightenment of passersby, inhabitants, and tourists.

The irony in the narrator's tone undercuts the impression that the display of historical tidbits on signs and the unfettered access to formerly privileged spaces represent an unmitigated triumph of "democratization" in postwar Austria. For one thing, as mentioned previously, the postwar democratic political process did not promote the questioning of National Socialism and its militarization of Austrian society. For another thing, the informational signs the narrator mentions give only enough information to provide basic orientation and the impression that further inquiry is no longer necessary. Transformed into a display environment, the city's buildings and heritage sites transmit enough information to inhibit the envisioning of alternate histories and social orders.[70] The suppression of alternate visions of the past illustrates the point made by Gerhard Roth—that Austrian bureaucracies operate through a quiet process of inscription and erasure. It is likewise a political problem, in the sense that Benjamin presents in his critique of state museums in his Eduard Fuchs essay, with museum display legitimizing existing power structures with a one-sided view of the past.[71] Yet the issue is also a temporal one, insofar as European cultural administrators learned in the nineteenth century that a whole complex of permanent museum displays and temporary installations and events could enhance political power.[72]

The constant gesturing toward a rich cultural heritage, paradoxically, works to deaden the ability of the past to serve life in the present. Part of what is deadening is that nothing seems capable of escaping the extension of museal processes and culture into ever greater areas of daily life, which the narrator cites when she states, "I am of course against every administration, against this worldwide bureaucracy that has taken over everything, from people and their images to potato bugs and their reproductions" (98). Part of what is deadening derives from state cultural administrators generating a steady supply of short-term events to keep past heritage appearing fresh and worth venerating. As the narrator comments, "I do not know why you or I should be proud, why we should want to attract the world's attention to ourselves with festival games, festival weeks, music weeks, memorial years, days of culture" (98). The world's attention mentioned by the narrator refers to more than ideological stability; it also refers to tourism and the fact that exhibitionary structures and events of all kinds enable the city and its heritage to be commodified. The narrator remarks: "[H]ere we are dealing . . . with the cult administration of an empire of the dead" (98). In the ritual veneration of the past, commodity fetish merges with the maintenance of an untouchable and constantly refreshed image of the greatness of the past. By creating such fervent displays of cultural heritage, no time and no space remain to remind us that anything other than high art and musical traditions were ever maintained in Austria. In this sense, Bachmann's novel anticipates the critique leveled by Gerhard Roth, who questions the displacement of violence through the aura of high culture.

The charge that Vienna's museum culture is deadening is a familiar one. On the one hand, the point that the museal ritualization of the past leaves little room for living in the present recalls concerns variously articulated by Goethe, Nietzsche, Benjamin, and Adorno about the potentially mummifying effects of museum culture. On the other, Austrian intellectuals have often blasted their countrymen's attitudes as museal. Hapsburg culture in particular often serves as a prime target for this kind of attack. In his seminal essay "Vienna's Gay Apocalypse Around 1880," Hermann Broch argued that in contrast to other German-speaking cities, Vienna had by 1880 already converted itself into a museum of its own past, contributing significantly to the fin-de-siècle cultural decline he famously called the "gay apocalypse." As Broch wrote, "The museal was reserved for Vienna, and indeed as a sign of decay, as an Austrian sign of decay. For in poverty, decay leads to a vegetative state; one in wealth, however, leads to the museum. The museal is a vegetative state under conditions of wealth, and Austria was still a wealthy country then."[73] Such a museal mode is also palpable in the thinking of Adolf Loos, when he refers to the Ringstrasse architecture as a "Potemkin city," a series of facades constructed for representative display purposes.

Several later texts by Bachmann's countryman Thomas Bernhard portray postwar Austrian culture as stagnant and museal, indeed, stagnant because it is museal. Such a stultifying cultural condition is diagnosed in *Auslöschung: Ein Zerfall* [Extinction: A Novel] when the irreverent Uncle Georg remarks about the lives of his family members in the small town of Wolfsegg, "How can you live the whole time half in the dark? You people live in a museum! Everything looks like it hasn't been used in years!"[74] As the literary scholar Jonathan Long argues, Uncle Georg's objection is meant to characterize a general Austrian cultural condition as well as an attitude that "conceives of culture as something living and dynamic."[75] Through Uncle Georg, objects and stories are brought into the present, where they disrupt the status quo and come alive in all their complexity. As Adorno argued about the example of Proust in his essay "Valery Proust Museum," the reactivation of meaning in museums always remained possible for an appropriately inclined museum goer.[76] Uncle Georg seems to be that rare Austrian (who lives in France) whose example can open up the past to the needs of the present.

Such a possibility seems more limited in Bernhard's *Alte Meister* [Old Masters]. In that novel, the figure of Reger regularly visits Vienna's Kunsthistorisches Museum for its singular ability to inspire what he considers to be philosophical modes of thinking.[77] Such a use of the museum is hardly what its past and present curators intended, however, since, in his opinion, they rigorously avoided collecting art that seems to challenge the social and political agendas of the ruling powers. He exclaims,

> It is so depressing always to see only one type of art [in the museum], art that has to be considered the art of the state, the anti-intellectual Hapsburg-Catholic art of the state. If we apply world-class standards, Reger said, then we have to say that the Kunsthistorisches Museum is, in spite of its reputation, no first-class museum, for it does not even have one picture by the great artist who surpasses all artists, Goya. . . . The Hapsburgs had little more regard for painting than for literature, because painting and literature always seemed to be *the most dangerous art* to them, in contrast to music, which could never hurt them. . . . All of Austria is in fact nothing but a Kunsthistorisches Museum, a Catholic-National Socialist Museum, a terrible museum.[78]

Though he does not explain the continuities he sees between the Hapsburg and National Socialist eras, it is clear that for him Austria's postwar cultural institutions bear the stamp of a long tradition of cultural administrators who preempt potential conflict by rendering dissenting voices invisible and thus as unusable as possible.

Bachmann's narrator offers a strikingly similar diagnosis of postwar Austrian cultural manifestations, though she also suggests that the only way to effectively counter these official renditions in the present requires a particular mode of refusal. A strategy is necessary that can frame cultural manifestations in such a way as to generate awareness of just how much has been erased, displaced, and masked. As she puts it, "The world could do nothing better than to look away assiduously [from the festivals] so as not to be horrified, for doing so could, in the best case, open its eyes to what still awaits it, and the more quietly things proceed here, the more secretly our gravediggers work, the more covertly everything is done, the more inaudibly the music is played and things are said in the end, the greater the true curiosity might become" (98–99). For Bachmann's narrator, only the ability "to look away" from official displays of history offers hope for the world. A notion typically associated with National Socialist "fellow travelers" and/or the postwar inability of Germans and Austrians to confront evidence of the Holocaust head on,[79] "looking away" in Bachmann's sense involves the avoidance of high culture that masks its capacity for brutality. Viewed askance, high culture's displacement of evidence of its aggression becomes a signifier of violent crime. Only by toning down the music, or by looking away from the high culture, can the destructive impulse of Austrian history be detected and engaged.

The inscription of a passage from the Army Museum's material record into the text can be interpreted accordingly. With the gesture of inclusion and minimal alteration, the narrative passes a small aspect of the museum's material record into the reader's life. In so doing, the narrative intervenes in the museal discourse by preparing a discursive space for notional contents that traditional narrative cannot contain without shearing those contents of their "fullness" and complexity. As a textual realization of "looking away," Bachmann's text invites the reader to follow the trail to the rest of the museum's record, where a generally suppressed level of collective memory can be "recollected."

Even if the reader failed to pick up on this gesture and had no knowledge of how prevalent the blood imagery was in the Nazi Army Museum, the museum in the novel should not be read as an innocent place. In *Malina,* enough of the 1960 catalog is presented for the reader to know that the museum enshrines the remains of a bloody event. Further supporting such an association of blood with brutality is Bachmann's use of words such as a "blood crime" (*Blutschande*) to describe the sexual abuse the narrator experiences at the hands of her Nazi father.[80]

Moreover, reading the museum catalog makes Malina's presence palpable to the narrator at the same time as she recognizes how the principles regulating the museum spaces operate in their home. The particulars of this transfer help to understand why Bachmann made Malina a museum employee in the text. As the narrator reads the 1960 catalog, she moves through the entire house, remarking: "I walk with the catalog of the Army Museum through all the rooms; the apartment looks as if it had not been lived in months, for when Malina is alone, disorder appears nowhere" (171). When Malina has the apartment to himself, he keeps it so extremely organized that it looks unlived in, like a museum. There is no great difference to him between work and home; for Malina both spaces are subject to the same sacred museal principle: order. A Smithsonian Institution appraisal of the Heeresgeschichtliches Museum in the early 1960s in fact noted its extreme sense of order and cleanliness.[81] For the art historian Donald Preziosi, sterile orderliness remains the modern museum's defining characteristic: "It is not by accident that the modern art museum tends to have the flavor of a well-kept contemporary suburb, with its stopped-time quality, its genteel banishment of dirt, disarray, and disorder, its air of being Williamsburgered."[82] The insistence on visible order defines all the spaces under Malina's domain, and it is partly for this reason that Malina cannot simply be a quiet bureaucrat in Bachmann's novel. Archival practices must be translated into the visual realm to have full potency in this novel, and only the museum can accomplish this.

For though she opposes Malina's museum principles and the dictates of order, the narrator's strategy of recording her existence likewise depends on a museal gaze. That is, the signs of her presence reside in her own disarranged displays, mounted for herself and for the eyes of anyone careful enough to detect them. Marking her presence with disorder, she carefully disarranges things around the apartment in obscure places such as a trash can, leaving traces of disorder that, if they could survive, would attest to her having been there. The narrator's attempt to resist through disordered displays faces difficulties because Malina has hired a cleaning lady whose allegiance to Malina's principles is shown by the similarity of her name to his: Lina. Standing in a hierarchical relationship to Malina, Lina promotes his principle of order in his living spaces in his stead (118). Besieged by Lina, the narrator constantly loses track of the material traces that confirm her existence: "Oftentimes, when Lina is alone in the morning, whatever alludes to me disappears into cabinets and cupboards; no dust settles; dirt and filth will only again appear in a few hours, because of me" (171). The narrator's battles against erasure throughout the text resemble the one at the end of the text, when she disappears into a crack in the wall.

The Domestic Space, Gender, and Narrative Strategy

Malina's museal method delimits and prefigures the actions that lead up to the murder of the narrative voice, the *Ich* [I]. Malina's approach to politics at the museum is decisively similar to his politics at home and in intimacy. In both areas, Malina advances by having things happen without being seen as an agent or revealing his position (11–12). From the beginning, Malina disregards the narrator completely until he is ready to start the love relationship. In one scene, while the narrator waits for confrontation because of her affair with Ivan, Malina silently lets her churn and does not get mixed up in it; he marks his ambivalence by reporting to her his schedule at the museum (87–88). In another scene, the narrator is disturbed by nightmarish flashbacks. Malina responds by showing an extreme disinterestedness in her, commanding her to be silent for the explicit reason that he is "on-call" (*Journaldienst*) the following day at the museum (209). And as I have already argued, Malina's commitment to his job at the museum likewise prevents his responding to his housemate's emergency return from vacation (170). Repeatedly, the museum appears precisely where Malina wishes to see its principles of order invoked, namely, when the narrator and her "disorder" bother him. The museum figures so prominently for quiet violence in the novel that *it* crops up where conflict might otherwise appear. This is not surprising, since much of the power of exhibiting resides in its ability to render unwanted ideas and perspectives invisible. The National Socialists took this museal principle to its logical extreme, for instance, in exhibits such as the one focusing on degenerate art. In Bachmann's text, the museum likewise emerges not only as an institution of cultural ossification, but also as one that can erase. Malina's invocation of the museum, and his disciplined duty to it, silences and renders invisible anything and anyone perceived as opposing him, including the narrator.

The conclusion of the novel can be read in precisely these terms. Without denying the richness and multilayered complexity of the image, I want to stress that the narrator's disappearing into a "crack in the wall" is also an unmistakably museal moment.[83] By the end of the text, the narrator cannot speak or bring Malina to acknowledge her by disrupting his exhibitionary gaze.[84] In desperation, she attempts, as she does throughout the text, to draw attention to herself by using strategies of disordered display. After preparing a stack of her letters to be found (332–33), she then enters the wall, creating not an absolute absence, but a trace in the form of a visible but inconspicuous rift. Held in the wall, she can see without sounds being able to emerge from this space (335–37). Earlier in the text, the narrator had insisted that these walls remain blank. At the novel's end, this piece of information now becomes significant, since the crack remains in full view because no pictures hang over it: "[B]ut the wall opens, I am in the wall, and visible for Malina is only the crack that we have seen for a long time" (336).

Malina reacts decisively to the situation. A powerful notion deriving from theories of exhibition holds that the structure of a display can inhibit the viewer's ability to envision what remains invisible, making it difficult to conceive of anything but the physical reality in view. In accordance with his museal gaze, he acts in every respect to make her absence permanent. First, Malina arranges the narrator's room to reflect his sense of order and seriousness, breaking her glasses and record albums, throwing away her sleeping pills and legal will, and hiding her prized candlestick (336). Not only are the disposed-of objects intimately connected to day-to-day existence; the narrator equates them with her being: "[H]e has smashed my glasses, he throws them into the wastebasket, those are my eyes" (336). As if to demarcate his control, Malina leaves only a small bowl with green edges in the room, a bowl that belonged to him.

Once Malina has arranged the display to reflect his notional reality, he speaks of the narrator not merely as absent, but as never having been there. He says to Ivan on the phone, "There is no woman here. I am telling you, there was never anyone here with that name" (337). By the same token, he confirms his own presence by what remains: "Malina looks around himself in a precise manner; he sees everything, but he is no longer listening. Only his small bowl with green edges is still there, it alone; it is his evidence that he is alone" (336). As a result of his new "installation," his physical environment matches his internal reality. Governed by Malina's controlling gaze, museal order marks the space of murder, the space Malina takes over in every sense.

Malina's museal takeover corresponds with Bachmann's notions of gendered violence and narrative perspective. As Bachmann stated in one interview, "Fascism is the first thing in the relationship between a man and a woman, and I have tried to say, in this society there is always war."[85] But Bachmann also described her novel as turned "inward" and constructed as if staged on an internal theater (*Gedankenbühne*), so that the novel is also about psychological dynamics and personality qualities that are rooted in societal conventions and experience.[86] Bachmann did not understand gender in essentialist terms. Instead, men and women were both equipped with abstractly rational (Malina) and immediately emotional capacities (the *Ich*) that are attributed to men and women more by societal convention than by biological necessity.[87] Bachmann described Malina and the narrator as gendered doppelgangers, locked in a dialectical conflict in which Malina would eventually prevail.[88]

Bachmann related this conflict in terms of finding a poetic voice appropriate to her society and material. After writing hundreds of exploratory pages for the "Death Styles" project, she realized that *Malina* had to come first in what was emerging as a trilogy. Following a musical structure, *Malina* represented the "overture" for the other two novels, *Requiem für Fanny Goldmann* [Requiem for Fanny Goldmann] and *Der Fall Franza* [The Franza Case]. That is, the "voice" constructed in *Malina* would relate the events of the latter two novels.[89] Bachmann thought, paradoxically, that she could narrate *Malina* only with a male voice. As she said in an interview with her friend Toni Kienlechner, "For me it is one of the oldest memories ... that I have always known that I needed to write this book.... That I have always sought this leading character. That I knew: that character will be male. That I can only narrate from a masculine position.... Now, it has been like finding myself, namely not to deny this feminine 'I' and nevertheless to emphasize the masculine 'I.'"[90] *Malina* stages the processes and exclusions necessary to give the traditional, masculine narrative position traction by the end of the novel, where telling changes occur in the narrative's use of both pronouns and tense. With respect to the former, a significant shift takes place at the end of the novel, where the first-person *Ich* gives way first to an indifferent *es* [it] and then to *er* [he]. As Sigrid Weigel has argued, Roland Barthes describes the taking on of the authorial *er* for the purposes of creating a novel precisely as a "death," reminding us that Bachmann is not alone in linking death to the question of narration.[91] And with respect to tense, significantly, *Malina* is narrated almost completely in the present tense until the end of the novel. There, the tense changes from "If Malina does not stop me, it is murder" (335) to "It was murder" (337).[92] Read in terms of traditional narrative, which takes place retrospectively using past tense, the tense change at the end of the novel represents the notion that all the experiences contained in the text have gone prior to their telling. Referring to this shift, Jost Schneider has described *Malina* as the transformation of an experiential consciousness (*erlebendes Ich*)—the *Ich* I have been calling the female narrative voice—into Malina, a semi-omniscient narrative consciousness (*erzählendes Ich*).[93] Weigel characterizes the process in a different but compatible way, understanding the two figures as embodying a gendered dialectic of enlightenment. For her, the *Ich* and Malina are mutually constitutive of each other, even though the experiences of the *Ich* necessarily precede what the narrative instance (Malina) can relate.[94] The *Ich* is a contrivance that works against traditional narrative by inserting experiences, emotions, and perspectives into the text in order that they be apprehended in the moment that a narrating consciousness suppresses them by using language.

By employing a Benjaminian topography of memory, the narrative expresses the deleterious effects of the narrative process in terms of encoded space. As such, the crack in the wall amounts to more than a metaphor of exclusion. Because the crack conceals its contents to anyone looking conventionally, it functions on one level in a semiotic fashion. As I mentioned in my discussion of the museal gaze at work in the notional museums of Rilke's poetry (Chapter 6), modern museums construct objects as aesthetic by ensuring that they remain properly spaced. Malina's bowl proclaims his presence only against the backdrop of conventionally blank spaces. That is, Malina's object can signify only because of the exclusions that structure its status. Yet Bachmann's point, I am convinced, goes beyond even this. While in the wall, the *Ich* goes on thinking, feeling, and remembering. Rich narratives that weave together personal and collective experiences running the gamut from rhapsodic love to trauma, from aesthetic beauty to military violence, await the reader who finds the *Ich* by "looking away" from conventional display and culture.

One of *Malina*'s strata, then, depicts a gendered drama of the conditions of postwar authorship in German-speaking literature. In different ways, this terrain has also figured in literary texts by the two authors that Suhrkamp's Siegfried Unseld engaged to edit *Malina,* Uwe Johnson and Martin Walser.[95] As Julia Hell has demonstrated in her analysis of these two writers, masculine authorship breaks down and slips into a feminine voice at moments when the narrators cannot evade recognizing themselves as part of a society of perpetrators of the Shoah.[96] *Malina* represents a stage running up to the dramas of authorship portrayed in Johnson's *Jahrestage* and Walser's public speeches, which focus on the breakdown of a (provisionally) established authorial voice in post-Holocaust, German-speaking society. The emergence of a female voice in Johnson's and Walser's texts makes some sense if authorship is constituted by the violent exclusion or silencing of the experiential, female voice. As *Malina* suggests, that experiential voice is not annihilated, but rather suppressed when the standard narrative perspective is constituted.[97] Put into a distanced position at the edge of perception from where, for all practical purposes, it cannot be heard, that voice emerges only in the moments of extreme crisis that Johnson's and Walser's texts depict.

Malina shows that potent, unperceived museal operations structure and enforce not only masculinity and femininity, but also the possibility of speaking and being heard in post-1945 society. Bachmann's deployment of the Army Museum in a Benjaminian topography of memory is a brilliantly apt way of challenging the culturally specific mechanisms and processes by which traditional authorial status perpetuates the violence and oppression of Austrian history. By locating this process in a museum practice circulating beyond museum walls via catalogs, films, and personal practices, *Malina* raises the unsettling notion that the highly determined structure of exhibits represents only one of many causes for concern. Bachmann's literary strategy exemplifies writers' ability to engage with and lay bare the processes by which museums operate and structure consciousness, and in fact offers something in opposition: a museum of the mind, a notional museum, which contains a fuller history than the institution in its current form presents to visitors. In the next chapter, I show how another writer uses narrative informed with Benjaminian principles to engage with the museum's "invisible" cultural hegemony and to construct a museum of the mind that seeks to render visible what museum culture renders out of sight but not out of mind in postwar German-speaking culture. With regard to Austrian history, it can be said that in the aftermath of Bachmann's work, business as usual in either literature or the museum may remain possible, but a return to innocence, to a state where their costs can remain hidden, is much more difficult.

8

(Re)collecting the Twentieth Century: Lenz's *Heimatmuseum*

Siegfried Lenz's 1978 novel *Heimatmuseum* [The Heritage] rests on a counterintuitive premise: the only chance of saving a local history (*Heimat*) museum and its artifacts is in its total physical destruction. The museum's owner, Zygmunt Rogalla, sets fire to his beloved artifacts, the reader learns, in order to thwart attempts by extreme right-wing political forces to take over the museum.[1] As Rogalla explains, his view of the impending appropriation was shaped from his intimate acquaintance with the objects and from the problematic concept his museum represented—Heimat [homeland].[2] Precisely because of its pivotal role in the construction of German identity since the late nineteenth century, Heimat had seen so much abuse that all conventional means of representing and preserving it had reached a political dead end. Rather than see Heimat and his objects again serve nationalist political purposes—in this case, the cause of reviving German claims to regions of Poland known as Masuria—Rogalla prefers to see them in ashes.

But while the blaze makes the misappropriation of the objects impossible, not everything goes according to plan. The fire spreads to Rogalla's neighboring home, destroying it and burning him badly. After the inferno, Rogalla lies near death in the hospital, capable of little more than speaking. There, blinded and reduced to orally recounting his museum's past,[3] he receives fifteen visits from his future son-in-law, Martin Witt, who prompts him to explain his act of destruction. Through their dialogue, the reader visits the museum notionally again and again, in a rich narrative "built" from a private collector's memories. Rather than spell the end for the objects in his museum, then, Rogalla's actions transform the objects into a textual museum, which, I show, redresses certain shortcomings of traditional museum environments.

Readers misunderstand Lenz's novel if they ignore the perspective of the private collector at the book's center. Reading as a collector reveals that the book offers a multifaceted series of "guided tours" through a museum that changes over time. The narrative thus seeks to capture the multivalent meanings of the artifacts in a serially unfolding form. Taken together over the whole of the book, these renderings come to indicate the historical fullness of the objects, or what Walter Benjamin terms their "fate."[4] As Benjamin points out with respect to that fate, the private collector is peculiarly equipped to ascertain, learn, and act in accordance with it. This notion has implications for both personal and collective memory and identity formation, all of which are central to the dynamics at work in *Heimatmuseum*. On the one hand, the collector's telling his objects' stories can be thought of productively as a cognitive and linguistic "talking cure" that operates in parallel with the healing of Rogalla's skin grafts.[5] At the same time, the fact that the telling is done through dialogic exchange with Martin serves the purpose of giving the "objects their due in the present." The resulting dialogic exchange represents an act of cultural transmission that arises from the private collector's commitment to his or her objects. Here it is significant that when it comes to the collection, the dialogue is a male-male one that functions as a medium for homosocial bonding, which anticipates Martin's eventual integration into Zygmunt's family. I also show the narrative stages of the process by which it is created in such a way that it remains indelibly marked by its transmission into the present, much as the scars of Rogalla's skin might prevent him from ever appearing to be exactly the man he was before the blaze.[6]

On the other hand, the "displacement" of the narrator's collections into narrative form enables a mass circulation of the objects with certain affinities to what Benjamin valued in the publishing projects of his exemplary private collector Eduard Fuchs. *Heimatmuseum* achieves this cultural function because the "fullness" of the objects remains incommensurate with the objects that the narrative describes. Here *Heimatmuseum* partakes of a dynamic similar to counter- or antimonuments (*Negativ-* or *Gegen-Denkmäler*), which in the 1980s and 1990s proliferated in Germany and Austria as strategies designed to challenge the materiality, permanence, and limitations of the traditional monument in the name of promoting improved remembrance of the Holocaust. The shifts in cultural terrain that have favored the implementation of countermonuments help to sharpen my understanding of *Heimatmuseum*'s attempt to rescue the concept of Heimat from its postwar ill-repute, so that it can be engaged and allowed to decay in a way that blunts whatever force it might have as a forbidden, but nevertheless longed-for, component of German identity and history. At the same time, *Heimatmuseum* raises important questions about the role of artifice in the transmission of cultural memory.

The Private Collector's Museum: Ownership and "Fate"

The private collector's perspective pervades every aspect of *Heimatmuseum,* making the collector's concerns the novel's central concerns. Chief among these concerns, as Rogalla repeatedly intimates, is the idea that his museum remains owned by a private collector committed to his objects' well-being. When, for instance, Nazi authorities threaten to exert control of the collections leading up to the Second World War, Zygmunt averts a takeover by invoking his rights as the owner and officially closing the museum. At the text's conclusion, when the reactionary Lucknower Heimatverein [The Homeland Association of Lucknow] is about to assert a legal claim to the objects, the issue again turns on who owns the collection. Zygmunt's burning of the museum represents his final assertion of ownership and control.

The latter takeover attempt results from a dispute between Zygmunt and his former brother-in-law and one-time ally, Conny Karrasch. The dispute arises following a visit to the museum by a Polish documentary filmmaking team working on the history of Masuria. Conny, a figure sensitive to the political nuances of events surrounding him, perceives before anyone else that the filmmakers had managed to use the museum's artifacts so as to interpret the museum's very existence as an on-going sign of suspect German intentions toward Poland. The unflattering but revealing Polish interpretation leads Conny to demand that the museum respond by reorganizing its objects to confirm in no uncertain terms that Germans want Masuria back. Moreover, the museum displays must advance the strongest possible case for the reclamation of this territory. Accordingly, Germans should be shown only as the one-time possessors of Masurian territory who were unfairly driven from these lands. Though Conny once opposed the Nazis, he now demands the purging of all evidence that German aggression and oppression in the Nazi era factored into Germans having to evacuate the Polish territories. Without this and other material documenting Slavic contributions to Masurian culture, the expellees can appear as unambiguous victims, wrongfully displaced from land that had supposedly belonged only to them.

Conny's desire to purge the museum of Nazi propaganda posters (645) repulses Zygmunt, not only because it recalls Nazi plans to gut the museum thirty years prior (382), but also, and mostly, because it violates his ownership. As he tells Martin:

> This time it was Conny who saw a reason for a sorting and purging of the collection, and indeed in such a way that you had the impression that he had the say under the roof of our museum. . . . I reminded him that we founded and built and installed this Heimat museum as a private matter, and that we, the founders, wanted

to see it serve one purpose only: to protect the world of Lucknow as we knew it from being forgotten, the single purpose it was to serve. (646)

Zygmunt's indignation at Conny's order ("that he had the say under the roof of our museum") directly relates to his views as a private collector. For Rogalla, private ownership means ensuring that the objects are saved and documented to the fullest extent possible. Suppressing any aspects of the world known to the private collector, whether they be good or bad from any particular standpoint, is tantamount to an attack on his very sense of being.

Rogalla's deep personal investment resonates with Benjamin's characterization of the collector's relationship to his objects. As Benjamin writes, "For inside [the collector] there are spirits, or at least little genii, which have seen to it that for a collector . . . ownership is the most intimate relationship that one can have to objects. Not that they come alive in him; it is he who lives in them."[7] Because the collector feels that he lives in his objects, he experiences a powerful sense of obligation to them. Rogalla learns this commitment from his uncle, Adam, the collector who starts Rogalla's museum and who initiates Rogalla into the world of collecting. In one scene, Adam takes Zygmunt into the cellar to see the collections in their entirety. When Adam reveals the objects, Rogalla obtains "a view of afflicted yet patient life . . . which [Uncle Adam] taught me to regard as my own" (168). So deeply ingrained is the sense of the collector's responsibility that the objects are equated with Rogalla's own life. If the collector treats his objects the way he would treat himself, then one might expect the fiercest acts of loyalty and protection on the part of the collector. The collection serves, as it were, as a proxy of self.

The collector's commitment to private ownership involves acting in accordance with what Benjamin describes as the object's "fate" [*Schicksal*]. Fate, in this understanding, relates everything that can be known about the object and its past ("All that is remembered, thought, known, becomes the base, frame, pedestal, and seal of its possession").[8] The notions at work in Lenz's text resonate strongly with this conception. When Zygmunt is introduced to Uncle Adam's collections, his uncle asks him to handle the objects, practice interpreting them, and learn their histories. History especially animates Zygmunt, or as he puts it: "I could not hear enough of the history and stories that he knew about each piece, of its origins, of its meaning and fate . . . in this way, Uncle Adam also had something to say about everything, legends and anecdotes, indeed, or 'moral tales,' of which one noticed that they had gathered rings as the stories were repeated an infinite number of times" (169). Resonating with Benjamin's notion (including the use of the word "fate"), Rogalla links each object to the complete history of its making, the places it has been, who has owned it before, what has been thought or told about it. That fate is referenced in the rings, traces of variation added by each teller as the objects were passed down countless times. This notion, which comes strikingly close to the notion of "memory" as Benjamin describes it in "The Storyteller," undergirds the novel's notions of history and cultural transmission.

The collector's commitment to the fullness of the objects' past prompts him or her to act so as to deliver them and their accompanying stories to future generations. Writing in reference to the collector's knowing the objects' fate, Benjamin observes, "Here . . . it can be surmised how the great physiognomists—and collectors are the physiognomists of the object world—are turned into interpreters of fate. One only has to observe a collector as he handles the objects in his vitrines. He hardly holds them in his hands and he seems inspired through them to look into their distance."[9] Uniquely positioned to interpret the larger trajectory of the object, the collector strives to give the object its due.[10] This means determining under what circumstances the collector can best deliver his or her objects into the future.

Zygmunt's responses to the threatened gutting of his museum illustrate his desire to find the optimal strategy for delivering his objects to present and future generations. Among the various strategies Zygmunt considers, including the destruction of the objects valued by the Nazis (424), invoking the museum's private status proves the most effective means of ensuring the overall integrity of the objects. Insisting on private status means refusing further public subsidies and closing the museum to the public (426–27). But while it preserves the objects, as a collector Zygmunt senses that his strategy nonetheless compromises the objects. As he explains to Martin,

> What I missed in particular? Definitely not the joy of discovery or even a certain devotional cows-eyed gaze; rather, I could not come to terms with the fact that the collected remnants of our past life were no longer seen. Do you understand? The value of all these things consisted only in others being able to see them, in others learning something about themselves by seeing them. Now they were alone together, the remnants of our past, labeled and carefully distributed in boxes, vitrines, shelves, freed of earth and ashes, and yet again in new dark hiding places—almost as if they had died a second, representative death. But we accepted this; we had to accept it. (428)

Rogalla's trade-off ("we had to accept it") turns on the risk of trying to give the objects their due in the present ("being seen by others") versus the demand that he also deliver them in their entirety to the future, however uncertain the future may be. Indeed, when Rogalla tries to explain what he thought his duty was at this time, he says concisely, "[A]ll that was asked of me was to bring our museum through the times" (401). That he cannot show the objects and ensure their survival at all times is the source of considerable anguish, so much so that he eventually quietly reopens the museum once the war has started so that the war's futility might become apparent (464–65, 479). Until that time, though, he is filled with a sense that he has allowed the objects to die "a second representative death." Such language recalls the dialectic between cultural ossification and renewal that Adorno saw in museums, with objects undergoing a cultural death when they enter the museum and a rebirth when connected with a visitor's personal circumstances. For Rogalla, depriving the objects of this possibility of rebirth is particularly distressing, since he had played a crucial role in bringing them "back from the dead" by unearthing them or freeing them from ashes in the first place.

Such an idiom, in which the collector offers nothing less than "new life" to the objects by bringing them into his possession, is striking. On one level, Rogalla's idiom recalls Benjamin's point that "for the true collector, the acquisition of an old book is its rebirth ... renewing the old world is the deepest drive in a collector's desire to acquire new things."[11] In an expansion of Benjamin's thinking, however, Rogalla's sense of renewal applies not only to the collector but to anyone who comes into contact with the collected objects. When the presentation enables something that approaches the fullness of history to be revealed, the objects supply something that can sustain the life of others (581). This conception resonates with Rogalla's oddly suggestive image of history as a swamp: "[F]or us history represented, for better or worse, a swamp, fickle, a dark, deceptive pool that has never been illuminated to the bottom; we had to mistrust anyone involuntarily who showed how good he was with rules or who attempted to bring light into the *life-supporting* morass" (427–28; my emphasis). If history offers life-supporting properties as Rogalla claims it does, these arise from discerning and respecting history's entirety, complexity, and precariousness. This entails recognizing one's limited understanding and hence the futility of locating a unitary origin or forming a totalizing comprehension of it.

Such a "swampy" condition does not translate into utter chaos or a sense of "anything goes" in the museum setting. Instead of literally assembling a morass, Rogalla imparts order to his museum by cleaning his objects, hanging them on the wall with labels, or sorting them into "boxes, vitrines, and shelves" (428). In some sense, Rogalla's task resides in overcoming the limitations of this museal order, so that visitors are able to grasp the often invisible fullness and complexity of past life (540). This goal entails constructing displays that resist their being used to form any simple conclusion about the past. As Rogalla indicates at one point in a conversation with Conny about possible abuses of his collection, the "story" the objects tell does not line up in a straightforward manner or emerge in one voice. Rather, the Heimat museum contains "irreplaceable witnesses of which very many absolutely do not use the official language but rather represented something you can call the silent opposition of things" (401). Duly noting the challenge Rogalla's collection poses to a simple understanding of the past, Conny confirms, "[Y]ou have all the tactile counterproofs: with their help you can show that history includes everything, the wonderful and inconspicuous junk" (402). The museum displays accordingly frustrate a Germanophile professor hoping to see an unequivocally Germanic version of the Masurian past. Unable to detect the movement of a grand idea through the objects, the professor derides what he calls the displays' "moving randomness" (368). Though the professor has not appreciated its value, the order determined by Rogalla constrains the conclusions a visitor can reach about what his collections mean.

Politics and Memory: Ownership's Advantages and Limits

Rogalla tends to believe that he has more control over visitor interpretations than he does, however, in part because ownership enabled him to preserve the museum during the Nazi era. This point is crucial, because Rogalla's overestimation of his ability to control both the objects and their interpretation prevents him from anticipating their attractiveness to right-wing organizations in the postwar years. According to Rogalla, maintaining ownership provided the major impulse to take objects with him when the Germans evacuated Masuria at the end of the Second World War: "I did not prepare the discoveries and documents, the evidence, and the numerous proofs of our deeply interwoven existence because they should one day ground a claim or get someone his due; *rather, I packed and took care of everything because it simply belonged to us.* It belonged to our region, to our lives, to the known insights about ourselves, without which we could not retrace the crooked path of our heritage" (537; my emphasis). Rogalla realizes only with hindsight that for others, the principle of ownership does not automatically function as a shorthand for being able to remember the fullness of the past. As a collector committed to a complex approach to the past, Rogalla instinctively gravitates toward taking Germanic and non-Germanic objects—the remnants of his "mixed exhibition space"—on his journey (537). Yet because Rogalla focuses too narrowly on his own uses of the objects, he fails to anticipate that others regard parts of the collection as a weapon in the fight to restore German control over lost territories. Though critical, ownership in itself does not ensure the transmission of a "full" past.

Rogalla is blinded to potential compromises of his collection—including those of his own making—in part because of emotional exigencies. During the evacuation from Masuria to Schleswig, Rogalla loses not only half of his prized collection, but also his son and wife. Stung by his losses, Rogalla reinvents his museum in the town of Egenlund under a nostalgic, past-directed program of "preserving the world of Lucknow as it was known to them" (591, 646). By pressing his collections into a compensatory function, Rogalla prevents them from having a full relationship to the present in two ways. First, Rogalla stops incorporating material from post-evacuation Masuria into his collections, in some sense denying that the history of the land continues even after the Germans have departed. The Polish team making its documentary film would have doubtless reacted differently had the museum openly acknowledged the post–World War II reality. Second, Rogalla regards his museum as a nearly sacred space (the "shed of devotion," as the narrator's son, Bernhard, likes to quip, 636), which attempts to keep a rigid notion of the past alive in the present. This prevents young people from finding meaning in the objects on their terms. Symptomatic of this condition is Rogalla's offense at the young people who play Glenn Miller records on the museum's old gramophone, who use the old implements in untraditional ways, and otherwise act irreverently (606–7).

In light of his previous pride at allowing visitors to touch, try on, and otherwise try out the objects, Rogalla's postwar attitude represents an important moment in the text's logic (329). As indebted as the novel is to the collector's viewpoint, it nonetheless seeks to reveal the limitations the collector can impose on the transmission of cultural heritage. Part of this problem derives from the limitations of physical museum environments, which Lenz seeks to redress by transforming the museum into narrative form. Since I examine this issue in a separate section, here I wish to observe only that the narrative form addresses the limitations created by Rogalla's nostalgia. In his conversation with Martin, Rogalla mentions, at least twice, visits from Poles who relate the postwar condition of Lucknow. Similarly, the narrative enables certain experiences such as the witnessing of Nazi atrocities in Eastern Europe to be included (469–78). In addition, the narrative form offers other benefits I delve into in a moment.

For now, I want to stress that the emotional resolution Rogalla eventually achieves comes about only because his postwar attitude translates into a collecting regime that compromises the objects. Rogalla's museal program of preserving anything that had to do with past life "as the expellees knew it" makes him willing to "take in everything that once had to do with Masuria" (591). Driven only to restore the losses sustained in the evacuation, Rogalla takes gifts and donations without noticing that gifts often come with strings attached. He is therefore surprised when his one-time friend, Conny, not only threatens to take over the museum, but also rejects Rogalla's assertion that the museum can be regarded as a "private matter":

> There was no sharpness, but rather displeasure in [Conny's] voice as he reminded me of the regular subventions that we had received from the Lucknower Heimat association. Then I proposed something I had considered internally for the longest time, namely to cut the subventions, to which Conny responded that this would not change anything on the rights of possession and disposition: too much had been brought in by others; all the gifts and loans could in all probability not be handled as private property. (646)

Perhaps because the Heimat association had supported the museum since before the war, Rogalla recognizes only belatedly what he should have learned in the Nazi era, namely, that financial support from *any* public entity potentially brings unwelcome compromises with it. He has been outflanked by Conny on the issue of accepting donated objects.

It is by acting too much the private collector that Rogalla has let himself be outmaneuvered. In the Benjaminian conception, the collector acquires objects through any number of tactical means, for instance, borrowing without returning, accepting gifts, or inheriting. One of Rogalla's earliest lessons as a collector stemmed from his uncle's instilling in him the collector's perspective on acquisition. Rogalla tells Martin about his uncle's notions of acquisition: "If you were to assume that 'putting aside,' indeed stealing, some document, some conclusive object filled uncle Adam with gratification and did not trouble him, you would not be mistaken" (171–72). If the collector tends to be largely deaf to the legal ramifications of such modes of acquisition, then Rogalla would likely not have given much thought to the possibility that donated objects might have strings attached.

In Zygmunt's retrospective analysis, Conny's arrival at the museum appears part of a larger campaign to use donations to undermine Zygmunt's control over the museum's collections. The museum's first postwar donation comes through Conny, which he immediately hangs in a prominent place without consulting Zygmunt (608). Moreover, Conny tours and photographs the museum with the express purpose of creating an illustrated catalog of its holdings, which makes up the first of Conny's five newspaper articles written to stimulate public interest in the museum (618, 621). Reproductions of the holdings impart such moving impressions that readers feel compelled to donate their objects. Shortly after the first couple of articles are published, "streams of gifts and donations" begin to arrive (618), with so many pouring in that the museum is eventually forced to depart from its avowed program of "taking everything in" because it has run out of space (620).

In other ways, the articles attack the museum's autonomy by strongly affecting the expectations of visitors. Conny's articles were

> fanatical, richly illustrated reports that moved many visitors to come out to us.... Often they carried the reports from the "Lucknow Messenger" in their hands, using them for orientation; sometimes I saw them sitting on the wood benches after their visit, again immersed in our Heimat newspaper precisely as if they were trying to align what had been advertised with what they had experienced. Not a single time did we find a copy of the "Lucknow Messenger" in one of our trashcans. (621)

As a man sensitive to the processes involved in the interpretation of his objects, Rogalla cannot help but notice the newspaper's ability to direct the experience of the objects. While a few visitors seem to struggle with the gap between reproduction and material object ("what was advertised" versus "what was experienced"), no evidence suggests that visitors reject the version of history promoted by the newspaper.

Rogalla has begun to lose control even before his confrontation with Conny. Rogalla sees the parallel strands of Conny's takeover strategy only when Conny reveals his use of the newspaper as an instrument of control (647). At this point, Conny has already backed Rogalla into a corner. As Rogalla says following the inferno, "[I]t was he, Conny Karasch, in the end who ... forced me to make this decision, who only left me this decision" (17). In part a result of the newspaper and of the Heimat association shrewdly positioning itself as the sole representative of public concern, Rogalla learns too late that the value and interpretability of what resides in the museum fundamentally depends on the circulation of information about its holdings *outside* the museum. Because it gives rise to his dialogic narrative, Rogalla's decision to destroy the objects addresses this issue by turning the museum into something that circulates in textual form.

The End of Object-Based Cultural Memory

The fact that a newspaper boycott could eliminate the museum's visitor stream reveals that it relies on an increasingly narrow segment of the population for cultural legitimacy. In its postwar incarnation, the museum attracts practically only expellees who are aging and slowly dying off (628–29). With few teenagers willing to treat his objects with the respect Rogalla deems necessary, and with his growing inability to reach schoolchildren with stories of his own past (630–31), a newspaper boycott would simply speed the end of the museum's relevance. Without a public to engage with his objects, preserving them in their traditional form no longer makes automatic sense.

Rogalla learned from his experience with the schoolchildren that he cannot control how subsequent generations regard the past and his experiences. As he says to Martin when they discuss the incident,

> Yes, Martin, you are right in that: the value of our experiences cannot be transmitted in just any way we desire. We have to agree, we who conspire with shadows, that others will call into question what means so much to us; maybe everything is condemned to decay, and our attempts to give immortality to some things that seem exemplary to us are only an expression for the hopeless rejection of a secretly recognized futility. I am not certain . . . but let's leave that be. (635)

In spite of his despair, Rogalla inserts the collector's project of cultural transmission into a temporal dialectic in which hope revolts against the certain futility of laboring for the future. Yielding to Martin, Rogalla agrees that cultural transmission requires that the next generation take possession on that generation's terms. Younger people give hard-fought experiences and prized insights critical scrutiny and doubt, or they potentially ignore, discard, or misuse them. Paradoxically, Rogalla must endanger the objects and their histories (his burning them represents the extreme of this condition) in order to save them.

The acceptance of this condition of cultural transmission precedes the conversations between Zygmunt and Martin. As a result, it is wrong to assume, as some critics have, that Rogalla seeks to inculcate Martin with an idyllic and problematic view of the Masurian Heimat. Rogalla wants to motivate Martin to appropriate the past and even to understand his perspective, to be sure. But his conversations with Martin figure as the latest in a series of generationally mediated transfers of past traditions and stories, first from Uncle Adam to Rogalla, and then from Rogalla to Martin. The didactic moment in the text consists of Martin (and the reader) learning how to think as a private collector. Despite the lack of physical collections, Martin learns that the collector renews the objects and their stories by taking possession of them, necessarily subjecting them to his scrutiny and his needs, until a subsequent collector takes them over. Each collector functions as a conduit.

Crucially, when it comes to the collection, the intergenerational exchange takes places between men. Women can be masters of weaving and compilers of history in various forms, but collecting is a male domain in this text. Rogalla's daughter, Henrike, for instance, is disqualified from being initiated into matters having to do with the collection, because she is too passionate and fanatical, too immediately connected to Heimat to be able to grasp the hard logical necessities Rogalla faces. Rogalla's wife, Carola, is at most his collectorly muse, a stimulant for rebuilding the museum, but someone who, no matter how much research she gets involved in, will never be admitted to his level. Instead, the collection functions as a medium that brings a father and a future son-in-law together. Indeed, before their conversations, Rogalla hardly knows Martin, and it is only through their exchanges via the medium of the collection that Rogalla fully constitutes his familial links to the future. By helping to establish kinship relations, this homosocial interaction somewhat recalls the collection's role in kinship formation that I drew attention to in Stifter's *Nachsommer* (Chapter 4). And yet there is a crucial difference, in that the collection has been translated into narrative form in *Heimatmuseum*. Every reader becomes a potential guardian of the collection's stories regardless of gender, though the condition for this might well be that the objects themselves no longer exist in physical form. Whether it be in the form of the textual museum or of Sonja Turk's book, narrative, rather than object-based history, seems to offer the more gender-inclusive path to history and memory.

It is perhaps worth mentioning that Rogalla structures his narrative so as to foreground his role as a conduit for passing down the objects and practices he knows about, a function that applies not only to his collecting but also to the knowledge of weaving traditions he inherits from Sonja Turk, his mentor, the master weaver. In both cases, Rogalla mediates the past, necessarily shaping it and the way it can be viewed. As Rogalla takes pains to make clear, his taking over the museum from his uncle leads to a reordering not only of the objects but also of the museum's priorities, for instance, in the decision to reverse his uncle's policies of showing only replicas of important artifacts and of not allowing people to touch things (292–93). By the same token, the loss of Sonja Turk's book in the fire requires that Rogalla rewrite it from memory in his own hand (13). In this quintessentially Benjaminian approach to storytelling, objects, anecdotes, and the stories of past happenings literally pass through him conceptually and physically on their way to the future, leaving traces of his own life on them like rings on a tree (an image Rogalla himself uses to describe the object-based transmission of the past).

Just as his appropriations change the imprint of those who came before him, Rogalla accepts that transferring ownership of the past to Martin requires Martin to scrutinize Rogalla's priorities and the past in terms of his own exigencies. Referring to Martin at one point as a kind of inspector of his past (468), Rogalla later remarks that Martin reminds him of his son, Bernhard, in the way he expresses critical doubt and skepticism (604). Over the course of their dialogues, Martin's perspective also affects how Rogalla tells his story. Rogalla begins to shorten his account of events in the course of the novel when Martin can read documents such as a post-fire newspaper report on his own. As Rogalla notes, "I saved the issue of the paper for you, here, in the lowest drawer of the nightstand; you can take it with you when you have heard everything ... indeed *I do not doubt that by now, you insist on creating your own image [of things]*" (618; my emphasis). As the "by now" signals, Rogalla endorses that Martin will decide for himself how to piece together what he has been told. This is why Rogalla approves of Martin and his daughter going to visit contemporary Masuria, where, as Rogalla points out, seeing things for himself will require Martin to revise what Rogalla has told him (397). Since not even Rogalla thinks Martin will mindlessly share his perspective, I disagree with critics such as Marilyn Sibley Fries who argue that Rogalla attempts, unsuccessfully or otherwise, to inculcate in Martin a nostalgic view of the Masurian past.[12] Even if Martin shared Rogalla's physical and emotional traumas—and Martin's losses are not precisely Rogalla's—the fact that the objects' stories pass through Rogalla first means that Martin inherits them with the traces of Rogalla's life and possession. However nostalgic Rogalla may be, Martin is free to think of the objects without nostalgia.

The Collector's Memory in Crisis: Order, the "Talking Cure," and Narrative

Rogalla cannot in fact pass objects and anecdotes down without Martin's witnessing how Rogalla has summoned them from the depths of his memory. Martin's visits to Rogalla constitute as important an element of Rogalla's convalescence as the healing of his skin grafts. Those visits force Rogalla to talk through the mental disarray left by the destruction of his museum, mental disarray occasioned by the loss of an indexing mechanism similar to that which Benjamin believes keeps the collector from lapsing into sickness. Linking order, chaos, and memory, Benjamin writes, "Every passion borders on chaos; the passion of the collector borders on the chaos of memories ... for what is this possession [of the collector] other than disorder, in which habituation has made itself so at home that it can appear to be order? You have already heard of people who have become invalids at the loss of their books.... All order is, especially in these areas, nothing other than a state of hovering over the abyss."[13] Like the collector who becomes an invalid at the loss of his books, Rogalla plunges himself into a crisis by destroying his familiar mechanism of control, his museum. Rogalla becomes even more overwhelmed when he considers that he has, in a sense, taken utter possession of the objects. As he puts it, "I know how much got reduced to ashes, and I alone know that all the catalogs burned up in which each individual piece was drawn and elaborated. It gets harder to think about it with every passing day" (339). No other person can come close to the mass of information Rogalla continues to hold in memory following the museum's destruction, and this burden imperils Rogalla's identity. Rogalla comes to terms with his overload of memory by constructing a dialogic narrative that enables him to gain control of his memories and to share his knowledge with Martin (and by implication, with the reader).

Zygmunt's need to regain mastery over the chaos of memories coursing through him matches the seriousness of his burns and other physical injuries. From the beginning, the narrative highlights parallel tasks of restoring proper order to memory and healing of damaged skin. The two processes cause similar kinds of pain (14), and, after stating that he will be able to recommit Sonja Turk's book to paper because it lies open before him in his memory (13), Zygmunt points out, "[L]et's hope that the new skin heals well, the islands of new skin that they have grafted onto me.... I am ready for anything; skin has its memory, too" (13). The remark "skin has its memory, too" makes it clear that recovering experience entails more than a conscious reflection. In this regard, *Heimatmuseum* resembles other novels of Lenz's, such as *Die Deutschstunde,* in which writing is shown to emerge in a Proustian fashion.[14] As far as Rogalla is concerned, the shape, direction, and success of the future bodily reconstruction must be thought of as being dialectically bound by the experiences and condition of the skin. When he is ready to leave the hospital, he will look like a different man, but he cannot be transformed into just anyone. The same applies to how he thinks. In fact, who he is and will be depends foremost on three elements from his past, all of which constrain him and all of which are "remade" in the present: the reconstruction of Sonja Turk's book, the healing of his body, and making the full history of his objects available to Martin.

Rogalla's burden of memory is compounded by his sense that only his moods, which are constantly shifting and unreliable (340), guide him. Lacking orientation, Rogalla sometimes has to break off his conversation because he cannot handle certain memories as they surface (372). At other times, Rogalla' is so feverish and weak that he makes deeply troubling utterances his "otherwise highly reliable memory" fails to register (425), lapses Rogalla interprets as signs that he cannot yet confront the truth of the past head on (245). Even on good days, he feels "an unwanted agitation" because he is now aware of the "hoard of stored moments and memories that have not gone away" (397). In these various ways, the destruction of the museum creates the requisite condition for Rogalla to gain access to the mass of stored memories that his pre-fire measures had effectively enabled him to bracket in his day-to-day life.

By the end of the novel, Zygmunt's improved ability to withstand the past has diminished both his previously insatiable thirst and his need to make pauses in his storytelling (650). Talking at length gets Zygmunt to this point. Though it concerns the medical staff, Zygmunt exclaims,

> Exhaustion? I'm exhausting myself by talking? To the contrary, Sister Margret; the more I get rid of the easier and more bearable it becomes; it seems to me as if I were distributing myself, as if I were giving back their part to all of the people who made me who I am, indeed—where I myself have the feeling of getting to know myself better and better. Our qualities namely, they only emerge clearly when we have given away everything we received from others. (364)

Sharing his past with Martin offers Rogalla therapeutic relief, but only because Rogalla feels as if he were repaying a debt to predecessors by passing his knowledge on to Martin.[15] Martin, in turn, bears a similar obligation to Rogalla, so that Martin is no mere, indifferent interlocutor.[16] Rather, he becomes the latest recipient in a chain of transfers that had begun long before he was born, setting him into conversation with a number of people. The identity that Rogalla establishes for himself resides in coming to see himself as a conduit (a synonym for his being a collector) that connects the generations before and after him.

Zygmunt cannot get a handle on his mass of memories alone. He needs dialogue with Martin in order to put his museum memories into some semblance of order and to achieve a relatively stable sense of identity. For this reason, it is tempting to speak of the novel as depicting a "talking cure," in which identity represents the composite product of memory mediated by bodily/material and cognitive/linguistic factors. Indeed, some critics have understood the dialogic structure, the question of personal identity, and the negligible difference between the first names Zygmunt and Sigmund as cues to understand the novel's dynamic solely as a (confused) depiction of the scene of Freudian analysis.[17] I want to differentiate my usage of the term, however, because the Freudian paradigm associated with "the talking cure" only partially captures the dynamic at work in the novel. If it is correct, for instance, to understand the scene of Freudian analysis as one in which the analyst remains detached and unaffected by the narrative constructed by the patient, crucial dimensions of Lenz's novel either go unaccounted for or are registered as grave inconsistencies. In light of the fact that Rogalla functions as a conduit to transmit his collections to Martin, it does not make sense to regard Martin as detached and unaffected. As the text progresses, moreover, Rogalla indicates his increasing involvement in Martin's personal life.

Beyond asking Martin point blank to talk about his plans with Rogalla's daughter, Henrike (407), Rogalla poses questions to hospital staff who know about Martin's life story, and he also refers to Martin's career as a biologist, which he has learned about through contexts not presented in the narrative (192, 407). This latter point requires us to acknowledge that the dialogues are only one facet in the flow of information between Rogalla and Martin, again making the model of analyst and patient seem unsuitable for characterizing their relationship.

In narrating his memories, Rogalla follows the logic of the private collector. In Benjamin's writings, the collector constructs identity as a function of the way he or she acquires, possesses, and arranges the objects of a collection. The basis for such a construction is an intertwining of the known history of the object and the recollections of how it was acquired, which together become personal memories that are always ready to swell up in the collector.[18] Rogalla speaks about precisely this when he tells Martin what he learned from his Uncle Adam: "I do not have to tell you, my dear Martin, that a double history was bound to each piece, namely the history of its origin and that of its acquisition through the Heimat researcher" (171). According to Benjamin, habitual order typically prevents memories from immobilizing the collector. "This or any other procedure [of maintaining order]," Benjamin writes, "is merely a dam against the spring tide of memories which surges toward any collector as he contemplates his possessions."[19] Seen this way, the physical presence of the object in a familiar exhibition environment works less to trigger or stimulate memory than to *stem* its flow. So long as order is maintained, memories continue to exist but are tucked away, "out of mind." Any one manifest order of the objects works to block conscious access to certain memories.[20]

In *Heimatmuseum,* the collector relies on order to control memory to such an extent that he can summon memories by carefully manipulating objects. When Uncle Adam shows his objects to Zygmunt, no memory flows until he takes the objects from their habitual resting places and hands them to Zygmunt:

> As always, Uncle Adam whispered with the objects, he murmured, yes, and renewed intimate relations [with them]. . . . Suddenly he froze, turned around quickly, and handed me something with both hands, something sparkling, a necklace made out of hammered white silver. . . . For a while he watched as I fingered the necklace, also examined my facial expression, and this story began like each of his stories, abruptly, as if it were taking him over. (169)

Phrases such as "as always" and "each of his stories" indicate that Adam repeats this process whenever he wishes to access his memories. Adam's undeniably strange behavior when he handles his objects recalls the ritual employed by Durs Grünbein (Chapter 2) to probe his memories by using the natural history diorama. Adam must take an object out of its display environment and hand it to Zygmunt before he can recall anything. Not only must habitual order be disrupted for Adam to tell stories, but he needs someone to receive the object and story.

Zygmunt's mind works in the same way, particularly in its reliance on habitual order to limit his emotional responses to painful memories. At the end of World War II, Rogalla leaves his museal objects packed away in crates for a long time. Eventually, however, his second wife pushes him to unpack the crates of rescued Masurian objects. Rather than be flooded with memories, Rogalla imposes order on them in his mind's eye before he confronts them. As he explains, "It was her impetus, her suggestion, it was her enthusiasm that revealed the next task. Even before she said it, I saw in a dreamy layout the slumbering inventory spread out, ordered, entrusted with expanded testimony, and not in a chamber or a back room, but rather on its own terms and in its own building" (591). Before his wife can even mention unpacking and sorting the objects for the new museum, Rogalla already has a framework in mind with which to approach them. In his mind, he constructs a rigid, detached vision of past life with an unmistakable sense of place and order (591). The desire to construct the museum with a suitably Masurian architectural style betrays the fact that the separate building puts the objects at a remove from his daily life for the first time since he took over the collections. Rogalla's need to keep the objects in place and out of the way offers one possible reason for his no longer approving of having objects moved around, manipulated, and connected to the fabric of daily life, as the younger generation does on the opening day of the museum (606–7). Though he retains a commitment to his objects in the postwar period, he cannot withstand the full force of personal memory. Order and physical dissociation enable him to disavow those memories that exist in him, at least until the objects are destroyed.

The museum's destruction creates a crisis that requires Rogalla to create new, ordered contexts for his memories. Though Rogalla's ability to withstand the past increases as he establishes context, Rogalla cannot control how his memories appear. As they surface, he is driven forward by associations he has with previous contexts. Roughly in the middle of the book, Rogalla reflects on his difficulties at what is a decidedly low point in his convalescence. Referring to memories as images that are carried as a kind of "invisible baggage," he explains, "The collected images, they, too, are not available to be used as we desire; they have their moments; they suddenly light up and then they darken again; they arise out of the depths; they are visible for a moment and they sink down again—just like these thin unpredictable plankton fields that make mounds in the Sargasso Sea, as you once mentioned" (407).[21] Images ebb and flow in their accessibility without a readily intelligible mechanism behind their appearance, recalling the passive side of memory that Nietzsche described in "Use and Disadvantages of History for Life." While Rogalla knows the general outline and eventual goal of the narrative he wants to produce, he does not know a priori all the details, the course, and the speed of his narrative. Just as with his skin grafts, he cannot know whether the narrative remedy will "take," or how his life and his relationships to others will be if and when he is able to leave the hospital. When Martin wants to know whether Rogalla will patch things up with his estranged daughter, Rogalla replies, "What plans should I have with [Henrike], since I still do not have a plan for myself? All I know is: that my third beginning awaits me when they release me healed" (310). Rogalla must discover and put too much into place for him to say more.

Together, the uncertainty and the associative process of the situation impel Rogalla to capture the appearance of an image in as much detail as he can while the moment presents itself. For to use Rogalla's own unusual metaphor for history, he must retrace his own way through the swampy morass of his own life (604). Every time he fends off Martin's request to take a straight path to the end, Rogalla insists on following all the twists and turns (106–7, 294, 494). As he admonishes Martin, "Patience, my dear Martin, have a little more patience; for you have to hear this, too, because it belongs to the story and because, often enough, I create the necessary impulse for myself from inconspicuous details" (51). For all the meandering of Rogalla's story, he narrates with remarkable consistency, at least from the standpoint of the collector enacting cultural transmission. Because it requires taking inventory of what and who is relevant from moment to moment, the form of Rogalla's narrative structures his consciousness in a specific and highly revealing way.

The Narrative as Museum: Inventoried Consciousness and the Accumulation of Narrated Guided Tours

Some critics have argued that Lenz cast Rogalla in the mode of Homer, the ancient oral teller of epic tales. According to Albert B. Lord in *The Singer of Tales,* the epic storyteller composes his tales from memory "on the fly," following certain internalized patterns such as rhyme, tag phrases, and the rhythm of the language to suit the audience. If one views Zygmunt as composing his tales in a similar fashion, then the collection emerges as a paradigmatic mnemonic that structures modern consciousness.[22] The fact that most critics have had no difficulty at all in decoding this structure lends weight to the argument that, at the end of the twentieth century, paradigms of collecting were "second nature" in German-speaking societies. As I discuss in Chapter 2, since 1989, increasing numbers of writers have reflected on these structures, with texts by W. G. Sebald, Durs Grünbein, Michael Krüger, and Walter Kempowski, among others, manifesting various kinds of inventoried storytelling or consciousness. Lenz's text is an important precursor to these narratives of inventoried consciousness, a precursor whose museal environment helps us understand the centrality of the museum in recent forms of inventoried consciousness.

Zygmunt's storytelling proceeds by taking inventory. Already in the third paragraph of the book, Rogalla tells Martin how the fire spread by following it through the museum's rooms, focusing on the individual objects as they burned:

> So you also know: I set the fire with refuse from the weaving room that I dowsed in gasoline and then lit both in the tapestry room of the museum as well as in the room that primarily contained Masurian toys: rag toys and wooden instruments and carved and painted birds that easily went up in flames. Only Simon Gayko, carpenter and cartwright whom I also know from Lucknow, was initiated in my plans, Simon Gayko, who had built the museum according to my suggestions, as a tiered house with a prominent wood balcony. . . .
>
> I set the fire in the evening, I said that already, after our seven weaving students had gone home; there was a weak north west wind that blew the sparks and smoke over the water, over the Schlei, as calculated. There was no danger [for the house] when the fire reached the document room and texts and records went up swirling in an unanticipated shower of sparks, including the city's letter in which the Great Elector awarded Lucknow a fourth fair; the rest of the letters and records got pulled into the drift as well and sailed away like flakes and went down onto the water. Or it got hung up on the hawthorn bush where it has made it up the cliff. Odd: while the museum was burning two fishing cutters passed Egenlund; their crews obviously did not want to take note of the fire; they slipped through the smoke cloud and the black flakes falling moving toward the mouth of the river. (7–8; ellipsis in original)

Though this passage goes on to describe other spaces such as the jewelry room as they go up in flames, the layout of the museum provides the underlying organization for the narrative into which Zygmunt interweaves comments. The long, winding sentences promote a sense that all these objects exist simultaneously and in relation to one another in the museum before coming into view when attention is focused on them. The writing produces an effect like that of a themed guided tour, where the narrative follows a particular itinerary through the museum, passing over some elements while expanding on others that contribute to the development of the narrative at that moment.

In *Heimatmuseum,* Rogalla offers a large number of "guided tours" through the museum, the surrounding environs, and the people.[23] While no single guided tour exhausts all the meanings or the range of stories that can be told about its artifacts, a structure of repetition emerges as passes are made through the museum. Over the course of the entire book, information accumulates about the museum and its respective objects. Certain objects and people appear again and again, in different orders, and in different contexts. As they build up layer by layer, the repeated appearance of objects primes Martin and the reader (whose positions may not be collapsed) to make comparisons with previous narrative strands. Such a palympsistic transposition of display environments into narrative works, in Rogalla's words, is to take people and things "under the magnifying glass" (15). Much like film techniques such as montage and slow-motion, narrative functions on one level as an analytical tool for uncovering heretofore latent aspects of Rogalla's past and identity. Yet on another level, this tool works by priming the reader to make critical comparisons with the museum he or she constructs notionally by using previous "guided tours."[24]

I must limit my analyses of the many "guided tours" to a few exemplary instances. One of the richest descriptions of the pre–World War II Heimat museum emerges when Zygmunt and his mother move in with Zygmunt's Uncle Adam. In the museum's overcrowded and unfamiliar environment, Zygmunt finds it hard to unpack:

> [W]e moved into our rooms, both facing the river; neither was large enough to be able to take in all of our household things because each room of the museum was used for the museum, with the innumerable artifacts and documents that Uncle Adam had passionately collected. So we stowed away our things, partially in the shed, partially on the floor, and while my mother had to accept her bed being surrounded by "devil's violins," droning pots, and woven hoops that made the *Bügeltanz* [a carnival dance] so beloved in Masuria, I had to come to terms above all with the presence of old Masurian wedding dresses, limp, worn out costumes preserved against moths that hung around with slightly elevated arms, which is why in some nights it seemed like they were reaching out to grab me. I must not forget the bed, with its turned ball feet, nor the painted chest, nor the decorated washboards and mangles, and you have to imagine that a board ran

> over my bed that held historic kitchen devices: cabbage mashers, herb mashers, wooden molds shaped like blossoms, or six-cornered stars. (160)

The overloaded grammar in this passage conveys not only the packed quality of these rooms, but also the slightly unsettling qualities of objects that held the inventorying gaze long enough to add attributes to them. After a brief respite, the inventory continues:

> But I adjusted to the plate and spoon racks; I even got to like the leather-trimmed wooden clogs that occupied a shelf like unshapely model boats. I sat on an historic chair with a carved back. Only I couldn't stand the old irons: with their toothed iron covers they reminded me of dog snouts baring their teeth.
>
> What surrounded, admonished, inspired, and estranged me in my room was of course only a small part of the collection that Uncle Adam found worthy of bearing witness to the long history of Masuria; the prize pieces, the precious discoveries and exhibits, the prehistoric goodies stood and hung in the front hall and the living room, the work room, and the kitchen, and last but not least in the secret cellar. You can assume, my dear Martin, that every corner of the house held remnants; they were stuffed into corners, occupied table tops, climbed the walls, and even if you were only out to get a swig of buttermilk, you had think that the jug you fetched from the cupboard might be a Sudauese funerary urn. (161)

With only rudiments of order structuring his description, Zygmunt takes stock by inventorying objects by type in their respective locations. The sheer mass of unfamiliar objects outside his room ensures that the pieces creep into daily life when least expected, as might happen by discovering that one's drinking glass is an ancient burial urn. These two passages, despite their length, offer precious little information about most objects. They help primarily to visualize the museum's contours behind the scenes (private rooms), while creating a framework for future reference.

Subsequent tours, for instance, the one that catalogues the "visit" to the museum paid by a Russian military officer a few pages later, enrich this framework. Following the officer's movements, the narrative tracks how particular objects draw his interest: "He stopped before early weapons, bent over a vitrine with historical coins, read the labels on the straw, wood, and rag dolls, doing everything seriously and with impenetrable interest. He drummed his fingertips on a crusader's chain mail. Before the two oldest spinning wheels of Masuria he shook his head thoughtfully, and the historical tools that were hanging there beautifully he glanced at with a snide look" (164). In simulating the officer's view of the museum, the text presents the objects and reactions that figure prominently in the Russian's tour, highlighting pieces Zygmunt has identified as the museum's prizes but that he has not described in detail. By not repeating this information, the text achieves narrative economy as it increases the resolution of its presentation of the museum.

With additional passes through some of the same spaces, for instance, the tour Zygmunt's classmates receive from his Uncle Adam, the selective quality of the respective tours becomes apparent. As Rogalla recalls, once

> Uncle Adam offered my twenty-two fellow pupils a tour through the museum. He gathered them in front of carvings, took them to the wall of weapons, asked them to admire tools and ancient jewelry, and while he explained with increasing enthusiasm and let the discoveries speak for their times, I moved around the edges among our uninterested misfits. [Uncle Adam] spoke to us, as I said, with increasing enthusiasm; his stories seemed inspired by the need to arouse participation by divulging knowledge in a spirited way. He found their interest and courted their cheap attention when he plucked the woven horsehair over the droning pot and slammed the "devil's violin" to the floor so that it banged and rattled. Noise—that's how you could reach them, outrageous, enduring noise for its own sake—tellingly enough, they all pressed in to provoke the simple instruments, yet they overheard what Uncle Adam had to tell them about the carnival music. (186–87)

This tour of the museum accents a different itinerary, one that emerges as a function of the visitors' disinterest in many of the objects. Whereas the narrative distinguishes the historical tools because the Russian reacts to them with a snide look, it presents an unembellished list of object categories when the students are relatively bored (wood pieces, weapons, tools, and old jewelry), and no mention is made of the dolls, coins, or spinning wheels that interested the Russian officer. Detail emerges only when the narrative centers on those objects that grab the students' attention, in the process quietly adding to the reader's knowledge of them. Having encountered the musical instruments in Zygmunt's description of his mother's room, the reader can now learn how and when they are played for the *Bügeltanz*.

Over time, the repetitions in the narrative structure enable Martin and the reader to construct a notional museum with ever increasing richness, yet one not contained representationally within the text. Much in line with Lenz's stated intention of creating a text that requires the active participation of the reader, interpretation of the guided tours relies upon detecting subtle changes in the presentation of objects and the concepts they represent. The repeated appearance of objects in varying contexts primes Martin and the reader, respectively, to make comparisons with previous presentations without the text's explicitly spelling them out. By comparing the tours over time, for instance, the tour given to Rogalla's class, the tours he gives prior to World War II, and his rules restricting the use of objects in Egenlund, the reader can see that Rogalla's own ideas about the collections undergo radical shifts. In the first tour, Rogalla is horrified when his schoolmates handle objects (188); in his own tours he insists that objects be worn and touched (293), and in Egenlund he is again horror stricken when young Germans play Glenn Miller records on old phonographs and dance in the museum (605–7). In spite of the highly introspective quest of his narrative, Rogalla seems not to share these insights. Rather, they result from a mode of interpretation the reader carries out through attention to semiotic encodings. Because the text promotes a critical view of Rogalla and the limitations of his perspective, Rogalla is not necessarily the mouthpiece of Lenz the author, as some critics have argued.

The guided tours prompt the reader to consider the construction of meaning through museal display. I have argued several times in this book that the power of museal display resides in part in its ability to render certain notions "invisible" and therefore much more difficult to think about. The narrative structure of "guided tours" beckons readers to understand that exclusions of various sorts go hand in hand with practically any act of interpretation, even those that are not motivated by extreme ideologies. The text sustains this point solely because it represents instances in which ideological commitments require contradictory evidence to be purged, as, for instance, with Conny's demand that Nazi propaganda be removed from the museum (644–45). Yet the guided tours also demonstrate, by using linguistic means, how ideology depends on the museal process of rendering invisible.

The text comments on this property of the guided tours, leaving little doubt that the reader is supposed to comprehend the reduction of meaning that particular orderings produce. Such a moment occurs when, shortly after the Nazi rise to power, a high-ranking National Socialist professor and brigade leader named Melzer-Tapiau arrives to inspect the collections. As in other guided tours, the narrative registers his impression of the objects:

> The Brigade Leader at first did not let it be seen if he was impressed; he examined all the objects with unchanging expression, thoughtfully, as if he were comparing them to set norms and

> patterns. However, in front of the Masurian musical instruments, in front of the droning pot and the "devil's violin," he began to smirk, and smiling thinly he took in the "animals of the Heimat," the carved kitchen devices, and my toy collection, which many have said was the richest, the most significant one of the entire south-eastern region. The professor praised the contents of the "Solkolk box"; he admired a piece of glass-beaded embroidery.
>
> Nodding, Melzer-Tapiau inspected the weapon room; he took the talon de lance and the dagger from the wall, turned them in the light, and decided: iron offering from the grave of a vandal warrior, last century B.C.E. In the tool room he determined the age of a wooden plow and set a spinning wheel in motion without a single blunder; afterwards he needed a drink of schnapps. (367)

Though the professor encounters all the objects, the narrative highlights details of those objects that bear on his fairly rigid, norm-based interpretation. While some objects receive an ambivalent response in spite of their relative cultural importance, only the weapons and tools seem to find his unabashed approval.[25]

This passage becomes crucial in light of Melzer-Tapiau's museological critique. He mutters disapprovingly,

> What good does it do to accumulate object after object [if you fail to see that] the objects only gain their meaning by being organized, that is to say, when they are put in the service of an idea, a great conception. . . . What matters is this: that the objects be employed as a proof that the Masurians have always understood themselves to be a German outpost in the east. The objects not only have to vouch for something; they also have to demonstrate, they have to agitate. The professor gave an example: if weapons and farm implements are combined appropriately, they allow warriorhood and belonging to the earth to appear on their own as conditions with a binding fate. (368)

The brigade leader rejects the museum not strictly for its content, but because it fails to use principles of organization to present objects in an ideological order. The narrative attention given to the handling of weapons and peasant tools neatly anticipates the linkage he claims would naturalize his "blood and soil" vision. So neat is this correspondence, however, and so overt is the museological commentary, that the reader aware of the museum's notional "fullness" cannot overlook how the narrative itself shunts the bulk of the museum's objects out of view precisely as it foregrounds Melzer-Tapiau's favorites. Melzer-Tapiau's application of "fixed patterns and norms" results in a highly selective appropriation of objects, which tends to render alternative concepts unthinkable, at least to the unreflective visitor. The reader of Lenz's novel who constructs a notional museum is not likely to be such a visitor.

No single pass through the museum can capture the complexity and the multivalent nature of the displays. As individual guided tours accumulate, it becomes easier to see how each tour diverges from the others and "fails" the fullness of the past, or what Benjamin refers to as an object's "fate." The novel, too, must fail in this quest, for even though it as a whole represents the possibility of coming closer to the fullness of the past better than any one rendering or interpretation of the objects, it must "misinterpret" that fate. In my reading, the novel does not strive for some putative state of metaphysical purity, as some critics have alleged.[26] It instead supplies a narrative structure with which to critique the desire for an absolute, enduring, or complete—in Benjamin's terms, a nonallegorized—interpretation.

Memory, Materiality, Incommensurability, and Translation

Lenz deploys Zygmunt as narrator with detectable blind spots as part of a critique of interpretive purity, particularly with regard to questions of memory and materiality. The text presents these questions in the guise of Zygmunt's response to his personal disaster, which up until now I have considered primarily in terms of the physical injury and memory burdens he faces as a collector. Yet Zygmunt's disaster and burden also derive from the loss of a unique, handwritten book on Masurian weaving techniques compiled over many years by his mentor, Sonja Turk. As one of the few remaining Masurian master weavers, Zygmunt carries on the traditions that Turk describes and interprets in her compilation. Its loss places additional burdens on Zygmunt, since he feels he must rewrite it from memory once he leaves the hospital.

Rewriting Turk's book differs from the narrative reconstruction of his Heimat museum primarily in Rogalla's view of the two tasks. Whereas Rogalla believes he can restore the book because he has "learned it completely by heart" (12), the museum's loss is irretrievable. As he tells Martin, "I, too, am assuming that [the book] was burned up, even if it has not been lost, totally lost in these that the Heimat museum's objects were, since it lies ready in my memory [*Gedächtnis*], and since I have the intention of rewriting it in the language of Sonja Turk" (13). The book's destruction threatens, but does not amount to, its final loss, for, according to Rogalla, the language and content of Turk's book can be recalled and recommitted to paper. The material objects once held in the museum, in contrast, cannot be remade in a way that would make the copy and the original identical. The political efficacy of Rogalla's act relies on this impossibility.

Yet Rogalla's distinction between material objects and linguistic representations of memory breaks down in two ways, both of which inform the core project of the novel. On the one hand, the museum artifacts are in fact not totally lost. Like the book on Masurian weaving, they continue to exist in human memory, and, as the novel itself attests, they can on some level be reconstructed through language. On the other hand, Rogalla's plan to rewrite Sonja Turk's tome on weaving "in the language of Sonja Turk" rests on a conception of language as an immaterial medium that reliably transmits information, ideas, and memory (in Chapter 1, I critique this notion in light of the institutional development of the museum).[27] Even though he plans to write in Sütterlin, Zygmunt's handwriting differs from Sonja Turk's, and his selection of paper and binding will make his book materially different from Sonja Turk's. In my reading, developments in the novel also question the viability of such a conception at the same time as they show why someone such as Zygmunt might cling to them.

I argue previously that Zygmunt's museum in Egenlund allows him to retreat into a nostalgic evocation of his lost homeland. At the postwar opening of the museum, Zygmunt discovers how powerful an effect memory can have. As he recalls, it was "[e]xciting . . . that memory succeeded in returning to the lost city. However, the city itself changed in being revived: I realized for the first time that every past is partially an invention. Certainly, it was still Lucknow that we made come to life, though it could not be overlooked that we had made the city at once poorer and richer with its past life" (596–97). Distinguishing between material remnants and internal memory, Zygmunt seems aware that the reanimation of the past arises from a dialectical movement between material and imaginary realms that is at once too little and too much with respect to the past.[28] Curiously, however, Zygmunt's insight leaves him relatively untroubled.

This lapse is explained in part by Zygmunt's belief that much more egregious falsifications of the past occur when one lacks historical remnants. For Zygmunt, Conny Karasch can maintain his "unreal" view of the Masurian past only because he lives in quarters containing no Masurian decoration or objects (623). Because Conny and the other members of the Heimat association prefer memory unchecked by physical realities such as evidence of Slavic culture, he berates them when the members make Conny an honorary citizen of Lucknow, calling them "lovers of the unreal" for their willingness to honor "the first honorary citizen of a city . . . that only exists in memory" (628). Yet Zygmunt represents not a fundamentally different position from Conny and his ilk, but rather the other end of a spectrum. To be sure, Zygmunt's reliance on physical objects to correct his inventions of the past prevents him from forgetting certain lessons from the past, for instance, that Slavic peoples and Germans always shared Masuria. Yet in spite of his object-based views, Zygmunt, too, invents a distorted past.

Zygmunt draws inferences about the falsifications induced by memory only when forced to do so by Martin, and even then, he can go only so far. In the middle of Zygmunt's critique of Conny's becoming an honorary citizen of Lucknow, Martin forcefully interrupts Zygmunt to get him to admit to a general point about memory: "Yes,
. . .
that is probably true: in our memory things lead a purer existence, undamaged, unimperiled . . . ah, let's let this be" (628; original ellipses). The ellipses that represent Martin's comments require careful scrutiny. Given Zygmunt's confirmatory statement ("that is probably true"), Zygmunt's first utterance summarizes Martin's point that the realm of memory—including Zygmunt's—lends things a wholeness, a purity, a truth that differs from the messiness of everyday life. This is a deeply relevant insight into the dynamics of memory for this text. The second ellipsis represents either a comment by Martin or a thought—which, it is impossible to know—that has irritated Zygmunt. Followed by the comment "ah, let's let this be," the second ellipsis marks a crucial moment in the text that cannot be reconstructed. Together they denote a limit Zygmunt does not cross and a gap the reader cannot smooth over.

Zygmunt's "ah, let's let that be" (or its slight variant, "but let's let that be") generally signifies Zygmunt's unwillingness to continue a train of thought. The leitmotif appears at least ten times in the second half of the text, surfacing when Zygmunt must confront something unpleasant, conflictual, or abstract. When expressing his distaste about his student Marian's theory of weaving, for instance, Zygmunt says: "[Marian] is a great weaver, no question. However, for his benefit I never attempted to take him at his word as soon as he got going on transparency, on 'transparency as an undulating back and forth in areas distributed in counterpoint.' *But let's let that be.* Every theory contains its author's disappointment at life's unwillingness to go according to plan; *let's let that be;* tell me instead something about Henrike, about you and Henrike" (407; my emphasis). Occurring twice, the leitmotif signals that Zygmunt prefers not to engage with something disagreeable to him, here his student's theoretical perspectives. Zygmunt rejects this and all theory because he believes that theory is compensatory, a way of conveying a deceptive form of mastery over the material world. By rejecting this kind of thinking, Zygmunt articulates a desire to leave life's wounds recognizable as such, untransformed by language, memory, or generalizing conceptions. Gaps that the reader cannot adequately fill likewise function as a textual strategy of representing such a desire.

In several key moments, however, Zygmunt's strategy of turning away from generalizing conceptions permits the distorting effects of his memory to continue. In some instances, Zygmunt utters his tag phrase when he must confront the nostalgia that informed his postwar view of the museum (598, 609, 618). And when Martin finally pushes Zygmunt to grasp the way that memory can make things appear pure and untainted, Zygmunt refuses to explore why notions of purity and wholeness might exert a powerful hold on someone experiencing loss (628). Though Zygmunt has healed considerably by the end of the text, he still craves the feeling of belonging and wholeness that his nostalgic view of Heimat provides. In fact, Zygmunt's impulse to turn away only surfaces around the middle of the novel, when his cure begins to take hold, and it appears with an increasing cadence thereafter (by my count, it appears on pages 300, 337, 392, 407, 494, 598, 609, 618, 628, and 635). Moreover, the text concludes with the on-going, pained quest for this kind of memory, not for its attainment. As Zygmunt laments, "[T]he treasured objects have disintegrated, the traces erased. The past has gotten back what it only lent us temporarily. However, memory [*Gedächtnis*] is already stirring; memory [*Erinnerung*] is already seeking and collecting in the uncertain silence of the no-mans-land" (655).

The text depicts Zygmunt as a character condemned to have memory fill in the gaps. He represents a figure for whom, against his better judgment, the illusion of a pure and untouched memory remains attractive, at times even irresistible.[29] By virtue of this depiction, Lenz's text primes the reader to ponder memory. To put it in the idiom of translation—an idiom favored by Benjamin in his thinking about the construction of the past in the present—the text helps us realize that memory situates past and present, constantly translating back and forth between past and present contexts.[30] *Heimatmuseum* de-naturalizes that translation process, preventing it from happening smoothly and revealing when "gaps" are filled in.[31] Much as Rogalla's scar tissue will always testify to that moment when he irrevocably transformed his museum and his life, the story of the objects' destruction marks a special layer forever added to their history. Even as past and present are linked, the connective tissue that runs between them (scar tissue and story) serves as a reminder that remains inassimilable to past or present.

I want to make two related points about this novel. First, its creation as a textual museum makes its contents fundamentally incommensurate with the material objects it replaces. Supporting this point is the running commentary in the text about the inability of a reproduction ever to become interchangeable with its original, for instance, in Sonja Turk's thesis on original weavings (419–20) or Zygmunt's ideas about original artifacts being irreplaceable in the museum (401–2). The anecdotes, stories, and histories transmitted in the text differ from those that a materially existing museum would transmit, in no small part because the reader cannot get around the fact that the text exists only because Rogalla has physically destroyed his objects. The reasons for the text's existence are inscribed into the narrative in a way that forces reflection on the differences between physical and textual museum.

Second, the staging of the moment of cultural transmission as a dialogue, which the reader views as a third party, affects the appropriation of the past. I therefore disagree with Marilyn Sibley Fries when she argues that the positions of Martin and the reader are interchangeable.[32] By virtue of the "guided tours," the reader can construct a notional museum that cannot be contained by the text or compared with whatever museum Martin might have in mind. As I have argued, the dialogue contains important moments that the reader cannot reconstruct and which remain inassimilable. But just as important, many more of Martin's comments can be reconstructed all too easily, so easily that one wonders whether Lenz really expected to challenge the reader by excising the dialogue at these moments. Moreover, Martin's commentary and questions might not at all correspond with the reader's, prompting the reader to develop an independent line of questioning or at least to realize that the conversation between Martin and Zygmunt occurs between two limited instances of consciousness at some temporal distance from the reader, a distance that only grows as the novel ages. Martin's perspective demarcates a divide that the reader must translate across in order to activate meaning, allowing the past to be delivered into the present in ways the text shapes but cannot fully determine.

The Activation of Meaning and the Shaping of Memory in *Heimatmuseum* and Countermonuments

Contemporary theorists following Adorno and Benjamin have argued that modern museum environments constitute a realm dialectically spanning cultural ossification and renewal.[33] In this view, objects enter the museum when they lose an organic connection to the fabric of social and cultural life. Severed from immediate cultural relevance, for instance, owing to obsolescence or changes in the relationship of artistic production to the cultural sphere (art produced for commercial or display purposes), museum objects undergo a kind of cultural "death." In theory, however, objects can regain a contemporary relevance when conditions permit visitors to draw them into their lives and generate meaning.

Heimatmuseum presents a nuanced account of how, in the case of one object-rich environment in postwar West Germany, this theoretical promise threatens to go unrealized. On one level, rigid visitor expectations about what objects in a Heimat museum can and cannot mean—and the inability to attract new visitors amounts to the same thing—prevent the dynamic reexamination of the objects and the concepts based on them. Paradoxically, the museum as institution represents part of the problem. At the end of the twentieth century, the notion that a museum's primary cultural mission always involves the preservation of objects and artifacts has become an article of faith. Though questioning this notion rightly seems tantamount to cultural barbarity, the unquestioned preservation of artifacts as an end in itself does not necessarily ensure on-going engagement with the past. When the past becomes too secure in either a physical or an interpretive sense, the result can be a kind of cultural forgetting predicated on a ritual, rather than rational, basis. *Heimatmuseum*'s disruption of the traditional museum paradigm suggests that the perceived permanence of physical artifacts can promote ritual forgetting.

Such a linkage of physical environment and cultural and historical amnesia likewise serves as the underpinning for commemorative projects known as anti- or countermonuments (*Negativ-* or *Gegendenkmäler).* Arising in the 1980s and 1990s in Germany and Austria, countermonuments were developed primarily to foster dynamic examination of the place of the Holocaust in German-speaking culture.[34] Advocates of countermonuments deemed nontraditional commemorative strategies necessary because National Socialists had abused monumental forms in their architectural and commemorative projects, making the very idea of the monument suspect when it comes to remembering the National Socialists' victims. Yet advocates of countermonuments also resist the idea that memory can be instilled in a lasting way in a single encounter, let alone be permanent. Too often, they assert, the erection of a traditional monument leads the spectator not to increased engagement with the past, but rather to a sense that the past has been dealt with. To counter this form of ritual forgetting and to involve visitors in the construction of the monument's meaning, countermonuments challenge the perceived permanence and immutability of monuments.

Often, the physical component of a countermonument exists only for a finite time and/or is shown to change as a function of the specific time, place, and visitors' interaction. An often cited countermonument is Jochen and Esther Shalev-Gerz's "Harburg Monument Against Fascism, War, Violence—For Peace and Human Rights." This monument consisted of a hollow aluminum column erected temporarily in a suburb of Hamburg. Sheathed in lead, the cylinder was to be inscribed by passers-by with their thoughts about what the monument said about their city, community, and country. When a section of column became covered, the artists sank it into the ground, where it eventually disappeared. From that point, only photographs and stories remained from the countermonument. Much as with the museum objects in *Heimatmuseum,* the monument's physical component is accessible only through the mediation of photographs and textual accounts of its contents and changes, yet it is primarily in this form that the monument has gained prominence.

Other forms of countermonuments, particularly *Negativdenkmäler,* also resonate with *Heimatmuseum,* such as the "Mahnmal gegen Rassismus" in Saarbrücken or Horst Hoheisel's inverted Aschrott-Brunnen in Kassel. In both cases, these monuments are installed underground, so that it is very difficult to view them or even to detect their presence. In Saarbrücken, the project consisted of inscribing the names of Jewish cemeteries around Germany on the undersides of cobblestones in a public square.[35] Because artists took and replaced the cobblestones surreptitiously at night, the public became aware of the project only through announcements of its completion. Hoheisel's fountain in turn replicated a fountain, originally erected in 1908 as a gift from the Jewish businessman Sigmund Aschrott to the city of Kassel, but destroyed by the Nazis and condemned to being forgotten. Hoheisel's completed monument is a full-size replica of the fountain, inverted, so that the viewer stands at the base, able to hear the sounds of rushing water and perhaps see a glimpse of the monument through a window. Without wanting to oversimplify the web of meanings that the monuments make available, particularly in their being subterranean,[36] I wish to point out that this form of countermonument relies so heavily on narrative that the question arises as to whether anything physical would have had to be put in place for the effect of the monument to have been achieved. To be sure, the possibility exists that the underground presences could be verified if necessary. But since the usual experience of the monument (e.g., the visitor to the square in Saarbrücken trying to imagine the inscribed stones beneath his or her feet) does not include this eventuality, this form of countermonument works foremost by constructing a narrative about the event and installation.

How different, then, are these monuments from *Heimatmuseum?* Even if it is granted that *Heimatmuseum* would, theoretically, be a different text if photographs of a burning museum or a pile of charred museal remains actually existed, the logic of both countermonuments and *Heimatmuseum* fundamentally relies on denying the role commonly given to material objects and monumental inscriptions at the end of the twentieth century. Both construct narrative as notional equivalents of the physical installation or component, equivalents that nonetheless manifest the moment(s) of transformation from physical to notional states as a nonreducible part of narrative. In other words, if part of the story cannot be left out, it is precisely that aspect of the narrative that relates the decay, transformation, or change of the material environment. This element is what gets updated in the act of receiving one of these countermonumental "texts": it forces the recipient to position him- or herself temporally and spatially with respect to the site, space, or act, confirming the change and/or dispersion of the story. In Lenz's novel, the destruction of the museum will always accompany its transmission into the present. It is therefore tempting to regard *Heimatmuseum* as attempting to situate the concept of Heimat in such a way that it remains accessible only on the condition that recipients of its story learn about the physical environment and its related concepts reaching a dead end. Like narrative scar tissue, this dead end marks the point across which Heimat's attractive features—its timeless sense of purity, wholeness, and rooted identity—must always be translated. Such a strategy, while not without risks, might serve current and future generations better than a sheer repudiation of the German past. Rather than allowing that past to take on a forbidden allure, this strategy transforms aspects of the German past such as Heimat into historically contingent concepts. Brought into the open, those concepts can change and decay over time, however long their half-lives may be.

Part of what makes *Heimatmuseum* such a fascinating text is that, in the end, no photographs of a burning museum or a pile of charred rubble in fact exist alongside it. Using only language, this novel evokes the vivid sense perceptions and knowledge more usually produced by objects encountered in physical environments in the mind's eye. The notional environment enabled by the narrative's serial presentation of "guided tours" works in the metaphorical registers shaped by the museal presentation of the world. By intervening in these discourses, the novel seeks to shape inventoried consciousness in ways that provide readers with an unparalleled sense of the past's richness and complexity. For historical, political, and cultural reasons, this sense of the past is harder to achieve at the end of the twentieth century by using traditional museum and memorial forms. *Heimatmuseum* represents a corrective intervention in the prevailing museum culture, one that claims a singular ability to transmit museal memory and experience. Yet what makes *Heimatmuseum* such a pivotal text in revealing the literary stakes in inventoried consciousness is not that it substitutes writing for the museum per se. Instead, *Heimatmuseum* uses literary artifice to promote the construction of a notional museum. This kind of exhibitionary vision, constructed nowhere but in the reader's mind, is what matters in recollecting the age of the museum.

Conclusion

The idea that a literary text can contribute to the construction of a notional museum offers a productive way for continuing to think about inventoried consciousness in the age of the public museum. It is an idea, rescued from Renaissance conceptions, which points to the centrality of the collector's mind as the locus of greatest concern in thinking about how the museum best fulfills its purposes. It also reminds one that literary texts once could lay claim to the idea of the "museum" with just as much efficacy as an object-rich environment. But it is an idea that can be productive only if it is updated so as to have purchase with respect to the epistemic and disciplinary shifts that have taken place since 1800. This study's genealogy has undertaken this work, to show that the idea of the museum in the mind has been a concern—and received articulation—throughout the history of the public museum.

Some of the purchase of the concept of the notional museum, I believe, lies in the way it supports distinctions between literary and museal environments and the cognitive "work" enabled by interpretation and reflection. Even in cases when literary texts might be considered to operate as textual museums (Rilke's *Neue Gedichte,* Lenz's *Heimatmuseum*), what the readers can construct, as a notional museum in the mind, diverges from the aesthetic artifact. Whatever narrative strategies are pursued to tell stories with objects–very often they tend to involve an ekphrastic form infused with the perceptions and cognitive acts of a narrating consciousness—the readers must take those stories into their lives in order to make them signify.

For the writers in my study, the cognitive work related to the telling of stories with objects has seemed to hold the key to addressing pressing cultural problems. In the postwar era, one such issue, brought to the fore by Bachmann's, Lenz's, and Sebald's writing in particular, involves the use of objects and anecdotes to relate, make meaning out of, and remember catastrophic events such as the Holocaust, war, and destruction. Such traumatic events, along with the accelerating pace of historical and cultural change and obsolescence that have driven the construction of modern museums from their outset, have tended to disrupt the ability of the contemporary mind to maintain ordered continuities with past objects and discourses. In these writers' diagnoses, the past remains accessible in the present era, albeit not in a completely or consciously controllable way. If museum spaces and certain kinds of literary texts have been identified as two indispensable ways of improving one's ability to navigate cognitively in today's digital world, it is because both can, with some sense of regularity and communicability, refer conscious and unconscious stimuli to inventoried consciousness.

In the imaginary worlds of German-speaking literature, the dynamics of collecting and exhibiting are figured again and again as a solely and stubbornly male domain. Even in the twenty-first century, with few exceptions, men collect and exhibit far more readily in Germany and Austria than do women. To my mind, it is most productive to conceive of the persistence of speaking about collecting and exhibiting in gendered terms as an expression of real and desired power relations. The ability to acquire and possess material objects, to order and shape them, to invest them with pasts, to gaze upon them, and to be able to consign them to storage or oblivion, all of these convey considerable imagined and real advantages and thus give rise to a variety of power differentials. These might extend beyond the collector/collected relationship to the communication between the collector and the viewer of an exhibition. The construction and expression of these differentials in terms of sexual difference and sexual economies signal that these processes are profoundly connected to our core needs, fears, and experiences as human beings, however these are perceived and articulated in a particular time, culture, and set of discourses.

One thing the persistent literary perception of collecting and exhibiting as a "masculine domain" might express is that a power asymmetry inheres to accumulation and display. Thus the possibility exists that collecting and exhibiting shift power relations in the favor of the collector, regardless of his or her gender. Critics such as Douglas Crimp, Andreas Huyssen, Roger Silverstone, Mieke Bal, and Tony Bennett have all expressed a certain anticipation that diversifying curatorial staff, postmodern installations, and increased interactivity with audiences shift power relations in favor of audiences by revealing alternatives that curators and exhibitors have rendered invisible through their decision making. It continues to be a valid and open question, however, whether these attempts to counteract the asymmetries completely succeed in shifting or reversing power imbalances within museums. While efforts of this kind no doubt have progressive intentions and should not be abandoned, the limits and effects of these strategies in domains governed by structural power inequalities should be recognized. Women might well benefit in some ways from increasing their numbers as collectors or shifting certain display practices, but this might not result in dominance being eliminated per se. The point would not be to preserve collecting and exhibiting as "masculine" domains in Germany or elsewhere, but rather to attend to the effects of power asymmetries even as the gendered exclusivity of collecting is reduced.

The possibility that collecting inherently creates asymmetrical power relations does nothing to diminish the importance of literature in its relationship to the dynamics of collecting and exhibiting. If anything, literature is all the more valuable as a result. I have argued that the thought experiments and notional museums established in literature permit imaginative explorations of the dynamics of collecting and exhibiting. From Goethe's *Elective Affinities* and Stifter's *Indian Summer* to Raabe's "Keltische Knochen" and even Rilke's *Dinggedichte,* writing offers the means of probing social configurations, behavior, bodily experience, and material reality in ways that might be more difficult or even impossible in the actual world, given the political and financial costs of creating and maintaining assemblages of objects and catalogs. Particularly in the later twentieth century, as museums and related institutions have proliferated and become "second nature," that literary exploration has taken the form of an engagement opposing many of these tendencies. Bachmann's and Lenz's novels correspondingly work against institutions, army and Heimat museums that offer inroads for retrenchment of reactionary political and social values.

Though many postwar intellectuals such as Bachmann and Lenz seem to favor narrative constructs over object-rich environments for promoting the cognitive "work" of a notional museum, it is, I think, too simple to conclude that literary texts should always prevail over museum settings or vice versa. At this juncture, the institutional and disciplinary forces that gave rise to the oppositional relationship between notions of the material museum and the immaterial literary text continue to exist. This is not to say that digital media and electronic databases, on the one hand, and interdisciplinary approaches to cultural problems, on the other, do not affect these configurations. Hal Foster, for one, has written that electronic databases seem to be splitting certain mnemonic functions off from the traditional mode of museum display. These shifts seem only to deepen the dominance of political economy over the institution's functions.[1] But whatever form these configurations take and however their functions become differentiated, literary texts, databases, and museums will continue to exist in relation to, and exert pressure on, one another.

This is perhaps another way of saying that future developments might well lead to a different configuration of archives, museums, and literature than is currently the case. Yet, as I have sought to show in many chapters of this study, German writers and museum makers have differentiated museums from other archival institutions. In many of the texts in this study, most prominently in writing by Goethe, Bachmann, Lenz, Grünbein, and Sebald, museums have singular effects on the mind, body, culture, and memory, which cannot be produced by other kinds of institutions that categorize, store, and preserve cultural artifacts.

With regard to the question of the "archive," I hope to have made a case for the need for greater historical and theoretical precision.

With respect to the advantages of literature versus museums, I have also raised concerns, particularly in my reading of W. G. Sebald's texts, about the relationship of artifice to the authenticity of memory and experience. In this regard, the genealogy offered by this study indicates that neither museums nor literary texts may be capable of offering more than artifice, in the sense that there is some "reality" outside these discourses. In Goethe's *Wahlverwandtschaften,* for instance, collections are shown to induce a dreamlike state in the characters encountering them; this allows the text to be read on one level as a warning about social hazards potentially arising from the widespread public exhibition of art. Yet the text transmitting this insight is not only one of the most sophisticated literary constructs in the German tradition, but also one that presents those encounters in an ekphrastic mode that evokes their effects in the mind's eye. Even if that exhibitory vision prepares readers to take the text's warning to heart and learn to better navigate a world beset with dream images, the basis for this ability does not spring from having left artifice behind. This notion applies for practically all the writing in this study, whether the dream images take the form of the Germanic past, commodities, acculturation, the nation, or digital simulacra. In the texts presented here, the inability to separate "factual reality" from "fictional invention" derives from the fact that the metaphorical regimes that allow museums and literary texts to construct their worlds are the same metaphorical regimes that construct *the* world.

This realization undercuts a perennial function of the museum, namely, to lend material backing to, indeed to authenticate, concepts and myths by means of displayed objects ("this is how it is"). This does not mean that from now on, everything must be considered fake or simulated and that distinctions between material and virtual environments cannot be maintained (for beings who inhabit bodies and three-dimensional space, material constraints will, so far as I can tell, continue to matter). Rather, museum-backed notions of authenticity underwriting so many modern-day myths—from the acculturated soul schooled by exposure to "true art" to the "historical destiny" of the German people—are notions that properly belong, like so many historical relics, "in the museum."

The ability of literary texts and museum environments to access the same metaphorical regimes also means that museums and collections, like their literary counterparts, succeed when they contribute to visitors' ability to construct and maintain notional museums. At stake in these notional museums is an enhanced sense of the past and present-day world that, so the thinking goes, might help people find greater satisfaction in their lives and their relationships to others.

The propensity to realize this theoretical promise, this study suggests, depends foremost on what people bring, in their minds, to those real and imagined environments. Insofar as the texts in this study depict as well as promote the kind of vivid mental frameworks that can be developed in response to organized spatial environments, recognizing this point seems to be key—not only for unlocking these revealing texts, but also for understanding that the world and our lives are only as rich as they can be envisioned in the mind's eye.

Notes

Chapter 1

1 Peter Weiss, Die Ästhetik des Widerstands (Frankfurt am Main: Suhrkamp, 1983), 11.

2 Weiss, *Die Ästhetik des Widerstands,* 11.

3 While I have adapted and expanded this concept for my purposes, I encountered the term "museum function" in my studies with Jann Matlock. Matlock's influence on my thinking, particularly in the early stages of this project, has been considerable, and I am grateful for her contribution. Art historians Carol Duncan and Alan Wallach have an earlier, unelaborated usage of the "museum function" that discusses the ceremonial display features of older architectural forms such as temples and cathedral chapels. See Carol Duncan and Alan Wallach, "The Universal Survey Museum," *Art History* 3, no. 4 (1980): 449.

4 Weiss, *Die Ästhetik des Widerstands,* 7. This translation is mine, as the English translation of the novel's first volume will not be available until 2005.

5 Walter Benjamin, "Eduard Fuchs: Der Sammler und der Historiker," in *Gesammelte Schriften,* ed. Rolf Tiedemann et al. (Frankfurt am Main: Suhrkamp, 1980), 2: pt. 2, 465–506 [hereafter *Gesammelte Schriften*].

6 Benjamin, "Eduard Fuchs: Der Sammler und der Historiker," in *Gesammelte Schriften,* 2: pt. 2, 502. Walter Benjamin, "Eduard Fuchs: Collector and Historian," in *Selected Writings: 1935–1938,* ed. Howard Eiland and Michael W. Jennings (Cambridge: Belknap/Harvard University Press, 2002), 3:282 [hereafter Edward Fuchs].

7 Erk Grimm uses the notion of inventory repeatedly in analyzing contemporary poetry, but, so far as I can tell, he does not use the phrase "inventoried consciousness." I intend a precise usage with different goals than Grimm's (see note 9 below). See Erk Grimm, "Fathoming the Archive: German Poetry and the Culture of Memory," *New German Critique* 88 (2003): 107–40.

8 Hans Haacke, "Museums, Managers of Consciousness," in *Hans Haacke Unfinished Business,* ed. Brian Wallis (Cambridge: MIT Press, 1986), 60.

9 By calling the story of Noah's Ark an instance of inventoried consciousness, I wish to argue against the tendency of contemporary scholars to see in it a "museum" or an "archive," as found, for instance, in Erk Grimm, "Fathoming the Archive: German Poetry and the Culture of Memory," 136. See Martin Luther, trans., *Die Bibel* (Stuttgart: Deutsche Bibelstiftung, 1978), 7:1–3. I am thinking of the Lay of the Lament of the Lost Survivor in *Beowulf.* See *Beowulf. A Verse Translation,* ed. Daniel Donoghue, trans. Seamus Heaney (London: Norton, 2002), 57–58.

10 Michel Foucault, *The Order of Things: An Archaeology of the Human Sciences* (New York: Pantheon Books, 1971), xvii–xviv. This shift can be similarly described using Luhmannian thinking. See Wolfgang Ernst, "Archi(ve)textures of Museology," in *Museums and Memory,* ed. Susan A. Crane (Stanford: Stanford University Press, 2000), 18–20.

11 Ernst, "Archi(ve)textures of Museology," 19.

12 Paula Findlen, "The Modern Muses: Collecting and the Cult of Remembrance in Renaissance Italy," in *Museums and Memory,* ed. Susan A. Crane (Stanford: Stanford University Press, 2000), 177–78.

13 Ernst, "Archi(ve)textures of Museology," 19.

14 Ernst, "Archi(ve)textures of Museology," 21. See also Eugenio Donato, "The Museum's Furnace: Notes Towards a Contextual Reading of Bouvard et Pécuchet," in *Textual Strategies:*

Perspectives in Post-Structuralist Criticism, ed. Josue V. Harari (Ithaca: Cornell University Press, 1979), 218. Suzanne L. Marchand, *Down from Olympus: Archaeology and Philhellenism in Germany, 1750–1970* (Princeton: Princeton University Press, 1996), 104–6. Narrative collections and even entire journals continued to be referred to as "museums" well into the nineteenth century. As late as 1814, the Romantic writer Jean Paul collaborated with the museum society of Frankfurt to produce the *Museum of Jean Paul,* a written volume whose title is justified with the reminder that "there are both written as well as built museums." As examples of both kinds, Jean Paul enumerates "the German museum—the fatherland museum—Schlegel's museum—the British museum—the Scandinavian museum—Baumgärtner's museums of the curious and of luxury." The "German museum" probably refers to H. C. Boie's "Deutsches Museum," published from 1776 to 1791. See Jean Paul Richter, "Museum von Jean Paul," in *Jean Pauls Sämtliche Werke,* ed. Preussische Akademie der Wissenschaften (Weimar: Herman Böhlau Nachfolger, 1938), 3.

15 See Durs Grünbein and Heinz-Norbert Jocks, *Durs Grünbein im Gespräch mit Heinz-Norbert Jocks* (Cologne: Dumont, 2001), 50–51.

16 Andreas Huyssen, *Twilight Memories: Marking Time in a Culture of Amnesia* (New York: Routledge, 1995), 18.

17 See discussions in Huyssen, *Twilight Memories,* 18f., and Mark W. Rectanus, *Culture Incorporated: Museums, Artists, and Corporate Sponsorships* (Minneapolis: University of Minnesota Press, 2002), 175–77. Salvos against broad audience appeal when the focus shifts from aesthetic perception were articulated in the following: James Cuno, ed., *Whose Muse? Art Museums and the Public Trust* (Princeton: Princeton University Press, 2004), 17–20, 53–55, 70f., 131–33, 138, 146f., 157f., 165f.

18 Huyssen, *Twilight Memories,* 18. Hal Foster, "Archives of Modern Art," *October* 99 (2002): 81–95.

19 Huyssen, *Twilight Memories,* 18. Foster, "Archives of Modern Art," 81–95.

20 Rectanus, *Culture Incorporated,* 216–25.

21 Though collecting is a fundamentally human activity, studies of medieval and Renaissance collecting have demonstrated radically different assumptions about collecting and exhibiting than are manifested in the post-Enlightenment. See Eilean Hooper-Greenhill, *Museums and the Shaping of Knowledge* (New York: Routledge, 1992), 5–15, 105–32. Lorraine Daston and Katherine Park, *Wonders and the Order of Nature, 1150–1750* (New York: Zone, 1998), 14.

22 See Carol Duncan, *Civilizing Rituals: Inside Public Art Museums* (London: Routledge, 1995), 20. Tony Bennett, *The Birth of the Museum: History, Theory, Politics* (London: Routledge, 1995), 57–105.

23 This phrasing is taken from James Rolleston.

24 James L. Rolleston, "The Politics of Quotation: Walter Benjamin's Arcades Project," *PMLA* 104, no. 1 (1989): 15.

25 Rolleston, "The Politics of Quotation," 15.

26 Rolleston, "The Politics of Quotation," 24–25.

27 Grünbein and Jocks, *Grünbein im Gespräch.* 33.

28 This phrasing is taken from Eric Downing, *Dirty Pictures: Photography, Archaeology, Psychoanalysis, and the Tradition of Bildung* (Detroit: Wayne State University Press, 2006), 15f. I have also drawn on the phrasing of Catherine Gallagher and Stephen Greenblatt, *Practicing New Historicism* (Chicago: University of Chicago Press, 2000), 30.

29 Mieke Bal, *Double Exposures: The Subject of Cultural Analysis* (New York: Routledge, 1996), 3.

30 Bal, *Double Exposures,* 3.

31 Bal, *Double Exposures,* 3–4. Ball cites Gananath Obeyesekere, *The Apotheosis of Captain Cook: European Mythmaking in the Pacific* (Princeton: Princeton University Press, 1990), 10–11. See also the argument of Robert Bud, "Science, Meaning, and Myth in the Museum," *Public Understanding of Science* 4 (1995): 1–16.

32 Worlds of difference obtain between prevailing conceptions of the archive. Foucault, on one

hand, defines the archive as "the law of what can be said, the system that governs the appearance of statements as unique events." Derrida, on the other, finds it necessary to think of the "archive" in terms of patriarchal law, Freudian drives and desires, and memory. Foucault's notion, as Boris Groys, Aleida Assmann, and Hal Foster have all made clear, is divorced from the physical records normally associated with the archive. See Michel Foucault, *The Archaeology of Knowledge,* trans. Alan Sheridan (New York: Pantheon Books, 1972), 129–30. Foster, "Archives of Modern Art": 81–95. Boris Groys, *Über das Neue: Versuch einer Kulturökonomie* (Munich: C. Hanser, 1992), 49. Aleida Assmann, *Erinnerungsräume: Formen und Wandlungen des kulturellen Gedächtnisses* (Munich: C. H. Beck, 1999), 346f. Derrida, in an ahistorical manner, distinguishes between the operations of conscious memory (*mneme*), the capacity for recall (*anamnesis*), and the use of prosthetic extensions of memory (*hypomnesis*). See Jacques Derrida, *Archive Fever: A Freudian Impression,* trans. Eric Prenowitz (Chicago: University of Chicago Press, 1996), 2–3, 7, 11, 25–31. See also Nancy Armstrong, *Fiction in the Age of Photography: The Legacy of British Realism* (Cambridge: Harvard University Press, 1999), 15–16. Michal Kobialka, "Historical Archives, Events, and Facts: History Writing as Fragmentary Performance," *Performance Research* 7, no. 4 (2002): 3–11. The collective term "archive" loses much of its ability to apply to a huge range of phenomena as soon as one insists upon conceptual rigor. This is particularly true of approaches derived from Derrida's theorization, which are seldom rigorously historicized, leading any and all, real or imagined, forms of knowledge production having something to do with accumulation and classification to be described as "archival."

33 Representative of this tendency is a study such as Thomas Richards's *The Imperial Archive,* which breezily moves between "knowledge producing institutions like the British Museum, the Royal Geographical Society, the India Survey, and the universities" (p. 4). The fantasy of total, classifying knowledge might well have exerted a powerful hold on people, enabling them to conceive of the British Empire, but this premise cannot do sufficient "work" unless it is equipped to make meaningful distinctions between institutions whose operating assumptions and methods diverge as much as they resemble one another. Symptomatically, Richards's claim that Jules Verne's submarine in *10,000 Leagues Under the Sea* represents the realization of André Malreaux's "museum without walls" seems not quite in the spirit of the French original, which translates literally as "the imaginary museum" and which involves the ability to construct alternative museums using photographs and other means of reproduction. Thomas Richards, *The Imperial Archive: Knowledge and the Fantasy of Empire* (New York: Verso, 1993), 4–6, 116–18.

34 Archivists, librarians, and curators understand their practices as related yet distinct. See Eckhardt G. Franz, "Archive, Bibliotheken, Museen—Gemeinsamkeiten und Besonderheiten, Grenzen und Zusammenspiel: Protokoll des Prodiumsgesprächs auf dem 51. deutschen Archivtag," *Der Archivar* 31, no. 1 (1978): 23–28. Two exceptions are Ernst, "Archi(ve)textures of Museology," 18–20; and Foster, "Archives of Modern Art," 81–95.

35 Some perspectives on libraries and archives include Markus Krajewski, *Zettelwirtschaft: Die Geburt der Kartei aus dem Geiste der Bibliothek* (Berlin: Kulturverlag Kadmos, 2002), 7–15; Hedwig Pompe and Leander Scholz, eds., *Archivprozesse: Die Kommunikation der Aufbewahrung* (Cologne: DuMont, 2002), 238–68, 291–315.

36 See, for instance, Anne Fuchs, "'Phantomspuren': Zu W. G. Sebalds Poetik der Erinnerung in Austerlitz," *German Life and Letters* 56 (2003): 281–98.

37 Eric Gidal, *Poetic Exhibitions: Romantic Aesthetics and the Pleasures of the British Museum* (Lewisburg: Bucknell University Press, 2001), 16. Barbara J. Black, *On Exhibit: Victorians and Their Museums* (Charlottesville: University Press of Virginia, 2000), 1–19. Catherine E. Paul, *Poetry in the Museums of Modernism: Yeats, Pound, Moore, Stein* (Ann Arbor: University of Michigan Press, 2002), 2–11.

38 Arendt writes of Benjamin as someone "whose spiritual existence had been formed and informed by Goethe." See Hannah Arendt, "Introduction," in *Illuminations,* ed. Hannah Arendt (New York: Harcourt Brace Jovanovich, 1967), 14. Some of Benjamin's affinities to Goethe are self-acknowledged, while others are not. See Daniel Purdy, "Weimar Classicism and the Origins of Consumer Culture," in *Unwrapping Goethe's Weimar: Essays in Cultural Studies and Local Knowledge,* ed. Burkhard Henke, Susanne Kord, and Simon Richter (Rochester, N.Y.: Camden House, 2000), 36–62.

39 On Nietzsche's museum critique, see James J. Sheehan, *Museums in the German Art World* (Oxford: Oxford University Press, 2000), 140–43. Only Goethe's writing was more valued by Nietzsche than was *Der Nachsommer.* On the relationship of *Der Nachsommer* to Nietzsche's thought, see Ernst Bertram, *Nietzsche: Versuch einer Mythologie* (Bonn: Bouvier, 1965), 238–48; and Renate Müller-Buck, "'Oktober-Sonne bis ins Geistige hinauf': Anfängliches zur Bedeutung von Goethes 'Novelle' und Stifters 'Nachsommer' für Nietzsches Kunstauffassung," *Nietzsche-Studien* 18 (1989): 537–49. In "Das Nutzen und Nachteil der Historie für das Leben" (The Use and Disadvantage of History for Life), Nietzsche distinguished between monumental history, antiquarian history, and critical history, showing how each in extreme form could endanger life. The antiquarian mode is most commonly linked to musealized forms of culture, though, as Walter Benjamin's critique of Wilhelminian *Kulturgeschichte* makes clear, museums may also serve as a means of enacting monumental history. Friedrich Nietzsche, "Das Nutzen und Nachteil der Historie für das Leben," in *Sämtliche Werke. Kritische Studienausgabe,* ed. Giorgio Colli and Mazzino Montinari (Berlin: de Gruyter, 1980), 1:243–334. Benjamin, "Eduard Fuchs," in *Gesammelte Schriften,* 502.

40 Arendt, "Introduction," 24, 39, 42–46.

41 "Imaginary topography" is a phrase I borrow from Sigrid Weigel, *Ingeborg Bachmann: Hinterlassenschaften unter Wahrung des Briefgeheimnisses* (Vienna: P. Zsolnay Verlag, 1999), 369. In regard to Grünbein and Benjamin, I am thinking of an essay such as "Kindheit im Diorama," which explicitly cites Benjamin's Arcades Project and the phrase "the Age of Mechanical Reproducibility," developing a number of his notions from the "Work of Art" essay with respect to the way the diorama structures memory and consciousness. See the essay in the collection by Durs Grünbein, *Galilei vermißt Dantes Hölle und bleibt an den Massen hängen: Aufsätze, 1989–1995* (Frankfurt am Main: Suhrkamp, 1996), 117–28, esp. 118, 122.

42 Hooper-Greenhill and Bennett make use of Foucault's notion of the episteme. Hooper-Greenhill, *Museums and the Shaping of Knowledge,* 7–18. Bennett, *Birth of the Museum,* 33. The excellent collection by Daniel J. Sherman and Irit Rogoff represents general Foucauldian approaches. Daniel J. Sherman and Irit Rogoff, eds., *Museum Culture: Histories, Discourses, Spectacles* (Minneapolis: University of Minnesota Press, 1994), 213–38. See also Douglas Crimp, *On the Museum's Ruins: With Photographs by Louise Lawler* (Cambridge: MIT Press, 1993), 44f. See Donato, "The Museum's Furnace."

43 On the possibility of alternative regimes of knowledge being enabled by alternative groupings of objects, see, for instance, James Clifford's notion of the art-culture divide. James Clifford, *The Predicament of Culture: Twentieth-Century Ethnography, Literature, and Art* (Cambridge: Harvard University Press, 1988), 220. On the implications for art history, see Donald Preziosi, *Rethinking Art History: Meditations on a Coy Science* (New Haven: Yale University Press, 1989), 70. Norman Bryson, "The Gaze in the Expanded Field," in *Vision and Visuality,* ed. Hal Foster (Seattle: Bay Press, 1988), 87–133.

44 For historical accounts of this issue, see Daniel J. Sherman, *Worthy Monuments: Art Museums and the Politics of Culture in Nineteenth-Century France* (Cambridge: Harvard University Press, 1989). Pierre Darbel and Alain Darbel with Dominique Schnapper Bourdieu, *The Love of Art: European Art Museums and Their Public,* trans. Caroline Beattie and Nick Merrima (Stanford: Stanford University Press, 1990).

45 Bennett rejects attempts such as Crimp's to use Foucauldian thinking to assert a fundamental likeness of the museum to an enclosed and enclosing prison space. Bennett, *Birth of the Museum,* 69. See Crimp, *On the Museum's Ruins,* 44f.

46 Bennett, *Birth of the Museum,* 69.

47 See Ackbar Abbas, "Walter Benjamin's Collector: The Fate of the Modern Experience," in *Modernity and the Text: Revisions of German Modernism,* ed. Andreas Huyssen and David Bathrick (New York: Columbia University Press, 1989), 216–39.

48 Abbas, "Walter Benjamin's Collector," 231.

49 Benjamin, "Ich packe meine Bibliothek aus," in *Gesammelte Schriften,* ed. Tilmann Rexroth (Frankfurt am Main: Suhrkamp, 1991), 4: pt. 1, 389. Similarly, in the Work of Art essay, "of course, the history of the artwork encompasses more than this. The history of the *Mona Lisa,* for instance, encompasses the kind and number of its copies made in the 17th, 18th, and

nineteenth centuries." Benjamin, "Das Kunstwerk . . . ," in *Gesammelte Schriften*, ed. Rolf Tiedemann et al. (Frankfurt am Main: Suhrkamp, 1980), 1: pt. 2, 476, note 2. "The Work of Art in the Age of Mechanical Reproduction," in *Illuminations*, ed. Hannah Arendt (New York: Schocken, 1968), 243. In the translation, this is note 1.

50 Michael P. Steinberg, "The Collector as Allegorist: Goods, Gods, and the Objects of History," in *Walter Benjamin and the Demands of History*, ed. Michael P. Steinberg (Ithaca: Cornell University Press, 1996), 88–89.

51 Eduard Fuchs, *Dachreiter und verwandte chinesische Keramik des 15. bis 18. Jahrhunderts* (Munich: Albert Langen, 1924), 5–6. Quoted in Benjamin, "Eduard Fuchs," in *Gesammelte Schriften*, 2: bk. 2, 502.

52 One prominent exception is the excellent essay by Daniel J. Sherman, "Quatremére/Benjamin/Marx: Art Museums, Aura, and Commodity Fetishism," in *Museum Culture: Histories, Discourses, Spectacles*, ed. Daniel J. Sherman and Irit Rogoff (Minneapolis: University of Minnesota Press, 1994), 123–43.

53 Benjamin, "Das Kunstwerk," 484 [emphasis original]. "Work of Art," 225. Compare remarks by Beatrice Hanssen, *Walter Benjamin's Other History: Of Stones, Animals, Human Beings, and Angels* (Berkeley and Los Angeles: University of California Press, 1998), 78.

54 Reproductions are, in other words, a way of augmenting the objects' exhibition value. Benjamin, "Das Kunstwerk," 484.

55 Foster, "Archives of Modern Art," 93. In note 29, p. 93, Foster points to precisely this transformation of original to authentic as underpinning the notion he has in mind.

56 Walter Benjamin, *Das Passagenwerk*, ed. Rolf Tiedemann et al., *Gesammelte Schriften* (Frankfurt am Main: Suhrkamp, 1980), 5: bk. 1, 274. Walter Benjamin, *The Arcades Project*, trans. Howard Eiland and Kevin McLaughlin (New York: Belknap, 2002), 206.

57 Benjamin, "Das Kunstwerk," 474–75. "The Work of Art," 222.

58 Esther Leslie, *Walter Benjamin: Overpowering Conformity* (London: Pluto Press, 2000), 150–51.

59 Benjamin, "Ich packe," 390. See also Abbas, "Walter Benjamin's Collector," 231.

60 Walter Benjamin, "Unpacking My Library," in *Illuminations*, ed. Hannah Arendt (New York: Schocken, 1968), 57–64.

61 Walter Benjamin, "The Storyteller," in *Illuminations*, ed. Hannah Arendt (New York: Schocken, 1968), 83–109.

62 See Chapter 6 in this volume. See also the analysis offered in Weigel, *Ingeborg Bachmann*, 368f.

63 Benjamin, *Passagenwerk*, 279. Benjamin, *The Arcades Project*, 211.

64 Walter Benjamin, "Ich packe meine Bibliothek aus," 395. Benjamin, "Unpacking My Library," in *Illuminations*, ed. Hannah Arendt (New York: Schocken, 1968), 58–68.

65 In addition to the essays and books I have already cited, I have in mind works such as Susan M. Pearce, *Museums, Objects, and Collections: A Cultural Study* (Washington, D.C.: Smithsonian Institution Press, 1992). Ivan Karp and Steven D. Lavine, eds., *Exhibiting Cultures: The Poetics and Politics of Museum Display* (Washington, D.C.: Smithsonian Institution Press, 1991). Ivan Karp, Christine Mullen Kreamer, and Steven D. Lavine, eds., *Museums and Communities: The Politics of Public Culture* (Washington, D.C.: Smithsonian Institution Press, 1992). Gwendolyn Wright, ed., *The Formation of National Collections of Art and Archaeology* (Washington, D.C.: National Gallery of Art, distributed by University Press of New England, 1996). John Elsner and Roger Cardinal, eds., *Cultures of Collecting* (Cambridge: Harvard University Press, 1994). Andrew McClellan, *Inventing the Louvre: Art, Politics, and the Origins of the Modern Museum in Eighteenth-Century Paris* (Cambridge: Cambridge University Press, 1994). Linda Nochlin, "Museums and Radicals: A History of Emergencies," in *Museums in Crisis*, ed. Brian O'Doherty (New York: G. Braziller, 1972).

66 It is worth pointing out that I have been using the pronoun "he" deliberately, since, with few exceptions, the collector is gendered "masculine" in the period I am considering.

67 Martin Roth, *Heimatmuseum: Zur Geschichte einer deutschen Institution* (Berlin: Mann, 1990), 108, 173. Lars-H. Thümmler, *Das Zeughaus Berlin im Zweiten Weltkrieg.* [Internet] (Deutsches Historisches Museum, 2003); [cited November 11, 2006]; available from http://www.dhm.de/texte/zhwk2.html.

Chapter 2

1 Durs Grünbein and Heinz-Norbert Jocks, *Durs Grünbein im Gespräch mit Heinz-Norbert Jocks* (Cologne: Dumont, 2001), 68.

2 Kempowski, for instance, accumulates quotes, observations, anecdotes, and historical tidbits that strike his fancy but that might sit in waiting for an indeterminate time before being attached to a character or a situation.

3 Fabian Lampart, "'Jeder in *seiner* Welt, so viele Welten.' Durs Grünbeins Dante," *Text und Kritik: Zeitschrift für Literatur* 153 (2002): 49.

4 Juvenal is the coiner of phrases such as "bread and circuses" to describe the quotidian pursuits of the Roman people and also the notion "who shall watch the watchmen?" See also Manfred Fuhrmann, "Juvenal-Barbier—Grünbein: Über den römischen Satiriker und zwei seiner tätigen Bewunderer," *Text und Kritik: Zeitschrift für Literatur* 153 (2002): 65–67. Helmut Böttiger, *Nach den Utopien: Eine Geschichte der deutschsprachigen Gegenwartsliteratur* (Vienna: Paul Zsolney, 2004), 122–23.

5 Durs Grünbein, "Zwischen Antike und X," in *Warum schriftlos leben: Aufsätze* (Frankfurt am Main: Suhrkamp, 2003), 117.

6 Grünbein, "Zwischen Antike und X," 114.

7 Riedel differentiates the term "poetics of presence" in this context from that espoused by George Steiner. Wolfgang Riedel, "Poetik der Präsenz: Idee der Dichtung bei Durs Grünbein," *Internationales Archiv für Sozialgeschichte der deutschen Literatur* 24, no. 1 (1999): 90.

8 Riedel, "Poetik der Präsenz," 90.

9 Riedel, "Poetik der Präsenz," 96.

10 Durs Grünbein, *Galilei vermißt Dantes Hölle und bleibt an den Massen hängen: Aufsätze 1989–1995* (Frankfurt am Main: Suhrkamp, 1996), 25.

11 Grünbein, *Galilei,* 32.

12 Eshel makes a similar point. Amir Eshel, "Diverging Memories? Durs Grünbein's Mnemonic Topographies and the Future of the German Past," *German-Quarterly* 74, no. 4 (2001): 410.

13 Grünbein's position seems close to that articulated by linguist George Lakoff and philosopher Mark Johnson, in their book *Metaphors We Live By* (Chicago: University of Chicago Press, 1980) and their subsequent work on the problem of what has come to be known as the "embodied mind."

14 Grünbein, *Galilei,* 23–24.

15 Grünbein, *Galilei,* 23.

16 [Emphasis original.] Grünbein and Jocks, *Grünbein im Gespräch.* 35.

Grünbein's equation of mental image and visual perception differs from the assessment of researchers in this field, who would differentiate between the richness of a visual perception and that of a mental image.

17 John Hollander, *The Gazer's Spirit: Poems Speaking to Silent Works of Art* (Chicago: University of Chicago Press, 1995). 7–29.

18 Grünbein, *Galilei,* 33. [My emphasis.]

19 See the arguments made by Donald Preziosi, *Rethinking Art History: Meditations on a Coy Science* (New Haven: Yale University Press, 1989), 68–70.

20 Böttiger, *Nach den Utopien: Eine Geschichte der deutschsprachigen Gegenwartsliteratur,* 120.

21 This is because, as Amir Eshel rightly points out, the poet produces historically informed images shaped both by unconsciousness memories and a "brain constantly perceiving the world, collecting images, and turning them into words, poems." Eshel, "Diverging Memories?" 410.

22 The italics are my emphasis; the ellipsis appears in the original. Grünbein, *Galilei,* 30.

23 Leading up to the quoted section, Grünbein discusses the effects of the Shoah in terms of damage to the brain that, in the process of healing, requires the training of other sections to take over the functions once carried out by the original section. Grünbein, *Galilei,* 32.

24 Both Amir Eshel and Erk Grimm gloss over this point in their discussions of this passage, an omission that is especially peculiar in Grimm's analysis. So far as I can tell, the archive is conceived of there as an entity that functions as intended, whether as a repository of written texts or as electronic databases. Though Grünbein can be seen as a representative of a contemporary literature given over to inventoried consciousness, thinking of modern consciousness in terms of a functioning archive seems to contradict Grünbein's thinking. Compare Eshel, "Diverging Memories?" 410. Erk Grimm, "Fathoming the Archive: German Poetry and the Culture of Memory," *New German Critique* 88 (2003): 137.

25 On Grimm's view of the Stasi files, see Grimm, "Fathoming the Archive," 130–31.

26 The structural element of the essay "Bevor der Mensch mit sich allein ist: 150 Jahre Zoologischer Garten Berlin" [Before Humankind Is Alone with Itself: 150 Years of the Berlin Zoological Garden] is the use of changing zoo architectures—meaning both styles of buildings and modes of display—highlighting the functions of the zoo in the colonial period and today. Grünbein, *Galilei,* 229–36.

27 Grünbein, *Galilei,* 221–22.

28 Grünbein, *Galilei,* 222–28.

29 Grünbein and Jocks, *Grünbein im Gespräch,* 51f..

30 Andreas Huyssen, *Twilight Memories: Marking Time in a Culture of Amnesia* (New York: Routledge, 1995), 32–35, 255. Hal Foster's articulation of this problematic in his "Archives of Modern Art" is also worth looking at. Hal Foster, "Archives of Modern Art," *October* 99 (2002): 81–95.

31 Foster, "Archives of Modern Art," 94–95. See also Ursula Frohne, "Motive der Zeit," in *Kunst der Gegenwart: Museum für Neue Kunst: ZKM Zentrum für Kunst und Medientechnologie Karlsruhe,* ed. Heinrich Klotz, Horst Bredekamp, and Ursula Frohne (Munich: Prestel, 1997), 38–50.

32 Grünbein and Jocks, *Grünbein im Gespräch,* 52f., 68f. Grünbein, *Galilei,* 33.

33 Grünbein, *Galilei,* 122.

34 Grünbein, *Galilei,* 122–23.

35 Walter Benjamin, "Charles Baudelaire: Ein Lyriker im Zeitalter des Hochkapitalismus," in *Gesammelte Schriften,* ed. Rolf Tiedemann et al. (Frankfurt am Main: Suhrkamp, 1974), 1: bk. 2, 611. Walter Benjamin, "On Some Motifs in Baudelaire," in *Illuminations,* ed. Hannah Arendt (New York: Schocken, 1968), 159.

36 Benjamin, "Charles Baudelaire: Ein Lyriker im Zeitalter des Hochkapitalismus," 611. Benjamin, "On Some Motifs in Baudelaire," 159.

37 Grünbein, *Galilei,* 123f.

38 Compare to Grimm's analysis of the diorama, which regards the function of what he calls the "visual archive" as consisting primarily in storage. Grimm, "Fathoming the Archive," 135.

39 See the remarks in Grünbein, *Galilei,* 117–19.

40 See James L. Rolleston, "The Politics of Quotation: Walter Benjamin's Arcades Project," *PMLA* 104, no. 1 (1989): 15.

41 Grünbein, *Galilei,* 119.

42 Durs Grünbein, *Falten und Fallen: Gedichte* (Frankfurt am Main: Suhrkamp, 1994), 123. This translation is mine.

43 Grünbein and Jocks, *Grünbein im Gespräch,* 68.

44 Grünbein, *Galilei,* 229–36.

45 "Creative forgetting" is Andreas Huyssen's phrase, which he uses to describe a theoretical potential for museums and exhibitionary spaces in the digital age. Huyssen, *Twilight Memories,* 34.

46 Theodor W. Adorno, *Minima Moralia: Reflexionen aus dem beschädigten Leben* (Frankfurt am Main: Suhrkamp, 1980), 210–12. In another essay, Grünbein predicts that the future of the diorama, an outmoded display technique, resides in its ability to represent extinct species in the manner convenient to us. Grünbein, *Galilei,* 119, 234–35.

47 Indeed, recent analyses have pointed out that prominent initiatives to spur innovation of computer technologies use the museum as a paradigm for exploring and thinking through computer functionality. Mark W. Rectanus, *Culture Incorporated: Museums, Artists, and Corporate Sponsorships* (Minneapolis: University of Minnesota Press, 2002), 221, 216.

48 Grünbein is particularly articulate in this respect, but he is by no means an exception in contemporary Germany. See Wolfgang Emmerich, "German Writers as Intellectuals: Strategies and Aporias of Engagement in East and West from 1945 Until Today," *New German Critique* 88 (2003): 37–54.

49 W. G. Sebald and Michaël Zeeman, "Max Sebald Interviewed by Michaël Zeeman: Programme: Kamer Met Uitzicht 12 July 1998 (VPRO—Netherlands TV). Transcribed by Gordon Turner, 2003," in *W. G. Sebald: History—Memory—Trauma,* ed. Scott Denham and Mark R. McCulloh (Berlin: de Gruyter, 2006). forthcoming. I am grateful to Gordon Turner for supplying me with this transcript.

50 [Emphasis original.]. Sebald and Zeeman, "Max Sebald Interviewed by Michaël Zeeman," forthcoming. This card appears in *Austerlitz* as a document collected by Austerlitz's mentor, the history teacher André Hilary. W. G. Sebald, *Austerlitz* (Munich: Hanser, 2001), 108. W. G. Sebald, *Austerlitz* (New York: Random House, 2001), 74. [Subsequent references cite these editions.]

51 Walter Benjamin, "Unpacking My Library," in *Illuminations,* ed. Hannah Arendt (New York: Schocken, 1968), 63. [Translation modified.]

52 Walter Benjamin, *Das Passagenwerk,* ed. Rolf Tiedemann et al. *Gesammelte Schriften* (Frankfurt am Main: Suhrkamp, 1980), 5: bk. 1. Walter Benjamin, *The Arcades Project,* trans. Howard Eiland and Kevin McLaughlin (New York: Belknap, 2002), 207.

53 Sebald and Zeeman, "Max Sebald Interviewed by Michaël Zeeman," forthcoming.

54 Benjamin, "Unpacking My Library," in *Illuminations,* ed. Hannah Arendt (New York: Schocken, 1968), 64.

55 See, for instance, Richard Crownshaw, "Reconsidering Postmemory: Photography, the Archive, and Post-Holocaust Memory in W. G. Sebald's 'Austerlitz'," *Mosaic* 37, no. 4 (2004): 215–36. See also Anne Fuchs, "'Phantomspuren': Zu W. G. Sebalds Poetik der Erinnerung in Austerlitz," *German Life and Letters* 56 (2003): 281–98. Eshel, "Diverging Memories?" 413–14.

56 Russell J. A. Kilbourn, "Architecture and Cinema: The Representation of Memory in W. G. Sebald's 'Austerlitz'," in *W. G. Sebald: A Critical Companion,* ed. J. J. Long and Anne Whitehead (Seattle: University of Washington Press, 2004), 144.

57 Sebald scholarship has presented his characters in terms of these figures. See, for instance, Massimo Leone, "Textual Wanderings: A Vertiginous Reading of W. G. Sebald," in *W. G. Sebald: A Critical Companion,* ed. J. J. Long and Anne Whitehead (Seattle: University of Washington Press, 2004), 89–101. Simon Ward, "Ruins and Poetics in the Works of W. G. Sebald," in *W. G.*

Sebald: A Critical Companion, ed. J. J. Long and Anne Whitehead (Seattle: University of Washington Press, 2004), 59–71.

58 "Dissonant language systems" is James Rolleston's phrase. See Rolleston, "The Politics of Quotation," 13–27.

59 The translation is from Benjamin, "Unpacking My Library," in *Illuminations,* ed. Hannah Arendt (New York: Schocken, 1968), 67. Original publication: Walter Benjamin, "Ich packe meine Bibliothek aus," in *Gesammelte Schriften,* ed. Tillmann Rexroth (Frankfurt am Main: Suhrkamp, 1991), 4: bk. 1, 396.

60 For perspectives on this practice in earlier Sebald texts, see Ruth Franklin, "Rings of Smoke," *The New Republic,* September 23, 2002, p. 37. See also Ward, "Ruins and Poetics in the Works of W. G. Sebald," 59–71.

61 See Huyssen, *Twilight Memories,* 34.

62 Benjamin, "Ich packe meine Bibliothek aus," In *Gesammelte Schriften*, 4: bk. 1, 388–96. Benjamin, "Unpacking My Library," in *Illuminations,* ed. Hannah Arendt (New York: Schocken, 1968), 58–68.

63 This emphasis on catastrophe has been critiqued for its proximity to "metaphysics and the apocalyptic philosophy of history so prominent in the German tradition." See Andreas Huyssen, "On Rewritings and New Beginnings: W. G. Sebald and the Literature About the Luftkrieg," *Zeitschrift für Literaturwissenschaft und Linguistik* 124 (2001): 72–90. See also Amir Eshel, "Against the Power of Time: The Poetics of Suspension in W. G. Sebald's Austerlitz," *New German Critique* 88 (2003).

64 See Peter M. McIsaac, "Autorschaft und Autorität bei W. G. Sebald," in *Deutsche Gegenwartsliteratur seit 1989: Zwischenbalanzen—Analysen—Vermittlungsperspektiven,* ed. Clemens Kammler and Torsten Pflugmacher (Heidelberg: Synchron, 2004), 139–52.

65 In interviews, Sebald sometimes described his method in terms of "bricolage." See Peter Pfeiffer, "Korrespondenz und Wahlverwandtschaft: W. G. Sebalds 'Die Ringe des Saturn,'" in *Gegenwartsliteratur: Ein germanistisches Jahrbuch/A German Studies Yearbook,* ed. Paul Michael Lützeler (Tübingen: Narr, 2003), 226–44; Arthur Williams, "W. G. Sebald: A Holistic Approach to Borders, Texts, and Perspectives," in *German-Language Literature Today: International and Popular?* ed. A. Williams, S. Parkes and J. Preece (Bern: Peter Lang, 2000), 107-11.

66 On the consistent beginnings of Sebald's texts, see Leone, "Textual Wanderings," 96. On the role of ritual in breaking down the difference between voluntary and involuntary memory, see Benjamin, "Charles Baudelaire: Ein Lyriker im Zeitalter des Hochkapitalismus," 611. Benjamin, "On Some Motifs in Baudelaire," 159–60.

67 McIsaac, "Autorschaft und Autorität bei W. G. Sebald," 139–52.

68 The generally depopulated condition of Sebald's writings has been recognized. See Ward, "Ruins and Poetics in the Works of W. G. Sebald," 58–59. Thomas Kastura, "Geheimnisvolle Fähigkeit zur Transmigration: W. G. Sebalds interkulturelle Wallfahrten in die Leere," *arcadia* 31 (1996): 209. Eva Juhl, "Die Wahrheit über das Unglück: Zu W. G. Sebald Die Ausgewanderten," in *Reisen im Diskurs: Modelle der literarischen Fremderfahrung von den Pilgerberichten bis zur Postmoderne,* ed. Anne Fuchs and Theo Harden (Heidelberg: C. Winter, 1995), 653. Juhl, "Die Wahrheit über das Unglück: Zu W. G. Sebald Die Ausgewanderten."

69 Ernestine Schlant, *The Language of Silence: West German Literature and the Holocaust* (New York: 1999).

70 A similar point is made by Leone, "Textual Wanderings," 97. See also Fuchs, "'Phantomspuren': Zu W. G. Sebalds Poetik der Erinnerung in Austerlitz," 281–98.

71 Sebald and Zeeman, "Max Sebald Interviewed by Michaël Zeeman," forthcoming. With respect to Sebald and the problem of literary realism, I am thinking of the argument mounted by Robert Holub in his *Reflections of Realism,* where he discusses modernist writing (specifically Rilke and Kafka, the latter of whom is central to Sebald's scholarly and literary writing) as deploying realist conventions in a way that exposes and comments on the impossibility of realism and the violent exclusions that realism must bring about in order to function.

72 Eshel, "Against the Power of Time: The Poetics of Suspension in W. G. Sebald's Austerlitz," 72f. Pfeiffer, "Korrespondenz und Wahlverwandtschaft," 226–44. See also Kilbourn, "Architecture and Cinema," 152.

73 Carolin Dittlinger, "Traumatic Photographs: Remembrance and the Technical Media in W. G. Sebald's 'Austerlitz'," in *W .G. Sebald: A Critical Companion,* ed. J. J. Long and Anne Witehead (Seattle: University of Washington Press, 2004), 156.

Chapter 3

1 Carol Duncan and Alan Wallach, "The Universal Survey Museum," *Art History* 3, no. 4 (1980): 451–56. Linda Nochlin, "Museums and Radicals: A History of Emergencies," in *Museums in Crisis,* ed. Brian O'Doherty (New York: G. Braziller, 1972), 7–11. Daniel J. Sherman, "The Bourgeoisie, Cultural Appropriation, and the Art Museum in Nineteenth-Century France," *Radical History Review* 38 (1987), 38–43. Eilean Hooper-Greenhill, *Museums and the Shaping of Knowledge* (New York: Routledge, 1992), 179–88.

2 See, for instance, the account by James J. Sheehan, *Museums in the German Art World* (Oxford: Oxford University Press, 2000), 18–22, 33–49.

3 Theodore Ziolkowski, *German Romanticism and Its Institutions* (Princeton: Princeton University Press, 1990), 313.

4 Alfred Stix, *Die Aufstellung der ehedem kaiserlichen Gemälde Galerie in Wien im 18. Jahrhundert* (Vienna: Museion, 1929). Quoted in Ziolkowski, *German Romanticism,* 313.

5 Volker Plagemann, *Das deutsche Kunstmuseum, 1790–1870: Lage, Baukörper, Raumorganisation, Bildprogramm* (Munich: Prestel-Verlag, 1967), 17–18.

6 Susan A. Crane has rightly argued that the impulses behind certain practices of collecting and the rise of a certain form of historical consciousness in Prussia and other parts of Germany in the early 19th century cannot be accounted for solely through external factors such as the French Revolution and the Napoleonic wars. Susan A. Crane, *Collecting and Historical Consciousness in Early Nineteenth-Century Germany* (Ithaca: Cornell University Press, 2000), 7, 14.

7 Duncan and Wallach, "Universal Survey Museum," 451–56.

8 Andrew McClellan, *Inventing the Louvre: Art, Politics, and the Origins of the Modern Museum in Eighteenth-Century Paris* (Cambridge: Cambridge University Press, 1994), 95.

9 Hooper-Greenhill, *Museums,* 182.

10 Hooper-Greenhill, *Museums,* 182. See also Duncan and Wallach, "Universal Survey Museum," 451–56.

11 Hooper-Greenhill, *Museums,* 180, 186. See also Nochlin, "Museums and Radicals," 7–11.

12 McClellan, *Inventing the Louvre,* 120–21.

13 Hooper-Greenhill, *Museums,* 188–90.

14 Sulpiz Boisserée, "Lebensbeschreibung," in *Sulpiz Boisserée: Tagebücher, 1808–1854,* ed. Mathilde Boisserée (Stuttgart: Cotta, 1862), 21.

15 Elisabeth Décultot has argued that while Goethe enjoyed a deep friendship with Vivant Denon, the head of the administration of confiscations, he in fact viewed the French undertakings negatively and as potentially destroying the fabric of arts and letters in Europe. Elisabeth Décultot, "Le Cosmopolitisme en Question: Goethe Face aux Saisies Françaises d'Oeuvres d'art sous la Revolution et sous l'Empire," *Revue Germanique Internationale* 12 (1999): 163–64.

16 Wilhelm von Humboldt wrote to Schiller after his arrival in 1797 in Paris: "I have not yet seen many things here; a few plays, the museum, and a collection of French antiquities, as one

might call it [the Musée des Monuments Français], a collection of statues and monuments that were removed from palaces, churches, vaulted rooms, and so on in various epochs of the Revolution, and [then] assembled and chronologically ordered." Wilhelm von Humboldt, "to Friedrich Schiller, Paris, December 7, 1797," in *Wilhelm von Humboldt, sein Leben und Wirken, dargestellt in Briefen, Tagebüchern, und Dokumenten seiner Zeit,* ed. Rudolf Freese (Berlin: Verlag der Nation, 1953), 307.

17 Johann Wolfgang Goethe, "Flüchtige Übersicht über die Kunst in Deutschland," in *Sämtliche Werke: Frankfurter Ausgabe* (Frankfurt am Main: Deutscher Klassischer Verlag, 1985), 807–10. Quoted in Décultot, "Le Cosmopolitisme en Question," 172. Helmut Börsch-Supan also notes that Goethe regarded such a mode of display as a hindrance to the development of artistic talent. Helmut Börsch-Supan, "Goethes Kenntnis von der Kunst der Goethezeit," in *Goethe und die Kunst,* ed. Sabine Schulze (Stuttgart: Hatje, 1994), 275. Goethe's experiences with the Dresden gallery remained pivotal for his entire life, although he became critical of the gallery's arrangement over time.

18 Susan A. Crane mounts a similar argument when she discusses the concept of public opinion. She points to an observation made by Christian Garve, who upon visiting Paris in 1798 noted that while the term "public opinion" was French, the idea behind it was familiar to the Germans. See Crane, *Collecting and Historical Consciousness,* 170. See Christian Garve, "Über die öffentliche Meinung," in *Gesammelte Werke* (Hildesheim: Olms, 1985), 293.

19 Ziolkowski, *German Romanticism,* 313.

20 Ziolkowski, *German Romanticism,* 314.

21 Peter Böttger, *Die Alte Pinakothek in München: Architektur, Ausstattung, und museales Programm* (Munich: Prestel, 1972), 13.

22 Karl Friedrich Schinkel, "Reisen nach Italien," in *Tagebücher, Briefe, Zeichnungen, Aquarelle,* ed. Gottfried Riemann (Berlin: Rütten and Loening, 1979), 126. Quoted in Ziolkowski, *German Romanticism,* 318.

23 In the planning for the founding of the new university in Berlin, which opened in 1810, Humboldt had been instrumental in deliberations that judged which of the royal holdings was most suitable for scholarship and research and thus the university and which should be preserved as aesthetic treasures and made available for the educational benefit of the public at large in the museum. He also toured Italian collections with the Prussian king in 1822, where he tried to argue for the desirability of creating a comparable venue for the Prussian collections. Barbara Segelken, "Sammlungsgeschichte zwischen Leibniz und Humboldt: Die königlichen Sammlungen im Kontext der akademischen Institutionen," in *Theater der Natur und Kunst: Essays,* ed. Horst Bredekamp, Jochen Brüning, and Cornelia Weber (Berlin: Henschel, 2000), 49–50. Douglas Crimp, *On the Museum's Ruins: With Photographs by Louise Lawler* (Cambridge: MIT Press, 1993), 296. See also Sheehan, *Museums in the German Art World,* 78–80.

24 Hermann Lübbe, "Wilhelm von Humboldt und die Berliner Museumgründung, 1830," *Deutsche Vierteljahrsschrift für Literaturwissenschaft und Geistesgeschichte* 54, no. 4 (1980): 656–76. It is worth noting that other countries, notably Spain, confronted a similar situation, with the establishment of prominent public collections being furthered by the Napoleonic wars.

25 Douglas Crimp argues that the terms of Schinkel's museum are Hegelian, and that it is upon the "wresting of art from its necessity in reality that idealist aesthetics and the ideal museum are founded." While Crimp claims to be after a materialist aesthetics and materialist art, his labeling of Schinkel's museum as the "ideal museum" seems to locate a single origin for the creation of the public art museum, which in my view cannot account for the multiple museum designs that proliferated in the German-speaking realm and remains beholden to a metaphysics of origin. Crimp, *On the Museum's Ruins,* 302.

26 Ziolkowski, *German Romanticism,* 317.

27 Plagemann, *Das deutsche Kunstmuseum, 1790–1870: Lage, Baukörper, Raumorganisation, Bildprogramm,* 74–75. Plagemann quotes Paul Ortwin Rave, *Schinkelwerk der Akademie des Bauwesens, Berlin: Teil I* (Berlin: 1941), 3:35.

28 This is a position forcefully argued by Ziolkowski, who also points to the adoption of a classical architectural style as an invocation of the temple-like status of the museum. Ziolkowski,

German Romanticism, 316–20. See also Gudrun Calov, *Museen und Sammler des 19. Jahrhunderts in Deutschland* (Berlin: De Gruyter, 1969), 26.

29 As Wackenroder put it in his 1797 book *Herzensergießungen eines kunstliebenden Klosterbruders:* "Picture galleries are regarded as fairs . . . and they ought to be regarded as temples, where one may admire the great artists . . . in still and quiet humility . . . I compare the enjoyment of the more noble artworks with prayer." Wilhelm Heinrich Wackenroder, *Herzensergiessungen eines kunstliebenden klosterbruders,* ed. Silvio Vietta and Richard Littlejohns, vol. 1: *Sämtliche Werke und Briefe: historisch-kritische Ausgabe* (Heidelberg: C. Winter, 1991). Quoted in Calov, *Museen und Sammler,* 25.

30 Ziokowski argues that Schinkel's museum was designed to create conditions in which the Romantic *Galleriegespräch* would be possible (Ziolkowski, *German Romanticism,* 372–77). Goethe was to have favored a model of exhibition in which exchanges of ideas could take place, in which the collector's motivations and recollections could be discerned through his objects. Carrie Asman, "Kunstkammer als Kommunikationsspiel: Goethe inszeniert eine Sammlung," in *Johann Wolfgang von Goethe: Der Sammler und die Seinigen,* ed. Carrie Asman (Amsterdam: Verlag der Kunst, 1997), 134–36.

31 Börsch-Sepan claims that other of Schinkel's products, most strikingly the frescoes he painted for the Museum in Berlin, would have appealed to Goethe, especially since Goethe had met Schinkel in 1820 and praised his drawings. Börsch-Sepan, "Goethes Kenntnis von der Kunst," in *Goethe und die Kunst,* ed. Sabine Schulze, 277.

32 Sheehan stresses that through *Bildung,* museums in the early nineteenth century were believed capable of supplying social cohesion, thereby compensating for forces that seemed to be rending society. James J. Sheehan, "From Princely Collections to Public Museums: Toward a History of the German Art Museum," in *Rediscovering History: Culture, Politics, and the Psyche,* ed. Michael S. Roth (Stanford: Stanford University Press, 1994), 175.

33 Lübbe, "Wilhelm von Humboldt," 662. Scherer and Ziolkowski discuss the symbolic capital available in the art works that were returned at the conclusion of the Napoleonic wars. Ziolkowski, *German Romanticism,* 311. Valentin Scherer, *Deutsche Museen: Entstehung und kulturgeschichtliche Bedeutung unserer öffentlichen Kunstsammlungen* (Jena: Diederichs, 1913), 102.

34 Lübbe, "Wilhelm von Humboldt," 662. As Nochlin and Bennett demonstrate, there were real concerns about museums and collections becoming the target of mass violence. See Nochlin, "Museums and Radicals," 6–40. Bennett, *Birth of the Museum: History, Theory, Politics* (London: Routledge, 1995), 69f.

35 Wilhelm von Humboldt, "Bericht des Ministers Wilhelm Freiherrn von Humboldt an den König vom 21. August 1830," in *Aus Schinkel's Nachlass: Reisetagebücher, Briefe, und Aphorismen, mitgetheilt und mit einem Verzeichniss sämmtlicher Werke Schinkel's versehen,* ed. Karl Friedrich Schinkel and Alfred Freiherr von Wolzogen (Berlin: Verlag der Königlichen geheimen Oberhofbuch Druckerei, 1862), 299. Quoted in Lübbe, "Wilhelm von Humboldt," 662.

36 Ziolkowski, *German Romanticism,* 314, 317. See the similar point made by Carrie Asman, "Le Trésor de Goethe: Le Collectionneur et Ses Dons," *Revue Germanique Internationale* 12 (1999): 155.

37 Böttger, *Die Alte Pinakothek,* 170.

38 Böttger, *Die Alte Pinakothek,* 170.

39 Böttger, *Die Alte Pinakothek,* 170. Böttger argues that Ludwig's intentions were more general and were related to his intention of putting the new capital of Bavaria "on the map." He supposedly said: "Out of Munich I want to make a city that will bestow such an honor on Germany that one does not know Germany if he has not seen Munich." Quoted in Benno Hubensteiner, *Bayerische Geschichte* (Munich: Richard Pflaum, 1951), 328.

40 Scherer, *Deutsche Museen,* 102.

41 The French destroyed the palace that held the collection in 1799. Böttger, *Die Alte Pinakothek,* 12.

42 Böttger, *Die Alte Pinakothek,* 13.

43 Böttger, *Die Alte Pinakothek,* 12–13.

44 Ziolkowski, *German Romanticism,* 316–17.

45 See Henning Bock, "Das Profane und das Heilige: Die Sammlungen Solly und Boisserée im Wettstreit um die Übernahme durch Preussen," in *Kunst als Kulturgut: Die Sammlung Boisserée, ein Schritt in der Begründung des Museums,* ed. Annemarie Bethmann-Siefert and Otto Pöggeler (Bonn: Bouvier, 1995), 109–11.

46 Ziolkowski, *German Romanticism,* 311. As Crane notes, political tensions caused Rhinelanders to mistrust the Prussians and their inventories. Crane, *Collecting and Historical Consciousness,* 50.

47 Crane, *Collecting and Historical Consciousness,* 50.

48 Crane, *Collecting and Historical Consciousness,* 50–51.

49 Crane, *Collecting and Historical Consciousness,* 50.

50 Suzanne Marchand, "Ancients and Moderns in German Museums," in *Museums and Memory,* ed. Susan A. Crane (Palo Alto: Stanford University Press, 2000), 184–85.

51 Erich Trunz, "Goethe als Sammler," *Goethe-Jahrbuch* 89 (1972): 16–17. Trunz notes how excited Goethe was in 1808 when he received a prayer book with Dürer reproductions in it.

52 Johann Wolfgang Goethe, *Kunst und Altertum am Rhein und Main, Goethes Werke: Weimarer Ausgabe* (Weimar: Böhlau, 1902), 34:80.

53 Crane, *Collecting and Historical Consciousness,* 50.

54 Calov, *Museen und Sammler,* 27–28.

55 Annemarie Gethmann-Siefert, "Einleitung," in *Kunst als Kulturgut: Die Sammlung Boisserée—ein Schritt in der Begründung des Museums,* ed. Annemarie Gethmann-Siefert and Otto Pöggeler (Bonn: Bouvier, 1995), vi–vii.

56 Gethmann-Siefert, "Einleitung," vii.

57 This notion resonates with Wackenroder's conception of the gallery. Gethmann-Siefert, "Einleitung," vi.

58 Eva Schulz, "Das Museum als wissenschaftliche Institution: Neue Ideen und tradierte Vorstellungen am Beispiel der Sammlung Boisserée," *Wallraf-Richartz-Jahrbuch* (1990): 302.

59 Boisserée, *Lebensbeschreibung,* in *Suliz Boisserée: Tagebucher, 1805–1854,* ed. Mathilde Boisserée (Stuttgart: Cotta, 1862), 1:1. Schulz, "Das Museum als wissenschaftliche Institution," 297, 302.

60 Scherer, *Deutsche Museen,* 123.

61 In a letter to the Boisserées, their collaborator Johann Bertram describes the sensation generated by the collections following their arrival in Stuttgart. Bertram laments having to turn away as many as 86 visitors in a single day, and he notes that interest in the collection is rising in all classes to such an extent that thousands are anticipated to visit. Though anxious about the crowd-control implications, he and Stuttgart natives believe that the collections will draw "large numbers of foreigners" to see the new cultural institution. Johann Bertram, July 1819. Quoted in Scherer, *Deutsche Museen,* 122–23.

62 Calov, *Museen und Sammler,* 27–28. Schulz, "Das Museum," 285–317. See also Gethmann-Siefert, "Einleitung," ii.

63 Boisserée, "Lebensbeschreibung," 1:1f. Scherer, *Deutsche Museen,* 119–22. See also Crane, *Collecting and Historical Consciousness,* 11.

64 Sulpiz Boisserée, "Brief an Goethe," in *Sulpiz Boisserée: Tagebücher, 1808–1854,* ed. Mathilde Boisserée, 1:6.

65 Scholarship has long since demonstrated that Goethe took a hand in shaping the reception of his novel, particularly reviews of it in contemporary journals. One of the curious features of the novel, however, is that its force was felt more strongly in nineteenth-century Britain and the

United States, with the novel's significance and comparative legitimacy for scholarly study becoming widely recognized in Germany only in the twentieth century.

66 Goethe to Sulpiz Boisserée. Jena, Mai 15, 1810. Quoted in Heinz Härtl, ed., *Die Wahlverwandtschaften: Eine Dokumentation der Wirkung von Goethes Roman, 1808–1832* (Berlin: Akademie Verlag, 1983), 156.

67 According to his correspondence, Goethe was deeply impressed with the drawings, and he immediately invited Boisserée to visit him. Goethe would turn into a fairly strong advocate of Boisserée, particularly after having seen the collection and receiving a tour of the cathedral from Boisserée. As Goethe admitted in *Kunst und Altertum am Rhein und Main,* he had been interested in Gothic architecture (Strasbourg cathedral) and other related issues before his trip to the Rhineland in 1814.

68 How else can one account for the striking parallels between Boisserée's cathedral project and the depiction of Goethe's Architect chapel scheme? If it is assumed that the literary text and Boisserée are not completely independent, would this not show that Goethe's text is in fact directly shaping the museal developments of his day?

69 It seems unlikely that Goethe's Architect is some sort of commentary on Boisserée. Goethe met Boisserée only in 1810, the year after the novel appeared. Most contemporaries, among them Jakob Grimm, Bettina Brentano, Achim von Arnim, and Karl von Varnhagen, believed that the model for Goethe's figure was Johann Daniel Wilhelm Eduard Engelhardt, a young architect from Kassel. Some, such as Wilhelm Grimm, however, doubted the veracity of the claim: "for it is strange, that of all that is said of him in the *Wahlverwandtschaften* that none of it is true" (p. 175). Goethe himself seemed at best ambivalent when wrote in the *Tag- und Jahreshefte:* "Of the people who stopped in Weimar this year I find the following noted: Engelhardt, architect from Kassel, traveling to Italy. It was claimed that I was thinking of him in the *Wahlverwandtschaften*" (p. 316). Härtl, ed., *Die Wahlverwandtschaften: Eine Dokumentation der Wirkung von Goethes Roman, 1808–1832,* 34, 72, 78, 110, 128, 171–72, 175, 212, 214, 316, 398, 400, 406, 419, 425.

70 Hartmut Böhme, "Fetisch und Idol: Erinnerungsformen in Goethes Wilhelm Meister, Faust, und Der Sammler und die Seinigen," in *Goethe und die Verzeitlichung der Natur,* ed. Peter Matussek (Munich: C. H. Beck, 1998), 178–201. Décultot, "Le Cosmopolitisme en Question," 162–72. Asman, "Kunstkammer als Kommunikationsspiel," 119–77.

71 Décultot. "Le Cosmopolitisme en Question," 165–75, 297f. Ziolkowski, *German Romanticism and Its Institutions,* 376.

72 Asman, "Kunstkammer als Kommmunikationsspiel," 161–62.

73 Johann Wolfgang Goethe, *Tag- und Jahreshefte, 1749–1806: Goethes Werke: Weimarer Ausgabe* (Weimar: Hermann Böhlau, 1895), 1/35:204–25.

74 See Asman, "Kunstkammer als Kommmunikationsspiel," 161–62.

75 Asman, "Kunstkammer als Kommmunikationsspiel," 135.

76 Asman, "Kunstkammer als Kommmunikationsspiel," 135.

77 With the view that through the true collector the object receives proper ownership, Goethe anticipates a position that Walter Benjamin will take up with some vehemence in texts such as "Eduard Fuchs: Der Sammler und der Historiker." Such a position might well have resulted from Goethe's familiarity with Quatremère de Quincy, which was effected through F. H. Jacobi (Décultot, "Le Cosmopolitisme en Question," 164–65). As Daniel J. Sherman has shown, Quatremère's critiques of the rising commodification of art resonate powerfully with Benjamin's theory of collecting and notions of aura. Daniel J. Sherman, "Quatremére/Benjamin/Marx: Art Museums, Aura, and Commodity Fetishism," in *Museum Culture: Histories, Discourses, Spectacles,* ed. Daniel J. Sherman and Irit Rogoff (Minneapolis: University of Minnesota Press, 1994), 123–43.

78 In one part of *Kunst und Altertum,* Goethe analyzes the precarious situation of Wallraf's collection. He concludes that the lack of space is a real detriment to the collection, noting that the city of Cologne could offer a suitable space and save the collection from destruction or possible dispersal. Goethe then expresses the notion that "it would be surprisingly pleasant if the rooms were to be tastefully decorated, in a fashion that agrees with the objects." He goes

to say that a few museums have made small steps in this direction, "but there is [in Germany] no whole universal museum [*kein gänzliches allgemeines Museum*] decorated in this manner." (pp. 77–78.) [My emphasis.] In addition to pointing to the conditions lacking in Germany, Goethe stresses that the government has a crucial role to play in altering that state of affairs, even suggesting strategies governments can use to encourage the lending and donating of private holdings to public museums (p. 75). Goethe, *Kunst und Altertum,* 34:107.

79 Goethe, *Kunst und Altertum,* 34:75–76.

80 Goethe, *Kunst und Altertum,* 34:74. [My emphasis.] Asman considers this passage to express an almost grotesque means of treating objects. Asman, "Kunstkammer als Kommmunikationsspiel," 169.

81 Goethe, *Kunst und Altertum,* 34:78.

82 Goethe, *Kunst und Altertum,* 34:78.

83 Böhme writes that the fetish serves the function of overcoming divisions, for instance, between past and present. Böhme, "Fetisch und Idol," 195, 199.

84 According to Asman, the *Kästchen* as a mode of display appears repeatedly in Goethe's literary works, for instance, in *Wilhelm Meisters Wanderjahren.* Asman, "Kunstkammer als Kommunikationsspiel," 170.

85 As Brigitte Peucker has noted, this is a connection that Benjamin mentions in his essay on the *Wahlverwandtschaften.* Brigitte Peucker, "The Material Image in Goethe's Wahlverwandtschaften," *The Germanic Review* 74, no. 3 (1999): 195–213.

86 Peucker observes this relation as well. "Material Image," 195–213.

87 I am using this term in the sense described by Böhme, who argues that similar talismanic functions of fetishes appear in *Wilhelm Meister* and *Faust.* Böhme, "Fetisch und Idol," 196.

88 Calov, *Museen und Sammler,* 50–63, 107–10.

89 The text even mentions that she will perform the tableaux again in the coming carnival.

90 Norbert Puszkar, "Frauen und Bilder: Luciane und Ottilie," *Neophilologus* 73 (1989): 397–410.

91 *Morgenblatt für gebildete Stände* (1814): (34) 136; (35) 140; (36), 143–44. [Emphasis original.].

92 See, for instance. the discussion in Astrida Orle Tantillo, *The Will to Create: Goethe's Philosophy of Nature* (Pittsburgh: University of Pittsburgh Press, 2002), 58–59.

93 On these issues, see Tantillo, *The Will to Create.* 12–57, 104–51.

94 Johann Wolfgang Goethe, "Einfache Nachahmung der Natur, Manier, Styl," in *Goethes Werke: Hamburger Ausgabe in 14 Bänden,* ed. Erich Trunz (Munich: C. H. Beck, 1981), 12:30–34.

95 I am thinking, for instance, of Tantillo's treatment of gender in Goethe's writings about plants, which casts masculinity and femininity as parts of a larger whole that, while they oppose each other, exist in a kind of equality. In my reading, such a theorization has its limits, even in Goethe arguably most scientific literary text, *Die Wahlverwandtschaften.* While I don't question Tantillo's understanding of Ottilie's suicide as a kind of plant growth cut short, the fact remains that, by killing herself, she seems to violate Goethe's understanding of the ideal of nature's drive to create. See Tantillo, *The Will to Create,* 152–59.

96 Dagmar v. Hoff and Helga Meise, "Tableaux vivants: Die Kunst- und Kultform der Attitüden und lebenden Bilder," in *Weiblichkeit und Tod,* ed. Renate Berger and Inge Stephan (Cologne, Vienna: Böhlau, 1987), 76.

97 I resist reading this passage, and those where the narrator uses designations such as "natural imitation" for the tableaux, as an ironic commentary on and a criticism of mistaking cultural practices for expressions of nature. Aside from the fact that the insight this ironic criticism generates is rather flat, the narrator does not sustain an ironic perspective in describing the tableaux. In his discussion, Friedrich Nemec notes that the narrator's tone changes and that his critical distance disappears when he sees Luciane perform. Friedrich Nemec, *Die Ökonomie der Wahlverwandtschaften* (Munich: Fink, 1973) 81. Critical remarks are also absent during Ottilie's nativity scenes.

98 It is worth mentioning in passing that this indicates a kind of high/low cultural divide. *Tableaux vivants* were, in no small part owing to the popularizing impact of Goethe's *Wahlverwandtschaften,* an extremely commonplace form of entertainment in the nineteenth century. They were seldom accorded the status of "high culture," however. See August Langen, "Attitüde und Tableau in der Goethezeit," in *Jahrbuch der deutschen Schillergesellschaft,* ed. Fritz Martini, Walter Müller Seidel, and Bernhard Zeller (Stuttgart: Kröner, 1968), 221–22, 234–35. See also Hoff and Meise, "Tableaux vivants," 74–75.

99 Walter Benjamin, "Das Kunstwerk im Zeitalter seiner technischen Reproduzierbarkeit," in *Gesammelte Schriften,* ed. Rolf Tiedemann et al. (Frankfurt am Main: Suhrkamp, 1980), 1: bk. 2, 480–81.

100 Benjamin, "Das Kunstwerk," in *Gesammelte Schriften,* 1: bk. 2, 482–84.

101 Benjamin, "Das Kunstwerk," in *Gesammelte Schriften,* 1: bk. 2, 481.

102 Benjamin, "Das Kunstwerk," in *Gesammelte Schriften,* 1: bk. 2, 480–84.

103 [In parentheses in the original.] Benjamin, "Das Kunstwerk," in *Gesammelte Schriften,* 1: bk. 2, 481.

104 The chapel's ritual function thus operates in much the same way as the rearranged graveyard as analyzed by Benjamin in his *Wahlverwandtschaften* essay. See also his comments on the mausoleum motif in the novel. Walter Benjamin, "Die Wahlverwandtschaften," in *Gesammelte Schriften,* ed. Rolf Tiedemann et al. (Frankfurt am Main: Suhrkamp, 1980), 1: bk. 2, 123–201.

105 Nemec, *Ökonomie der Wahlverwandtschaften,* 97.

106 Ziolkowski, *German Romanticism,* 314.

107 By asserting that Ottilie and Eduard are sleeping, perhaps to be awakened one day, Goethe's text neatly inverts a view held by Novalis that galleries would lead to a kind of awakening. As Susan A. Crane has argued, metaphors of "awakening" were prominent among Romantic collectors contemporary with Goethe. In Goethe's novel, past Germanic culture is indeed actualized and brought into the present, but the effect is precisely not enlivening. Crane, *Collectors and Historical Consciousness,* 6–13.

108 Theodor W. Adorno, "Valéry Proust Museum," in *Prism* (Cambridge: MIT Press, 1981), 75–77.

Chapter 4

1 Friedrich Hebbel, ed., *Der Nachsommer,* vol. 3, *Werke* (Munich: Hanser, 1965), 682–83. Rainer Maria Rilke, "Letter to Gräfin Aline Dietrichstein, July 9, 1917," in *Briefe aus den Jahren 1914–1921,* ed. Ruth Rilke Sieber and Carl Sieber (Leipzig: Insel-Verlag, 1937), 146. Thomas Mann, *Die Entstehung des Doktor Faustus: Roman eines Romans, Werke* (Amsterdam: Besmann-Fischer, 1000), 123f., 168.

2 Adalbert Stifter, *Der Nachsommer,* ed. Alfred Doppler and Wolfgang Frühwald, 4:1–4:3, *Werke und Briefe: Historisch-kritische Gesamtausgabe* (W. Kohlhammer: Stuttgart, 1997), 4:3:282. The translation is: Adalbert Stifter, *Indian Summer,* trans. Wendell Frye (New York: Lang, 1985), 478–79. All subsequent references are made parenthetically, first to the volume and page number of the German edition and then to the translation.

3 Claude Levi-Strauss, *The Elementary Structure of Kinship* (Boston: Beacon Press, 1969), 480f. "Homosocial" is a term that is conceived to run parallel to notions of homosexuality. The term helps to uncover and relate structures of male-to-male interaction whose function is to obscure their relationship to homosexual and homoerotic desire. Eve Kosofsky Sedgwick, *Between Men: English Literature and Homosocial Desire* (New York: Columbia University Press, 1985), 25–27.

4 Gayle Rubin, "The Traffic in Women: Notes on the 'Political Economy' of Sex," in *Toward*

an *Anthropology of Women,* ed. Rayna R. Reiter (New York: Monthly Review Press, 1975), 157–210.

5 For an interesting discussion of Heinrich's *Bildung* in more general terms, see Peter Uwe Hohendahl, "Die gebildete Gemeinschaft: Stifters Nachsommer als Utopie der ästhetischen Erziehung," in *Utopieforschung: Interdisziplinäre Studien zur neuzeitlichen Utopie,* ed. Wilhelm Vosskamp (Stuttgart: Metzler, 1982), 333–56.

6 Tony Bennett, *The Birth of the Museum: History, Theory, Politics* (London: Routledge, 1995), 163–73.

7 Donald Preziosi, *Rethinking Art History: Meditations on a Coy Science* (New Haven: Yale University Press, 1989), 68–70. Eilean Hooper-Greenhill, *Museums and the Shaping of Knowledge* (New York: Routledge, 1992), 6–8. Bennett, *Birth of the Museum,* 167.

8 Hooper-Greenhill, *Museums and the Shaping of Knowledge,* 182. Debate has always existed over the pros and cons of issuing guides and catalogs to the exhibitions. See also Tony Bennett, "The Multiplication of Culture's Unity," *Critical Inquiry* 21, no. 4 (1995): 861–89.

9 Theodore Ziolkowski, *German Romanticism and Its Institutions* (Princeton: Princeton University Press, 1990), 311–15.

10 Volker Plagemann, *Das deutsche Kunstmuseum, 1790–1870: Lage, Baukörper, Raumorganisation, Bildprogramm* (Munich: Prestel-Verlag, 1967), 74–75. Plagemann quotes Paul Ortwin Rave, *Schinkelwerk der Akademie des Bauwesens, Berlin:* vol. 3 (Berlin: Deutsche Kunstverlag, 1941), 35.

11 Suzanne L. Marchand, *Down from Olympus: Archaeology and Philhellenism in Germany, 1750–1970* (Princeton: Princeton University Press, 1996).

12 Humboldt was deeply impressed with the historical arrangement of objects in the Musées des Monuments Français. See the series of letters he wrote to Goethe about his experiences: Wilhelm von Humboldt, "Musée des Petits Augustins: Letters to Goethe," in *Werke,* ed. Andreas Flitner and Klaus Giel (Stuttgart: Cotta, 1960), 519, 595–30. Susan A. Crane, *Collecting and Historical Consciousness in Early Nineteenth-Century Germany* (Ithaca: Cornell University Press, 2000), 122–23. Hermann Lübbe, "Wilhelm von Humboldt und die Berliner Museumgründung, 1830," *Deutsche Vierteljahrsschrift für Literaturwissenschaft und Geistesgeschichte* 54, no. 4 (1980): 656–76.

13 Plagemann, *Das deutsche Kunstmuseum,* 74.

14 Plagemann, *Das deutsche Kunstmuseum,* 77.

15 Plagemann, *Das deutsche Kunstmuseum,* 77.

16 Walther Rehm, *Nachsommer: zur Deutung von Stifters Dichtung* (Bern: A. Francke, 1951), 34.

17 James J. Sheehan, "From Princely Collections to Public Museums: Toward a History of the German Art Museum," in *Rediscovering History: Culture, Politics, and the Psyche,* ed. Michael S. Roth (Stanford: Stanford University Press, 1994), 175.

18 Sheehan, "From Princely Collections," 175.

19 Sheehan, "From Princely Collections," 175.

20 The museum is now known as the Heeresgeschichtlices Museum im Arsenal. See Franz Kaindl, "Das Wiener Heeresgeschichtliches Museum: Ein historisches Nationalmuseum von internationaler Dimension," in *Die Nation und ihre Museen,* ed. Marie-Louise Plessen (Frankfurt: Campus, 1992), 272–73. This museum has a crucial function in Bachmann's *Malina.*

21 Lieselotte Hoffmann, *Adalbert Stifter und Wien* (Vienna: Wiener Verlag, 1946), 50. Gustav Wilhelm, *Begegnung mit Stifter: Einblicke in Adalbert Stifters Leben und Werk* (Munich: K. Alber, 1943), 81f.

22 Otto Jungmair, *Adalbert Stifter als Denkmalpfleger* (Linz: Oberösterrischer Landesverlag, 1973), 77–79, 127–28. In the novel, Kefermarkt is called Kerberg and Saint Wolfgang is not mentioned by name. Otto Jungmair, *Adalbert Stifters Linzer Jahre: Ein Kalendarium* (Graz: Stiasny, 1958), 60, 86.

23 Jungmair, *Stifter als Denkmalpfleger,* 86–87, 99, 101, 106. Jungmair, *Stifters Linzer Jahre,* 151.

24 Jungmair, *Adalbert Stifters Linzer Jahre,* 125.

25 Adalbert Stifter, "Über die Schule," in *Sämtliche Werke,* ed. Konrad Steffen (Munich: Winkler, 1978), 14:256–317.

26 Jungmair, *Stifters Linzer Jahre,* 92, 145. In the Landesmuseum, Stifter was asked to assist in arranging the display of the Kain collection of Roman artifacts and the geological collection.

27 Jungmair, *Stifter als Denkmalpfleger,* 86. Some critics have argued that Risach is a mouthpiece for Stifter. See, for example, Jungmair, *Stifter als Denkmalpfleger,* 127–30.

28 See also Jungmair, *Adalbert Stifters Linzer Jahre,* 89.

29 This kind of project has been described by Susan A. Crane, who links these movements to Romantic attempts to envision a unique and glorious German antiquity. Crane, *Collecting and Historical Consciousness,* 60–104.

30 Stifter, "Über die Schule," [My emphasis.]

31 Wilhelm, *Begegnung mit Stifter,* 30, 149.

32 Margrit Wyder, "Vorhof zum Tempel: Der Anfang von Stifters Nachsommer," *Sprachkunst: Beiträge zur Literaturwissenschaft* 20, no. 2 (1990): 152–53.

33 For Wyder, this notion of cleansing before entering the temple explains why the business practices of Heinrich's father never enter the text. In this way she shows a contrast between the *Nachsommer* and Freytag's *Soll und Haben,* in which the rise of the bourgeoisie is depicted with an affirmation of business practices. See Wyder, "Vorhof zum Tempel," 152–59.

34 Heinrich Reitzenbeck, "Adalbert Stifter: Eine biographische Skizze," in *Libussa: Jahrbuch für 1853,* ed. Paul Aloys Klar (Prague: Verlag Calve, 1853), 26–28. Quoted in Adalbert Stifter, *Adalbert Stifters Leben und Werk in Briefen und Dokumenten* (Frankfurt am Main: Insel-Verlag, 1962), 293.

35 Ziolkowski, *Romanticism and Its Institutions,* 319–20.

36 Plagemann, *Das deutsche Kunstmuseum,* 78.

37 Schinkel's rotunda was designed to cleanse the visitor of everyday thoughts before he entered the galleries. See Ziolkowski, *Romanticism and Its Institutions,* 311–15. The monumental façade of von Klenze's Pinakothek was to perform a similar function. Sheehan. "From Princely Collections," 175. Hansen's Heeresmuseum modifies Schinkel's conception, presenting the visitor with fifty-two large sculptures that consecrate the space and inspire awe.

38 In the sculpture rooms of the Berlin museum, Schinkel constructed the height of each stand according to the height of its statue and the architectonic form of the room. Hansen did something similar in the Heeresmuseum Vienna. Von Klenze followed a different technique in Munich's Glyptothek. Plagemann, *Das deutsche Kunstmuseum,* 75.

39 Stifter's story "Abdias" provides an interesting and problematic elaboration of this dynamic. In this text, the desert Jew Abdias comes to reside in Austria with his daughter, who is likened to an exotic flowering plant like the *Cereus peruvianus* in the *Nachsommer.* See Adalbert Stifter, "Abdias," in *Sämtliche Werke,* ed. notes by Karl Pörnbacher (Munich: Winkler, 1978), 579–674.

40 Bennett, *The Birth of the Museum,* 77–88.

41 This ability to obscure is part of the great power of exhibiting, which inhibits visitors from imagining alternative orderings, stories, and histories. Preziosi, *Rethinking Art History,* 70. Bennett, *Birth of the Museum,* 163–73.

42 David Blackbourn and Geoff Eley, *The Peculiarities of German History: Bourgeois Society and Politics in Nineteenth-Century Germany* (Oxford: Oxford University Press, 1984), 226.

43 Alfred Stix, *Die Aufstellung der ehedem kaiserlichen Gemälde Galerie in Wien im 18. Jahrhundert* (Vienna: Museion, 1929). Quoted in Nikolaus Pevsner, *A History of Building Types* (Princeton: Princeton University Press, 1976), 117.

44 Bennett, *Birth of the Museum,* 73–75.

45 Heinrich often claims that he behaves politely by not staring at others, yet the text is replete with instances when it is clear that he is intensely aware of other people's clothing and their likely class and place of residence. In museal environments like the imperial painting collection and also on the streets, Heinrich openly observes the faces of young women (4.1:201; 117). On the gaze and discipline in exhibitionary environments and the growing tendency for streets to resemble display spaces, see Bennett, *Birth of the Museum,* 29–32, 73–75.

46 Hoffmann, *Stifter und Wien,* 50.

47 Gudrun Calov, *Museen und Sammler des 19. Jahrhunderts in Deutschland* (Berlin: De Gruyter, 1969), 151–56.

48 Calov, *Museen und Sammler,* 154–56.

49 Blackbourn and Eley, *Peculiarities,* 221–28.

50 Walter Benjamin, "Eduard Fuchs: Der Sammler und der Historiker," in *Gesammelte Schriften,* ed. Rolf Tiedemann et al. (Frankfurt am Main: Suhrkamp, 1980), 2: bk. 2, 465–506. Walter Benjamin, "Über den Begriff der Geschichte," in *Gesammelte Schriften,* ed. Rolf Tiedemann et al. (Frankfurt am Main: Suhrkamp, 1980), 1: bk. 2, 691f.

51 Benjamin, "Eduard Fuchs," in *Gesammelte Schriften,* 2: bk. 2, 465–506.

52 Walter Benjamin, "Ich packe meine Bibliothek aus," in *Gesammelte Schriften,* ed. Tillmann Rexroth (Frankfurt am Main: Suhrkamp, 1991), 4: bk. 1, 396. Walter Benjamin, "Unpacking My Library," in *Illuminations,* ed. Hannah Arendt (New York: Schocken, 1968), 67.

53 Altering the order would produce an "awful feeling" for Risach (4.2:112; 236). Compare Benjamin's claim that the collector creates a sense of order from the habit of having objects in a particular arrangement, an order that suppresses certain memories. Benjamin, "Bibliothek," in *Gesammelte Schriften,* 4: bk. 1, 388–89.

54 The translation is mine. Walter Benjamin, *Das Passagenwerk,* ed. Rolf Tiedemann et al., in *Gesammelte Schriften* (Frankfurt am Main: Suhrkamp, 1980), 5: bk. 1, 273. Benjamin quotes Max von Boehn, *Die Mode: Menschen und Moden im sechzehnten Jahrhundert, nach Bildern und Stichen der Zeit ausgewählt und Geschildert* (Munich: F. Bruckmann, 1923), 136.

55 I am using the word "suppression" in the manner of Derrida, who with respect to the operation of prosthetic memory devices uses 'suppression' to distinguish between Freudian repression and what Freud called "secondary repression." See Jacques Derrida, *Archive Fever: A Freudian Impression,* trans. Eric Prenowitz (Chicago: University of Chicago Press, 1996), 28.

56 Risach's destruction of the copper etchings is a thinly veiled political act. Though the dangers of destroying cultural property deemed to be "filthy" or "degenerate" in the name of "the general good of the people" seem especially obvious in the twentieth century, Risach might be expected to be a little more cautious given his contempt for past cultures that neglected art they considered inferior (4.1:113; 68–69).

57 Alexander Nehamas, *Nietzsche: Life as Literature* (Cambridge: Harvard University Press, 1985), 186. I am grateful to Eric Downing for this reference.

58 Nehamas, *Nietzsche,* 186.

59 Martin Swales, *The German Bildungsroman from Wieland to Hesse* (Princeton: Princeton University Press, 1978), 81. Russell A. Berman, *The Rise of the Modern German Novel: Crisis and Charisma* (Cambridge: Harvard University Press, 1986), 124. Berman generally concurs with Benjamin's well-known characterization of the "visual hypertrophy" of the novel that is understood to reduce acoustic phenomena, particularly verbal exchanges, to mere ornamental displays. I would simply point out that, for the reader, these exchanges are nevertheless subject to semiotic decoding much like the other visual displays in the text.

60 Both Margrit Wyder and Herbert Seidler make a similar point with different emphases. Wyder, "Vorhof zum Tempel," 155. Herbert Seidler, "Gestaltung und Sinn des Raumes in Stifters Nachsommer," in *Adalbert Stifter: Studien und Interpretationen,* ed. Lother Stiehm (Heidelberg: Stiehm, 1968), 205, 222–23.

61 My arguments as to the separation of rooms are indebted to Wyder, "Vorhof," 152–53, 155–56, 162–63. See also Hohendahl, "Die gebildete Gesellschaft," 333–56.

62 Seidler, "Gestaltung und Sinn," 205. Kirsten Belgum, *Interior Meaning: Design of the Bourgeois Home in the Realist Novel* (New York: P. Lang, 1991), 61–62.

63 Wyder, "Vorhof," 152.

64 Wyder, "Vorhof," 165.

65 Adalbert Stifter, "Vorrede: Bunte Steine," in *Sämtliche Werke,* ed. notes by Karl Pörnbacher (Munich: Winkler, 1978), 1:7–13.

66 Stifter, "Vorrede," 71–13.

67 Eric Downing, "Common Ground: Conditions of Realism in Stifter's 'Vorrede,'" *Colloquia Germanica* 1 (1995): 40–41.

68 E. J. Browne, *Charles Darwin: A Biography, Vol. 1: Voyaging* (Princeton: Princeton University Press, 1996), 3–340. Peter Raby, *Alfred Russel Wallace: A Life* (Princeton: Princeton University Press, 2001), 21f. Dolf Sternberger, *Panorama of the Nineteenth Century,* trans. Joachim Neugroschel (New York: Urizen Books, 1977), 104.

69 E. J. Browne, *Charles Darwin: A Biography, Vol. 2: The Power of Place* (New York: Alfred A. Knopf, 2002), 3–125. Raby, *Wallace,* 138–39.

70 Wyder, "Vorhof," 162–63. Seidler, "Gestaltung und Sinn," 53–56.

71 Rubin, "The Traffic in Women," 157–210. Sedgwick, *Between Men,* 25–27. See also Judith Butler, *Gender Trouble: Feminism and the Subversion of Identity* (New York: Routledge, 1990), 38–43.

72 My argument is not immediately concerned with the characterization of the homoerotic in this text, since that per se analysis would go too far afield. For my purposes, it is the general inadmissibility of the homoerotic in open relations between men that helps us to detect the "work" of collecting in the novel.

73 See also Crane, *Collecting and Historical Consciousness,* 60–104. Stifter was a follower of the Austrian version of this movement initiated by Anton Ritter von Spaun.

74 Sedgwick, *Between Men,* 25–26.

75 Benjamin, "Ich packe Bibliothek aus," in *Gesammelte Schriften,* 4: bk. 1, 389. See also Ackbar Abbas, "Walter Benjamin's Collector: The Fate of the Modern Experience," in *Modernity and the Text: Revisions of German Modernism,* ed. Andreas Huyssen and David Bathrick (New York: Columbia University Press, 1989), 230–31.

76 Benjamin, "Ich packe meine Bibliothek aus," in *Gesammelte Schriften,* 4: bk. 1, 393.

77 Berman, *Rise of the Modern German Novel,* 132.

78 Elisabeth Bronfen, *Over Her Dead Body: Death Femininity, and the Aesthetic* (New York: Routledge, 1992), 270–80.

Chapter 5

1 Raabe's narrative is not the only literary text of this era that addresses some of these concerns. A portion of Theodor Fontane's first novel *Vor dem Sturm* deals with similar debates about unearthed artifacts and national identity, only with the question there being whether prehistoric artifacts are Slavic or Germanic in origin. In other ways, Fontane's *Wanderungen durch die Mark Brandenburg* might also be read for its museum function. I have chosen to focus on Raabe's text because it captures with particular clarity the emerging moment of cultural tourism, an issue that is important in Chapter 6, on Rilke's *Neue Gedichte.* Raabe's text also appears before the realization of the German nation in 1871, allowing it to manifest a productive uncertainty about the ultimate question of German unification. I refer to Fontane's texts as asides during my argument.

2 It was, of course, no accident that the rise of archaeology was intertwined with the creation of modern Western historical consciousness, when the works of Droysen, Ranke, Mommsen, Marx, and Darwin were radically altering the ways in which the past could be considered, and the place of mankind in that past. Günter Smolla, "Archäologie und Nationalbewußtsein," in *Zwischen Walhall und Paradies: Eine Austellung des Deutschen Historischen Museums in Zusammenarbeit mit dem Museum für Vor- und Frühgeschichte SMPK,* ed. Heidemarie Anderlik (Berlin: Deutsches Historisches Museum, 1991), 12.

3 Smolla, "Archäologie und Nationalbewußtsein," 12. Wilfried Menghin, "Pfahlheim: Eine Ausgrabungsruine des 19. Jahrhunderts," in *Zwischen Walhall und Paradies: Eine Austellung des Deutschen Historischen Museums in Zusammenarbeit mit dem Museum für Vor- und Frühgeschichte SMPK,* ed. Heidemarie Anderlik (Berlin: Deutsches Historisches Museum, 1991), 85–86. Suzanne L. Marchand, *Down from Olympus: Archaeology and Philhellenism in Germany, 1750–1970* (Princeton: Princeton University Press, 1996), 154. Ingo Wiwjorra, "German Archaeology and Its Relation to Nationalism and Racism," in *Nationalism and Archaeology in Europe,* ed. Margarita Díaz-Andreu García and T. C. Champion (Boulder, Colo.: Westview Press, 1996), 164.

4 Marchand. *Down from Olympus,* 154–55. The study of objects found on German soil, first the domain of *Altertumskunde* and later that of various Roman-German and *Heimat* museums, was also rent by bitter, ideologically informed splits by those who privileged objects of the Romans over those of pre-Roman (Germanic, Celtic, and Slavic) origins, and vice versa.

5 Although these endeavors were often driven by patriotism and a desire to participate in debates about a particular region's oldest inhabitants being Celtic, Germanic or Slavic, other motivations existed. Some amateurs sought the erudition and education that accompanied the study of the past, while others saw in the digs possibilities for travel, adventure, and entertainment. Still others were motivated by material gain, either to add to their own collections or to sell found objects in the prospering museum market that existed for prehistoric and other archaeological material. Menghin, "Pfahlheim: Eine Ausgrabungsruine des 19. Jahrhunderts," 85.

6 Bruce G. Trigger, *A History of Archaeological Thought* (Cambridge: Cambridge University Press, 1989), 99.

7 Glyn Edmund Daniel, *A Hundred and Fifty Years of Archaeology* (Cambridge: Harvard University Press, 1975), 152.

8 The history of the dig therefore affords us a window on archaeological practices during the breakthrough years of the field, during the 1850s and early 1860s, when Darwin's *On the Origin of Species* crystallized a radically new way of thinking about the origins of humanity. Trigger, *A History of Archaeological Thought,* 94.

9 John Murray's 1853 English guide to the area, written just as the region was opening up to mass tourism, stresses that "the magnificent scenery of the Danube, the Bavarian Mountains, the Salzkammergut, and the Tyrol is almost without rival, and the fact that these districts are comparatively unfrequented by the crowds of ordinary tourists will prove an additional charm to the discriminating traveler." John Murray, *A Handbook for Travelers in Southern Germany: Being a Guide to Württemberg, Bavaria, Austria, Tyrol, Salzburg, Styria, &c., the Austrian and Bavarian Alps, and the Danube from Ulm to the Black Sea,* 6th, cor. and enl. ed. (London: J. Murray, 1853), 1.

10 Raabe used Baedeker's 1859 guide to Austria on his trip, and he made notes in it and referred back to it while writing the story. Wilhelm Karl Raabe, *Sämtliche Werke,* ed. Karl Hoppe, Hans Oppermann, and Hans Plischke (Freiburg, Switzerland: H. Klemm, 1951), 474–75. Most accounts of Hallstatt, whether archaeological monographs, private letters, popular reports, or fiction like Raabe's all make a point of recounting details of the journey to the cemetery and describing the site's surroundings. The archaeologist A. B. Meyer even includes an engraving of the area preceding his report. Joan Evans, *Time and Chance: The Story of Arthur Evans and His Forebears* (Westport, Conn.: Greenwood Press, 1974), 122. I am grateful to Eric Downing for this reference. See also Adolph Bernhard Meyer, *Das Grabfeld von Hallstatt: Anlässlich eines Besuches daselbst* (Dresden: Verlag von Wilhelm Hoffmann, 1885), title page, 1, 5.

11 Meyer, *Das Grabfeld von Hallstatt,* 7. Ludwig Pauli, *Die Gräber vom Salzberg zu Hallstatt: Erforschung, Überlieferung, Auswertbarkeit* (Mainz am Rhein: P. von Zabern, 1975). Bettina

Glunz, "Über einige 'historisierende' Schauspielrequisiten (und Kostüme) des 'Theaterherzogs' Georg II. von Sachsen-Meiningen," *Deutsches archäologisches Korrespondenzblatt* 24, no. 2 (1994): 227.

12 In the east, the debates turned on whether Germanic or Slavic predecessors had occupied the land first. See, for instance, Fontane's *Vor dem Sturm.* See also the work of Rudolf Virchow, a Renaissance man with a deep interest in prehistoric archaeology and the founding father of many museums.

13 Heidemarie Anderlik, "'Der Ring des Nibelungen': Bühnenkunst und Germananbild im 19. Jahrhundert," in *Zwischen Walhall und Paradies: Eine Austellung des Deutschen Historischen Museums in Zusammenarbeit mit dem Museum für Vor- und Frühgeschichte SMPK,* ed. Heidemarie Anderlik (Berlin: Deutsches Historisches Museum, 1991), 26–33. Glunz, "Über einige 'historisierende' Schauspielrequisiten," 228.

14 Glunz, "Über einige 'historisierende' Schauspielrequisiten," 226–27.

15 Wilhelm Raabe, *Keltische Knochen,* ed. Karl Hoppe, Hans Oppermann, and Hans Plischke, in *Sämtliche Werke* (Göttingen: Vandenhoeck and Ruprecht, 1962), 9:474–75. All subsequent references are given parenthetically to this edition. Jeffrey L. Sammons, *Wilhelm Raabe: The Fiction of the Alternative Community* (Princeton: Princeton University Press, 1987), 142.

16 Karl Hoppe and Hans Plischke, "Keltische Knocnen: Das Werk: Zur Entstehung," in *Wilhelm Raabe, Sämtliche Werke,* ed. Karl Hoppe, Hans Oppermann, and Hans Plischke (Göttingen: Vandenhoeck and Ruprecht, 1962), 474–75.

17 Sammons claims this is one of Raabe's intentions. Sammons, *Wilhelm Raabe,* 142.

18 Walter Kendrick, *The Secret Museum: Pornography in Modern Culture* (Berkeley and Los Angeles: University of California Press, 1996).

19 W. G. Sebald, "Thanatos: Zur Motivstruktur in Kafkas Schloss," *Literatur und Kritik* 8 (1972): 408–9.

20 Mikhail Bakhtin, *Rabelais and His World,* trans. Hélène Iswolsky (Bloomington: Indiana University Press, 1984), 28, 94.

21 Hoppe and Plischke, *Wilhelm Raabe: Sämtliche Werke,* 474–78.

22 Siegfried Kapper, "Die Hallstätter Ausgrabungen," *Westermann's Jahrbuch der Illustrirten deutschen Monatshefte* (1858): 510–19.

23 Kirsten Belgum points out that publications like *Westermann's* and the *Gartenlaube* had such diverse components that it would likely be erroneous to posit one ideal reader for an entire serial. Kirsten Belgum, *Popularizing the Nation: Audience, Representation, and the Production of Identity in Die Gartenlaube, 1853–1900* (Lincoln, Neb.: University of Nebraska Press, 1998), xxii–xxiii.

24 Rudolf Virchow, "Erinnerungen an Schliemann," *Die Gartenlaube* (1891): 66–68, 104–8, 299–303. Quoted in Justus Cobet, *Heinrich Schliemann: Archäologe und Abenteurer* (Munich: C. H. Beck, 1997), 73–74. Virchow was a politician, physician, anthropologist, archaeologist, and museum founder, who also served as a tireless popularizer of scientific knowledge.

25 Quoted in Cobet, *Heinrich Schliemann,* 73.

26 Cobet, *Heinrich Schliemann,* 73.

27 Heinrich Schliemann, *Trojanische Altertümer: Berichte über die Ausgrabungen in Troja* (Leipzig, 1874), 161; quoted in Cobet, *Heinrich Schliemann,* 7.

28 Theodor Fontane, *Vor dem Sturm. Roman aus dem Winter 1812 auf 13,* ed. Helmuth Nürnberger (Munich: Carl Hanser, 1990), on "Odin's Wagon," see pp. 95–101. Subsequent references are made parenthetically to this edition.

29 André Malraux, *Museum Without Walls* (Garden City, N.Y.: Doubleday, 1967), 16–17.

30 It has been claimed that certain of Heinrich's features in Stifter's *Der Nachsommer* were derived from Simony and his activities, and that the story "Bergkristall" also stems from an experience the two men shared while climbing a glacier in Oberösterreich.

31 Quoted in Karl Kromer, *Das Gräberfeld von Hallstatt* (Florence: Sansoni, 1959), 11.

32 Viennese officials, who received the first copy Ramsauer produced, probably would not have suspected that he would be willing to produce additional copies and so create a bidding war behind their backs.

33 Menghin, "Pfahlheim," 85.

34 Julia Bertschik, *Maulwurfsarchäologie: Zum Verhältnis von Geschichte und Anthropologie in Wilhelm Raabes historischen Erzähltexten* (Tübingen: M. Niemeyer, 1995), 52f.

35 "Especially since both initiated and uninitiated guests carry out a looting excavation here and there and smuggle out some pieces. As Mr. Straberger notes: 'It can be assumed with certainty that many high-ranking personalities and wealthy tourists have reached the same through influence and money what Hofrat von Az was permitted to do,' and I have become familiar with several such cases; I name only one such attempt on the part of the duke of Meingingen" (Meyer, *Das Grabfeld von Hallstatt,* 7). While Bettina Glunz disputes the claim that the Herzog of Meiningen tried to steal grave artifacts, she documents the impact that Celtic objects found in Hallstatt, and illustrated in books and other publications, had on the theater costumes the duke had designed for the Meiningen Court Theater. Glunz, "Über einige 'historisierende' Schauspielrequisiten." Similar costume combinations appeared in Wagner's productions in Bayreuth. See Anderlik, "'Der Ring des Nibelungen'," 26–33.

36 Meyer, *Das Grabfeld von Hallstatt,* 7.

37 Dean MacCannell, *The Tourist: A New Theory of the Leisure Class* (Berkeley and Los Angeles: University of Califrnia Press, 1999), 135–41.

Chapter 6

1 See Andreas Huyssen, *Twilight Memories: Marking Time in a Culture of Amnesia* (New York: Routledge, 1995). These critiques begin to take shape with the formation of the public museum in France. See Daniel J. Sherman, "Quatremére/Benjamin/Marx: Art Museums, Aura, and Commodity Fetishism," in *Museum Culture: Histories, Discourses, Spectacles,* ed. Daniel J. Sherman and Irit Rogoff (Minneapolis: University of Minnesota Press, 1994), 123–43. In some respects, Goethe's critical voice, which resonates with insights later advanced by Walter Benjamin, might also be named as one comparable to Quatremére's, also in that Goethe's accompanies the formation of the museum.

2 Rainer Maria Rilke, *Briefe aus den Jahren 1892 bis 1904,* ed. Ruth Rilke Sieber and Carl Sieber (Leipzig: Insel-verlag, 1939), 1:244–46.

3 Tony Bennett. *The Birth of the Museum: History, Theory, Politics* (London: Routledge, 1995).

4 A few critics have argued that the *Neue Gedichte* [New Poems] must be viewed as a museum of dead objects ("ein Museum toter Dinge"). As this phrase implies, these critics see the poems primarily as inert artifacts, organized to replicate a space conceived of as static and completed, frozen in time for all time. If nothing else, this assessment fails to do justice to the dynamic place of museal objects in Rilke's thinking and more generally in the cultural landscape. Other critics merely treat the specific exhibited objects in various museums as more or less unremarkable inspiration for many of Rilke's *Neue Gedichte* and for portions of *Die Aufzeichnungen des Malte Laurids Brigge* [The Notebooks of Malte Laurids Brigge]. Indeed, Rilke's poem "Der Panther" [The Panther] locates its object "in the Jardin des Plantes, Paris." Yet Rilke's correspondence mentions that the first inspiration for this poem came from the Bibliothèque Nationale and a casting Rodin possessed of that same figure. Claude David, "Die Leere und die Fülle," in *Rainer Maria Rilke,* ed. Rüdiger Görner (Darmstadt: Wissenschaftliche Buchhandlung, 1987), 321. Though Judith Ryan suggests that the *Neue Gedichte* invite being read in terms of the museum, she seems to discount such an approach, implying that it would require the poems to correspond to identifiable objects in an unambiguous fashion. Judith

Ryan, *Rilke, Modernism, and Poetic Tradition* (Cambridge: Cambridge University Press, 1999), 52. Frank Baron, *Rilke and the Visual Arts* (Lawrence, Kans.: Coronado Press, 1982), 8. Rainer Maria Rilke, *Neue Gedichte,* ed. Ruth Sieber-Rilke, *Sämtliche Werke* (Frankfurt am Main: Insel, 1955), 1:505. Subsequent references to poems from this collection are to this edition and are indicated with line and page number parenthetically. Unless otherwise indicated, translations are from Rainer Maria Rilke, *New Poems,* trans. Edward Snow (San Francisco: North Point Press, 1984) and Rainer Maria Rilke, *New Poems: The Other Part,* trans. Edward Snow (San Francisco: North Point Press, 1987).

5 Ryan, *Rilke, Modernism,* 52. John Hollander, *The Gazer's Spirit: Poems Speaking to Silent Works of Art* (Chicago: University of Chicago Press, 1995), 7–29. See also Peter Por's notion of Rilke's poetry creating imaginary space. Peter Por, "Rilke—Rodin, Cézanne, Klee: Die Schöpfung des Raumes in der Moderne," in *Proceedings of the XXIIth Congress of the International Comparative Literature Association,* ed. Roger Bauer and Fokkema Douwe (Munich: iuidicum, 1990), 54.

6 Rilke, letter to Clara Rilke, August 31, 1902, *Briefe aus den Jahren 1892–1904,* 246.

7 Karl Baedeker, *Paris and Environs with Routes from London to Paris: Handbook for Travelers,* 14th rev. ed. (Leipzig: K. Baedeker, 1900), 414–15. Leo Woerl, *Wörl's Führer durch Paris und Umgebung* (Leipzig: Woerl's Reisebücherverlag, 1900), 260.

8 Tony Bennett, *The Birth of the Museum,* 84.

9 Rainer Maria Rilke, letter to Clara Rilke, September 29, 1905, Rainer Maria Rilke, *Briefe aus den Jahren 1904 bis 1907,* ed. Ruth Sieber-Rilke and Carl Sieber (Leipzig: Insel, 1939), 2:100. [Addition as in original.]

10 Hélène Pinet, ed., *Rodin Collectionneur* (Paris: Musée Rodin, 1967).

11 Rainer Maria Rilke, *Auguste Rodin* (Frankfurt am Main: Insel, 1955), 232.

12 Ursula Emde, *Rilke und Rodin* (Marburg/Lahn: Verlag des Kunstgeschichtlichen Seminars der Universität Marburg, 1949), 61. The letter is dated August 1, 1903.

13 Emde, *Rilke und Rodin,* 69–70.

14 Rilke, letters to Clara Rilke, May 11, 1906, May 29, 1906, June 1, 1906, July 6, 1906, *Briefe aus den Jahren 1904–1907,* 132–33, 144–49, 149–53, 162–64.

15 Emde, *Rilke und Rodin,* 62.

16 Emde, *Rilke und Rodin,* 62. Ralph Freedman, *Life of a Poet: Rainer Maria Rilke* (New York: Farrar Straus and Giroux, 1996), 162.

17 Wolfgang Leppmann, *Rilke: Sein Leben, seine Welt, sein Werk* (Bern: Scherz, 1981), 229.

18 In letters from 1906 and 1907, Rilke writes about encounters that vibrantly recall the devastating impact of his initial experiences of the Parisian streets. See Rilke, letters to Clara Rilke, May 29, 1906, June 19, 1907, *Briefe aus den Jahren 1904–1907,* 144–49, 332–34.

19 Rilke, letter to Clara Rilke, July 6, 1906, *Briefe aus den Jahren 1904–1907,* 163–64.

20 Ibid.

21 Rilke, letter to Clara Rilke, May 29, 1906, *Briefe aus den Jahren 1904–1907,* 144–49.

22 Rilke, letter to Clara Rilke, March 8, 1907. *Briefe aus den Jahren 1904–1907,* 278–81. [Emphasis original.]

23 Herman Meyer, "Rilkes Cézanne-Erlebnis," in *Zarte Empirie: Studien zur Literaturgeschichte* (Stuttgart: Metzler, 1963), 260.

24 Norbert Bolz, Michelle Mattson, trans., "Farewell to the Gutenberg Galaxy," *New German Critique* 78 (1999): 109–31.

25 Norman Bryson, "The Gaze in the Expanded Field," in *Vision and Visuality,* ed. Hal Foster (Seattle: Bay Press, 1988), 107.

26 Bryson, "Gaze in the Expanded Field," 97.

27 Bryson, "Gaze in the Expanded Field," 97. Meyer, "Rilkes Cézanne-Erlebnis," 285.

28 Brigitte L. Bradley, *Rainer Maria Rilkes Neue Gedichte: Ihr zyklisches Gefüge* (Bern: Francke Verlag, 1967), 9. See also Stefan Schank, *Rainer Maria Rilke* (Munich: dtv, 1998), 90–91.

29 David Frisby, "The Flâneur in Social Theory," in *The Flâneur,* ed. Keith Tester (London: Routledge, 1994), 93. See also Huyssen, *Twilight Memories,* 122–24.

30 Walter Benjamin, *Das Passagenwerk,* ed. Rolf Tiedemann et al., in *Gesammelte Schriften* (Frankfurt am Main: Suhrkamp, 1980), 5: bk. 1, 272–73.

31 Benjamin, *Passagenwerk,* 272.

32 Bolz, Mattson, trans., "Farewell to the Gutenberg Galaxy," 115.

33 Benjamin, *Passagenwerk,* 273. Walter Benjamin, *The Arcades Project,* trans. Howard Eiland and Kevin McLaughlin (New York: Belknap, 2002), 206.

34 Janet Wolff, "The Artist and the Flâneur," in *The Flâneur,* ed. Keith Tester (New York: Routledge, 1994), 127. See also Frisby, "The Flâneur in Social Theory," 92–97.

35 Judith Ryan, *Umschlag und Verwandlung: poetische Struktur und Dichtungstheorie in R. M. Rilkes Lyrik der mittleren Periode (1907–1914)* (Munich: Winkler, 1972), 9.

36 Bradley, *Rilkes Neue Gedichte,* 75. Ryan, *Umschlag und Verwandlung,* 24.

37 On Rilke's view of the dog, see Meyer, "Rilkes Cézanne-Erlebnis," 282–83.

38 Hans Berendt, *Rainer Maria Rilkes Neue Gedichte: Versuch einer Deutung* (Bonn: H. Bouvier, 1957), 113.

39 Rainer Maria Rilke, letter to Clara Rilke, September 27, 1902, *Briefe aus den Jahren 1892–1904,* 272–74.

40 Ibid. See also Rilke, *Auguste Rodin,* 173.

41 Rilke, *Auguste Rodin,* 172.

42 Freedman, *Life of a Poet,* 170.

43 André Malraux, *Museum Without Walls* (Garden City, N.Y.: Doubleday, 1967), 16–17.

44 On Malraux's engagement with Benjamin, see Denis Hollier, "On Paper," in *Anymore,* ed. Cynthia Davidson (New York: Anyone Corporation, 2000). 60–61. Hal Foster, "Archives of Modern Art," *October* 99 (2002): 92–93.

45 Rosalind E. Krauss, "Postmodernism's Museum Without Walls," in *Thinking About Exhibitions,* ed. Reesa Greenberg, Bruce W. Ferguson, and Sandy Nairne (New York: Routledge, 1996), 344–45.

46 *Guide des plaisirs à Paris: Paris le jour: Paris la nuit: La "Tournée des Grands-Ducs": comment on s'amuse: ou l'on s'amuse: ce qu'il faut voir: ce qu'il faut faire: un plan des plaisirs de Paris,* (Paris: 1900), 35.

47 Albert Edward Elsen and Auguste Rodin, *In Rodin's Studio: A Photographic Record of Sculpture in the Making* (Oxford: Phaidon Press, 1980), 20.

48 In his 1846 essay "Why Sculpture Is Boring," Baudelaire had faulted sculpture precisely for its dual nature as commodity and aesthetic object. Alex Potts argues that Baudelaire defined the condition of modern sculpture in this essay, a condition that arises in part from its being produced directly for purchase by museums and galleries. Alex Potts, "The Reification and Disintegration of Sculpture in Rodin and Rilke," in *Sight and Insight: Essays on Art and Culture in Honour of E. H. Gombrich at 85,* ed. E. H. Gombrich and John Onians (London: Phaidon Press, 1994), 356–57.

49 Ruth Butler, *Rodin in Perspective* (Englewood Cliffs, N.J.: Prentice-Hall, 1980). Figs. 9 and 10 show Rodin's sculptures placed in highly conspicuous positions at the Salon of 1898.

50 Butler, *Rodin in Perspective,* 100.

51 Ibid.

52 Elsen and Rodin, *In Rodin's Studio,* 19–20.

53 Rodin's studio seemed to emulate the factory in his use of reproducibility, modularity, scaling, and fragmentation to produce a wide range of sculpture.

54 Before the advent of public museums, copper etchings and copyists brought into circulation artworks that were owned by nobility or were otherwise inaccessible. While the creation of public museums greatly increased the opportunity for the population at large to view collected paintings, the practice of copying in museums continued throughout the nineteenth century, in the training of artists and as a trade largely constituted by women. Perhaps a remnant of this trade can be seen when Malte notices the unbuttoned dresses of young girls, occupied with drawing in the Musée Cluny, who have left their families for work in the city and therefore no longer have anyone to help them dress. The now ubiquitous museum gift shop partakes of this dialectic with its postcards, reproductions such as posters and T-shirts, and museum catalogs. A Musée des Copies, housing copies of works of the Italian Renaissance, was maintained in Paris as late as 1872, although it was closed soon thereafter, in part because photography had proved especially useful for reproducing art works. Patricia Mainardi, *The End of the Salon: Art and the State in the Early Third Republic* (Cambridge: Cambridge University Press, 1993), 46. Rainer Maria Rilke, *Die Aufzeichnungen des Malte Laurids Brigge,* ed. Ruth Sieber, in *Sämtliche Werke* (Frankfurt am Main: Insel, 1966), 6:830–31. In calling attention to such a small detail in clothing, Malte conforms to the social practice of the day. The French debate over whether umbrellas needed to be checked in museums reveals that museum-goers of the late nineteenth century expended as much energy watching one another as they did examining the works of art. The umbrella, particularly its size, shape, and condition, was an indication of class status. With the increasing popularity of industrially manufactured clothing, small details became increasingly telling of class distinctions. Daniel J. Sherman, *Worthy Monuments: Art Museums and the Politics of Culture in Nineteenth-Century France* (Cambridge: Harvard University Press, 1989), 226–30.

55 Elsen and Rodin, *In Rodin's Studio,* 15.

56 Elsen and Rodin, *In Rodin's Studio,* 10.

57 Elsen and Rodin, *In Rodin's Studio,* 15.

58 Elsen and Rodin, *In Rodin's Studio,* 16.

59 Rilke, *Auguste Rodin,* 69.

60 Emde, *Rilke und Rodin,* 94.

61 John Milner, *The Studios of Paris: The Capital of Art in the Late Nineteenth Century* (New Haven: Yale University Press, 1988), 59–63.

62 Wolff, "The Artist and the Flâneur," 123.

63 Elsen and Rodin, *In Rodin's Studio,* 19–23.

64 Anne M. Wagner, "Rodin's Reputation," in *Eroticism and the Body Politic,* ed. Lynn Avery Hunt (Baltimore: Johns Hopkins University Press, 1991), 197. Potts, "The Reification and Disintegration of Sculpture in Rodin and Rilke," 366.

65 Wagner, "Rodin's Reputation," 196–97, 225–27. Alain Kirili, "The Scandal of Rodin and His Models," in *Rodin: Eros and Creativity,* ed. Rainer Crone and Siegfried Salzmann (Munich: Prestel, 1992), 210–13.

66 Emde, *Rilke und Rodin,* 71.

67 Wagner, "Rodin's Reputation," 201–2.

68 Wagner, "Rodin's Reputation," 196.

69 Wagner, "Rodin's Reputation," 223–25.

70 Wagner, "Rodin's Reputation," 223–25, 234–35.

71 Rilke, *Auguste Rodin,* 164–65.

72 Bram Dijkstra, *Idols of Perversity: Fantasies of Feminine Evil in Fin-de-Siècle Culture* (New York: Oxford University Press, 1986), 99–107.

73 Georg Simmel argues that Rodin showed that the classical style of sculpture, long held to be

absolute, is but one possible sculptural style. Simmel draws an analogy with Nietzsche, who showed that there is no absolute morality, but rather several moralities. Georg Simmel, "Rodins Plastik und die Geistesrichtung der Gegenwart," *Berliner Tageblatt,* September 29, 1902.

74 Rilke, *Auguste Rodin,* 53.

75 Marie Busco and David Finn, *Rodin and His Contemporaries: The Iris & B. Gerald Cantor Collection* (New York: Cross River Press, 1991), 36.

76 Rodin to H. C. E. Dujardin-Beaumetz, translated and quoted in Elsen and Rodin, *In Rodin's Studio,* 166.

77 Rilke, *Auguste Rodin,* 162.

78 Martin Luther, trans., *Die Bibel* (Stuttgart: Deutsche Bibelstiftung, 1978), 21–22.

79 Elisabeth Bronfen, *Over Her Dead Body: Death, Femininity, and the Aesthetic* (New York: Routledge, 1992), 216.

80 Patricia Linden, "Frauenkult und Weiblichkeit in Rainer Maria Rilkes Aufzeichnungen des Malte Laurids Brigge," *Germanistische Mitteilungen* 25 (1987): 4–5.

81 Linden, "Frauenkult und Weiblichkeit," 4–5. Bronfen, *Over Her Dead Body,* 218.

82 Kathleen L. Komar, "The Mediating Muse: Of Men, Women, and the Feminine in the Work of Rainer Maria Rilke," *Germanic Review* 64 (1989): 130.

83 Huyssen, *Twilight Memories,* 125.

84 Huyssen, *Twilight Memories,* 125.

85 By the time of his interactions with Rodin, Rilke was experiencing conflict between the demands of his creative work and the intimacy and commitment required to maintain quotidian marital life (Freedman, *Life of a Poet,* 160–67). Drawn in part to Rodin's imperative to work constantly, Rilke's move to Paris amounted to a renunciation of his wife and domestic responsibilities in an attempt to better devote himself to his work, ostensibly leading Rilke to feel affinities with the renunciation of famous female poets ("die grossen Liebenden") (see Komar, "The Mediating Muse," 130).

86 Rilke's mother is supposed to have been so disappointed at having had a boy that she named him René and then proceeded to pretend that his identity was that of a girl named Sophie. Wolff, "The Artist and the Flâneur," 128–31.

87 Wolff, "The Artist and the Flâneur," 128–31. See also Huyssen, who resists seeing Malte as a flâneur of any kind. *Twilight Memories,* 121–22.

88 Huyssen, *Twilight Memories,* 112.

89 Frances Mary Scholz, "Rilke, Rodin, and the Fragmented Man," in *Rilke and the Visual Arts,* ed. Frank Baron (Lawrence, Kans.: Coronado Press, 1982), 30–38.

90 Rilke, *Malte,* 732.

91 Bennett, *Birth of the Museum,* 179. The term "retrospective prophecy" is taken from Thomas Huxley, "On the Method of Zadig: Retrospective Prophecy as a Function of Science," in *Science and Culture and Other Essays* (London: Macmillan, 1882), 135–55.

92 Huyssen, *Twilight Memories,* 123–26.

93 Huyssen recognizes as much when he sees instances of fragmentation such as these as part of a larger modernist project that consists of Rilke's "spitting out his childhood in bits and pieces . . . in an aesthetically highly controlled way." Huyssen, *Twilight Memories,* 123.

94 I am using the notion of "just so" story in the manner of biologists such as Stephen J. Gould and Richard Lewontin, who critiqued the invention of unverifiable stories of past events that conveniently explain configurations of data and/or conditions. Stephen J. Gould and Richard Lewontin, "The Spandrels of San Marco and the Panglossian Paradigm: A Critique of the Adaptationist Programme," *Proceedings of the Royal Society* B205 (1979), 591–98. Their use of the term is inspired by Rudyard Kipling's *Just So Stories* (1902), which offer fanciful "explanations" of "How the Leopard Got Its Spots," "How the Camel Got Its Hump," and so on.

95 "Oh Lou, there is much more reality in a poem I write successfully than in any relationship or affection that I feel." Quoted in Leppmann, *Rilke: Sein Leben,* 229.

96 Albert Edward Elsen, "Rodin and the Partial Figure," in *The Partial Figure in Modern Sculpture: From Rodin to 1969* (Baltimore: Baltimore Museum of Art, 1969), 22.

97 Elsen, "Rodin and the Partial Figure," 22.

98 Elsen, "Rodin and the Partial Figure," 22.

99 Rilke, letter to Clara Rilke, September 2, 1902, *Briefe aus den Jahren 1892 bis 1904,* 252. [Ellipses as in original.]

100 Rainer Crone and David Moos, "A Biographical Narrative: Auguste Rodin, 1840–1917," in *Rodin: Eros and Creativity,* ed. Rainer Crone and Siegfried Salzmann (Munich: Prestel, 1992), 45.

101 Elsen and Rodin, *In Rodin's Studio,* 29.

102 Elsen and Rodin, *In Rodin's Studio,* 29.

103 Donald Preziosi, *Rethinking Art History: Meditations on a Coy Science* (New Haven: Yale University Press, 1989), 69. Museums also strip the objects of the contexts that would prevent them from appearing simultaneously.

104 Elsen and Rodin, *In Rodin's Studio,* 28.

105 Crone and Moos, "A Biographical Narrative: Auguste Rodin, 1840–1917," 11.

106 Elsen, "Rodin and the Partial Figure," 24.

107 Rilke, letter to Clara Rilke, September 2, 1902, *Briefe aus den Jahren 1892 bis 1904,* 252–53. [Ellipses in original.]

108 Translation modifies that published in Rilke, *New Poems,* 51.

109 Martina Kriessbach, *Rilke und Rodin: Wege einer Erfahrung des Plastischen* (Frankfurt am Main: Peter Lang, 1984), 70. Krießbach quotes a letter to Lou Andreas-Salomé (August 10, 1903) in which Rilke describes how he seeks to find the "cell" of his artistic method in language, in analogy to Rodin's use of the *modelé* as his "cell."

110 Rilke, letter to Clara Rilke, January 26, 1906, *Briefe aus de Jahren 1904 bis 1907,* 115–16.

111 Ibid.

112 Rilke, *Auguste Rodin,* 13.

113 Rilke, *Auguste Rodin,* 11–12.

114 Rilke, *Auguste Rodin,* 151.

115 Rilke, *Auguste Rodin,* 151.

116 Rilke, *Auguste Rodin,* 149–51. Kriessbach, *Rilke und Rodin,* 34–36.

117 Rilke, *Auguste Rodin,* 149–53. Witness Rilke's statement: "There were [for Rodin] only innumerably many living surfaces, there was only life, and the means of expression that he found for himself made a bee-line for this life."

118 Rilke, *Auguste Rodin,* 164.

119 Potts, "The Reification and isintegration of Sculpture in Rodin and Rilke," 362.

120 Rilke, *Auguste Rodin,* 164–65.

121 Bennett, *Birth of the Museum,* 179–81.

Chapter 7

1 Ingeborg Bachmann, *Werke,* ed. Christine Koschel and Inge von Weidenbaum, 4 vols. (Munich: Piper, 1978), 3:337. Subsequent references are to this edition, given parenthetically. Transla-

tions are my own unless otherwise noted.

2 Arguments of this sort have taken a variety of forms. See in particular Sigrid Weigel, *Ingeborg Bachmann: Hinterlassenschaften unter Wahrung des Briefgeheimnisses* (Vienna: P. Zsolnay Verlag, 1999), 526–35, and Jost Schneider, *Die Kompositionsmethode Ingeborg Bachmanns: Erzählstil und Engagement in Das dreissigste Jahr, Malina und Simultan* (Bielefeld: Aisthesis, 1999), 269–71.

3 Christine Koschel and Inge von Weidenbaum, eds., *Wir müssen wahre Sätze finden: Gespräche und Interviews* (Munich: Piper, 1991), 70, 144.

4 Bachmann Nachlass, Blatt 4679. Quoted in Hans Höller, *Ingeborg Bachmann: Das Werk von den frühesten Gedichten bis zum "Todesarten"—Zyklus* (Frankfurt am Main: Athenäum, 1987), 349, note 192.

5 Ingeborg Bachmann, *"Todesarten"-Projekt,* ed. Robert Pichl, Monika Albrecht, and Dirk Göttsche (Munich: Piper, 1995), 3.1:496–97. My translation.

6 Schneider, *Die Kompositionsmethode Ingeborg Bachmanns,* 270.

7 Weigel, *Ingeborg Bachmann,* 366–69.

8 Walter Benjamin, "Berliner Chronik," in *Gesammelte Schriften,* ed. Rolf Tiedemann and Hermann Schweppenhauser (Frankfurt am Main: Suhrkamp, 1980), 6:486. Walter Benjamin, "A Berlin Chronicle," in *Reflections: Essays, Aphorisms, Autobiographical Writings,* ed. Peter Demetz (New York: Schocken, 1978), 25–26.

9 Koschel and Weidenbaum, eds., *Wir müssen wahre Sätze finden,* 65.

10 Weigel, *Ingeborg Bachmann,* 369.

11 Benjamin, "Berliner Chronik," in *Gesammelte Schriften,* 6:486. Benjamin, "A Berlin Chronicle," 26.

12 On the need to differentiate between the modes of operation and effects of differing archival institutions, see the discussions in Chapters 1, 2, 3, and 8 in this volume.

13 Gerhard Roth, *Eine Reise in das Innere von Wien: Essays* (Frankfurt am Main: S. Fischer, 1991), 186.

14 Peter Schubert, *Das Wiener Arsenal: Ein historischer Überblick* (Vienna: Brüder Hollinek, 1975), 16. Roth, *Eine Reise,* 187. Carl E. Schorske, *Fin-de-siècle Vienna: Politics and Culture* (New York: Knopf, 1979), 30–31.

15 In recent years, significant changes have altered the role of the federal government in administering Austrian museums. In Bachmann's time, however, most national museums were federal institutions.

16 Roth, *Eine Reise,* 185.

17 Alfred Mell, *Heeresmuseum in Wien: Austellung ausgewählter Neuerwerbungen aus dem Zeitalter Kaiser Franz Josefs.* (Vienna: Heeresmuseum Wien, 1937), 3.

18 Heinz Zatschek, *Das Heeresegeschichtliche Museum in Wien* (Graz: Böhlau, 1960), 25.

19 Zatschek, *Das Heeresegeschichtliche Museum in Wien,* 25.

20 Schubert, *Das Wiener Arsenal,* 47. Lars-H. Thümmler, *Das Zeughaus Berlin im Zweiten Weltkrieg.* [Internet] (Deutsches Historisches Museum, 2003); [cited November 11, 2006]; available from http://www.dhm.de/texte/zhwk2.html. Section "Verwaltungsstrukturen." By 1941, the other museums carry the uniform designations and reflect the standardized hierarchy described by Thümmler. See the explanation in *Heeresmuseum Wien: Führer durch die Feldherrn- und durch die Ruhmeshalle* (Vienna: Heeresmuseum Wien, 1941), 1.

21 All army museums were to be named according to the rubric, *Heeresmuseum XX,* with XX being the name of the location of the museum, thus Heeresmuseum Wien, Heeresmuseum Dresden, and so on. See the 1941 guidebook and also Thümmler, *Das Zeughaus Berlin im Zweiten Weltkrieg.* [Internet] [cited November 11, 2006]; http://www.dhm.de/texte/zhwk2.html.

22 Recent analyses of "Aryanization" in Vienna have argued that its rapid and energetic implementation there served as a "model" for the rest of Germany. Hans Witek, "'Arisierungen' in Wien: Aspekte nationalsozialistischer Enteignungspolitik, 1938–1940," in *NS-Herrschaft in Österreich: Ein Handbuch,* ed. Emmerich Talos, Wolfgang Neugebauer, and Ernst Hanisch (Vienna: öbv and hpt, 2001), 798–800.

23 Martin Roth, *Heimatmuseum: Zur Geschichte einer deutschen Institution* (Berlin: Mann, 1990), 108–9.

24 Thümmler, *Das Zeughaus Berlin im Zweiten Weltkrieg.* [Internet] [Cited November 11, 2006].

25 Thümmler, *Das Zeughaus Berlin im Zweiten Weltkrieg.* [Internet] [Cited November 11, 2006].

26 Zatschek's narrative downplays the interaction between collection and temporary shows, underscoring how exceptional it was that "this or that piece from the old collections" was brought in for the temporary show "Kampfraum Südost" [Southeastern Battle Area]. Zatschek, *Das Heeresegeschichtliche Museum in Wien,* 26. Kaindl claims that the Nazi era represents "the most decisive caesura in the entire history of the museum." Franz Kaindl, "Das Wiener Heeresgeschichtliches Museum: Ein historisches Nationalmuseum von internationaler Dimension," in *Die Nation und ihre Museen,* ed. Marie-Louise Plessen (Frankfurt: Campus, 1992), 277.

27 Roth, *Heimatmuseum,* 173–74.

28 The few Wehrmacht units made up primarily of Austrians also were deployed to this region of the war, in part because of Austria's history of conflict in this area. Walter Manoschek and Hans Safrian, "Österreicher in der Wehrmacht," in *NS-Herrschaft in Österreich: ein Handbuch,* ed. Emmerich Talos, Wolfgang Neugebauer, and Ernst Hanisch (Wien: öbv and hpt, 2001), 124.

29 Christoph Zuschlag, *'Entartete Kunst': Ausstellungsstrategien im Nazi-Deutschland* (Worms: Wernersche Verlagsgesellschaft, 1995), 321.

30 Founded by Jews in 1906, the Prague museum was taken over by the Nazis after their invasion of Czechoslovakia (p. 56). Under the control of the Schutzstaffel (SS), a Jewish staff was retained to collect and document Jewish objects following deportations and confiscations of property that were part and parcel of the Shoah. See Wolfgang Ernst, "Archi(ve)textures of Museology," in *Museums and Memory,* ed. Susan A. Crane (Stanford: Stanford University Press, 2000), 24–25. For a lengthier analysis and information on the displays, see Dirk Rupnow, *Täter, Gedächtnis, Opfer: Das "Jüdische Zentralmuseum" in Prag, 1942–1945* (Vienna: Picus, 2000).

31 Rupnow, *Täter, Gedächtnis, Opfer,* 180. See also Dirk Rupnow, "'Ihr müsst sein, auch wenn ihr nicht mehr sein': The Jewish Central Museum in Prague and Historical Memory in the Third Reich," *Holocaust and Genocide Studies* 16 (2002): 23–53.

32 Zatschek, *Das Heeresegeschichtliche Museum in Wien,* 1960.

33 *Wehrmacht—Heer/Heeresmuseum Wien: Sonderschau Sowjetrussischer Beute,* (Vienna: Heeresmuseum Wien, 1942), 3–5.

34 *Sonderschau Sowjetrussischer Beute,* 3.

35 *Kampfraum Südost: Sonderschau veranstaltet vom Chef der Heeresmuseen im Heeresmuseum Wien: Juni-August 1944* (Vienna: Verlag des Heeresmuseums, 1944), 5.

36 See Zatschek, *Das Heeresegeschichtliche Museum in Wien,* 26.

37 *Heeresmuseum Wien* (1941), 3–4.

38 The title page of the 1943 catalog *Heeresmuseum Wien* is inscribed "Das Heeresmuseum in Wien: Dokumente zu einem großen Teil der deutschen Geschichte" [The Army Museum in Vienna: Documents on a Great Part of German History].

39 *Das Heeresmuseum in Wien* (Vienna: Heeresmuseum Wien, 1943), 3. *Heeresgeschichtliches Museum Wien* (Graz: Verlag Styria, 1988), 8.

40 *Heeresmuseum Wien* (1941), 5.

41 *Heeresmuseum Wien* (1941), 6.

42 *Heeresmuseum Wien* (1941), 8.

43 *Das Heeresmuseum in Wien* (1943), 6.

44 *Katalog des Heeresmuseum: Isonzofront Saal 1 und 2* (Vienna: Verlag des Heeresmuseums, 1934), 1–2.

45 Zatschek, *Das Heeresegeschichtliche Museum in Wien,* 53.

46 Roth, *Eine Reise,* 183–84.

47 TOP-ONLINE-Winterthur-Frauenfeld-W-1-Saint Gallen-Zurich. "Weltkrieg-Auslöser in Wien" [Internet] (2004) [cited May 1, 2005]; available from: http://www.toponline.(h/avea-l.vub-42. art-44223.tce.

48 Kaindl, "Das Wiener Heeresgeschichtliches Museum," 279.

49 Kaindl, "Das Wiener Heeresgeschichtliches Museum," 279.

50 Zatschek, *Das Heeresegeschichtliche Museum in Wien,* 27.

51 It could be claimed that the ambiguous design of the museum display anticipated visitors with an overriding sense of how to interpret the pathos and symbolism of the objects. When the display was created, however, no such clear consensus existed as to what the Hapsburg Empire, let alone its demise, meant. The terms related to the Hapsburg monarchy in the twentieth century were and continue to be seriously overdetermined. The versions of the "Hapsburg myth" familiar today, such as the one promulgated by Hemito von Doderer, were being formulated only in the 1950s and 1960s, with the term itself being coined by Claudio Magris in 1963. Jacques le Rider, "Hugo von Hofmannsthal and the Idea of Central Europe," in *The Habsburg Legacy: National Identity in Historical Perspective,* ed. Ritchie Robertson and Edward Timms (Edinburgh: Edinburgh University Press, 1994), 121–22. See Anton Pelinka, "Austrian Identity and the 'Ständesstaat.'" in *The Habsburg Legacy: National Identity in Historical Perspective,* ed. Ritchie Robertson and Edward Timms (Edinburgh: Edinburgh University Press, 1994), 174–75. Andrew Barker, "Doderer's Hapsburg Myth: History, the Novel, and National Identity," in *Austria, 1945–1955: Studies in Political and Cultural Re-emergence,* ed. Anthony Bushell (Cardiff: University of Wales Press, 1996), 44–49.

52 See Pelinka, "Austrian Identity and the 'Ständesstaat,'" 169–70.

53 Tina Walzer and Stephan Templ, *Unser Wien: "Arisierung" auf Österreichisch* (Berlin: Aufbau-Verlag, 2001), 198.

54 The plaque is in the Feldherrenhalle. The catalog contains praise from Drimmel, as well as photographs of his active participation in ceremonies. Manfried Rauchensteiner, *Phoenix aus der Asche* (Vienna: Heeresgeschichtliches Museum, 2005).

55 Vaclav Podany and Hana Barvikova, *Heinz Zatschek.* [Internet] (Archive of the Academy of Sciences of the Czech Republic, 2005) [cited November 11, 2006]; available from http://www.archiv.cas.cz/english/pages/histpers.htm.

56 Wolfgang Kos, "Entnazifizierung der Bürokratie," in *Verdrängte Schuld, verfehlte Sühne: Entnazifizierung in Österreich, 1945–1955,* ed. Sebastian Meissl, Klaus-Dieter Mulley, and Oliver Rathkolb (Munich: R. Oldenbourg, 1986), 54. Oliver Rathkolb, "NS-Problem und politische Restauration: Vorgeschichte und Etablierung des VdU," in *Verdrängte Schuld, verfehlte Sühne: Entnazifizierung in Österreich, 1945–1955,* ed. Sebastian Meissl, Klaus-Dieter Mulley, and Oliver Rathkolb (Munich: R. Oldenbourg, 1986), 79.

57 Anton Pelinka, "The Great Austrian Taboo: The Repression of the Civil War," in *Coping with the Past: Germany and Austria After 1945,* ed. Kathy Harms, Lutz R. Reuter, and Volker Durr (Madison: University of Wisconsin Press, 1990), 56–57.

58 Pelinka, "The Great Austrian Taboo," 56–57.

59 Pelinka, "The Great Austrian Taboo," 60–61. Rathkolb, "NS-Problem," 79–88.

60 The Österreichische Volkspartei (ÖVP; Austrian People's Party) and Socialdemokratische Partei (SPÖ; Social Democratic Party of Austria) had a secret committee to deal with rearming Austria's military. Christian Stifter, *Die Wiederaufrüstung Österreichs: Die geheime Remilitarisierung der westlichen Besatzungszonen, 1945–1955* (Innsbruck: Studien Verlag, 1997), 30, 191. Robert Kriechbaumer, "Der lange Weg in die Moderne: Ein mentatlitätsgeschichtlicher

Essay zur Geschichte der Zweiten Republik," in *Österreichische Nationalgeschichte nach 1945*, ed. Robert Kriechbaumer, Oliver Rathkolb, and Otto Maschke (Vienna: Böhlau, 1998), 28–30.

61 Stifter, *Wiederaufrüstung Österreichs*, 30–32.

62 While Kriechbaumer observes that a tension exists between the concept of neutrality and military emphases, Stifter shows that Austrians repeatedly insisted on having the option of developing offensive weapons. Kriechbaumer, "Der lange Weg," 29–30. Stifter, *Wiederaufrüstung Österreichs*, 184.

63 This secrecy was primarily directed toward the Austrian people, as the Allies were fully aware and supportive of these endeavors. The United States contributed 5 million dollars a year toward this end. Christine Stöckl, *Die Verteidigungspolitik der ÖVP und der Stellenwert der militärischen Landesverteidigung im österreichischen Neutralitätskonzept, 1955–1985* (Vienna: W. Braumüller, 1985), 39–42. Manfried Rauchensteiner, *Der Sonderfall: die Besatzungszeit in Österreich. 1945 bis 1955* (Graz: Styria, 1979), 305–6.

64 Stifter, *Wiederaufrüstung Österreichs*, 49–50, 160.

65 Stifter illustrates this point with a quote from Franz Winterer, a high-ranking lieutenant colonel in the Wehrmacht, who was also the first undersecretary of the office of the army under Karl Renner. See Franz Winterer, "Abschiedsbefehl Generalmajor Winterers vom 29. Dezember 1945," 76. Quoted in Stifter, *Wiederaufrüstung Österreichs*, 49.

66 Alexander Pollak, *Die Wehrmachtslegende in Österreich: Das Bild der Wehrmacht im Spiegel der österreichischen Presse nach 1945* (Vienna: Böhlau, 2002), 64–65.

67 Bachmann Nachlass, Blatt 4679. Quoted in Höller, *Ingeborg Bachmann*, 349, note 192.

68 Carol Duncan, *Civilizing Rituals: Inside Public Art Museums* (London: Routledge, 1995), 20.

69 Tony Bennett, *The Birth of the Museum: History, Theory, Politics* (London: Routledge, 1995), 84–86.

70 This sentence is a paraphrase of Donald Preziosi, *Rethinking Art History: Meditations on a Coy Science* (New Haven: Yale University Press, 1989), 70.

71 Walter Benjamin, "Über den Begriff der Geschichte," in *Gesammelte Schriften*, ed. Rolf Tiedemann et al. (Frankfurt am Main: Suhrkamp, 1980), 1: bk. 2, 691–706. Blasting open the "continuum of history" is an essential component of Benjamin's revolutionary project.

72 Bennett, *Birth of the Museum*, 84–86.

73 Hermann Broch, "Die fröhliche Apokalypse Wiens um 1880," in *Kommentierte Werkausgabe: Schriften zur Literatur*, ed. Paul M. Lützeler (Frankfurt am Main: Suhrkamp, 1975), 145–46.

74 Thomas Bernhard, *Auslöschung: Ein Zerfall* (Frankfurt am Main: Suhrkamp, 1986), 40.

75 Jonathan J. Long, *The Novels of Thomas Bernhard: Form and Its Function* (Rochester: Camden House, 2001), 164–65. See passages in *Auslöschung* such as those on pp. 22–23.

76 Theodor W. Adorno, "Valéry Proust Museum," in *Gesammelte Schriften* (Frankfurt am Main: Suhrkamp, 1977), 10.1: 181–74.

77 Thomas Bernhard, *Alte Meister: Eine Komödie* (Frankfurt am Main: Suhrkamp, 1985), 160–61.

78 Bernhard, *Alte Meister*, 304–5, 307.

79 Julia Hell, "Eyes Wide Shut, German Post-Holocaust Authorship," *New German Critique* 88 (2003): 9–36.

80 As Weigel perceptively notes, Bachmann's use of the term to mean "incest," as it generally meant in the pre-Nazi era, draws attention to the Nazi redefinition of it as a word to designate a crime arising from sexual contact between Germans and non-Germans. Weigel, *Ingeborg Bachmann*, 541–42.

81 J. Lee Westrate, *European Military Museums: A Survey of Their Philosophy, Facilities, Programs, and Management* (Washington, D.C.: Smithsonian Institution, 1961), 144.

82 Preziosi, *Rethinking Art History*, 68–70.

83 Schneider, *Die Kompositionsmethode Ingeborg Bachmanns,* 268. Eva Lindemann, "Die Gangart des Geistes," in *Ingeborg Bachmann: Neue Beiträge zu ihrem Werk: Internationales Symposion, Münster, 1991,* ed. Dirk Göttsche and Hubert Ohl (Würzburg: Königshausen & Neumann, 1993), 318, note 11. Neva Slibar, "Angst, Verbrechen, und das Unheimliche: Genre und Motivumwandlungen der Angstliteratur in Ingeborg Bachmanns Spätprosa," in *Ingeborg Bachmann: Neue Beiträge zu ihrem Werk; Internationales Symposion, Münster 1991,* ed. Dirk Göttsche and Hubert Ohl (Würzburg: Königshausen & Neumann, 1993), 167–86.

84 The passage reads, "I look at Malina in an undetached manner, but he does not look up. I get up and think, if he does not immediately say anything, it is murder, and I move away, because I cannot say it" (p. 354).

85 The omitted section refers to the second chapter of *Malina.* Koschel and Weidenbaum, eds., *Wir müssen wahre Sätze finden,* 144. At the end of her interview with Toni Kienlechner in the same book (p. 100), Bachmann endorses ways of approaching her book that do not recognize that the Ich and Malina are doppelganger.

86 Koschel and Weidenbaum, eds., *Wir müssen wahre Sätze finden,* 71.

87 See Weigel, *Ingeborg Bachmann,* 530.

88 Koschel and Weidenbaum, eds., *Wir müssen wahre Sätze finden,* 74, 87, 99–100. The narrator also indicates that this condition exists when she says that Ivan "does not know whom he is dealing with, that he is involved with an appearance that can be deceiving. I do not want to mislead Ivan, but he will never see that I am double. I am also Malina's creation" (pp. 103–4).

89 Koschel and Weidenbaum, eds., *Wir müssen wahre Sätze finden,* 95–96.

90 Koschel and Weidenbaum, eds., *Wir müssen wahre Sätze finden,* 99–100.

91 Weigel, *Ingeborg Bachmann,* 528–29.

92 As Schneider points out, the major exception to this is the Legend of the Princess of Kagran. Schneider, *Die Kompositionsmethode Ingeborg Bachmanns,* 283.

93 Schneider, *Die Kompositionsmethode Ingeborg Bachmanns,* 268–69, 272–74.

94 Weigel, *Ingeborg Bachmann,* 530.

95 Joachim Hoell, *Ingeborg Bachmann* (Munich: Deutscher Taschenbuch Verlag, 2001), 573.

96 Hell mentions in a footnote the potential utility of her framework for interpreting Bachmann's novel, precisely for its having been written in a "male voice." Hell, "Eyes Wide Shut," 17–21.

97 Jacques Derrida makes a similar distinction in how the archive affects the possibilities of cultural enunciation. See Jacques Derrida, *Archive Fever: A Freudan Impression,* trans. Eric Prenowitz (Chicago: University of Chicago Press, 1996), 28.

Chapter 8

1 Siegfried Lenz, *Heimatmuseum: Roman* (Munich: Deutscher Taschenbuch Verlag, 1981), 601. All subsequent references to the novel are made parenthetically.

2 *Heimat* is not fully rendered by the English word "homeland," so I retain the German term. While *Heimat* is now indicates a local and tangible region or area, the history of this concept is long and complex. Most scholars agree that the term refers to notions of community and belonging, although the contours of the community have varied over time, changing according to the context of enunciation. See Peter Blickle, *Heimat: A Critical Theory of the German Idea of Homeland* (Rochester, N.Y.: Camden House, 2002), 3–6. Elizabeth Boa and Rachel Palfreyman, *Heimat, a German Dream: Regional Loyalties and National Identity in German Culture, 1890–1990* (Oxford: Oxford University Press, 2000), 26–29. Alon Confino, *The Nation as a Local*

Metaphor: Württemberg, Imperial Germany, and National Memory, 1871–1918 (Chapel Hill: University of North Carolina Press, 1997), 151. Celia Applegate, *A Nation of Provincials: The German Idea of Heimat* (Berkeley and Los Angeles: University of California Press, 1990), 11.

3 There is more than a passing resemblance to Homer in the figure of Zygmunt. On this point, see Marilyn Sibley Fries, "The Interlocutor and the Narrative Transmission of the Past: On Siegfried Lenz's Heimatmuseum," *Monatshefte* 79, no. 4 (1987): 452–53. Zygmunt's scene of narration is likewise reminiscent of the inaugural site of narration, which Shoshana Felman claims to be "the deathbed, in which the dying man (or the original narrator) reviews his life (evokes his memories) and thus addresses the events and lessons of his past to those surrounding him." See Shoshana Felman, "Benjamin's Silence," *Critical Inquiry* 25 (1999): 207.

4 Walter Benjamin, "Ich packe meine Bibliothek aus," in *Gesammelte Schriften,* ed. Tillmann Rexroth (Frankfurt am Main: Suhrkamp, 1991), 4: bk. 1, 389.

5 The narrator's first name, Zygmunt, brings to mind the originator of psychoanalysis. The dialogic structure of the novel also can be seen as an integral part of the psychoanalytic setting. Fries, "The Interlocutor," 453.

6 The image of the scarred male body is no doubt to be understood in relationship to the image of a healthy, strapping German body often found in Nazi cultural production.

7 The translation is from Walter Benjamin, "Unpacking My Library," in *Illuminations,* ed. Hannah Arendt (New York: Schocken, 1968), 67. Original: Benjamin, "Ich packe meine Bibliothek aus," in *Gesammelte Schriften,* 396.

8 Benjamin, "Ich packe meine Bibliothek aus," in *Gesammelte Schriften,* 389.

9 Walter Benjamin, *Das Passagenwerk,* ed. Rolf Tiedemann et al., in *Gesammelte Schriften* (Frankfurt am Main: Suhrkamp, 1980), 5: bk. 1, 274–75.

10 Benjamin, *Passagenwerk,* in *Gesammelte Schriften,* 5: bk. 1, 274–75.

11 The entire passage reads, "[F]or the true collector, the acquisition of an old book is its rebirth. And therein lies the childlike quality that is intertwined with the qualities of an old man in the collector." Benjamin, "Unpacking My Library," in *Illuminations,* 66. Benjamin, "Ich packe meine Bibliothek aus," in *Gesammelte Schriften,* 389–90. A similar dialectic of death and renewal can be read in Adorno's famous essay, "Valéry Proust Museum." Theodor W. Adorno, "Valéry Proust Museum," in *Gesammelte Schriften* (Frankfurt am Main: Suhrkamp, 1977), 10.1:181–94.

12 Fries, "The Interlocutor," 451.

13 Benjamin, "Unpacking My Library," in *Illuminations,* 65–66.

14 With regard to *Die Deutschstunde,* Boa and Palfreyman argue that Lenz's technique evokes bodily memories in a "Proustian fashion . . . conjured up through sights and smells, sounds and tastes." Boa and Palfreyman, *Heimat, a German Dream,* 149–50. They argue more generally that such bodily memories typically accompany notions of *Heimat,* which they understand as a longed-for realm of childhood.

15 A strong sense of investment is thoroughly conveyed in the vocabulary that appears in the original of this passage. The phrases "Anteil zurückgeben," and "an etwas beteiligen" both carry economic connotations with them, corresponding respectively to the notions "to pay back interest" and "to invest in something/someone." Moreover, *verteilen* is a verb commonly used to describe the payment of profits or dividends, as in "Gewinn verteilen," "to distribute profits."

16 At the end of their first conversation, Rogalla observes that Martin will need to keep coming back, for one visit practically obligates him to return (p. 53). Martin also functions as a mediator in his own right, passing information to Rogalla about his daughter Henrike at a time when Henrike is utterly alienated from her father.

17 Fries, "The Interlocutor," 449–62.

18 Benjamin, "Ich packe meine Bibliothek aus," in *Gesammelte Schriften,* 4: bk. 1, 391. Shoshana Felman has recently located the coiling of the autobiographical and the theoretical/historical as a key paradigm for understanding the coordinates of all of Benjamin's writing and politics. See Felman, "Benjamin's Silence," 214.

19 "This or any other procedure is merely a dam against the spring tide of memories, which surges toward any collector as he contemplates his possessions. Every passion borders of the chaotic, but the collector's passion borders on the chaos of memories." Benjamin, "Ich packe meine Bibliothek aus," in *Gesammelte Schriften,* 4: bk. 1, 388.

20 I have in mind a distinction similar to that made by Derrida, who in his analysis of the archive in relation to memory highlights the use of prosthetic memory aids as performing a suppression of memory. For Derrida, suppressed memories do not enter the unconscious. See Jacques Derrida, *Archive Fever: A Freudian Impression,* trans. Eric Prenowitz (Chicago: University of Chicago Press, 1996), 20–28.

21 It is not clear whether Rogalla is referring here to a condition before the destruction of the objects, or whether he is explaining that such a condition always applies.

22 Rhetoric has a very long tradition of organizing thoughts according to the loci in a room or space. The use of the collection as I am positing it here would hark back to this tradition.

23 Rogalla also approaches extramuseal environments, occurrences and even people in a similar fashion. When Zygmunt first visits Conny's home on the prison grounds, he interprets his environment by taking stock of the objects and how they define their space and inhabitants. More than half a page is spent detailing the watch chain, sweater, vest, and Janus-head jewelry that Conny's father is wearing before Rogalla says anything about his face and mannerisms, which have to be brought into agreement with the objects on his person (p. 37). Similar instances are encountered again and again in the book, where inventories of objects (the list of cures his father can offer, p. 108), settings and rooms (pp. 66, 338), place names (p. 170), days of the week (pp. 269–72), and even the various noises people make while working (p. 213), serve as the royal road to Rogalla's past world.

24 In the "Kunstwerk" essay, Benjamin presents the possibility that film technology (slow motion, freeze frame, montage) can reveal aspects of the unconscious we cannot perceive in "normal" existence. Rogalla exploits these possibilities in a variety of display contexts, for instance when he takes his son past several carpets so that he can "experience them as in a film" (p. 389). At various points, he depicts certain scenes as if in a diorama (pp. 66–81, 165–67, 280), in a panorama (pp. 151–52, 176), as well as a procession through a gallery.

25 Melzer-Tapiau's response to these objects accords with National Socialist policy for re-organizing Heimat museums. In order to mobilize the public for the war, Heimat museums were to foreground whatever weaponry they had and work in parallel with the revamped army museums and armories. See Martin Roth, *Heimatmuseum: Zur Geschichte einer deutschen Institution* (Berlin: Mann, 1990), 108f., 173. See also an online study done by Lars-H. Thümmler, *Das Zeughaus Berlin im Zweiten Weltkrieg.* [Internet] (Deutsches Historisches Museum, 2003 [cited November 11, 2006]); available from http://www.dhm.de/texte/zhwk2.html.

26 On this point, see Fries, "The Interlocutor," 458–59.

27 See Fries, "The Interlocutor," 458–59.

28 This confirms the distinction that Derrida makes between external hypomnese (a prosthetic extension of memory) and internal mneme and amamnesis (a memory reserve and the ability to recall, respectively). Derrida, *Archive Fever,* 11–13.

29 Such a notion of "pure memory" recalls the qualities Zygmunt attributes to the concept of *Heimat.* In a central dispute with Martin about the concept of *Heimat,* Zygmunt states that despite his awareness of how abused the concept of *Heimat* was in the Nazi era, he wishes to recover some aspects of the concept, because he thinks people seek that feeling whether it is taboo or not (p. 120). In this sense, the dynamics of memory are crucially interrelated with the valences of *Heimat.*

30 I consider this point in Chapter 1, this volume. See also James L. Rolleston, "The Politics of Quotation: Walter Benjamin's Arcades Project." *PMLA* 104, no. 1 (1989): 13–27.

31 Zygmunt comments at one point that having lost his sight temporarily, he sees things with a fresh perspective, as if for the first time.

32 Fries, "The Interlocutor," 458–59.

33 Hal Foster, "Archives of Modern Art," *October* 99 (2002): 81–95. Andreas Huyssen, *Twilight*

Memories: Marking Time in a Culture of Amnesia (New York: Routledge, 1995).

34 There have been manifestations particularly in the former Soviet Union that seek to provide a corrective to official state culture without creating an utter void in the identities of those people who lived in those cultures.

35 For a description of the monument, see the Swiss art museum page "Jochen Gerz, *2146 Steine—Mahnmal gegen Rassismus.*" (November 1997 [cited November 11, 2006]. Available at http://www.kunstmuseum.ch/andereorte/portraits/jgerz/jgsteine.htm. See also Jochen Gerz, "Das lebende Monument: Interview with Guillaume Hillairet, Jan Kopp, und Véronique Loock, March 1996" [cited November 11, 2006]. Available at http://www.farm.de/gerz/gerzDE/respDE2/interDEText.html. In this interview, Gerz discusses his conscious engagement with the invisibility of the monument and its materiality.

36 Both monuments deploy notions of subterranean connections. In Saarbrücken, one part of this might be that the foundations of German civil organization (the city square) are related to an extinguished and/or absent Jewish life in Saarbrücken and all over Germany. Hoheisel intended his monument to be reflected in the groundwater, so that through the groundwater, it would be connected underground to all of Kassel. See Jochen Gerz, *2146 Steine.* James Young, *The Texture of Memory: Holocaust Memorials and Meaning* (New Haven: Yale Uniersity Press, 1993), 45.

Conclusion

1 See Hal Foster, "Archives of Modern Art," *October* 99 (2002): 94–95.

Works Cited

Abbas, Ackbar. "Walter Benjamin's Collector: The Fate of the Modern Experience." In *Modernity and the Text: Revisions of German Modernism,* edited by Andreas Huyssen and David Bathrick, 216–39. New York: Columbia University Press, 1989.

Adorno, Theodor W. *Minima Moralia: Reflexionen aus dem beschädigten Leben.* Frankfurt am Main: Suhrkamp, 1980.

———. "Valéry Proust Museum." In *Gesammelte Schriften,* 181–94. Frankfurt am Main: Suhrkamp, 1977.

———. "Valéry Proust Museum." In *Prisms,* 173–86. Cambridge: MIT Press, 1981.

Alter, Peter. "The Rhetoric of the Nation-State and the Fall of Empires." In *The Habsburg Legacy: National Identity in Historical Perspective,* edited by Ritchie Robertson and Edward Timms, 196–206. Edinburgh: Edinburgh University Press, 1994.

Anderlik, Heidemarie. "'Der Ring des Nibelungen': Bühnenkunst und Germananbild im 19. Jahrhundert." In *Zwischen Walhall und Paradies: Eine Austellung des Deutschen Historischen Museums in Zusammenarbeit mit dem Museum für Vor- und Frühgeschichte SMPK,* edited by Heidemarie Anderlik, 26–33. Berlin: Deutsches Historisches Museum, 1991.

Applegate, Celia. *A Nation of Provincials: The German Idea of Heimat.* Berkeley and Los Angeles: University of California Press, 1990.

Arendt, Hannah. "Introduction." In *Illuminations,* edited by Hannah Arendt, 1–58. New York: Harcourt Brace Jovanovich, 1967.

Armstrong, Nancy. *Fiction in the Age of Photography: The Legacy of British Realism.* Cambridge: Harvard University Press, 1999.

Asman, Carrie. "Kunstkammer als Kommunikationsspiel: Goethe inszeniert eine Sammlung." In *Johann Wolfgang von Goethe: Der Sammler und die Seinigen,* edited by Carrie Asman, 119–77. Amsterdam: Verlag der Kunst, 1997.

———. "Le Trésor de Goethe: Le Collectionneur et Ses Dons." *Revue Germanique Internationale* 12 (1999): 153–60.

Assmann, Aleida. *Erinnerungsräume: Formen und Wandlungen des kulturellen Gedächtnisses.* Munich: C. H. Beck, 1999.

Bachmann, Ingeborg. *"Todesarten"-Projekt,* vol. 3.1. Edited by Robert Pichl, Monika Albrecht, and Dirk Göttsche. Munich: Piper, 1995.

———. *Werke.* 4 vols. Edited by Christine Koschel and Inge von Weidenbaum. Munich: Piper, 1978.

———, Christine Koschel, Inge von Weidenbaum, and Clemens Münster. *Werke, Dritter Band, Todesarten: Malina und unvollendete Romane.* Munich: Piper, 1993.

Baedeker, Karl. *Paris and Environs with Routes from London to Paris: Handbook for Travellers.* 14th rev. ed. Leipzig: K. Baedeker, 1900.

Bakhtin, Mikhail. *Rabelais and His World.* Translated by Hélène Iswolsky. Bloomington: Indiana University Press, 1984.

Bal, Mieke. *Double Exposures: The Subject of Cultural Analysis.* New York: Routledge, 1996.

Barker, Andrew. "Doderer's Hapsburg Myth: History, the Novel, and National Identity." In *Austria, 1945–1955: Studies in Political and Cultural Re-emergence,* edited by Anthony Bushell, 37–54. Cardiff: University of Wales Press, 1996.

Baron, Frank. *Rilke and the Visual Arts.* Lawrence, Kans.: Coronado Press, 1982.

Bartmann, Dominik. "Berlin offiziell-Kunst und Kunstpolitik unter Wilhelm II." In *Berlin um 1900: Ausstellung der Berlinischen Galerie in Verbindung mit der Akademie der Künste zu den Berliner Festwochen, 1984,* edited by Gesine Asmus, 183–209. Berlin: Nicolai, 1984.

Beck, Hans-Joachim. "Malina oder die Romantik: Literarische Rezeption und Komposition in Ingeborg Bachmanns Romantrilogie Todesarten." *Germanisch-Romanische Monatsschrift* 38 (1988): 304–24.

Belgum, Kirsten. *Interior Meaning: Design of the Bourgeois Home in the Realist Novel.* New York: P. Lang, 1991.

———. *Popularizing the Nation: Audience, Representation, and the Production of Identity in Die Gartenlaube, 1853–1900.* Lincoln: University of Nebraska Press, 1998.

Benjamin, Walter. *The Arcades Project.* Translated by Howard Eiland and Kevin McLaughlin. New York: Belknap, 2002.

———. "A Berlin Chronicle." In *Reflections: Essays, Aphorisms, Autobiographical Writings,* edited by Peter Demetz, 3–60. New York: Schocken, 1978.

———. "Berliner Chronik." In *Gesammelte Schriften,* edited by Rolf Tiedemann and Hermann Schweppenhauser, 6:465–519. Frankfurt am Main: Suhrkamp, 1980.

———. "Charles Baudelaire: Ein Lyriker im Zeitalter des Hochkapitalismus." In *Gesammelte Schriften,* edited by Rolf Tiedemann, Hermann Schweppenhauser, Theodor W. Adorno, and Gershom Scholem, 1: bk. 23, 509–690. Frankfurt am Main: Suhrkamp, 1974.

———. "Eduard Fuchs: Collector and Historian." In *Selected Writings: 1935–1938,* edited by Howard Eiland and Michael W. Jennings, 260–302. Cambridge: Belknap/Harvard University Press, 2002.

———. "Eduard Fuchs: Der Sammler und der Historiker." In *Gesammelte Schriften,* edited by Rolf Tiedemann, Hermann Schweppenhauser, Theodor W. Adorno, and Gershom Scholem, 2: bk. 27, 465–506. Frankfurt am Main: Suhrkamp, 1980.

———. "Ich packe meine Bibliothek aus." In *Gesammelte Schriften,* edited by Tillmann Rexroth, 4: bk. 1, 388–96. Frankfurt am Main: Suhrkamp, 1991.

———. "Karl Kraus." In *Gesammelte Schriften,* edited by Rolf Tiedemann, Hermann Schweppenhauser, Theodor W. Adorno, and Gershom Scholem, 2: bk. 2, 334–67. Frankfurt am Main: Suhrkamp, 1980.

———. "Das Kunstwerk im Zeitalter seiner technischen Reproduzierbarkeit." In *Gesammelte Schriften,* edited by Rolf Tiedemann, Hermann Schweppenhauser, Theodor W. Adorno, and Gershom Scholem, 1: bk. 2, 471–508. Frankfurt am Main: Suhrkamp, 1980.

———. "On Some Motifs in Baudelaire." In *Illuminations,* edited by Hannah Arendt, 155–200. New York: Schocken, 1968.

———. "Paris, die Hauptstadt des XIX. Jahrhunderts." In *Gesammelte Schriften,* edited by Rolf Tiedemann, Hermann Schweppenhauser, Theodor W. Adorno, and Gershom Scholem, 5: bk. 1, 45–59. Frankfurt am Main: Suhrkamp, 1980.

———. *Das Passagenwerk.* Edited by Rolf Tiedemann, Hermann Schweppenhauser, Theodor W. Adorno, and Gershom Scholem. *Gesammelte Schriften.* Frankfurt am Main: Suhrkamp, 1980.

———. "Stifter." In *Gesammelte Schriften,* edited by Rolf Tiedemann, Hermann Schweppenhauser, Theodor W. Adorno, and Gershom Scholem, 2: bk. 1, 608–10. Frankfurt am Main: Suhrkamp, 1980.

———. "The Storyteller." In *Illuminations,* edited by Hannah Arendt. New York: Schocken, 1968.

———. "Über den Begriff der Geschichte." In *Gesammelte Schriften,* edited by Rolf Tiedemann, Hermann Schweppenhauser, Theodor W. Adorno, and Gershom Scholem, 1: bk. 2, 691–706. Frankfurt am Main: Suhrkamp, 1980.

———. "Unpacking My Library." In *Illuminations,* edited by Hannah Arendt, 59–67. New York: Schocken, 1968.

———. "Die Wahlverwandtschaften." In *Gesammelte Schriften,* edited by Rolf Tiedemann, Hermann Schweppenhauser, Theodor W. Adorno, and Gershom Scholem, 1: bk. 1, 123–201. Frankfurt am Main: Suhrkamp, 1980.

———. "The Work of Art in the Age of Mechanical Reproduction." In *Illuminations,* edited by Hannah Arendt. New York: Schocken, 1968.

Bennett, Tony. *The Birth of the Museum: History, Theory, Politics.* London: Routledge, 1995.

———. "The Multiplication of Culture's Unity." *Critical Inquiry* 21, no. 4 (1995): 861–89.

Beowulf. A Verse Translation. Translated by Seamus Heaney. Edited by Daniel Donoghue. London: Norton, 2002.

Berendt, Hans. *Rainer Maria Rilkes Neue Gedichte: Versuch einer Deutung.* Bonn: H. Bouvier, 1957.

Berman, Russell A. *The Rise of the Modern German Novel: Crisis and Charisma.* Cambridge: Harvard University Press, 1986.

Bernhard, Thomas. *Alte Meister: Eine Komödie.* Frankfurt am Main: Suhrkamp, 1985.

———. *Auslöschung: Ein Zerfall.* Frankfurt am Main: Suhrkamp, 1986.

Bertram, Ernst. *Nietzsche: Versuch einer Mythologie.* Bonn: Bouvier, 1965.

Bertschik, Julia. *Maulwurfsarchäologie: Zum Verhältnis von Geschichte und Anthropologie in Wilhelm Raabes historischen Erzähltexten.* Tübingen: M. Niemeyer, 1995.

Black, Barbara J. *On Exhibit: Victorians and Their Museums.* Charlottesville: University Press of Virginia, 2000.

Blackbourn, David, and Geoff Eley. *The Peculiarities of German History: Bourgeois Society and Politics in Nineteenth-Century Germany.* Oxford: Oxford University Press, 1984.

Blickle, Peter. *Heimat: A Critical Theory of the German Idea of Homeland.* Rochester, N.Y.: Camden House, 2002.

Boa, Elizabeth, and Rachel Palfreyman. *Heimat, a German Dream: Regional Loyalties and National Identity in German Culture, 1890–1990.* Oxford: Oxford University Press, 2000.

Bock, Henning. "Das Profane und das Heilige: Die Sammlungen Solly und Boisserée im Wettstreit um die Übernahme durch Preussen." In *Kunst als Kulturgut: Die Sammlung Boisserée, ein Schritt in der Begründung des Museums,* edited by Annemarie Bethmann-Siefert and Otto Pöggeler, 107–12. Bonn: Bouvier, 1995.

Boehn, Max von, and Oskar Fischel. *Die Mode: Menschen und Moden im neunzehnten Jahrhundert nach Bildern und Kupfern der Zeit,* vol. 2. Munich: F. Bruckmann, 1907.

Bohlen, Celestine. "Retrenching Guggenheim Closes Hall in Las Vegas." *The New York Times,* December 24, 2002, pp. 1, 10.

Böhme, Hartmut. "Fetisch und Idol: Erinnerungsformen in Goethes Wilhelm Meister, Faust, und Der Sammler und die Seinigen." In *Goethe und die Verzeitlichung der Natur,* edited by Peter Matussek, 178–201. Munich: C. H. Beck, 1998.

Boisserée, Sulpiz. "Brief an Goethe." In *Sulpiz Boisserée: Tagebücher, 1808–1854,* edited by Mathilde Boisserée, 1–6. Stuttgart: Cotta, 1862.

———. "Lebensbeschreibung." In *Sulpiz Boisserée: Tagebücher, 1808–1854,* edited by Mathilde Boisserée, 1–45. Stuttgart: Cotta, 1862.

Bolz, Norbert, and Michelle Mattson (trans.). "Farewell to the Gutenberg Galaxy." *New German Critique* 78 (1999): 109–31.

Börsch-Supan, Helmut. "Goethes Kenntnis von der Kunst der Goethezeit." In *Goethe und die Kunst,* edited by Sabine Schulze, 269–78. Stuttgart: Hatje, 1994.

Böttger, Peter. *Die Alte Pinakothek in München: Architektur, Ausstattung, und museales Programm.* Munich: Prestel, 1972.

Böttiger, Helmut. *Nach den Utopien: Eine Geschichte der deutschsprachigen Gegenwartsliteratur.* Vienna: Paul Zsolney, 2004.

Bourdieu, Pierre, and Alain Darbel, with Dominique Schnapper. *The Love of Art: European Art Museums and Their Public.* Translated by Caroline Beattie and Nick Merrima. Stanford: Stanford University Press, 1990.

Bradley, Brigitte L. *Rainer Maria Rilkes Der neuen Gedichte anderer Teil: Entwicklungsstufen seiner Pariser Lyrik.* Bern: Francke, 1976.

———. *Rainer Maria Rilkes Neue Gedichte: Ihr zyklisches Gefüge.* Bern: Francke Verlag, 1967.

Broch, Hermann. "Die fröhliche Apokalypse Wiens um 1880." In *Kommentierte Werkausgabe. Schriften zur Literatur,* edited by Paul M. Lützeler, 145–53. Frankfurt am Main: Suhrkamp, 1975.

Bronfen, Elisabeth. *Over Her Dead Body: Death, Femininity, and the Aesthetic.* New York: Routledge, 1992.

Browne, E. J. *Charles Darwin: A Biography, Vol. 1: Voyaging.* Princeton: Princeton University Press, 1996.

———. *Charles Darwin: A Biography, Vol. 2: The Power of Place.* New York: Alfred A. Knopf, 2002.

Bryson, Norman. "The Gaze in the Expanded Field." In *Vision and Visuality,* edited by Hal Foster, 87–113. Seattle: Bay Press, 1988.

Bud, Robert. "Science, Meaning, and Myth in the Museum." *Public Understanding of Science* 4 (1995): 1–16.

Busco, Marie, and David Finn. *Rodin and His Contemporaries: The Iris & B. Gerald Cantor Collection.* New York: Cross River Press, 1991.

Butler, Judith. *Gender Trouble: Feminism and the Subversion of Identity.* New York: Routledge, 1990.

Butler, Ruth. *Rodin in Perspective.* Englewood Cliffs, N.J.: Prentice-Hall, 1980.

Calov, Gudrun. *Museen und Sammler des 19. Jahrhunderts in Deutschland.* Berlin: De Gruyter, 1969.

Carvill, Barbara. "The Blind News Vendor in Rilke's Novel, Die Aufzeichnungen des Malte Laurids Brigge." In *Rilke and the Visual Arts,* edited by Frank Baron, 61–72. Lawrence, Kans.: Coronado, 1982.

Clifford, James. *The Predicament of Culture: Twentieth-Century Ethnography, Literature, and Art.* Cambridge: Harvard University Press, 1988.

Cobet, Justus. *Heinrich Schliemann: Archäologe und Abenteurer.* Munich: C. H. Beck, 1997.

———. "Troia, Jericho, und die historische Kritik." In *Archäologie und historische Erinnerung: Nach 100 Jahren Heinrich Schliemann,* edited by Justus Cobet and Barbara Patzek, 117–35. Essen: Klartext, 1992.

———, and Barbara Patzek, eds. *Archäologie und historische Erinnerung: Nach 100 Jahren Heinrich Schliemann.* Essen: Klartext, 1992.

Cohn, Dorrit. "Optics and Power in the Novel." *New Literary History* 26 (1995): 3–20.

Confino, Alon. *The Nation as a Local Metaphor: Württemberg, Imperial Germany, and National Memory, 1871–1918.* Chapel Hill: University of North Carolina Press, 1997.

Crane, Susan A. *Collecting and Historical Consciousness in Early Nineteenth-Century Germany.* Ithaca: Cornell University Press, 2000.

Crimp, Douglas. *On the Museum's Ruins: With Photographs by Louise Lawler.* Cambridge: MIT Press, 1993.

Crone, Rainer, and David Moos. "A Biographical Narrative: Auguste Rodin, 1840–1917." In *Rodin: Eros and Creativity,* edited by Rainer Crone and Siegfried Salzmann, 35–56. Munich: Prestel, 1992.

Crownshaw, Richard. "Reconsidering Postmemory: Photography, the Archive, and Post-Holocaust Memory in W. G. Sebald's 'Austerlitz.'" *Mosaic* 37, no. 4 (2004): 215–36.

Cuno, James, ed. *Whose Muse? Art Museums and the Public Trust.* Princeton: Princeton University Press, 2004.

Daniel, Glyn Edmund. *A Hundred and Fifty Years of Archaeology.* Cambridge: Harvard University Press, 1975.

Das Heeresmuseum in Wien. Vienna: Heeresmuseum Wien, 1943.

Daston, Lorraine, and Katherine Park. *Wonders and the Order of Nature, 1150–1750.* New York: Zone, 1998.

David, Claude. "Die Leere und die Fülle." In *Rainer Maria Rilke,* edited by Rüdiger Görner. Darmstadt: Wissenschaftliche Buchhandlung, 1987.

Décultot, Elisabeth. "Le Cosmopolitisme en Question: Goethe Face aux Saisies Françaises d'Oeuvres d'art sous la Revolution et sous l'Empire." *Revue Germanique Internationale* 12 (1999): 161–75, 297–98.

Derrida, Jacques. *Archive Fever: A Freudian Impression.* Translated by Eric Prenowitz. Chicago: University of Chicago Press, 1996.

Dijkstra, Bram. *Idols of Perversity: Fantasies of Feminine Evil in Fin-de-Siècle Culture.* New York: Oxford University Press, 1986.

Dittlinger, Carolin. "Traumatic Photographs: Remembrance and the Technical Media in W. G. Sebald's 'Austerlitz.'" In *W. G. Sebald: A Critical Companion,* edited by J. J. Long and Anne Whitehead, 155–71. Seattle: University of Washington Press, 2004.

Dolent, Jean (Charles-Antoine Fournier). *Maître de sa joie.* Paris: A. Lemerre, 1902.

Donato, Eugenio. "The Museum's Furnace: Notes Towards a Contextual Reading of Bouvard et Pécuchet." In *Textual Strategies: Perspectives in Post-Structuralist Criticism,* edited by Josue V. Harari, 213–38. Ithaca: Cornell University Press, 1979.

Downing, Eric. "Common Ground: Conditions of Realism in Stifter's 'Vorrede.'" *Colloquia Germanica* 1 (1995): 35–53.

———. *Dirty Pictures: Photography, Archaeology, Psychoanalysis, and the Tradition of Bildung.* Detroit: Wayne State University Press, 2006.

———. *Double Exposures: Repetition and Realism in Nineteenth-Century German Fiction.* Stanford: Stanford University Press, 2000.

Duncan, Carol. *Civilizing Rituals: Inside Public Art Museums.* London: Routledge, 1995.

———, and Alan Wallach. "The Universal Survey Museum." *Art History* 3, no. 4 (1980): 448–69.

Eisel, Franz. "Geschichts- und Altertunsvereine als Keimzellen und Wegbereiter der Heimatmuseen." *Neue Museumskunde* 27 (1984): 173–82.

Elsen, Albert Edward. *The Partial Figure in Modern Sculpture: From Rodin to 1969.* Baltimore: Baltimore Museum of Art, 1969.

———, and Auguste Rodin. *In Rodin's Studio: A Photographic Record of Sculpture in the Making.* Oxford: Phaidon Press, 1980.

Elsner, John, and Roger Cardinal, eds. *Cultures of Collecting.* Cambridge: Harvard University Press, 1994.

Emde, Ursula. *Rilke und Rodin.* Marburg/Lahn: Verlag des Kunstgeschichtlichen Seminars der Universität Marburg, 1949.

Emmerich, Wolfgang. "German Writers as Intellectuals: Strategies and Aporias of Engagement in East and West from 1945 Until Today." *New German Critique* 88 (2003): 37–54.

Ernst, Wolfgang. "Archi(ve)textures of Museology." In *Museums and Memory,* edited by Susan A. Crane, 17–34. Stanford: Stanford University Press, 2000.

Eshel, Amir. "Against the Power of Time: The Poetics of Suspension in W. G. Sebald's Austerlitz." *New German Critique* 88 (2003): 71–96.

——— "Diverging Memories? Durs Grünbein's Mnemonic Topographies and the Future of the German Past." *German Quarterly* 74, no. 4 (2001): 407–16.

Evans, Joan. *Time and Chance: The Story of Arthur Evans and His Forebears.* Westport: Conn. Greenwood Press, 1974.

Felman, Shoshana. "Benjamin's Silence." *Critical Inquiry* 25 (1999): 201–34.

Feuerlicht, Ignace. "Der 'Erzähler' und das 'Tagebuch' in Goethes Wahlverwandtschaften." *Goethe-Jahrbuch* 103 (1986): 316–43.

Findlen, Paula. "The Modern Muses: Collecting and the Cult of Remembrance in Renaissance Italy." In *Museums and Memory,* edited by Susan A. Crane, 161–78. Stanford: Stanford University Press, 2000.

Fontane, Theodor. *Vor dem Sturm: Roman aus dem Winter, 1812 auf 13.* Edited by Helmuth Nürnberger. Munich: Carl Hanser, 1990.

Foster, Hal. "Archives of Modern Art." *October* 99 (2002): 81–95.

Foucault, Michel. *The Archaeology of Knowledge.* Translated by Alan Sheridan. New York: Pantheon Books, 1972.

———. *Discipline and Punish: The Birth of the Prison.* Translated by Alan Sheridan. New York: Vintage, 1977.

———. "Nietzsche, Genealogy, History." In *The Foucault Reader,* edited by Paul Rabinow, 76–100. New York: Pantheon Books, 1984.

———. *The Order of Things: An Archaeology of the Human Sciences.* New York: Pantheon Books, 1971.

———. "What Is an Author?" In *Textual Strategies: Perspectives in Post-Structuralist Criticism,* 141–60. Ithaca: Cornell University Press, 1979.

Franklin, Ruth. "Rings of Smoke." *The New Republic,* September 23, 2002, p. 39.

Franz, Eckhardt G. "Archive, Bibliotheken, Museen—Gemeinsamkeiten und Besonderheiten, Grenzen und Zusammenspiel: Protokoll des Prodiumsgesprächs auf dem 51. deutschen Archivtag." *Der Archivar* 31, no. 1 (1978): 23–28.

Freedman, Ralph. *Life of a Poet: Rainer Maria Rilke.* New York: Farrar Straus and Giroux, 1996.

Fries, Marilyn Sibley. "The Interlocutor and the Narrative Transmission of the Past: On Siegfried Lenz's Heimatmuseum." *Monatshefte* 79, no. 4 (1987): 449–62.

Frisby, David. "The Flâneur in Social Theory." In *The Flâneur,* edited by Keith Tester, 81–110. London: Routledge, 1994.

Frohne, Ursula. "Motive der Zeit." In *Kunst der Gegenwart: Museum für Neue Kunst: ZKM Zentrum für Kunst und Medientechnologie Karlsruhe,* edited by Heinrich Klotz, Horst Bredekamp and Ursula Frohne, 28–50. Munich: Prestel, 1997.

Fuchs, Anne. "'Phantomspuren': Zu W. G. Sebalds Poetik der Erinnerung in Austerlitz." *German Life and Letters* 56 (2003): 281–98.

Fuchs, Eduard. *Dachreiter und verwandte chinesische Keramik des 15. bis 18. Jahrhunderts.* Munich: Albert Langen, 1924.

Fuhrmann, Manfred. "Juvenal-Barbier—Grünbein: Über den römischen Satiriker und zwei seiner tätigen Bewunderer." *Text und Kritik: Zeitschrift für Literatur* 153 (2002): 60–69.

Gallagher, Catherine, and Stephen Greenblatt. *Practicing New Historicism.* Chicago: University of Chicago Press, 2000.

Garve, Christian. "Über die öffentliche Meinung." In *Gesammelte Werke,* edited by Kurt Wölfel, 291–334. Hildesheim: Georg Olms, 1985.

Gates, Lisa. "The Bild and the Body." Unpublished paper. Cambridge: Harvard University, 1992.

Gerz, Jochen. 1997. *2146 Steine—Mahnmal gegen Rassismus.* [cited May 30, 2003]. Available at http://www.kunstmuseum.ch/andereorte/portraits/jgerz/jgsteine.htm.

———, Guillaume Hillairet, Jan Kopp, and Véronique Loock. 1996. "Das lebende Monument: Interview with Guillaume Hillairet, Jan Kopp, und Véronique Loock." [cited May 30, 2003]. Available at http://www.farm.de/gerz/gerzDE/respDE2/interDEText.html.

Gethmann-Siefert, Annemarie. "Einleitung." In *Kunst als Kulturgut: Die Sammlung Boisseré—Ein*

Schritt in der Begründung des Museums, edited by Annemarie Gethmann-Siefert and Otto Pöggeler, I–XXVIII. Bonn: Bouvier, 1995.

Gidal, Eric. *Poetic Exhibitions: Romantic Aesthetics and the Pleasures of the British Museum.* Lewisburg: Bucknell University Press, 2001.

Glaser, Horst Albert. *Die Restauration des Schönen: Stifters "Nachsommer."* Stuttgart: Metzler, 1965.

Glunz, Bettina. "Über einige 'historisierende' Schauspielrequisiten (und Kostüme) des 'Theaterherzogs' Georg II. von Sachsen-Meiningen." *Deutsches archäologisches Korrespondenzblatt* 24, no. 2 (1994): 223–29.

Goethe, Johann Wolfgang. "Einfache Nachahmung der Natur, Manier, Styl." Edited by Erich Trunz. In *Goethes Werke: Hamburger Ausgabe,* 12:30–34. Munich: C. H. Beck, 1981.

———. *Elective Affinities.* Translated by R. J. Hollingdale. New York: Penguin, 1971.

———. "Flüchtige Übersicht über die Kunst in Deutschland." In *Sämtliche Werke: Frankfurter Ausgabe,* 1:18, 807–10. Frankfurt am Main: Deutscher Klassiker Verlag, 1985.

———. *Kunst und Altertum am Rhein und Main.* Vol. 34, *Goethes Werke: Weimarer Ausgabe,* 69–200. Weimar: Böhlau, 1902.

———. *Tag- und Jahreshefte. 1749–1806.* In Vol. 1/35, *Goethes Werke: Weimarer Ausgabe,* 1–224. Weimar: Hermann Böhlau, 1895.

———. *Die Wahlverwandtschaften.* Edited by Erich Trunz. In *Goethes Werke: Hamburger Ausgabe,* 6:242–490. Munich: C. H. Beck, 1981.

———, and Carrie Asman. *Der Sammler und die Seinigen.* Amsterdam: Verlag der Kunst, 1997.

Gould, Stephen J., and Richard Lewontin. "The Spandrels of San Marco and the Panglossian Paradigm: A Critique of the Adaptationist Programme." *Proceedings of the Royal Society* B205 (1979): 581–98.

Grasskamp, Walter. *Museumsgründer und Museumsstürmer: Zur sozialgeschichte des Kunstmuseums.* Munich: C. H. Beck, 1981.

Greenberg, Reesa, Bruce W. Ferguson, and Sandy Nairne. *Thinking About Exhibitions.* London: New York, 1996.

Grimm, Erk. "Fathoming the Archive: German Poetry and the Culture of Memory." *New German Critique* 88 (2003): 107–40.

———. "Mediamania? Contemporary German Poetry in the Age of New Information Technologies: Thomas Kling and Durs Grunbein." *Studies-in-Twentieth-Century-Literature* 21, no. 1 (1997): 275–301.

Grote, Ludwig, ed. *Deutsche Gärten des 18. Jahrhunderts.* Stuttgart: H. Günther, 1946.

Groys, Boris. *Über das Neue: Versuch einer Kulturökonomie.* Munich: C. Hanser, 1992.

Grünbein, Durs. *Falten und Fallen: Gedichte.* Frankfurt am Main: Suhrkamp, 1994.

———. *Galilei vermißt Dantes Hölle und bleibt an den Massen hängen: Aufsätze, 1989–1995.* Frankfurt am Main: Suhrkamp, 1996.

———. "Zwischen Antike und X." In *Warum schriftlos leben: Aufsätze,* 111–17. Frankfurt am Main: Suhrkamp, 2003.

———, and Heinz-Norbert Jocks. *Durs Grünbein im Gespräch mit Heinz-Norbert Jocks.* Cologne: Dumont, 2001.

Guide des plaisirs à Paris: Paris le jour: Paris la nuit: La "Tournée des Grands-Ducs": comment on s'amuse: ou l'on s'amuse: ce qu'il faut voir: ce qu'il faut faire: un plan des plaisirs de Paris. Paris, 1900.

Görner, Rüdiger. *Rainer Maria Rilke.* Darmstadt: Wissenschaftliche Buchgesellschaft, 1987.

Haacke, Hans. "Museums, Managers of Consciousness." In *Hans Haacke. Unfinished Business,* edited by Brian Wallis, 60–73. Cambridge: MIT Press, 1986.

Hanssen, Beatrice. *Walter Benjamin's Other History: Of Stones, Animals, Human Beings, and Angels.* Berkeley and Los Angeles: University of California Press, 1998.

Harari, Josué V. *Textual Strategies: Perspectives in Post-Structuralist Criticism.* Ithaca: Cornell University Press, 1979.

Hebbel, Friedrich. *Der Nachsommer.* Edited by Gerhard Fricke. In *Werke,* 3:682–83. Munich: Hanser, 1965.

Heeresgeschichtliches Museum Wien. Graz: Verlag Styria, 1988.

Heeresmuseum Wien: Führer durch die Feldherrn- und durch die Ruhmeshalle. Vienna: Heeresmuseum Wien, 1941.

Hell, Julia. "Eyes Wide Shut: German Post-Holocaust Authorship." *New German Critique* 88 (2003): 9–36.

Hoell, Joachim. *Ingeborg Bachmann.* Munich: Deutscher Taschenbuch Verlag, 2001.

Hoff, Dagmar von, and Helga Meise. "Tableaux vivants: Die Kunst- und Kultform der Attitüden und lebenden Bilder." In *Weiblichkeit und Tod,* edited by Renate Berger and Inge Stephan, 69–86. Cologne: Böhlau, 1987.

Hoffmann, Lieselotte. *Adalbert Stifter und Wien.* Vienna: Wiener Verlag, 1946.

Hohendahl, Peter Uwe. "Die gebildete Gemeinschaft: Stifters Nachsommer als Utopie der ästhetischen Erziehung." In *Utopieforschung: Interdisziplinäre Studien zur neuzeitlichen Utopie,* edited by Wilhelm Vosskamp, 333–56. Stuttgart: Metzler, 1982.

Hollander, John. *The Gazer's Spirit: Poems Speaking to Silent Works of Art.* Chicago: University of Chicago Press, 1995.

Hollier, Denis. "On Paper." In *Anymore,* edited by Cynthia Davidson, 58–61. New York: Anyone Corporation, 2000.

Holub, Robert C. *Reflections of Realism: Paradox, Norm, and Ideology in Nineteenth-Century German Prose.* Detroit: Wayne State University Press, 1991.

Hooper-Greenhill, Eilean. *Museums and the Shaping of Knowledge.* New York: Routledge, 1992.

Hoppe, Karl, and Hans Plischke. "'Keltische Knochen': Das Werk; Zur Entstehung." In *Wilhelm Raabe: Sämtliche Werke,* edited by Karl Hoppe, Hans Oppermann, and Hans Plischke, 474–78. Göttingen: Vandenhoeck and Ruprecht, 1962.

Hubensteiner, Benno. *Bayerische Geschichte.* Munich: Richard Pflaum, 1951.

Humboldt, Wilhelm von. "Bericht des Ministers Wilhelm Freiherrn von Humboldt an den König vom 21. August 1830." In *Aus Schinkel's Nachlass: Reisetagebücher, Briefe, und Aphorismen, mitgetheilt und mit einem Verzeichniss sämmtlicher Werke Schinkel's versehen,* edited by Karl Friedrich Schinkel and Alfred Freiherr von Wolzogen. Berlin: Verlag der Königlichen geheimen Oberhofbuch Druckerei, 1862.

———. "Musée des Petits Augustins: Letters to Goethe." In *Werke,* edited by Andreas Flitner and Klaus Giel, 519–52. Stuttgart: Cotta, 1960.

———. "to Friedrich Schiller, Paris, December 7, 1797." In *Wilhelm von Humboldt, sein Leben und Wirken, dargestellt in Briefen, Tagebüchern, und Dokumenten seiner Zeit,* edited by Rudolf Freese, 305–10. Berlin: Verlag der Nation, 1953.

Huxley, Thomas. "On the Method of Zadig: Retrospective Prophecy as a Function of Science." In *Science and Culture and Other Essays,* 135–55. New York: D. Appleton, 1884.

Huyssen, Andreas. "On Rewritings and New Beginnings: W. G. Sebald and the Literature about the Luftkrieg." *Zeitschrift für Literaturwissenschaft und Linguistik* 124 (2001): 72–90.

———. *Twilight Memories: Marking Time in a Culture of Amnesia.* New York: Routledge, 1995.

Härtl, Heinz, ed. *Die Wahlverwandtschaften: Eine Dokumentation der Wirkung von Goethes Roman, 1808–1832.* Berlin: Akademie Verlag, 1983.

Höller, Hans. *Ingeborg Bachmann: Das Werk von den frühesten Gedichten bis zum "Todesarten"-Zyklus.* Frankfurt am Main: Athenäum, 1987.

Jelinek, Elfriede. "Der Krieg mit anderen Mitteln." In *Kein objektives Urteil, nur ein lebendiges: Texte zum Werke von Ingeborg Bachmann,* edited by Christine Koschel and Inge von Weidenbaum, 311–19. Munich: Piper, 1989.

Juhl, Eva. "Die Wahrheit über das Unglück: Zu W. G. Sebald Die Ausgewanderten." In *Reisen im Diskurs: Modelle der literarischen Fremderfahrung von den Pilgerberichten bis zur Postmoderne,* edited by Anne Fuchs and Theo Harden, 640–59. Heidelberg: C. Winter, 1995.

Jungmair, Otto. *Adalbert Stifter als Denkmalpfleger.* Linz: Oberösterrischer Landesverlag, 1973.

———. *Adalbert Stifters Linzer Jahre: Ein Kalendarium.* Graz: Stiasny, 1958.

Kaindl, Franz. "Das Wiener Heeresgeschichtliches Museum: Ein historisches Nationalmuseum von internationaler Dimension." In *Die Nation und ihre Museen,* edited by Marie-Louise Plessen. Frankfurt: New York, 1992.

Kampfraum Südost: Sonderschau veranstaltet vom Chef der Heeresmuseen im Heeresmuseum Wien: Juni–August 1944. Vienna: Verlag des Heeresmuseums, 1944.

Kapper, Siegfried. "Die Hallstätter Ausgrabungen." *Westermann's Jahrbuch der Illustrirten deutschen Monatshefte* (1858): 510–19.

Karp, Ivan, Christine Mullen Kreamer, and Steven D. Lavine, eds. *Museums and Communities: The Politics of Public Culture.* Washington, D.C.: Smithsonian Institution Press, 1992.

Karp, Ivan, and Steven D. Lavine, eds. *Exhibiting Cultures: The Poetics and Politics of Museum Display.* Washington, D.C.: Smithsonian Institution Press, 1991.

Kastura, Thomas. "Geheimnisvolle Fähigkeit zur Transmigration: W. G. Sebalds interkulturelle Wallfahrten in die Leere." *arcadia* 31 (1996): 197–216.

Katalog des Heeresmuseum: Isonzofront Saal 1 und 2. Vienna: Verlag des Heeresmuseums, 1934.

Katalog des Heeresmuseum: Mörsersaal. Vienna: Verlag des Heeresmuseums, 1934.

Kaufmann, Thomas Dacosta. "From Treasury to Museum: The Collections of the Austrian Hapsburgs." In *The Cultures of Collecting,* edited by John Elsner and Roger Cardinal, 137–54. Cambridge: Harvard University Press, 1994.

Kendrick, Walter. *The Secret Museum: Pornography in Modern Culture.* Berkeley and Los Angeles: University of California Press, 1996.

Kilbourn, Russell J. A. "Architecture and Cinema: The Representation of Memory in W. G. Sebald's 'Austerlitz.'" In *W. G. Sebald: A Critical Companion,* edited by J. J. Long and Anne Whitehead, 140–54. Seattle: University of Washington Press, 2004.

Kirili, Alain. "The Scandal of Rodin and His models." In *Rodin: Eros and Creativity,* edited by Rainer Crone and Siegfried Salzmann, 210–13. Munich: Prestel, 1992.

Kobialka, Michal. "Historical Archives, Events, and Facts: History Writing as Fragmentary Performance." *Performance Research* 7, no. 4 (2002): 3–11.

Kohn-Waechter, Gudrun. *Das 'Problem der Post' in Malina von Ingeborg Bachmann und Martin Heideggers der Satz vom Grund.* Edited by Anita Runge and Lieselotte Steinbrügge. Stuttgart: J. B. Metzler, 1991.

Komar, Kathleen L. "The Mediating Muse: Of Men, Women, and the Feminine in the Work of Rainer Maria Rilke." *Germanic Review* 64 (1989): 129–33.

Kos, Wolfgang. "Entnazifizierung der Bürokratie." In *Verdrängte Schuld, verfehlte Sühne: Entnazifizierung in Österreich, 1945–1955,* edited by Sebastian Meissl, Klaus-Dieter Mulley, and Oliver Rathkolb, 52–72. Munich: R. Oldenbourg, 1986.

Koschel, Christine, and Inge von Weidenbaum. *Registratur des literarischen Nachlasses von Ingeborg Bachmann.* Edited by Robert Pichl. Vienna: Austrian National Library, 1981.

———, eds. *Wir müssen wahre Sätze finden: Gespräche und Interviews.* Munich: Piper, 1991.

Krajewski, Markus. *Zettelwirtschaft: Die Geburt der Kartei aus dem Geiste der Bibliothek.* Berlin: Kulturverlag Kadmos, 2002.

Krauss, Rosalind E. "The Cultural Logic of the Late Capitalist Museum." *October* 54 (1990): 3–17.

———. "Postmodernism's Museum Without Walls." In *Thinking About Exhibitions,* edited by Reesa Greenberg, Bruce W. Ferguson, and Sandy Nairne, 341–48. New York: Routledge, 1996.

Kriechbaumer, Robert. "Der lange Weg in die Moderne: Ein mentatlitätsgeschichtlicher Essay zur Geschichte der Zweiten Republik." In *Österreichische Nationalgeschichte nach 1945,* edited by Robert Kriechbaumer, Oliver Rathkolb, and Otto Maschke, 17–48. Vienna: Böhlau, 1998.

Kriessbach, Martina. *Rilke und Rodin: Wege einer Erfahrung des Plastischen.* Frankfurt am Main: P. Lang, 1984.

Kromer, Karl. *Das Gräberfeld von Hallstatt.* Florence: Sansoni, 1959.

Lakoff, George, and Mark Johnson. *Metaphors We Live By.* Chicago: University of Chicago Press, 1980.

Lampart, Fabian. "'Jeder in *seiner* Welt, so viele Welten.' Durs Grünbeins Dante." *Text und Kritik: Zeitschrift für Literatur* 153 (2002): 49–59.

Lange, Viktor. "Interpretation des Nachsommers." In *Der deutsche Roman vom Barock bis zur Gegenwart,* edited by Benno von Wiese, 34–75. Düsseldorf: A. Bagel, 1963.

Langen, August. "Attitüde und Tableau in der Goethezeit." In *Jahrbuch der deutschen Schillergesellschaft,* edited by Fritz Martini, Walter Müller Seidel, and Bernhard Zeller, 194–258. Stuttgart: Kröner, 1968.

Lennox, Sara. "In the Cemetery of the Murdered Daughters." *Studies in Twentieth Century Literature* 5, no. 1 (1980): 75–105.

Lenz, Siegfried. *Heimatmuseum: Roman.* Munich: Deutscher Taschenbuch Verlag, 1981.

Leone, Massimo. "Textual Wanderings: A Vertiginous Reading of W. G. Sebald." In *W. G. Sebald: A Critical Companion,* edited by J. J. Long and Anne Whitehead, 89–101. Seattle: University of Washington Press, 2004.

Leppmann, Wolfgang. *Rilke: Sein Leben, seine Welt, sein Werk.* Bern: Scherz, 1981.

Leslie, Esther. *Walter Benjamin: Overpowering Conformity.* London: Pluto Press, 2000.

Levi-Strauss, Claude. *The Elementary Structure of Kinship.* Boston: Beacon Press, 1969.

Lillyman, William J. "Monasticism, Tableau Vivant, and Romanticism: Ottilie in Goethe's Die Wahlverwandtschaften." *Journal of English and Germanic Philology* 81 (1982): 347–66.

Lindemann, Eva. "Die Gangart des Geistes." In *Ingeborg Bachmann: Neue Beiträge zu ihrem Werk: Iinternationales Symposion Münster, 1991,* edited by Dirk Göttsche and Hubert Ohl, 281–98. Würzburg: Königshausen & Neumann, 1993.

Linden, Patricia. "Frauenkult und Weiblichkeit in Rainer Maria Rilkes Aufzeichnungen des Malte Laurids Brigge." *Germanistische Mitteilungen* 25 (1987): 3–28.

Long, Jonathan J. *The Novels of Thomas Bernhard: Form and Its Function.* Rochester, N.Y.: Camden House, 2001.

Lübbe, Hermann. "Wilhelm von Humboldt und die Berliner Museumgründung, 1830." *Deutsche Vierteljahrsschrift für Literaturwissenschaft und Geistesgeschichte* 54, no. 4 (1980): 656–76.

MacCannell, Dean. *The Tourist: A New Theory of the Leisure Class.* Berkeley and Los Angeles: University of California Press, 1999.

Mainardi, Patricia. *The End of the Salon: Art and the State in the Early Third Republic.* Cambridge: Cambridge University Press, 1993.

Malraux, André. *Museum Without Walls.* Garden City: N.Y. Doubleday, 1967.

Mann, Thomas. *Die Entstehung des Doktor Faustus: Roman eines Romans, Werke,* Amsterdam: Bormann-Fischer, 1949.

Manoschek, Walter, and Hans Safrian. "Österreicher in der Wehrmacht." In *NS-Herrschaft in Österreich: Ein Handbuch,* edited by Emmerich Talos, Wolfgang Neugebauer, and Ernst Hanisch, 331–60. Vienna: öbv and hpt, 2001.

Marchand, Suzanne. "Ancients and Moderns in German Museums." In *Museums and Memory*, edited by Susan A. Crane. Palo Alto: Stanford University Press, 2000.

Marchand, Suzanne L. *Down from Olympus: Archaeology and Philhellenism in Germany, 1750–1970.* Princeton: Princeton University Press, 1996.

Marx, Karl. *Capital: A Critique of Political Economy*, vol. 1. Translated by Ben Fowkes. New York: Vintage, 1977.

McClellan, Andrew. *Inventing the Louvre: Art, Politics, and the Origins of the Modern Museum in Eighteenth-Century Paris.* Cambridge: Cambridge University Press, 1994.

McCulloh, Mark. *Understanding W. G. Sebald.* Columbia, S.C.: Camden House, 2003.

McIsaac, Peter M. "Autorschaft und Autorität bei W. G. Sebald." In *Deutsche Gegenwartsliteratur seit 1989: Zwischenbalanzen—Analysen—Vermittlungsperspektiven*, edited by Clemens Kammler and Torsten Pflugmacher, 139–52. Heidelberg: Synchron, 2004.

Mell, Alfred. *Heeresmuseum in Wien: Austellung ausgewählter Neuerwerbungen aus dem Zeitalter Kaiser Franz Josefs.* Vienna: Heeresmuseum Wien, 1937.

Menghin, Wilfried. "Pfahlheim: Eine Ausgrabungsruine des 19. Jahrhunderts." In *Zwischen Walhall und Paradies: Eine Austellung des Deutschen Historischen Museums in Zusammenarbeit mit dem Museum für Vor- und Frühgeschichte SMPK*, edited by Heidemarie Anderlik, 85–115. Berlin: Deutsches Historisches Museum, 1991.

Meyer, Adolph Bernhard. *Das Grabfeld von Hallstatt: Anlässlich eines Besuches daselbst.* Dresden: Verlag von Wilhelm Hoffmann, 1885.

Meyer, Herman. "Rilkes Cézanne-Erlebnis." In *Zarte Empirie: Studien zur Literaturgeschichte*, 244–86. Stuttgart: Metzler, 1963.

Milner, John. *The Studios of Paris: The Capital of Art in the Late Nineteenth Century.* New Haven: Yale University Press, 1988.

Müller, Wolfgang. *Rainer Maria Rilkes 'Neue Gedichte': Vielfältigkeit eines Gedichttypus.* Meisenheim a. Glan: Hain, 1971.

Müller, Wolfgang G. "Der Weg vom Symbolismus zum deutschen und angloamerikanischen Dinggedicht des beginnenden zwanzigsten Jahrhunderts." *Neophilologus* 53, no. 2 (1974): 157–79.

Müller-Buck, Renate. "'Oktober-Sonne bis ins Geistige hinauf': Anfängliches zur Bedeutung von Goethes 'Novelle' und Stifters 'Nachsommer' für Nietzsches Kunstauffassung." *Nietzsche-Studien* 18 (1989): 537–49.

Murray, John. *A Handbook for Travellers in Southern Germany: Being a Guide to Würtemberg, Bavaria, Austria, Tyrol, Salzburg, Styria, &c., the Austrian and Bavarian Alps, and the Danube from Ulm to the Black Sea.* 6th, cor. and enl. ed. London: J. Murray, 1853.

Nehamas, Alexander. *Nietzsche: Life as Literature.* Cambridge: Harvard University Press, 1985.

Nemec, Friedrich. *Die Ökonomie der Wahlverwandtschaften.* Munich: Fink, 1973.

Neue deutsche Biographie. Edited by Historische Kommission Bayerische Akademie der Wissenschaften. Berlin: Duncker & Humblot, 1966.

Nietzsche, Friedrich. "Das Nutzen und Nachteil der Historie für das Leben." In *Sämtliche Werke: Kritische Studienausgabe*, edited by Giorgio Colli and Mazzino Montinari, 1:243–334. Berlin: de Gruyter, 1980.

———. "Ecce homo." In *Sämtliche Werke: Kritische Studienausgabe*, edited by Giorgio Colli and Mazzino Montinari, 13:615–35. Berlin: de Gruyter, 1980.

———. "Menschliches, Allzumenschliches II." In *Sämtliche Werke: Kritische Studienausgabe*, edited by Giorgio Colli and Mazzino Montinari, 2:307–704. Berlin: de Gruyter, 1980.

Nochlin, Linda. "Museums and Radicals: A History of Emergencies." In *Museums in Crisis*, edited by Brian O'Doherty, 6–40. New York: G. Braziller, 1972.

Obeyesekere, Gananath. *The Apotheosis of Captain Cook: European Mythmaking in the Pacific.* Princeton: Princeton University Press, 1990.

Oppert, Kurt. "Das Dinggedicht: Eine Kunstform bei Mörike, Meyer, und Rilke." *Deutsche Vierteljahresschrift für Literaturwissenschaft und Geistesgeschichte* 4 (1926): 747–83.

Paul, Catherine E. *Poetry in the Museums of Modernism: Yeats, Pound, Moore, Stein.* Ann Arbor: University of Michigan Press, 2002.

Pauli, Ludwig. *Die Gräber vom Salzberg zu Hallstatt: Erforschung, Überlieferung, Auswertbarkeit.* Mainz am Rhein: P. von Zabern, 1975.

Pearce, Susan M. *Museums, Objects, and Collections: A Cultural Study.* Washington, D.C.: Smithsonian Institution Press, 1992.

Pelinka, Anton. "Austrian Identity and the 'Ständesstaat.'" In *The Habsburg Legacy: National Identity in Historical Perspective,* edited by Ritchie Robertson and Edward Timms, 169–77. Edinburgh: Edinburgh University Press, 1994.

———. "The Great Austrian Taboo: The Repression of the Civil War." In *Coping with the Past: Germany and Austria After 1945,* edited by Kathy Harms, Lutz R. Reuter. and Volker Durr, 56–65. Madison: University of Wisconsin Press, 1990.

Perrot, Michelle. *A History of Private Life.* Cambridge, Mass.: Belknap Press, 1990.

Peucker, Brigitte. "The Material Image in Goethe's Wahlverwandtschaften." *The Germanic Review* 74, no. 3 (1999): 195–213.

Pevsner, Nikolaus. *A History of Building Types.* Princeton: Princeton University Press, 1976.

Pfeiffer, Peter. "Korrespondenz und Wahlverwandtschaft: W. G. Sebalds 'Die Ringe des Saturn.'" *Gegenwartsliteratur: Ein germanistisches Jahrbuch/A German Studies Yearbook* (2003): 226–44.

Pichl, Robert, Monika Albrecht, and Dirk Göttsche. *Ingeborg Bachmanns "Todesarten"-Projekt: Neue Teilregistratur des literarischen Nachlasses in der Österreichischen Nationalbibliothek.* Vienna: Edition Praesens, 1995.

Pichl, Robert, and Alexander Stillmark. *Kritische Wege der Landnahme: Ingeborg Bachmann im Blickfeld der neunziger Jahre.* Vienna: Hora Verlag, 1994.

Pinet, Hélène, ed. *Rodin Collectionneur.* Paris: Musée Rodin, 1967.

Plagemann, Volker. *Das deutsche Kunstmuseum, 1790–1870: Lage, Baukörper, Raumorganisation, Bildprogramm.* Munich: Prestel-Verlag, 1967.

Plessen, Marie-Louise. *Die Nation und ihre Museen.* Frankfurt: Campus, 1992.

Podany, Vaclav, and Hana Barvikova. 1999. Heinz Zatschek. In Archive of the Academy of Sciences of the Czech Republic [cited November 11, 2006]. Available at http://www.cas.cz/aa/pages/histpers.htm.

Pollak, Alexander. *Die Wehrmachtslegende in Österreich: Das Bild der Wehrmacht im Spiegel der österreichischen Presse nach 1945.* Vienna: Böhlau, 2002.

Pompe, Hedwig, and Leander Scholz, eds. *Archivprozesse: Die Kommunikation der Aufbewahrung.* Cologne: DuMont, 2002.

Por, Peter. "Rilke—Rodin, Cézanne, Klee: Die Schöpfung des Raumes in der Moderne." In *Proceedings of the XXIId Congress of the International Comparative Literature Association,* edited by Roger Bauer and Fokkema Douwe, 50–56. Munich: iuidicum, 1990.

Potts, Alex. "The Reification and Disintegration of Sculpture in Rodin and Rilke." In *Sight and Insight: Essays on Art and Culture in Honour of E. H. Gombrich at 85,* edited by E. H. Gombrich and John Onians, 355–78. London: Phaidon Press, 1994.

Preziosi, Donald. *Rethinking Art History: Meditations on a Coy Science.* New Haven: Yale University Press, 1989.

Purdy, Daniel L. "Weimar Classicism and the Origins of Consumer Culture." In *Unwrapping Goethe's Weimar: Essays in Cultural Studies and Local Knowledge,* edited by Burkhard Henke, Susanne

Kord, and Simon Richter, 36–62. Rochester, N.Y.: Camden House, 2000.

———. *The Tyranny of Elegance: Consumer Cosmopolitanism in the Era of Goethe.* Baltimore: Johns Hopkins University Press, 1998.

Puszkar, Norbert. "Frauen und Bilder: Luciane und Ottilie." *Neophilologus* 73 (1989): 397–410.

Raabe, Wilhelm. *Keltische Knochen.* Edited by Karl Hoppe, Hans Oppermann, and Hans Plischke, In *Sämtliche Werke,* vol. 91. Göttingen: Vandenhoeck and Ruprecht, 1962.

Raabe, Wilhelm Karl. *Sämtliche Werke.* Edited by Karl Hoppe, Hans Oppermann, and Hans Plischke. Freiburg: H. Klemm, 1951.

Raby, Peter. *Alfred Russel Wallace: A Life.* Princeton: Princeton University Press, 2001.

Rathkolb, Oliver. "NS-Problem und politische Restauration: Vorgeschichte und Etablierung des VdU." In *Verdrängte Schuld, verfehlte Sühne: Entnazifizierung in Österreich, 1945–1955,* edited by Sebastian Meissl, Klaus-Dieter Mulley, and Oliver Rathkolb, 73–100. Munich: R. Oldenbourg, 1986.

Rauchensteiner, Manfried. *Der Sonderfall: Eie Besatzungszeit in Österreich, 1945 bis 1955.* Graz: Styria, 1979.

———, et al. *Phoenix aus der Asche.* Vienna: Heeresgeschichtliches Museum, 2005.

Rave, Paul Ortwin. *Karl Friedrich Schinkel Lebeswerk,* vol. 3. Berlin: Deutscher Kunstverlag, 1941.

Reckenfelder-Bäumer, Christel. "'Wissen ist Macht—Macht ist Wissen.'" In *Berlin um 1900: Ausstellung der Berlinischen Galerie in Verbindung mit der Akademie der Künste zu den Berliner Festwochen 1984,* edited by Gesine Asmus, 405–19. Berlin: Nicolai, 1984.

Rectanus, Mark W. *Culture Incorporated: Museums, Artists, and Corporate Sponsorships.* Minneapolis: University of Minnesota Press, 2002.

Rehm, Walther. *Nachsommer: Zur Deutung von Stifters Dichtung.* Bern: A. Francke, 1951.

Reiter, Rayna R. *Toward an Anthropology of Women.* New York: Monthly Review Press, 1975.

Reitzenbeck, Heinrich. "Adalbert Stifter: Eine biographische Skizze." In *Libussa: Jahrbuch für 1853,* edited by Paul Aloys Klar. Prague: Verlag Calve, 1853.

Richards, Thomas. *The Imperial Archive: Knowledge and the Fantasy of Empire.* New York: Verso, 1993.

Richter, Jean Paul. "Museum von Jean Paul." In *Jean Pauls Sämtliche Werke,* edited by Preussische Akademie der Wissenschaften, 3–168. Weimar: Herman Böhlau Nachfolger, 1938.

Rider, Jacques le. "Hugo von Hofmannsthal and the Idea of Central Europe." In *The Habsburg Legacy: National Identity in Historical Perspective,* edited by Ritchie Robertson and Edward Timms, 121–35. Edinburgh: Edinburgh University Press, 1994.

Riedel, Wolfgang. "Poetik der Präsenz: Idee der Dichtung bei Durs Grünbein." *Internationales Archiv für Sozialgeschichte der deutschen Literatur* 24, no. 1 (1999): 82–105.

Riemann, Gottfried. "Das Museum am Lustgarten. 1823–1830." In *Karl Friedrich Schinkel. 1781–1841,* 135–52. Berlin: Henschelverlag Kunst und Gesellschaft, 1982.

Rilke, Rainer Maria. *Die Aufzeichnungen des Malte Laurids Brigge.* Edited by Ruth Sieber. In *Sämtliche Werke,* vol. 6. Frankfurt am Main: Insel-Verlag, 1966.

———. *Auguste Rodin.* Frankfurt am Main: Insel-Verlag, 1955.

———. *Briefe aus den Jahren 1892 bis 1904,* vol. 1. Edited by Ruth Rilke Sieber and Carl Sieber. Leipzig: Insel-Verlag, 1939.

———. *Briefe aus den Jahren 1904 bis 1907,* vol. 2. Edited by Ruth Sieber-Rilke and Carl Sieber. Leipzig: Insel-Verlag, 1939.

———. "Letter to Gräfin Aline Dietrichstein, July 9, 1917." In *Briefe aus den Jahren 1914–1921,* edited by Ruth Rilke Sieber and Carl Sieber. Leipzig: Insel-Verlag, 1937.

———. *Neue Gedichte.* Edited by Ruth Sieber-Rilke. In *Sämtliche Werke,* vol. 1. Frankfurt am Main: Insel-Verlag, 1955.

———. *New Poems.* Translated by Edward Snow. San Francisco: North Point Press, 1984.

———. *New Poems: The Other Part.* Translated by Edward Snow. San Francisco: North Point Press, 1987.

———. *Sämtliche Werke.* Edited by Ruth Sieber. Frankfurt am Main: Insel-Verlag, 1962.

Rodin, Auguste. *Les Cathédrales de France.* Paris: A. Colin, 1921.

Rolleston, James L. "The Politics of Quotation: Walter Benjamin's Arcades Project." *PMLA* 104, no. 1 (1989): 13–27.

Roth, Gerhard. *Eine Reise in das Innere von Wien: Essays.* Frankfurt am Main: S. Fischer, 1991.

Roth, Martin. *Heimatmuseum: Zur Geschichte einer deutschen Institution.* Berlin: Mann, 1990.

Rubin, Gayle. "The Traffic in Women: Notes on the 'Political Economy' of Sex." In *Toward an Anthropology of Women,* edited by Rayna R. Reiter, 267–319. New York: Monthly Review Press, 1975.

Rupnow, Dirk. "'Ihr müsst sein, auch wenn ihr nicht mehr sein': The Jewish Central Museum in Prague and Historical Memory in the Third Reich." *Holocaust and Genocide Studies* 16 (2002): 23–53.

———. *Täter, Gedächtnis, Opfer: Das "Jüdische Zentralmuseum" in Prag, 1942–1945.* Vienna: Picus, 2000.

Ryan, Judith. *Rilke, Modernism. and Poetic Tradition.* Cambridge: Cambridge University Press, 1999.

———. *Umschlag und Verwandlung: Poetische Struktur und Dichtungstheorie in R. M. Rilkes Lyrik der mittleren Periode (1907–1914).* Munich: Winkler, 1972.

Sacken, Eduard Freiherr von. *Das Grabfeld von Hallstatt in Oberösterreich und dessen Alterthümer.* Vienna: W. Braumüller, 1868.

Sammons, Jeffrey L. *Wilhelm Raabe: The Fiction of the Alternative Community.* Princeton: Princeton University Press, 1987.

Schank, Stefan. *Rainer Maria Rilke.* Munich: dtv, 1998.

Scherer, Valentin. *Deutsche Museen: Entstehung und kulturgeschichtliche Bedeutung unserer öffentlichen Kunstsammlungen.* Jena: Diederichs, 1913.

Schinkel, Karl Friedrich. "Reisen nach Italien." In *Tagebücher, Briefe, Zeichnungen, Aquarelle,* edited by Gottfried Riemann. Berlin: Rütten and Loening, 1979.

Schlaffer, Hannelore. "Frauen als Einlösung der frühromantischen Kunsttheorie." *Jahrbuch der deutschen Schillergesellschaft* 21 (1977): 274–96.

Schlant, Ernestine. *The Language of Silence: West German Literature and the Holocaust.* Routledge, 1999.

Schliemann, Heinrich. *Trojanische Altertümer: Berichte über die Ausgrabungen in Troja.* Leipzig, 1874.

Schneider, Jost. *Die Kompositionsmethode Ingeborg Bachmanns: Erzählstil und Engagement in Das dreissigste Jahr, Malina und Simultan.* Bielefeld: Aisthesis, 1999.

Scholz, Frances Mary. "Rilke, Rodin, and the Fragmented Man." In *Rilke and the Visual Arts,* edited by Frank Baron, 27–44. Lawrence, Kans.: Coronado Press, 1982.

Schorske, Carl E. *Fin-de-Siècle Vienna: Politics and Culture.* New York: Knopf, 1979.

Schubert, Peter. *Das Wiener Arsenal: Ein historischer Überblick.* Vienna: Brüder Hollinek, 1975.

Schulz, Eva. "Das Museum als wissenschaftliche Institution: Neue Ideen und tradierte Vorstellungen am Beispiel der Sammlung Boiserée." *Wallraf-Richartz-Jahrbuch* (1990): 285–317.

Schulze, Sabine, Friedmar Apel, and Johann Wolfgang von Goethe. *Goethe und die Kunst.* Stuttgart: Hatje, 1994.

Sebald, W. G., and Michael Zeeman. "Max Sebald interviewed by Michael Zeeman: Programme: Kamer met Uitzicht July 12, 1998 (VPRO—Netherlands TV). Transcribed by Gordon Turner, 2003." In *W. G. Sebald: History—Memory—Trauma,* edited by Scott Denham and Mark R. McCulloh. Berlin: de Gruyter, 2006. Forthcoming.

Sebald, Winfried Georg. *Austerlitz.* Munich: C. Hanser, 2001.

———. *Luftkrieg und Literatur: Mit einem Essay zu Alfred Andersch.* Munich: C. Hanser, 1999.

Sedgwick, Eve Kosofsky. *Between Men: English Literature and Homosocial Desire.* New York: Columbia University Press, 1985.

Segelken, Barbara. "Sammlungsgeschichte zwischen Leibniz und Humboldt: Die königlichen Sammlungen im Kontext der akademischen Institutionen." In *Theater der Natur und Kunst: Essays,* edited by Horst Bredekamp, Jochen Brüning, and Cornelia Weber, 46–51. Berlin: Henschel, 2000.

Seidler, Herbert. "Gestaltung und Sinn des Raumes in Stifters Nachsommer." In *Adalbert Stifter: Studien und Interpretationen,* edited by Lother Stiehm, 203–26. Heidelberg: Stiehm, 1968.

Sheehan, James J. "From Princely Collections to Public Museums: Toward a History of the German Art Museum." In *Rediscovering History: Culture, Politics, and the Psyche,* edited by Michael S. Roth, 170–82. Stanford: Stanford University Press, 1994.

———. *Museums in the German Art World.* Oxford: Oxford University Press, 2000.

Sherman, Daniel J. "The Bourgeoisie, Cultural Appropriation, and the Art Museum in Nineteenth-Century France." *Radical History Review* 38 (1987): 38–57.

———. "Quatremére/Benjamin/Marx: Art Museums, Aura, and Commodity Fetishism." In *Museum Culture: Histories, Discourses, Spectacles,* edited by Daniel J. Sherman and Irit Rogoff, 123–43. Minneapolis: University of Minnesota Press, 1994.

———. *Worthy Monuments: Art Museums and the Politics of Culture in Nineteenth-Century France.* Cambridge: Harvard University Press, 1989.

———, and Irit Rogoff, eds. *Museum Culture: Histories, Discourses, Spectacles.* Minneapolis: University of Minnesota Press, 1994.

Simmel, Georg. "Rodins Plastik und die Geistesrichtung der Gegenwart." *Berliner Tageblatt,* September 29, 1902.

Slibar, Neva. "Angst, Verbrechen, und das Unheimliche: Genre und Motivumwandlungen der Angstliteratur in Ingeborg Bachmanns Spätprosa." In *Ingeborg Bachmann: Neue Beiträge zu ihrem Werk; Internationales Symposion, Münster, 1991,* edited by Dirk Göttsche and Hubert Ohl, 167–86. Würzburg: Königshausen and Neumann, 1993.

Smolla, Günter. "Archäologie und Nationalbewußtsein." In *Zwischen Walhall und Paradies: Eine Austellung des Deutschen Historischen Museums in Zusammenarbeit mit dem Museum für Vor- und Frühgeschichte SMPK,* edited by Heidemarie Anderlik, 10–15. Berlin: Deutsches Historisches Museum, 1992.

Steinberg, Michael P. "The Collector as Allegorist: Goods, Gods, and the Objects of History." In *Walter Benjamin and the Demands of History,* edited by Michael P. Steinberg, 88–118. Ithaca: Cornell University Press, 1996.

Sternberger, Dolf. *Panorama of the Nineteenth Century.* Translated by Joachim Neugroschel. New York: Urizen Books, 1977.

Stiehm, Lothar, ed. *Adalbert Stifter: Studien und Interpretation: Gedenkschrift zum 100. Todestage.* Heidelberg: L. Stiehm, 1968.

Stifter, Adalbert. "Abdias." In *Sämtliche Werke,* edited by and notes by Karl Pörnbacher, 5:579–674. Munich: Winkler, 1978.

———. *Adalbert Stifters Leben und Werk in Briefen und Dokumenten.* Frankfurt am Main: Insel-Verlag, 1962.

———. *Indian Summer.* Translated by Wendell Frye. New York: Lang, 1985.

———. *Der Nachsommer.* Edited by Alfred Doppler and Wolfgang Frühwald. In *Werke und Briefe: Historisch-kritische Gesamtausgabe,* 4:1–4:3. Stuttgart : W. Kohlhammer, 1997.

———. "Über die Schule." In *Sämtliche Werke,* edited by Konrad Steffen, 256–317. Munich: Winkler, 1978.

———. "Vorrede: Bunte Steine." In *Sämtliche Werke,* edited and notes by Karl Pörnbacher, 1:7–13. Munich: Winkler, 1978.

Stifter, Christian. *Die Wiederaufrüstung Österreichs: Die geheime Remilitarisierung der westlichen Besatzungszonen, 1945–1955.* Innsbruck: Studien Verlag, 1997.

Stix, Alfred. *Die Aufstellung der ehedem kaiserlichen Gemälde Galerie in Wien im 18. Jahrhundert.* Vienna: Museion, 1929.

Stöckl, Christine. *Die Verteidigungspolitik der ÖVP und der Stellenwert der militärischen Landesverteidigung im österreichischen Neutralitätskonzept, 1955–1985.* Vienna: W. Braumüller, 1985.

Swales, Martin. *The German Bildungsroman from Wieland to Hesse.* Princeton: Princeton University Press, 1978.

Tantillo, Astrida Orle. *The Will to Create: Goethe's Philosophy of Nature.* Pittsburgh: University of Pittsburgh Press, 2002.

Theweleit, Klaus. *Männerphantasien.* 2 vols. Reinbek bei Hamburg: Rowohlt, 1980.

Thümmler, Lars-H. 2003. Das Zeughaus Berlin im Zweiten Weltkrieg. In Deutsches Historisches Museum [cited June 20, 2005]. Available at http://www.dhm.de/texte/zhwk2.html.

Tomberger, Corinna. "Die Wiederkehr des Künstler-Helden: Jochen Gerz im 'Duell mit der Verdrängung.'" In *Gedächtnis und Geschlecht: Deutungsmuster in Darstellungen des nationalsozialistischen Genozids,* edited by Insa Eschebach, Sigrid Jacobeit, and Silke Wenk, 395–415. Frankfurt: Campus, 2002.

Trigger, Bruce G. *A History of Archaeological Thought.* Cambridge: Cambridge University Press, 1989.

Trunz, Erich. "Goethe als Sammler." *Goethe-Jahrbuch* 89 (1972): 13–61.

Virchow, Rudolf. "Erinnerungen an Schliemann." *Die Gartenlaube* (1891): 66–68, 104–8, 299–303.

Wackenroder, Wilhelm Heinrich. *Herzensergiessungen eines kunstliebenden klosterbruders.* Edited by Silvio Vietta and Richard Littlejohns. In *Sämtliche Werke und Briefe: Historisch-kritische Ausgabe,* 1:51–145. Heidelberg: C. Winter, 1991.

Wagner, Anne M. "Rodin's Reputation." In *Eroticism and the Body Politic,* edited by Lynn Avery Hunt. Baltimore: Johns Hopkins University Press, 1991.

Wallach, Duncan. *Exhibiting Contradiction: Essays on the Art Museum in the United States.* Amherst: University of Massachusetts Press, 1998.

Walzer, Tina, and Stephan Templ. *Unser Wien: "Arisierung" auf Österreichisch.* Berlin: Aufbau-Verlag, 2001.

Ward, Simon. "Ruins and Poetics in the Works of W. G. Sebald." In *W. G. Sebald: A Critical Companion,* edited by J. J. Long and Anne Whitehead, 58–71. Seattle: University of Washington Press, 2004.

Wehrmacht—Heer/Heeresmuseum Wien: Sonderschau Sowjetrussischer Beute. Vienna: Heeresmuseum Wien, 1942.

Weigel, Sigrid. *Ingeborg Bachmann: Hinterlassenschaften unter Wahrung des Briefgeheimnisses.* Vienna: P. Zsolnay Verlag, 1999.

———. *Die Stimme der Medusa: Schreibweisen in der Gegenwartsliteratur von Frauen.* Dülmen-Hiddingsel: Tende, 1987.

———. *Topographien der Geschlechter: Kulturgeschichtliche Studien zur Literatur.* Reinbek bei Hamburg: Rowohlt, 1990.

Weiss, Peter. *Die Ästhetik des Widerstands.* Frankfurt am Main: Suhrkamp, 1983.

Westphal-Hellbusch, Sigrid. *Zur Geschichte des Museums,* vol. 21. Berlin: D. Reimer, 1973.

Westrate, J. Lee. *European Military Museums: A Survey of Their Philosophy, Facilities, Programs, and Management.* Washington, D.C.: Smithsonian Institution Press, 1961.

Wilhelm, Gustav. *Begegnung mit Stifter: Einblicke in Adalbert Stifters Leben und Werk.* Munich: K. Alber, 1943.

Williams, Arthur. "The Elusive First Person Plural: Real Absences in Reiner Kunze, Bernd-Dieter Hüge, and W. G. Sebald." In *Whose Story? Continuities in Contemporary German-Language Literature,* edited by A. Williams, S. Parkes, and J. Preece, 85–113. Bern: Peter Lang, 1998.

———. "W. G. Sebald: A Holistic Approach to Borders, Texts, and Perspectives." In *German-Language Literature Today: International and Popular?* edited by A. Williams, S. Parkes, and J. Preece, 99–118. Bern: Peter Lang, 2000.

Witek, Hans. "'Arisierungen' in Wien: Aspekte nationalsozialistischer Enteignungspolitik 1938–1940." In *NS-Herrschaft in Österreich: ein Handbuch,* edited by Emmerich Talos, 199–214. Vienna: öbv and hpt, 2001.

Wiwjorra, Ingo. "German Archaeology and Its Relation to Nationalism and Racism." In *Nationalism and Archaeology in Europe,* edited by Margarita Díaz-Andreu García and T. C. Champion, 164–88. Boulder, Colo.: Westview Press, 1996.

Woerl, Leo. *Wörl's Führer durch Paris und Umgebung.* Leipzig: Woerl's Reisebücherverlag, 1900.

Wolf, Ernest M. *Stone into Poetry: The Cathedral Cycle in Rainer Maria Rilke's Neue Gedichte.* Bonn: Bouvier, 1978.

Wolff, Janet. "The Artist and the Flâneur." In *The Flâneur,* edited by Keith Tester, 111–37. New York: Routledge, 1994.

Wright, Gwendolyn, ed. *The Formation of National Collections of Art and Archaeology.* Washington, D.C.: National Gallery of Art, distributed by University Press of New England, 1996.

Wyder, Margrit. "Vorhof zum Tempel: Der Anfang von Stifters Nachsommer." *Sprachkunst: Beiträge zur Literaturwissenschaft* 20, no. 2 (1990): 149–75.

Young, James Edward. *The Texture of Memory: Holocaust Memorials and Meaning.* New Haven: Yale University Press, 1993.

Zatschek, Heinz. *Das Heeresegeschichtliche Museum in Wien.* Graz: Böhlau, 1960.

Ziolkowski, Theodore. *German Romanticism and Its Institutions.* Princeton: Princeton University Press, 1990.

Zuschlag, Christoph. *'Entartete Kunst': Ausstellungsstrategien im Nazi-Deutschland.* Worms: Wernersche Verlagsgesellschaft, 1995.

Index

www.ingramcontent.com/pod-product-compliance
Lightning Source LLC
LaVergne TN
LVHW061219100826
845148LV00004B/800

* 9 7 8 0 2 7 1 0 5 8 7 0 2 *